2006

NIGERIA'S URBAN HISTORY

Past and Present

Edited by
Hakeem Ibikunle Tijani

University Press of America,® Inc.
Lanham · Boulder · New York · Toronto · Oxford

Copyright © 2006 by
University Press of America,® Inc.
4501 Forbes Boulevard
Suite 200
Lanham, Maryland 20706
UPA Acquisitions Department (301) 459-3366

PO Box 317
Oxford
OX2 9RU, UK

Library of Congress Control Number: 2006920829
ISBN-13: 978-0-7618-3433-8 (paperback : alk. paper)
ISBN-10: 0-7618-3433-5 (paperback : alk. paper)

∞™ The paper used in this publication meets the minimum
requirements of American National Standard for Information
Sciences—Permanence of Paper for Printed Library Materials,
ANSI Z39.48—1984

This book is dedicated to

the late Professor Gabriel Ogundeji Ogunremi

and the late Dr. Nina Mba

Table of Contents

List of Tables and Ilustrations   vii
Acknowledgments   ix
Foreword by Professor Toyin Falola   xi
Abbreviations   xiii

Chapter 1: Reflection on Nigeria's Urban History   1
Hakeem I. Tijani
Chapter 2: Human Factor in Urbanization   15
Jare Ajayi
Chapter 3: Gender, Urbanization and Socio-economic Development   27
Wole Atere & Akeem Akinwale
Chapter 4: The Impact of Road Transportation   45
Dipo Olubomehin
Chapter 5: Role of Theater and Drama in Political and Urban Development   57
Patrick Ebewo
Chapter 6: Prostitution and Urban Social Relations   75
Saheed Aderinto
Chapter 7: Policing Urban Prostitution   99
Saheed Aderinto
Chapter 8: Urban Neglect and Underdevelopment of a Border Town   119
Abolade Adeniji & Hakeem I. Tijani
Chapter 9: Transformation of the Sabongari   133
Rasheed Olaniyi
Chapter 10: Colonial and Postcolonial Architecture and Urbanism   145
Seyi Fabiyi
Chapter 11: Legal Aspect of Urban Development   167
Mosope Fagbongbe & Hakeem I. Tijani
Chapter 12: Industries as Catalyst of Urban Development: A Microanalysis   183
Hakeem I. Tijani
Chapter 13: Urbanism and Traditional Religion   191
Danoye Oguntola-Laguda
Chapter 14: Urbanism and Ethnic Crises Since the 1980s   201
Olayemi Akinwunmi and Hakeem I. Tijani
Chapter 15: Managing Rural and Urban Poverty   211
Adoyi Onoja

Chapter 16: The Development of a Federal Capitol Territory – Abuja   227
    Ibrahim Umaru

About the Editor and Contributors   247
Index   251

List of Tables

Table 3.1. Gender Distribution Of Person By Industry   39
Table 3.2. Percentage Distribution of Persons by Occupational Groups (%)   40
Table 3.3. Federal Civil Service Staff by Gender 1990-1993   40
Table 3.4. Medical Practitioners in Nigeria by Sex   41
Table 3.5. Distribution of Primary School Teachers by Sex   41
Table 3.6. Distribution of Teaching Staff By Tertiary Institution by Gender 1980/81-1992/93   42
Table 3.7. Distribution of Persons Holding Political Positions (1999-2003) by Gender   42
Table 8.1. Badagry Population 1846 – 1890   123
Table 8.2. Badagry Population 1890 – 1911   123
Table 9.1. Persons of Northern Nigerian Origins, Sabongari, Zaria 1913   136
Table 9.2. Population of Muslims and Christians in Sabongari, Kano 1939   138
Table 9.3. Schools in Sabongari, Kano, 1925-1973   141
Table 12.1. List of Some Industries within Mushin Area   185
Table 12.2. Industrial Estates in Lagos State   185
Table 12.3. Works Department Capital Projects 1983   187
Table 14.1. Population of the Largest Towns in Nigeria, 1921 – 1963   203
Table 16.1: Phased Development of the Capital City Plan   236
Table 16.2. Estimated Population of the FCT by Area Council (1986-1988)   238
Table 16.3. Estimated Population of the FCT by Area Council (1990-1995)   238

Acknowledgments

This volume is a celebration of the interdisciplinary approach and teamwork of the contributors to whom I'm grateful. I thank each and every one of them for their resilience and dedication in the last two years. Their zeal to meet reviewers' comments and excel is commendable.

To Professor Falola, I say thank you for reading the drafts and accepting to write a Foreword – an indication of your acceptance of the authors' scholarship and positive disposition towards the project. I would like to thank Sam Severance for helping with Camera-Ready and formatting of chapters. Students in my senior history seminar class at USF assisted in identifying words and terms for index. Singular praise goes to Michelle Molloy for compiling and typing words and terms that aided Sam in outlining index proper.

I'm indebted to my wife and children for enduring months of fiscal strain required by the project. To David Chao, Michael Marino, and other staff at University Press of America (and the in-house reviewers), I say thanks for the opportunity. It's an indication of your trust and acceptance of our scholarship.

Hakeem Ibikunle Tijani, PhD
USF Joliet, Illinois,
November 2005

Foreword

Nigerian cities present a multitude of faces: those of tradition, of modernity, of globalization, of order, of chaos; and of many more, both pretty and ugly. All these faces are depicted, in one way or the other, in this highly focused book that will benefit students and researchers, historians and social scientists, policy makers and planners. We see the representation of history, with some chapters showing the growth of cities during the colonial era in the first half of the twentieth century, and some others analyzing the changes of recent years. The encounter with colonialism led to the expansion of cities, the creation of new ones, and the emergence of new urban cultures relating to such aspects as religion, music, art, dance, leisure, theater, and drama. Since independence, an oil economy has added to the remarkable nature of urban life and culture.

In various engaging chapters, an enormous amount of data has been generated to reveal the nature of obstacles facing Nigeria's urbanism. The volume shows us the nature of human agency in building communities within cities. Also, we see the significant role of gender issues, including how women have broken down barriers and vigorously contributed to nation building. Nigerian cities have to overcome problems of poverty, crime, and prostitution, all human problems that attract refreshing comments in this book.

The volume enriches our knowledge in other ways as well: the analysis of the crucial relevance of transportation; the visible pockets of transformation and success; and the eagerness and ingenuity of millions of Nigerians to survive. It is gratifying to note the linkage that the authors have established between cities and economic development. One chapter shows the growth of industrialization, and another focuses on how to overcome structural poverty.

The organic nature of urbanism is clearly revealed, in relation to how occupations are created, how the countryside is connected to cities, how people live and where they live, how conflicts are generated and resolved, and how diversity (defined by ethnic and religious differences) are negotiated. It is clear from the accounts presented in this book that investments have been rich and diverse, creating a compelling picture of livable cities.

Dr. Hakeem Tijani and his disciples are astute in successfully telling us about issues of urban neglect, urban poverty, and criminal incarceration of the poor, spread of diseases, and a host of other issues emerging out of modern urbanism. Thus, they have analyzed important problems and offered some suggestions for their resolution.

Furthermore, there is a sustained commitment to telling us about city cultures in ways that are fresh and engaging. Among the critical highlights is how cultures are lived and formulated, how people of different ethnicities cohabitate, and how tensions are mediated in cultural terms. In spite of people's levels of wealth and status, they create cultural spaces for themselves, finding opportunities for happiness and creating limitless moments of joy.

Those who are interested in understanding how Nigerian cities have grown to become what we know today must turn to this book. Great insights are offered to the readers on various aspects of Nigerian cities: the process of urbanization; the management of cities; and the conflicts and challenges embedded in human interactions in urban settings. Dr. Hakeem Tijani and his contributors have revealed the many-headed hydra of Nigeria's urbanism. Thanks to them, we are no longer like Hercules facing the many-headed beast.

Toyin Falola
Frances Higginbothom Nalle Centennial Professor in History
Fellow of the Nigerian Academy of Letters
The University of Texas at Austin

Abbreviations

ADB	African Development Bank
ADI	African Development Indicators
ARODIST	Arochukwu District
ASCON	Administrative Staff College of Nigeria
BAI	Battle Against Indiscipline
CSO	Chief Secretary Office
CALPROF	Calabar Province
COMCOL	Commissioner for the Colony
DG	Millennium Development Goals
DFRRI	Directorate of Food, Roads and Rural Infrastructures
ERA	European Reservation Areas
EIA	Environmental Impact Assessment
FCT	Federal Capital Territory
FEPA	Federal Environmental Protection Agency
FHA	Federal Housing Authority
FMBN	Federal Mortgage Bank of Nigeria
FMFL	Federal Mortgage Finance Limited
FOS	Federal Office of Statistics
GAD	Gender and Development
GDP	Gross Domestic Product
GRA	Government Reserve Areas
IKOTDIST	Ikot Ekpene District
MAMSER	Mass Mobilization for Social and Economic Recovery
NA	Native Authority
NAE	National Archives Enugu
NAI	National Archives Ibadan
NDE	National Directorate of Employment
NEEDS	National Economic Empowerment and Development Strategy
NEPAD	New Partnership for African Development
NICOLA	Non-Indigenes Community Leaders Association
NISER	Nigeria Institute for Social and Economic Research
NNDC	Northern Nigeria Development Company

NMTU	Nigerian Motor Transport Union
NSUDIST	Nsukka District
SHA	Kaduna State Housing Authority
SOAS	School of Oriental and African Studies
SONTA	Society of Nigerian Theater Artists
UCLA	University of California Los Angeles
UDB	Urban Development Bank
UNIYSH	United Nation's International Year of Shelter for the Homeless
URS	Urban Renewal Scheme
WAD	Women and Development
WAI	War Against Indiscipline
WID	Women in Development

1

Reflection on Nigeria's Urban History

Hakeem I. Tijani

Defining Urban History

Urban history is both national and international in its approach to questions about the society. In its national form, urban history is associated with local history when the study focuses on a particular locality or when some aspect of life in a local community is being analyzed or described. National could be a regional or country study depending on the scope and period. In addition, its internationalism implies comparative analysis to determine the similarities and inferences from different parts of the world. Professor H.J. Dyos (1921-1978), perhaps the father of urban history, gave it its internationalism in his seminal works *Victorian Suburbs* (1961) and *Urban History Yearbook* (1974) - which is now known as *Urban History*. We must stress that urban history, whether in its local or international form attempts to answer some of the basic questions about the nature of our societies. For our purpose, urban history is defined as the historical analysis of societal transformation – transformation being both human and physical, man's interaction with his environment, and his ability to change it to meet his needs. An urban history of Nigeria thus implies the development of the country in all ramifications. However, since we cannot adequately cover the totality of the Nigerian experience, the chapters in this book focus on development since the imposition of colonial rule emphasizing administrative development as a form of urban history and how the country was transformed aesthetically, legally, structurally and physically.

The Context

Urbanization as used in this book involves the familiar process of historical development. It is not the sociological terminology of the process such as acculturation, diffusion, assimilation, or amalgamation, but rather a process of historical development in its entirety. What should be stressed is that the process of urbanization itself is applicable both to the "urbanites" and the "ruralites" or "urban centers" and "rural areas". Used in this sense, urbanization or urban history connotes the historical transformation of the society from rural to urban or developed centers. The process, arguably, is multifaceted and numerous. However, impliedly urbanization of Nigeria, like many Third World countries, seems to be a planned development. Historically the various ethnic groups have shown attempts since the Neolithic age to transform areas now known as Nigeria. Pre-colonial, colonial, and post-colonial experiences have shown strides in the historical transformation of the country that made its urban history necessary.

There are four approaches available to the urban historian. The approaches are: *urbanization process, urban biography, thematic, and cultural studies*. The *urbanization process* provides an essential context for more localized studies. It includes the element of demographic concentration, a structural or systems approach, and the behavioral aspects of urbanization. A detailed description of the related elements of urbanization is Gilbert Stelter's "Introduction" which is in his book, (ed.) *Cities and Urbanization: Canadian Historical Perspectives* (Toronto: Copp Clark Pitman, 1990, pp 1-15). Secondly, *urban biography* is the most popular form of urban history as far as the general public is concerned. The best of the biographies attempt to relate the many complex facets of a city - such as transportation, municipal government, physical expansion, society and social organization - to a larger context of the total city. Thus, the city itself becomes a distinct collective personality, and capable of action. Therefore, the city is seen as more than just a place where interesting events happen. Thirdly, the *thematic approach* deals, with a variety of themes such as economic, social, architectural, etc. It emphasizes a wholist approach to understanding the history of the society. The *cultural studies approach*, is a fairly recent development and post-modern in its analyses. It stems from an interdisciplinary body of theory including the literary theory of Jacques Derrida and the cultural anthropology of Clifford Geertz. Perhaps the most provocative example is Alan Mayne's *The Imagined Slum: Newspaper Representation in Three Cities, 1870-1914* (1993), which is a study of how slums were represented in the popular press in Sydney, San Francisco, and Birmingham. Mayne argues that slums were the constructions of the imagination, and that these representations led directly to the contemporary schemes of slum clearance and city improvement. Thus, an urban historian relies on multidisciplinary tools to reconstruct the society. It is not unusual to find an art historian, social historian, architectural historian, a geographer, a planner, a sociologist, an anthropologist, economic historian, or a literary critic engaging in urban history such as contributors to this book. In addition, the chapters cover all of the approaches emphasizing specificity of urbanization in Nigeria.

Previous scholarships have concentrated on some of the approaches. Akin Mabogunje, (perhaps, the "father of urban study in Nigeria") in *Urbanization in Nigeria* uses a combination of the approaches detailing urban planning in the country. His seminal study however did not cover important issues such as policing, prostitution, postcolonial urban renewals etc. Other important studies are that of Abner Cohen (1969) and Kenneth Little (1973) although scholarly doctoral dissertations have since emerged to cover areas hitherto neglected. Unlike Cohen, Atere, Olaniyi, Olayemi, and Laguda in their chapters gave a historical narrative of strangers and hosts. What is distinctive is the ability to transcend anthropological conceptualization of Cohen and his ilk. Colonial urban policy of segregation cannot be understood without knowledge of the relationship between the host and stranger community. While it's obvious that harmonious inter-group relations took place between the host community and the strangers in the two stranger quarters, their relationship was not devoid of hostility and antipathy. It is in the light of this that this work looks at all the socio-economic, political and most importantly religious factors, which contributed in escalating tension between the host and strangers on one hand, and as a harbinger of urbanization or aftermath of such contact.

Scholars seem to agree that a turning point in academic scholarship on urbanization can be noticed in the work of Kenneth Little. The essays in this volume depart from previous scholarships that emphasized urbanization being predominantly a structural development of the physical human environment. Hence, emphasis was on economic growth, population increase and other closely connected themes. History of urban architecture for instance, also revolves round the development of heterogeneous community and influx of new values. On the contrary, Kenneth discusses urbanization as the aftermath of the growth of cities or urban center. This aftermath is the new value and ethos of urbanization. The strength of the work lie in an understanding of urbanization not purely as structural, economic and population growth, but as social interaction in urban domains in some selected urban centers in Africa. His work can be described as a contribution to urban sociology and anthropology. The only limitation of the work is undue and open-ended generalizations. Although, the author discusses the nature of contact between African and outside world before colonialism, the academic persuasion of the author as urban sociologist did not allow him to historicize Afro-European relations and the role it played in colonial social urbanization.

Historical Antecedents

Historians, anthropologists, archaeologists, and ethno-linguists adequately document the transformation of Africa from the Paleolithic Age to the Neolithic Age. Following the Neolithic age was the Bronze Age, when more cities and urban centers emerged all over Africa. People who lived in what later became Nigeria, in 1914, had already experienced stages in the development of humans, as we know them today. It suffices to say that Nigerian societies were not isolated from this development. The NOK culture had proved Herodotus and Pliny wrong in their erroneous views about Africans (Tijani, 1994). Indeed, there was predominant transformation of life as it changed from nomadic to sedentary and rural to urban in different parts of what is now modern Nigeria. With the largest and one of the most rapidly growing cities in sub-Saharan Africa, Nigeria has experienced the phenomenon of urbanization as deeply as any other African nation, which is, perhaps, unparallel in the continent. Of course, this has historical antecedents dating back to prehistoric times.

Modern urbanization in Nigeria fits into the popular model called "central place theory." This implies the dominance and growth of a single primate city, which became the central place (the political and commercial center of the nation). Lagos (and later many administrative centers) seemed to be the perfect central place in the Nigerian context. Its emergence was largely a result of geographical location and contact with Europeans on the coast. Also important is the emergence of Lagos as a consular post for the British, its emergence as a colony, and its continuous development during colonial period as a center of administrative development and penetration of the hinterland. There is no doubt that the British colonial rule set in motion the emergence of other cities of major size and importance, a number of which were larger than most other colonies. For instance, in the Yoruba region of the southwest and the Hausa-Fulani and Kanuri areas of the north, there were a number of cities with historical roots stretching back well before the advent of British colonial rule, giving those distinctive physical and cultural identities. Also, amongst the Acephalous or "stateless societies," such as the Igbo of the southeast Nigeria, few urban centers emerged before the institution of British colonialism. In addition, throughout the colonial period, there emerged urban centers (the colonial administrative headquarters largely serving as the central place) all over Nigeria just as in any colonial enclave. Perhaps the most distinctive deduction about urbanization in Nigeria is the length of its historical extension and the geographic pervasiveness of its coverage.

Urban development in Nigeria, as in other parts of the world, is multidimensional. It is largely a function of politics, trade and commerce, population movement, government investment in new areas, and general growth. For instance, in the northern part of the country, the transformation of the rural communities to the great urban centers of Kano, Katsina, Zaria, Sokoto, the early Borno capitals (Gazargamo and Kuka), and other cities served as entreports to the Saharan and trans-Saharan trade, and as central citadels and political capitals for the expanding states of the northern savanna. According to Metz, "the northern savannah cities grew within city walls; at the center of each were the main markets, government buildings, and the central mosque." He continued, "Around them clustered the houses of the rich and powerful. Smaller markets and denser housing were found away from the core, along with little markets at the gates. There was also cleared land within the gates that were used for subsistence agriculture. Groups of specialized craft manufacturers (cloth dyers, weavers, potters, and the like) were organized into special quarters, with the enterprises often being family-based and inherited. Roads from the gates ran into the central market and the administrative headquarters. Cemeteries were outside the city gates" (Metz, 1991). The area attracted large numbers of traders and migrants from other region. These new settlers soon built homestead called "stranger quarters" (the Sabon Gari) which were solely for migrant traders and settlers from other areas and societies (Allyn, 1974; Olaniyi, 2004).

Also important is the fact that rural-urban interaction continue as surrounding large and older cities attracts migrants; the rural areas serving an important supplier of both food and cash crops, an essential part of growth and development. These areas have come to be known as close settled zones, and they were of major importance to the agricultural economies of the north. There is no doubt that Kano is the most urbanized of all northern cities. During the 1990s, the inner close settled zone around Kano, the largest of its kind, extended to a radius of about thirty kilometers, which was essentially the limit of a day trip to the city on foot or by donkey (a position it continued to enjoy). Suffice it to say that there had been continuous interaction between the close settled zone, the inner zone, and the outer zones; all acting as essential part of the multidimensional nature of urban development in Nigeria. In sum, there has long been a tradition of intensive interaction between the rural and urban populations, involving not just human, but non-human forces.

In the southern part of Nigeria, the Yoruba kingdoms, city-states, and the Benin Empire's zeal to trade with the Europeans on the coast, and the competition among the cultural centers partly made Lagos an important city. In addition, the activities of European traders also attracted people living in the central regions of the land to migrate to coastal cities such as Badagry, Brass, and Bonny, and later Calabar and Port Harcourt. Also, there were some similarities of origin and design in the forest and southern savanna cities of Yorubaland. Culture, landscape, and history generated a very different character for most of these cities. As in the north the earlier Yoruba towns often centered on the palace of a ruler (Aafin), which was surrounded by large open space and a market. This arrangement is still evident in older cities such as Ife. However, many of the important contemporary Yoruba cities, including the largest, Ibadan, were founded during the period of the Yoruba wars in the first half of the 19th century (Metz, 1991). Based on their origins as war camps, they usually contained multiple centers of power without a single central palace. Instead, the main market often assumed the central position in the original town, and there were several separate areas of important compounds established by the major original factions. Abeokuta, for example, had three main families from the Egba clan who had broken away from, and become important rivals of, Ibadan. Besides these divisions, separate areas were built for stranger migrants such as "Sabo" in Ibadan, which was where many of the Hausa migrants resided. These were complemented by colonial administrators', Government Reserve Areas (GRA), and built as centers for "native" habitation apart from the European settlers.

Despite its geographical location, Yorubaland witnessed a high population density in most of its cities and rural villages. This is one of the significant features of the region. Its cultural diversity was further polarized by the 19th Yoruba warfare (Falola & Oguntomisin, 1996). The distinctive Yoruba pattern of densification involved filling in compounds with additional rooms, then adding a second, third, or sometimes even a fourth story. Eventually, hundreds of people might live in a space that had been occupied by only one extended family two or three generations earlier. Fueling this process of densification were the close connections between rural and urban dwellers, and the tendency for any Yoruba who could afford it to maintain both urban and rural residences.

Although the next section is about British attempt at urban administrative development, we should note that adding sections to existing cities was an important aspect of new urban initiatives during the colonial period. Among the most important were Kaduna, the colonial capital of the Protectorate of Northern Nigeria, and Jos in the central highlands. Jos was the center of the tin mining industry on the plateau and a recreational town for expatriates and the Nigerian elite. These new cities lacked walls, but they did have centrally located administrative buildings and major road and rail transport routes, along which the main markets were developed. The routes became one of the main forces for the cities' growth. The result, according to Metz, is a basic linear city. The linear city differed from the circular pattern, which was largely based on defensive needs and characterized the earlier indigenous urban centers (Metz, 1991). Suffice it to say that the forest zone with its tall trees and thick bush was never a hindrance to urban transformation before colonial, during colonial, and in post-colonial periods.

As mentioned earlier, the other colonial addition was the segregated GRA (Kano, Kaduna, Ikeja, Ikoyi, and Victoria Island), which consisted of European-style housing, a hospital or nursing station, as well as educational, recreational, and religious facilities for the British colonials and the more prominent European trading community. The whole formed an expatriate enclave, which was deliberately separated from the indigenous Nigerian areas in order to control sanitation and limit the spread of diseases such as malaria. After independence, these areas generally became upper income suburbs, which sometimes spread outward into surrounding farmlands as well as inward to fill in the space that formerly separated the GRA from the rest of the city. New institutions, such as government funded industrial and housing estates, university campuses, government office complexes, hospitals, and hotels, were often located outside or on the fringes of the city in the 1980s. The space that originally separated them from the denser areas was then filled in as further growth occurred.

Factors such as the accumulation of wealth, prestige, political power, and religious learning in the cities attracted large numbers of migrants from the neighboring countryside and from distant regions. The growth in population often occasioned the building of additional sections to accommodate newcomers and strangers. In many of the northern cities, as Olaniyi analyze in chapter nine, there were separations between sections of the community. Often non-Muslim migrants, not subject to the religious and prohibitions of the Emir, lived in separate quarters. However, those who came from within the vicinity were subjects of the Emir. The former area was designated the "Sabon Gari," or new town (which in southern cities, such as Ibadan, has often been shortened to "Sabo"), while the latter was often known as the "Tudun Wada," an area often quite wealthy and elaborately laid out. The result, it seems, was that many of the northern cities grew from a single centralized core to being poly-nucleated cities. These cities contained areas whose distinctive character reflected their origins as well as the roles and positions of their inhabitants.

British Urban Administration

This section focuses on British colonial administrative development as an aspect of multidimensional nature of urbanization and development. We emphasize the eastern part of Nigeria partly because Adeniji, Olaniyi, and Olubomehin have respectively provided background as it relates to the northern and western parts of the country in chapter four, eight, and nine. Suffice it to say that the specificity here is not unique to eastern Nigeria. Rather the creation of urban administrative centers is common features of colonial enclaves. The historical narrative specifying eastern Nigeria is adequate for our purpose here. Urban administrative centers were thus central places where modern urban transformation began. British colonial dominance of what later became Nigeria began in 1849 when John Beecroft was appointed the first British consul for the Bight of Benin and Biafra. He was charged with the responsibility of stamping out the slave trade and promoting legitimate trade in areas under his jurisdiction. He was to offer protection to British traders on the Rivers, while the British naval squadron stationed along the coast of West African was placed at his disposal. The Consular period lasted from 1849 to 1899 when the Niger Coast Protectorate came to an end, and the consular administration was placed under the control of the Foreign office in London (National Archives Enugu [NAE] CSO3: Niger Coast Protectorate 1894-1899).

In 1900, the Protectorate of the Southern Nigeria was proclaimed. And 1906, when the Colony of Lagos and Protectorate of Southern Nigeria were merged, the colonial Secretary's office was created for Lagos to deal with matters relating to Lagos territory. In addition, a Secretary was appointed to deal with matters relating to Southern Nigeria, making sure they were amalgamated, and seeing that the office of Chief Secretary was created. It replaced the Colonial Secretary's office. In 1921, the Nigerian Secretariat (later abolished in 1958) was created and placed under the Chief Secretary to the Government. It had two branches namely, the Native Affairs Branch headed by a Secretary to Native Affairs, and the Statistical Branch responsible for collection and collation of statistical date and information required by the Government. In 1914, the Southern Nigeria Protectorate was merged with the Northern Protectorate. A Chief Secretary was appointed to assist the Governor who was in charge of the Protectorate. Lieutenant Governors were appointed for the Northern and Southern Provinces and were assisted by civil secretaries (NAE/CSO5: Lagos Confidential Dispatches).

Early on in the Eastern area, Calabar was created as a province in 1914 and was made up of the following districts and divisions: Abak, Arochuku, Eket, Ikot Ekpene, Itu, Opobo and Uyo. In 1959, the Calabar Province was split into Calabar, Uyo and Anang Provinces. The Abak district that was established in 1909 was placed under the District Commission at Uyo, and later in 1914; it became part of the Ikot Ekpene Division. In 1931, it formed part of the Uyo Division, and then in 1954 it was constituted into an independent division (NAE/IKOTDIST 1-14 Correspondence 1911-1960).

The Arochukwu District was constituted in 1902 after the Arochuku expedition. In 1914, Arochuku became a sub-district under the Ikot Ekpene Division, and in 1959, it formed part of Bende Division in Umuahia Province. The Eket station was opened in 1904, and in 1914, it became a District in the Calabar Division. Finally, in 1922 the Eket station was constituted into a separate District. Ikot Ekpene was established as a station in 1904 and in 1914, it became a Division in the Calabar Province. By 1927, it became a separate administrative unit. In 1959, the Division was transferred to the newly created Uyo Province. Itu first came into contact with the British in 1900, and in 1902, Mary Slessor of the Church of Scotland Mission opened a station at Itu. In 1908, part of the Ikot Ekpene was carved out and constituted into a sub-district. In 1914, Itu became a District under the Ikot Ekepene Division. In addition, in 1927 it became a separate Division and was renamed Enyong Division (NAE/ARODIST 1-28 Correspondence of Arochukwu 1907-1961).

The town of Opobo was founded in 1869 by Oko Jumbo-Jaja and was named Opobo in 1870, after King Opobo of Bonny. Opobo was constituted into a district under the Oil Rivers Protectorate administration. In 1914, it became part of the Owerri Province and in 1915; it was transferred to the Calabar Province. In 1954, it became a Division. Uyo station was opened in 1905 and was then known as Aka. In 1914, Uyo became part of the Ikot Ekpene Division. In 1959, it was constituted into a Province. Ogoja Province was established in 1914, after the splitting of the former Eastern Province. It comprised three divisions: Ogoja Abakaliki and Obubra. Each of these divisions was sub-divided into districts that included Ogoja, Obudu, Abakaliki, Afikpo, Obubra and Ikom (NAE/ARODIST).

Abakaliki was one of the Northern Districts of the Eastern Province before the amalgamation of the Northern and Southern Protectorates. In 1959, Abakaliki was constituted into a Province in the Eastern Region of Nigeria. Afikpo District was one of the districts under the Eastern Province, and was situated on the Cross River. The district (Ediba) came under the British focus in 1896 during the Niger-Cross River Expedition. In 1902, Ediba was made the headquarters of the Cross River Division and in 1905, the headquarters moved from Ediba to Afikpo. In 1914, Bende District ceased from being administered from Afikpo and in 1923; it became an independent district again. In 1955, Afikpo Division was created (NAE/ARODIST).

Obubra District was situated on the Northern bend of the Cross River and was bounded by the District of Ogoja, Ikom, Oban, Afikpo and Abakaliki. British influence in Obubra dated back to 1902, when British Soldiers occupied Obubra Hill. Obubra became a District in 1905 in the Cross River Division. In 1906, it became a separate district under Afikpo Division. In 1916, the Obubra Division was constituted and comprised Obubra and Ikom. Obudu District was situated in the extreme northeastern corner of the protectorate and was conterminous with Northern Nigeria, the German Cameroon, and the District of Ikom and Ogoja. Obudu came under British influence in 1909 during the Niger-Cross River Expedition. In 1914 Obudu became part of the Ogoja Province and a District within the Ogoja Division.

The Central or Niger Province that was created, after the cession of the territories of the Royal Niger Company to the protectorate of Southern Nigeria in 1900, was divided into a number of districts for administrative purposes. Among them was the Onitsha District formed in 1904, with a station established at the Onitsha town. In 1906, the Central and Western Province were merged, while Onitsha maintained its position as a district (NAE/CSO2: Oil Rivers Protectorate Dispatches 1891-1893; CSO3: Niger Coast Protectorate Dispatches 1894-1899).

Onitsha became a province after 1914 amalgamation of southern and northern protectorates. It comprised the Onitsha, Awka, Udi and Okwoga Districts that became the Obole District. Later, it became the Nsukka Division under Onitsha Province. It was enlarged in 1922 with the following divisions: Onitsha, Awka, Awgu, Enugu and Nsukka. The Awka District, east of the Niger District of Onitsha, was created in 1904 and was bounded by Udi and Okigwi. In 1914, Awka became a District in the new Onitsha Province (NAE/ONITDIST 1-5 Correspondences 1914-1956).

The Nsukka Division formed the Igbo-speaking areas of the Okwoga District. The Okwoga District, in the central or Niger Province, was forced on the opening up of that part of Southern Nigeria by the Niger-Cross River expedition of 1908-1909, with headquarters at Okwoga. In 1918, the Obolo Division was created out of the Okwoga Division, comprising the Igbo-speaking areas of the Division. In 1922 the Division was renamed Nsukka Division. The Udi District was situated on the eastern border of the Central Province, and was bounded by the Districts of Abakaliki, Afikpo, and Okigwi in the Eastern Province, and by Awka, Onitsha, and Okwoga in the Central Province. Udi first became a district in 1907, and in 1914 the Udi Division was created. It was later renamed Enugu Division, and in 1955 it was reconstituted into a Division. Owerrri Province was constituted in 1914 following the amalgamation of the Northern and Southern Protectorates of Nigeria, and the splitting of the Eastern or Calabar Province. Some of the districts in the Eastern Province were grouped together to form the new province. The districts were Aba, Ahiada, Bende, Bonny, Brass, Degema, Okigwi, Orlu, Owerri, Opobo, and Afikpo. In 1915, Opobo and Afikpo Districts were transferred to Calabar and Ogoja Provinces respectively. The remaining districts were regrouped into four divisions and a district, which included Aba, Degema, Okigwi, Owerri and Bende Districts. In 1931 Owerri Provinces was reorganized into six administrative divisions that were called Aba, Ahoada, Bende, Degema, Okigwi and Owerri (NAE/CSO3: Niger Coast).

And in April 1947, the Rivers Province was created out of the Owerri Province, with its headquarters at Port Harcourt. Ahoada, Bonny, Brass, and Degema were transferred to the new province. In 1959, the Provincial system of administration in the Eastern Nigeria was reorganized, leading to the creation of Umuahia Province from Owerri Province, and Port Harcourt, Degema and Yenagoa Provinces from the Rivers Province (NAE/CSO3: Niger Coast).

On the other hand, Aba District was first created in 1906, following the establishment of the Eastern or Calabar Province. It was situated between two rivers, Imo and Achacha, a tributary of the Kwa-Ibo, and was bounded by the districts of Bende, Ikot, Ekpene, Abak, Opobo, Degema, and Owerri. The Principal towns of the District included Aba (the headquarters), Akwete, Asa, Azumini, Obegu, Obohia, Ohambele, and Omo-Elele. Ahoada District was created in 1906 as part of the Eastern or Calabar District. The districts of Owerri, Degema, Brass, and Abo surrounded it. In 1931, it was constituted into a division in the Owerri Province. In 1947, Ahiada became a division in the Rivers Province. The Bende District was situated between the Cross and Imo Rivers. It was conterminous with the districts of Afikpo, Arochuku, Ikot Ekpene, Aba, Owerri, and Okigwi. From 1914 to 1916, the Bende District was being administered from Afikpo. In 1955, the Bende District became a Division and headquarters of the Bende County Council (NAE/CALPROF 1: General Correspondence of Calabar Province Office, 1906-1963).

The Brass District was situated in the extreme Southeast corner of the Eastern Province, and occupied the greater part of the delta region of the River Niger. It first became a district in 1906 in the Eastern or Calabar Province. In 1914 when Owerri Province was created, it was transferred to the new Province. In 1947 when Rivers Province was created, it was transferred to the new Province. In 1956, Bras became a Division and the headquarters of the Central Ijaw County Council. The Degema District was first created in 1906 in the Eastern Province, and it extended from the Rivers Santa Barbara and Sombreiro in the west to the Rivers Bonny and Imo in the east. The principal towns included Bakana, Bugama, Degema (Dist. Headquarters), Egbedda and Omo-Nelu. Degema was in Owerri Province until 1947, when Rivers Province was created and it was transferred to the new Province. In 1956, Degema Division was created and Degema town became the headquarters of the Oil Rivers county Council (NAE/CALPROF 1: Correspondence).

The Okigwi District was situated at the head of the Rivers Imo and Orashi. The Districts of Onitsha, Awka, Udi, Afikpo, Bende and Owerri bound it. The Okigwi District was created in 1906 as part of the Eastern District and in 1914; it became part of the Owerri Province. Its principal towns were Amoda, Eziachi, Eziama, Ihube and Ishiaga. By 1906, Orlu was created as a sub-district under

Okigwi. However, in 1914 it became a full district in the Owerri Province. In 1955, Orlu became a Division and the headquarters of the Orlu County Council. Owerri District was situated on the Western border of the Eastern Province. It shared boundaries with the District of Bende, Okigwi, Aba, Degema, Ahoada and the District of Abo in the Central Province. Part of the Province was taken away to form part of the sub-District of Orlu, which was attached to Okigwi District. In 1914, the Owerri Province was created, while Owerri District continued to exist until 1955 when Owerri Division was created. Also created were the Owerri county Council and Owerri Urban (NAE/CALPROF: General Correspondence). Thus narrated, it is clear that Colonial urban administrative centers provide the needed economic impetus and condition for the entrenchment and consolidation of colonial policy of exploitation. Arguably, they also served as centers of political modernization and development.

Conclusion

Nigeria, since independence, has become an increasingly urbanized and urban-oriented society. The oil boom of the 1970s spurred development and urban transformation in Nigeria. There were massive improvements in roads and the increase importation of vehicles, construction of bridges, development of industrial estates, and housing complex. During the 1970s, it enjoyed the position of the fastest urbanization growth rate in the world. Because of the great influx of people into urban areas, the growth rate of urban population in Nigeria since the late 1980s is estimated to be close to 6 percent per year, more than twice that of the rural population. The trend will continue giving all indices of development and government rural-urban renewal projects.

Now, there are thirty-six state capitals in Nigeria, each estimated to have more than 100,000 inhabitants. It is assumed that seventeen of these capitals, plus a number of other cities, probably had populations exceeding over 200,000 inhabitants. Virtually all of these were growing at a rate that doubled their size every fifteen years. Abuja, the Federal capital city, is fast growing and had exceeded the estimated population of 1 million by the end of the twentieth century. Umaru has succinctly described its transformation from a village to a vibrant Federal capitol city in chapter sixteen.

The most significant transformation in the development of rural areas to urban centers is the development of industrial estates and continuous rural-urban population shifts. Many of the major cities had growing manufacturing sectors, such as textile mills, steel plants, car assembly plants, large construction companies, trading corporations, and financial institutions. They also included government-service centers, large office, and housing estates, along with a great variety of small business enterprises, many in the "informal sector". This is the focus of Ajayi and Tijani in chapter one, two, and thirteen. Of course, some of the negative effects of this phenomenon are slum areas and congestions. Perhaps most devastated areas are the border towns that continued to suffer or lack many modern facilities as explained in chapter eight by Adeniji and Tijani. The social and religious impact of the process of urbanization is the focus of Aderinto, Akinwale and Atere, Ebewo, Oguntola-Laguda, and Aderinto. Assurance of urban facilities and its maintenance would not be effective without government policing. Hence, Aderinto, and Fagbongbe and Tijani focused on various enactments by government to take care of social ills in urban centers, and efforts at ensuring the legality of urbanization laws in contemporary time. Governmental efforts at reducing the growing poverty level of migrants in urban areas are the focus of Onoja. The development of aesthetic and foreign architectural construction is the focus of Fabiyi in chapter ten. Here, he discussed precolonial, colonial, and postcolonial architectural outline of urban centers in Nigeria. On the other hand, Olayemi focuses on the emergent militia group in recent time that transcends the role of veterans such as Omo pupa and Bayo Success. An essential aspect of his discourse is the role of non-governmental agencies in resolving the perennial ethnic clashes. Suffice it to say that chapters in this book not only focus on specific issues, policies, and events, but more importantly, aspects of multidimensional urban growth, development, or urban neglect that had remained on the archival shelves or as footnotes in previous studies. We do not however claim to have covered all aspects of urban history of Nigeria. Areas not covered are intentional to provide avenue for further inquiries and scholarship. We hoped reviewers would take this into consideration when they critique chapters in this book in the future.

Notes and References

A Mabogunje, *Urbanization in Nigeria* (London, 1968)

----------- *Cities and Social Order* (Ibadan, 1974)

A Cohen, *Custom and Politics in Urban Africa: A Study of Hausa Migrants in Yoruba Towns* (London, 1969)

G Stelter (ed.) *Cities and Urbanization: Canadian Historical Perspectives* (Toronto, 1990)

HJ Dyos, *Victorian Suburbs* (London, 1961)

----------- *Urban History Yearbook* (London, 1974)

K Little, *Urbanization as a Social Process: An African Case Study* (London, 1973)

A Mayne, *The Imagined Slum Newspaper Representation in Three Cities* (London, 1993)

HC Metz (ed.) *Nigeria: Country Studies* (Library of Congress, 1991)

D Allyn, "The Sabon Gari System in Northern Nigeria, 1911-1940", PhD History, UCLA, 1974

DM Anderson & R Rathbone (eds.) *Africa's Urban Past* (Oxford, 2000)

L Plotnikov, *Strangers to the City: Urban Man in Jos* (Pittsburgh, 1967)

C Coquery-Vidrovitch, "The Process of Urbanization in Africa from the Origins to the Beginning of Independence: An Overview Paper," *African Studies Review* 34, no 1 (1991)

T Falola & S Salm (eds.) *Nigerian Cities* (New Jersey, 2004)

----------- *Urbanization and African Cultures* (Durham, 2005)

T Chandler & G Fox, *3000 Years of Urban Growth* (New York, 1974)

JDY Peel, "Urbanisation and Urban History in West Africa," *Journal of African History*, Volume 21, 1980

U Esse, *Guide to Sources of Nigerian History at the National Archives Enugu* (Enugu, 1991)

L Fourchard, "African Urban History: Past and Present," *Lagos Historical Review*, Volume 5, 2005

A Simone and A Abouhamu (eds.) *Urban Africa – Changing Contours of Survival in the City* (Dakar, 2005)

Archival sources from NAI and NAE are identified in parentheses in the paragraphs

2

Human Factor in Urbanization

Jare Ajayi

The Context

The human factor plays an essential role in multidimensional nature of urbanization and development. It could be argued that it is the main factor upon which other factors relied. This chapter continues the tone in chapter emphasizing the indispensable human factor in urbanization and development in Nigeria. The two keywords in this chapter, **Urbanization** and **Development** are linked by two other concepts: *socialization* and *growth*. The basis of this linkage is clear enough; we cannot talk of urbanity where socialization has not gone beyond the family unit. In the same vein, development presupposes a positive change from the original state of the socio-economic condition of the society in question or an edification of the original situation.

It was often assumed that increasing economic growth measured in Gross Domestic Product (GDP) is tantamount to development. By this it is assumed that an expansion in the value (both in quality and quantity) of goods and services produced in a country would result in the reduction if not elimination of poverty and inequality. The dividend and benefit of economic growth "it was assured, would fall into the laps of all, whether rich or poor, male or female".[1] However, reality from country to country and from decade to decades has proved this to be a very wrong assumption indeed. While expansion in economic activity promotes urbanization, much more is required (a) to have a sustainable growth and development and (b) for the increased economic activity not to be overtaken by the number of people that would flock to this new center of economic promise. Therefore, an unplanned concentration of people may give rise to slums, shanties, ghettos and their by-products – squalors crime etc.

A UNICEF study of 49 nations shows that countries which had a baseline in 1980 of low child mortality and low income poverty advanced socially and economically; while the economies that actually shrank in that decade were those that all started in 1980 with high child mortality, high income poverty or both[2] Thus by the 1990's, the assumption that economic growth in itself would result in human development was realized to be flawed; however, it was realized that the opposite was true as when human development enhances, this was often a condition for economic development. For, while a developed individual in terms of education and capacity building is in a position not only to induce and generate enviable economic undertakings, he/she is also better placed to sustain it. An uneducated (non-intellectually developed) individual, on the other hand is not only likely to need help but may not fully appreciate initiated project and sustain it unaided. Japan, Cuba, and, for a different reason, Israel exemplify the 'miracle' that developed citizens can perform. These countries, among others, possess virtually no mineral resources, yet they are among nations whose citizens enjoy a high living standard. This is due to their high level of education that encouraged a high level of infrastructure.

Incidentally when urbanization is discussed as a concept, the human content is higher than its material content. A given urban unit is measured in terms of its human population vis-à-vis available facilities and resources. Development, in its holistic sense, should herald socio-political reforms that will usher in such indices as the democratization of the political system, economic prosperity, public services that are both efficient and effective, visionary leadership, a vibrant legislature, an independent judiciary that is dynamic, and a citizenry that is conscious of its well-being and is ever-ready to edify its orientation and worldview. Development economists have put down a framework through which a country's development indices can be measured. The framework is in five stages:

1   The first is the traditional society. Here, social and economic systems hardly change over a long period of time. Economic output is low with just enough to meet the basic needs of the population. In traditional societies such as this, there is nothing to induce economic growth or to make society want to achieve growth.

2   The second is the transitional stage at which changes begin to occur in what have been societal norms. Often the stimulus for this change comes from outside influence(s). Outsiders may bring new methods of production to exploit natural resources available locally; although, the level of technology involved might be fairly low. The kind of industries featuring here might be primary.

3   Here the economy has developed to a point in which it can generate investment from its own resources by using technology that is sufficiently advanced to sustain its own growth. The economy (unlike what it obtains in most developing countries today) does not rely much on outside support. Primary industry is still dominant, but with a gradual appearance of secondary industries.

4   A 'drive-to-maturity' is the fourth stage. Advanced technology features result in the setting up of new industries, which are mainly secondary and tertiary industries as against the primary industry. Citizens begin to enjoy low unit cost of products and services as a result of mass production mechanism that has been introduced.

5   The fifth stage is one in which the economy attains its maximum level of sophistication. Standard of living is high, services are efficient, and the population is materially affluent or at least very comfortable. The rate of consumption of goods and services is high which induces more productions. Leisure hours are increased as most methods of production are automated.

It is a known fact that most African countries are still between the second and third stages while there are still a few between the first and the second. In a situation like that, the kind of habitat that would exist is hampered as a result of the death of both human and material resources. Citizens drift from one area to another in search of better prospect for living. This is how migration, particularly rural-to-urban, normally comes about. Because the existing population in the town has not been adequately catered for nor is there a plan that anticipated the influx of new people, the town to which the immigrants headed soon degenerate. Whatever facilities are available become inefficient. Decay sets in and hampers further growth and development. Such a society cannot move out of its situation unless there is an intervention from an outside influence.

Urbanization is one of the major consequences of economic growth and development. Paradoxically, urbanization itself serves as an impetus for enhanced economic activities and development. Thus any action taken in bringing about a properly planned Urbanisation Policy is an important step on the path to economic growth and development.

Normally, urbanization comes about as a result of an expansion of human settlement. This expansion can be as a result of three occurrences:

(a) Natural increase in population through high birth rate with a corresponding low death rate.
(b) Increase in population due to immigration
(c) Combination of (a) and (b).

Ideally, such increase in population should occur simultaneously with an increase in infrastructures such as housing, electricity, telecommunications, educational facilities, health care provisions, etc. But this is not the case in most of the third world countries where things began to deteriorate as a result of various policies instituted by governments in these countries. The deterioration is in the failure to achieve the basic desire of the individual such as food, clothing, a decent environment, and a reasonable accommodation to live in. The year 2004 edition of a World Bank publication contains African Development Indicators (ADI), which presents data for more than 500 indicators of development in 53 countries. Unfortunately, the ADI paints an unwholesome picture as it states, "Half of the region's population still lives in extreme poverty and Africa still houses about three quarters of the world's poorest countries." It goes on to lament that persistent low growth rates, weak commodity prices, civil wars, anemic aid regimes, and the rapid spread of HIV/AIDS "threaten gains of the recent years in overall poverty alleviation and may jeopardize Africa's chances of attaining some of the Millennium Development Goals (MDG) by 2015." To the list must be added lack of transparency in the management of resources by the countries' leaders.

Hope was very high as nations in Africa and other colonized countries prepared for an independence in which the citizens' conduction would be enhanced and their living standard highly improved. But after a few decades into independence, the situation became worse. "Hunger and want became more widely spread due to a combined effects of reduced economic activity, falling national incomes, reduced purchasing power, unemployment and arising food prices." [3] Reasons for this include the cumulative effect of colonial resource exploitation resulting in economic stagnation and social crisis of commodity export earnings, allocation of scarce resources to unproductive ventures, political instability, lack of continuity in policies, corruption, mismanagement, and absence of requisite skills in management and misplacement of priority.

Compared to Asia, and perhaps Europe, Africa, particularly its sub-Sahara, is more of *land-surplus* rather than *labour surplus*. This land-to-human ratio ought to be an advantage in terms of meeting the need of the average citizen. Unfortunately, this is not the case due in part to demographic dislocation stemming from the slave trade era, successions of social strife, political instability, activities of multinational corporations and the biased configuration of the world economy by the super powers. Countries in the first category sell primary products to countries in the second category and buy secondary products in return at prices that are decidedly against the primary products suppliers.

The effect of all these are harsh socio-economic conditions which are creating internal displacement in legion of these developing countries. Unfortunately, many governments in these countries pursue policies that are urban-biased at the expense of rural communities. The atmosphere in increasingly urbanized areas keeps enticing people to urban centers to the detriment of the rural native settings. Whereas, government and their policy makers are aware of this trend, they do little or nothing about in concrete and meaningful terms.

Consequently, two major challenges begin to emerge: depopulation and *spoliation* of the rural areas and the *"ghettorization"* of urban and sub-urban areas. With the high increase in people flocking into the emerging urban centers, governments in Africa are overwhelmed, particularly by the dwindling economic resources that they have to spread into so many areas. The enormity of the challenges is such that many resort to escapism such as borrowing and/or inhuman policies that would force urban-slum dwellers to relocate. The latter policies, such as pulling down makeshift shelters built by poor urban-dwellers, are often conceived and carried out to the detriment of the citizens. The paradox here is that in order for any nation to develop its citizens must have a base in form of tolerable accommodations in addition to proper feeding and skill empowerment. For any human being, "the right to shelter has to be a suitable accommodation which would allow him to grow in every aspect – physical, mental and intellectual."[4]

Practical Hints on Urban Renewal

There is a legion of literature on various aspects of development and urbanization – the latter, a by-product of the former. What is rare are literatures and canons detailing practical aspects of these two concepts?

The rest of this chapter provides recipes for an urbanized community without the side-effects common with many urban and sub-urban communities in developing countries. Perhaps more so than any other aspect of socio- economic conundrum, the success or failure of urban planning depends on the involvement or participation of the people in the area under focus. History of habitation presents us sufficient lessons in this regard. When the head of a clan resolves to establish a settlement, he discusses the plan with adult members of the community. They contribute ideas, labour and resources that not only 'create' or establish the settlement, but also aide in running it. Thus, sustenance and maintenance of such a community continue to be a responsibility of virtually all members of the community.

Two things are noteworthy in the foregoing. One is this idea of 'carrying along'. The other is the authority that the executors of such programs must have over the area to be covered. We shall see how these work in practical terms in due course. An area meant for urbanization (or sub urbanization) must be large enough to encompass viable economic units that would be *interact ion*al first between inhabitants of the settlement and then by extension between members and those outside its immediate enclave. However, it must be small enough for possible interactions between inhabitants and its sub-units, and be amenable to studying and analysis. It can range from some hundreds of people to several thousands. In the words of Michael Goreliek,[6] "it is preferable that the area 'fit' within the confines of a governmental 'unit' – that is, fall within the same administrative boundaries and under the same administration."

Vertical and Horizontal Nuances

There are two broad nuances that must be observed. The first that percolates through different tiers of government is called *Vertical Nuances*. After settling the geographical issue (i.e. the location of the proposed settlement), the next thing is a framework that takes care of urban (or sub-urban) plans of governments at different levels with an intent to harmonize them. What is meant here is that whatever plan is conceived must not be in conflict with Town, Regional, or Urban Planning program at any level in a country that has different tiers of government (e.g. a federal republic). This is important if the program is not to encounter legal and/or bureaucratic blockade before and after take-off. Thus, it is important that there should be a *National Policy* on matters relating to urbanization.

Such a macro Policy must be compact enough to accommodate the country's *National Objective* and to espouse and guarrrantee cultural norms. This however must not be misconstrued to mean complete uniformity in the administrative and physical structure of centers'to be created or re-created under the Policy. Rather, such a Policy must leave room for peculiar features that may exist in different parts of the country. This is important to be borne in mind irrespective of whether the political structure in which the Policy is to be implemented is unitary, federal, or confederal. Each tier of government can then formulate its own Urban Program within the framework of the Policy. The same rule applies even if the planned urban project is by a non-governmental organization or a private individual. For instance, the housing policy of a given country may be that industries must not co-exist with residential apartments for obvious health reasons. Another might be that girls and boys cannot share a school as can be found in some countries with strong religious practice that discourages intermingling between heterogeneous sexes in public.

Whatever Urban Program or scheme conceived in such areas must take cognizance of the need to build different schools for boys and girls in the latter case as well as to ensure that industrial estates are separated from residential estates in the former. Same rule applies in multi-religious settings that must have separate plots of land reserved for adherents of major religions within its enclave so as to avoid conflict.

Horizontal Nuances

This concerns the range of activities, extant and anticipated, that would be taking place in the planned estate. Thus, project planners must take note of the type of businesses that may be featured in their planned estates. These fall under private and public. That is private undertakings that come under trade and commerce, agriculture, etc., and public services like health, education, and welfare schemes.

Whereas it could be possible, for instance, to have a full range of agriculture such as livestock, fisheries, greenhouses, field crops, etc. in a given estate, there are situations where the same is not feasible in another estate even under the same Urban Program. As already implied, the two Nuances just mentioned must be harmonized in order to have a viable urbanization program. Here, attention is drawn to a host of *area/region-specific factors* that can have a great implication for Developmental Process of the state. Thus, when the same framework in both Vertical and Horizontal Nuances is applied in the course of building different urban projects, the content of each project cannot be the same in all cases. So is the methodology. For instance, the type of materials, structure and activities that would be allowed for building purpose in earthquake-prone areas would be different from what could be approved for more stable ecological areas.

Feasibility

In Urban Planning, it is important to conceive plans that are feasible in terms of both building and maintenance. One major determinant here is affordability. To be affordable, a project must not be far above the income level of those who will occupy it. One way of achieving this is to ensure a high local content in the execution of the project and to be as simple and as practicable as possible.

Apart from cost, one important advantage of being simple, practical and local in material usage is the ease with which the local population would be able to replicate it as well as carrying out maintenance works whenever the need arises. However, advocating high local content and simplicity is not tantamount to using materials that are archaic or the designing of structures that can obviously not meet the need of the 21st century. It simply calls for a creative employment of available materials and ingenious application of it in a manner that would make future maintenance easy.

Cultural Factor

There is the socio-cultural factor that must be considered when planning an Urban Program. The case of Orissa, India is pertinent here. The authorities in the state of Orissa, India decided in 1997 to have an integrated (urban) development plan for Nayargh, a district within the state. Low school attendance by girls compare to boys was soon identified as a problem for the scheme. The team charged with the task refused to accept the assumed reason of 'gender-bias' as the cause of this practice. After a month of the team's study-stay in the area, it was found that the real reason for this disparity in school attendance is lack of adequate facilities and equipments. For biological (and to an extent, cultural) reason, this does not constitute much of a problem for boys as they could go behind the wall or nearby trees to answer the call of nature; however, "many girls and parents of girls didn't want to compromise female modesty, a core value in India society."[7] Proposal was made (and luckily, accepted) to construct toilets in form of outhouses for the schools. The number of girls attending schools increased tremendously thereafter. Housing design must take cultural sentiments about housing and living-style into consideration. For instance, a single bedroom apartment is not likely to be patronized by many in sub-Sahara Africa where extended family and dependants syndrome is still very much at play.

The Failure of Urban Programs

Most urban programs in developing countries fail because of their tall ambition, heavy reliance on exotic ideas and gargantuan designs that are too complex for the people/beneficiaries to maintain afterwards. A case study would be mentioned to drive the point home.

A case study can be found in Kaduna, which is a settlement largely brought into being by colonial administration in northern part of Nigeria. Lord Fredrick

Lugard, the Governor came up with the idea of building a place to accommodate government workers. He commissioned his officers to find a location that would be within a reasonable distance from administrative and commercial centers of the day – and one that would be easy for both domestic staff and officers to be punctual at their duty posts at the Government Reservation Area (GRA).

A site comprising 20 hectares of land was found. Named Lugard Administrative Quarters afterwards, the settlement provided homes for hopeful and happy low-income earners. It represented a model at the time and served a very useful purpose. After Nigeria's independence in 1960, the Quarter was renamed Ali Akilu Housing Estate. It was to come under the aegis of the Northern Nigeria Development Company (NNDC) as a legacy to states carved out of the defunct Northern Region from 1967. As the city of Kaduna grew in leap and bounds, the estate was neglected. Dilapidation set in only to be complicated by unanticipated rise in population due in part to paucity of good houses in other parts of the burgeoning city. In contrast to new settlements springing up around it, Ali Akilu Estate stagnated and became mired in obsolete fixtures. Two immediate reasons can quickly be adduced for this. One is that the owner of the property, the NNDC, a government parastatal, was not paying requisite attention to it; its major concern being collection of rents and sundry charges. The second reason is that occupants of the Estate were not treating the facilities as privately owned. As is common with Nigerians, little regard is often given to things that belong to the government, as successive administrations had not thought it fit to create a sense of patriotism in the people. The practice is to use public facility or opportunity for one's maximum advantage often at the expense of the public. As though to institutionalize the tradition of marginalizing the Estate, even those who grow up there, usually move out to 'a more befitting' area once they could afford doing so. Gradually the place became an abode of the less privileged with all the attendant deprivations. For example till as late as late 1980s, bucket-system latrines were the toilet facility available therein while many of the structures were in various stages of dilapidation.

Viewing it as an embarrassment, the property department of the NNDC thought of demolishing the structures and rebuilding them in a manner that would turn the area into a modern estate. Residents resisted this move in part because no alternative was provided and partly because of the realization that they were not going to have it back after reconstruction. They were able to stop the corporation through a court action. Frustrated by its inability to have its way, NNDC sold the estate to Kaduna State Housing Authority in 1985. The latter was content with just collecting rents from the estate's occupants. Rents that were grossly inadequate for the kind of reno-vation and maintenance required. Yet it was not prepared to sink money obtained elsewhere into it. The estate thus continued in its downward slide.

In May 1986, Archcon Nigeria Limited, which was headed by an architect, Gabriel Aduku, later showed interest in doing something about the estate. It came up with an Urban Renewal Scheme (Ali Akilu Housing Estate for Kaduna Housing Authority), Kaduna. The company received permission from the owner to carry out the desired reform in the estate. "The objective of the undertaking was to look into the feasibility of rehabilitating the people and develop appropriate structures which would be to the socio-economic advantage of both the state and the people"[8]

A survey of all households was carried out; thus, birth was given to a plan that would entail the building of 501 housing units to replace the existing 226. "The total population to be re-housed was 1,750 of which about 59% was made up of persons below 18 years of age. The average household size was 7.7 persons, and room occupancy rate was 3.3 persons per habitable room. Of the household heads, 58% of them had salaried jobs, 28% were self-employed while 14% were unemployed." [9]

The project, which is to be carried out in phases, was to be completed in three years at an estimated cost of N9, 803,947.37 by 1987. Considering the assurance given to the occupants that they would be re-housed since the new project would be carried out in phases, the designers received the co-operation of the people 'through a combined system of advocatory and participatory planning.' Thus, they received the tenants' blessing in the understanding that this, finally, was their project. Among the issues considered when formulating the plan was the need to ensure that the workplaces of the residents were not too far away. This was informed by the fact that transportation may become an acute problem in the near future, and that it would bring a measure of relief if a worker could walk or cycle to work.

Everyone concerned was excited including the Kaduna State Government which was then under Colonel Abubakar Umar who provided some funds for the project's initial take-off and adopted it as the state's contribution to the United Nations' International Year of Shelter for the Homeless (UNIYSH). Out of enthusiasm, the designers approached banks for funding. When commercial banks were reluctant, they approached the African Development Bank (ADB), which advised that Shelter Afrique was in a better position to assist.

With officers of KSHA in tow, Aduku led a team to the Shelter's headquarters in Nairobi, Kenya. But the team came back from subsequent (follow-up) trips disappointed. Shelter Afrique said it could not fund the project on the grounds that Nigeria was not facing housing problem nor was she a poor country. 'More importantly, *Shelter Afrique* would not hear of the demolishing of any existing building. They would rather mend derelict ones than knock them down; they would rather upgrade slums by modification than by radical surgery.'

The state government buoyed the spirit of those concerned by its readiness to provide more money for the realization of the original dream for the estate. Bureaucracy and political maneuvering set and caused some delays. It is in this condition that administration changed. Simply put, one of the recurrent problems is the lack of continuity between a departing government project and the new government. A combination of the two happened in the case of Urban Renewal Project meant for Ali Akilu Housing Estate, Kaduna, after the departure of Umar's administration. The old buildings in most cases were demolished and the occupants pushed out to their fate. Suffice it to say that Ali Akilu East Estate has completely metamorphosed from an unsanitary slum to a 'state of the art' and fancy neighborhood as it is entirely elitist and out of reach of those whose labour gave rise to the original development. A total negation of the social concern which inspired ARCHCON into the elaborate scheme for the upliftment of the working class tenants who had no where else to call their home.

Conclusion

Urban development is basically the expansion, edification and enhancement of existing facilities and opportunities. These could be social, economic or political. For a society, it is the combination of them all, as a nation cannot be said to be desirably developed if it is advanced (say politically) but has incipient or inchoate socio-economic system. In any case, such an *undeveloped* system would be a bane of the aspect that is assumed to be developed.

Whether the Renewal Project is for urbanization or a counter-urbanization, the need to observe the following is paramount:
1. Have the area to be used properly designated.
2. Be clear about the kind of estate intended.
3. Ensure that all stakeholders are informed and are involved.
4. Ensure that the stakeholders participate in the planning, execution and eventual utilization of the project in manner suggesting a neo-autonomous democratic government.
5. Ensure that the project is capable of sustaining the inhabitants in terms of household needs including transportation, security, health, and educational and other social and welfare facilities.
6. Have an idea of the maximum population that the estate can take when it has reached its optimum point.
7. The planned estate must be capable of sustaining its occupants for at least 50 years.
8. The design must conform to national urban policy and take cognizance of ecology-environmental regulations.
9. Must be designed in a manner that up to three quarters of the material needed could be sourced locally.
10. The cost must be such that the stakeholders would be able to afford. And in the event of a need for support, the amount that would be sourced from outside would be marginal such that the repayment would be easy.
11. There is the need for absolute transparency on the part of those in charge of day-to-day running of the project.
12. Engage the services of experts in all the technical areas. A great advantage is gained if stakeholders have skills that can be deployed for the establishment and running of the estate.
13. Let the design be culture-sensitive.

Notes and References

1. The State World's Children, 2004, UNICEF (New York, 2003) p 20
2. United Nations Children's Fund: Synergies, cost-benefit analysis and child policies UNICEF Division of Policy and Planning, Global Policy Section, 2003, p 14
3. Basic Facts about United Nations, 1992, p 123
4. A publication of Shelter Rights Initiative as reported by *Daily Comet* (a Nigeria news-paper) of February 18, 2003, p 33
5. We use Policy/Program for the overall framework conceived by a government in a given area while the term 'center' or 'estate' is used for a unit of settlement created there from. Thus a program may have many centers or estates, as is the case in many towns and cities.
6. Michael Gorliek, director, Weitz Center for Development Studies, Israel quoted *in Anatomy of the Rehovot Approach: Integrated Regional Development – Israel Style* by Danniela Askenazy, *Shallom Magazine*, No2, Jerusalem 2003 p 2.
7. Ibid. p 3.
8. Nnimmo Bassey and Okechukwu Nwaeze, *Beyond Simple Lines* (Kraft Books: Ibadan, 1993), p 64.
9. Ibid. p 65.

3

Gender, Urbanization and Socio-Economic Development

Adewole A. Atere & Akeem Ayofe Akinwale

Introduction

From the pre-colonial era till the present day, patriarchy, which is the basis of gender discrimination, dominates the social structure across societies (Nigeria inclusive). For example, in ancient Israel, the male's Morning Prayer was: "Blessing art thou who have not made me a Gentile or a slave or a woman". Also in France in 865 A.D., a conference was held to ascertain the biological status of women, and it was resolved "that woman are human beings but created purposely to worship men". Moreover, in many societies, especially those in Africa, women are regarded as their husbands' property (Ojo, 1997). Hence, some scholars now conceptualize gender as a relationship of permanent opposition between males and females.

Resulting from the above is the fact that-despite immense human and material resources endowment, Nigeria remains a sleeping giant as it is unable to wake up from the deep slumber of economic underdevelopment, high rate of rural- urban migration, urban problems (poverty, unemployment, crime), gender discrimination and so on. The constitution of the Federal Republic of Nigeria takes no cognizance of gender disparity in the various aspects of national life and therefore does not provide for gender equality in any sector of the society. The effect of this includes the disempowerment of women, which is rooted in discriminatory traditional practices such as disinheritance of females, humiliating widowhood practices, taboos against acquisition of properties and so on (Agina-Ude, 2003:4).

Unfortunately, an adequate explanation of the problem of Nigeria's socio-economic development remains elusive. Thus, the need to search deeper and identify social configurations that are supportive or inhibitive to the Nigerian socio-economic development is still a challenge to African scholars. As such, the problem of development in Nigeria is yet to be fundamentally addressed because the former and existing African values have given way to capitalist oriented development strategies. These strategies have pauperized women and relegated them to inactive players. Evidently, the traditional roles of women are ignored in categories that determine the development of a nation (especially in the European sense) such as the measurement of per capita income, Gross Domestic Products, and manpower. Therefore, the extent to which African nations imbibe or fail to imbibe European culture has been the yardstick for measuring their level of development.

Ironically, the more the attempt at grafting the European ideas in African societies the less the effects have been. For instance, developmental policies (Modernization by Design of the 1950s/1960s, Basic Needs Approach of the 1970s, the Human Resource Approach of the 1980s, and the Sustainable Development of the 1990s to date) are yet to yield desirable results. Policy makers adopt the economic approach to redress Africa's development problems whereas the root cause is political. Thus, an administration of wrong remedies has compounded the crisis due to failure of past development strategies (Nuhu, 2003:44; Olutayo, 2003:31; Omoweh, 2003: 34; NISER, 2003).

Hence, the most conspicuous effect of the European contact of the 20th century was the dramatic change in the entire traditional economic orientation of Nigerians. The quest for gender mainstreaming, guided urbanization and socio-economic development in Nigeria instigate this chapter. One distinctive feature of technologically advanced societies is that gender tolerance, urbanization, and industrialization contributed in no small measure to their development. In light of the above, it must be noted that the problem of gender issue, urbanization and socio-economic development are interlinked. Therefore, this chapter is guided by the following questions:

- How important is gender role to urbanization and socio-economic development?
- How does urbanization influence the pattern of Nigeria's socio-economic development?
- What are the factors that influence the Nigerian socio-economic development?
- In what ways do women/men contribute to or inhibit Nigeria's socio-economic development?
- How can men and women be adequately encouraged to support guided urbanization and sustainable socio-economic development?
- How effective are government machineries and policies aimed at supporting gender mainstreaming and development culture in Nigeria?

Gender and Sex Roles

Gender is a concept used to depict the different social, economic, political, and religious roles performed by male and female in the society in all human societies, from the most primitive to the most industrialized. Females and males have certain roles and responsibilities to perform with in a society; that is, there is a division of labour between both genders. Women are mostly recognized for their productive roles, which are regarded as the "primary" role of all women. Any role apart from this is regarded as "secondary" and a deviation from established norm. In contrast, the male gender is regarded as the custodian of law and order; the overall "primary breadwinner" of the household as well as the defender of the family in case of attacks (Oyakanmi, 2000). Both at home and at school, females are taught to be gentle, peaceful, and "norm" abiding while males are expected to be aggressive and playful. These stereotype behaviors are carried into adulthood (Olutayo, 2000). Thus, gender and sex roles could determine life the chances of both male and female as seen in the structure of urban life in Nigerian cities.

Rate of Urbanization in Nigeria

The rate of urbanization in Nigeria is one of the fastest in the world; indeed the growth rate of Nigeria's major cities such as Lagos, Abuja, and Kano is ranked among the world's fastest. Between 1963 and 1991, Nigeria's population census showed an increase of over 35 percent in the numbers of people living in urban areas. Between 1991 and 2001 the increase is estimated currently to be about 41 percent. This is largely a result of rural-urban and urban-urban migration. Such a phenomenal increase brings monumental problems in its wake. These problems usually include housing, water and sanitation, electricity, transportation, lack of opportunities for gainful employment, pollution of the environment, security problems, crime, and social risks. Men and women create all these and are in turn adversely affected with women usually being more disadvantaged than men.

Urban development in Nigeria can be described haphazardly as an uneven development in the towns as the very rich areas lie close to slum areas. Inhabited by squatters, the latter develops as rapidly as the population grows. No migrant has ever given his or her government a prior notice of intention to migrate. Therefore, the task has been undoubtedly frustrating and daunting. Additionally, the spiraling growth retards all efforts made to improve the situation. This is even more so in the face of inadequate regulatory regimes. Even where these regimes exist, people are reluctant to abide by them or even flaunt them. An example of this would be the defiant and fraudulent ways in which people acquire and build over sewerage lines, in green areas, and drainage areas with no consideration of the fact that these are part of the design of the city layout, which is meant to serve generations of Nigerians.

Existing services become overstretched. This especially occurs when illegal connections are continuously made, making the supply epileptic and grossly inadequate. Consequently, most urban dwellers become dissatisfied, if not perplexed, and often agitated. Reactions from these bottled up frustrations can eventually find expressions in a variety of ways (Nigerian Tribune 7th Jan 2003; Daily Trust 5 December, 2002).

Therefore, the question is this: Has the government done anything in the area of urban development and within the last three years, and if it has, can it continue to do so alone? The answer to the first part of the question is yes. Available evidence shows that the current administration has made an appreciable strive to improve the conditions in urban areas though these may not be glaringly evident. But sadly, the answer to the second question is a resounding no. The government needs the support, cooperation, and understanding of the people as well as the direct participation of the citizenry in the infrastructural development of towns and cities in Nigeria.

Without such cooperation, urban development in Nigeria can be seriously delayed. As things are, it is evident that most Nigerian cities tend to wear a drab and dilapidated look; buildings are placed in every available space-green area. The unregulated trading activities and the haphazard location of small-scale repair outfits along major roads disfigure city centers. As for the mountains of refuse in the cities, they are so much a part of the landscape that they actually serve as landmarks for directing people who may be new to an area. Again in the urban areas, people, and especially women, are so unconscious of the environment and pollution that they freely throw refuse about.

To address the above, the Nigerian government sets up a 15-man committee assigned with the task of recommending an appropriate organizational framework for housing development and to find ways of facilitating greater participation from the private sector in urban development. This gives an indication of the desire to change the morass of urban development in Nigeria. At the same time, it is a call for support and assistance from the public. The committee's report recommended far reaching actions to be carried out. Already the government is setting up a new Ministry of Housing and Urban Development designed specifically to deal with the urban problem. This is a clear indication of government's commitment to continue shouldering the responsibility. However, the participation of the citizenry is paramount.

Other specific actions taken by government indicating her commitment to urban development includes the direct inputs into housing, transportation, social amenities such as electricity, telecommunications, water and sanitation, etc. Government also has four parastatals directly involved in housing. These as follows: Federal Housing Authority (FHA), Federal Mortgage Bank of Nigeria (FMBN), Federal Mortgage Finance Limited (FMFL) and The Urban Development Bank (UDB). The Federal Housing Authority, responsible for implementing government housing programs by developing and managing real estates on commercial basis, has within the last 2 years completed 500 housing units in Abuja. It has gone into partnership with private developers to complete 1127 units in Abuja and Port Harcourt. In Lagos, work has resumed at sites which were previously abandoned (Satellite 2 and Abesan 1&4). In other states, the FHA encouraged the state governments to take over formerly abandoned housing projects in their states. The financial institutions have been working hard on housing provisions as they have been granting loans, mortgages, etc. to people to build their houses.

In 2001, the Urban Development Bank spent over $110million towards the implementation of some 23 projects which cover housing, markets and motor parks, upgrading of roads, development of cultural sites, and the construction of shopping complexes. UDB also supports and participates in the implementation of the sustainable city program in Enugu, Kano and Ibadan.

But with an ever-escalating demand in the housing sector, government efforts naturally pale; some estimates put the need for housing stock increases at 40,000 units every year. Can the government alone be realistically expected to provide all that? given all the other areas requiring attention, the answer cannot be yes. The Obasanjo administration also started the redevelopment of inner cities and urban renewal to reduce urban blight in 14 states! Access roads, drains, and electrification are in progress in Rivers, Anambra, FCT, Oyo, Kwara, Enugu, and Kano States. Urban Transport has not been neglected. By 2001, some 66-road projects had been completed and commissioned at a cost over $61.6million. There are still some 129 other on-going projects costing over $190.16million. As mentioned above, the FCT minister has recently completed arrangements for 5000 mass transit buses to ply Abuja municipals. Lagos, Abuja, Port Harcourt, Maiduguri, Yola, Kano, Ibadan, Abeokuta, Onitsha, Jos, Kaduna, Uyo, Ilorin, and Benin are also enjoying urban management strategies. In Addition, a pilot, Community project has been initiated in 2001 in Nyanya, Abuja on waste minimization through source reduction re-use, recycling and the use of biodegradable packing materials. Several ancillary facilities have been constructed such as refuse transfer stations, toilets wells, and a fertilizer plant was thrown into the bargain. This project is ready for replication around the country.

In light of the foregoing, it is obvious that women, more than men, create the bulk of urban problems through sewage disposal and informal sector activities. Unfortunately, women suffer more from urban problems due to disempowerment and urbanisation of poverty that is making urban household to practice urban food production-growing cassava, plantain, etc in their backyard. ILO's concept of aristocracy of labour explains these phenomenal multi occupational families in urban areas as well as rural urban linkages. For instance, in Ghana, every civil servant wife now raises chicken and eggs in her backyard or engages in selling clothes or food; in Kampala cassava and plantain grow in backyards of even affluent residential areas as Kalolo and Nakashero; in Akure (Nigeria) virtually all income classes practice urban food production (Chinery-Hesse, 1994; Okoko, 2000).

Gender Issues in Development Planning

In the 1970's, Nigeria attempted to join the global race for development through the indigenization exercise. This was unsuccessful because of inherent inadequacies in its implementation and management. Some decades ago, development planners in both developed and developing countries were gender blind. The planners in both developed programs which affected both males and females differently. Many development programs have been said to be unsuccessful because women's activities and roles were not taken into consideration. However, discrimination against women affects their contribution to social development.

In the pre-colonial era, women were not totally powerless. Worthy to mention is Queen Amina (Northern Nigeria), a notable military and political leader who ruled both men and women in Hausa land. Among the Igbo of Eastern Nigeria, women participated fully in decision making at most levels. The Obi (male king) and the Omu (female king) jointly ruled Villages and towns. The Omu is not the wife of the Obi. Omu ruled the women just as the Obi ruled the men. In places where there were no Obi and Omu, there were aged women groups at the village level. They attended village meetings along with men. In Yoruba land, Southern part of Nigeria, women were indispensable in the palace and community adminis-tration. Prominent among the women were Erelu (the head of the female Ogboni cult), Iya-Afin (mother of the palace), and Ayaba (wife of the king).

Therefore, a discourse on gender and development requires a critical analy-sis of the various gender theoretical explanations as this may partly explain why women have hitherto been neglected in the development process.

Biological Theory

This holds that the fundamental and psychological differences between males and females in the society make male supremacy and patriarchy inevitable. As George Peter Murdock suggests, the sexual division of labour is the most efficient way of organizing a society. Thus any attempt to abolish gender roles will go against "nature". However, it will be incorrect to assume that nature is responsible for holding women in servitude. For example, among the Gwaris in Niger State (Northern part of Nigeria), women mostly dominated the agricultural sector while men are mostly involved in petty trading. Also, in metropolitan Lagos, only males (especially the Hausas) worked as commercial load carriers (called "alabaru" in Yoruba language). The occupation has recently witnessed the influx of females from rural areas (notably Southern part of Nigeria). It therefore implies here that economic imperative determines the roles played by both males and females. The inadequacy of the biological determinant theory to provide convincing explana-tion on the subjugation of women in the society leads to the next theoretical expla-nation, that is, the cultural determinant perspective.

The Cultural Determinant Theory

The cultural determinant perspective postulates that culture, rather than biology, is responsible for the relegated position of women. Anne Oakley, a British sociologist, who is one of the proponents of this school of thought from her investigation of several societies (the Mbuti Pygmies of the Congo forests, the Australian Aborigines, China, Russia, Cuba, and Israel), concluded that apart from child bearing, there are tasks which are exclusively performed by women. Biological characteristics do not bar women from particular occupations; rather, the mother-role is a cultural construct and a validating myth for the "domestic oppression of women". In support of the above, Heidi Gottfried (1998) posits that gender relations are embedded in the way major institutions are organized. Also,

Sherry Ortar opined that it is not biology as such that ascribes women to their position in the society, but the way in which every culture defines and evaluates female biology.

The Marxian Approach

Karl Marx and Engel postulate that female subordination is the result of the emergence of private ownership of production means, which is protected by monogamous marriage. Certain individuals have accumulated surplus wealth, and they desire to bequeath this wealth to their "own flesh and blood", preferably a male child. Therefore, men need to dominate women to ensure the 'undisputed paternity' of their heirs (Haralambos and Holborn, 2000). However, the key to women's liberation will be their entry into paid labour market and their participation in the class struggle. In line with the Marxian argument, Ogionwo and Otite (1979) observed that in pre-colonial Nigeria, the society frowned on girls working while waiting to get married. Once married, they must keep to the duties of a wife and mother. The applicability of the theory to Nigeria is rather limited because control of the means of production by the male gender is inadequate to explain the domination of the female. Thus, the "Feminism theory" becomes necessary.

Feminist Theory

Feminism started in the Western world around the 1930s to ensure women's liberation and emancipation. For example, in Britain, the Equal Pay Act was enacted in 1970, sex discrimination Act in 1975, and Equal Employment Act in 1972. The Equal Pay Act provides that it is illegal to pay women less than men for doing the same work on jobs that require equivalent skill, effort, responsibilities, and under similar working conditions. There are several feminist theories (first wave feminism, Autonomous feminism and Post feminism), which originated from the Western society. Thus, Radical, Liberal, Social, and Marxian feminists agree that there is a patriarchal society that oppresses women. Feminism comes in different forms: Liberal feminism, Radical feminism, Socialist feminism, and Post feminism. The feminist writers submit that culturally defined gender roles should be abolished. To really appreciate why women, particularly Nigerian women, are clamoring for empowerment, the status of the "ordinary" Nigerian woman suffices.

Profile of the Nigerian Woman

The health status, especially reproductive health, of the Nigerian woman is very poor. Health services are inadequate and inaccessible to the rural women (Igbube, 2001). Female Genital Mutilation is prevalent in twenty-eight African countries. It is performed on two million young girls yearly. The practice leads to long-term morbidity, complications during childbirth, mental torture, and even death. The participation of women in Nigerian politics is minimal in that the political powers of women were drastically reduced with the introduction of native administration (Olurode, 1990). Wife battering rape, acid attack, forced prostitution, trafficking of women, and so on, are the order of the day as regards violence against women in Nigeria. According to Nigerian Human Development Index Report (1996), Nigeria's literacy rate is 54.1 percent. 62.5 percent of male are literate while 39.5 percent female are literate (Femi Olokesusi, 2001).

Development

Development has often been equated with economic growth, process of modernization, industrialization, social change and high achievement motivation, etc. Development being seen as social change is conceived in terms of an evolutionary and structural differentiation phenomena (Labinjo, 1995). To evolutionists like Charles Darwin, the development of a society is perceived as evolving from simple to an increasing complex form. On the basis of Parson's pattern variables, Hoselitz contend that industrialized societies exhibit the characteristics of universalism, achievement, specificity, affectivity, neutrality, and self-orientation, while industrialized societies exhibit their opposites. Wait Whitman Rostow in his major work, the stages of Economic Growth subtitled A Non-Communist Manifesto, identified five stages of economic development namely:

1. The traditional stage: characterized by primitive agricultural economy.
2. Stage of preparation or preconditions for take-off: at this stage, the manufacturing sector is gradually being developed.
3. Take-off Stage: The society is on the verge of development. There is substantial increase in the level of production and the society is attaining the level of self-sufficiency.
4. Drive to maturity: Economic growth at this stage is very fast and the society can produce virtually anything it desires.
5. Era of mass consumption: The leading sector shifts towards the production of durable consumer goods and services and has captured the world markets.

To Rostow, only the United States of America has reached the mass consumption stage, and he identifies the gap between the developed and developing nations in terms of these stages. However, Gunder Frank argues that the first two changes are fictional and the last two are utopian. In addition, Oyejide (1998) identified three key purposes of development which include:

1. The creation of wealth.
2. Poverty alleviation.
3. Raising the standard of living.

For these purpose to be achieved, two pre-requisites must be satisfied:

1. Investments in human capabilities, particularly in education, skill acquisition and health, which enable people to work productively and creatively.
2. Adaptation, transformation and creation of institution, which assist in channeling people's energy towards the achievement of the goals of development.

However, NISER (2003) noted that development encompasses physical development (e.g. housing), social development (health, crime rate, life expectancy, poverty, PLWHA, etc), political development (legislation, resources allocation), technological development (industrialization), and economic development (human resources).

Theories of Development

The Modernization theory and the Dependency theory are the two main competing paradigms of development.

Modernization Theory

Modernization theory was developed by Neo-evolutionists such as Richard Bendix, Nell Smelser, McClelland, Everett, etc. who posit the inevitable transformation from one type of social order to another and identified three types of society:
a. Pre-industrial or agrarian
b. Industrializing
c. Industrialized

Richard Bendix defined modernization as social change that has occurred in the `8th century in Europe and have led to economic or political breakthroughs in the pioneering societies. In summary, modernization theorists assume that development can be achieved in a lineal form through the transfer of institutions, technology, and attitudes from developed to under-developed nations. Europe is perceived as having a higher culture, and the "Europeanization" of the lower culture will lead to development in the less developed nations (Olutayo, 1999).

Dependency Theory

In contrast to the foregoing, Dependency theorists contend that global parity was disrupted by colonialism, which developed the first world and simultaneously underdeveloped the third world such that the rich nations grow richer and the poor nations become poorer. Thus, the first world countries have concentrated global resources while producing massive debts in third world thereby creating barriers to economic development in the third world. In reaction to this, Chinery-Hesse (1994) noted that there are two opposing views of the causes of African underdevelopment: Externalist view (belief in decline in international prices and foreign influence) and Internalist view (belief in economic management of African government). However, if development is associated with growth as claimed by the modernization and dependency theorists, there should be progress and improvement over the previous state of affairs in rural societies (Igbo, 2000).

Approaches to the Integration of Women in Development Programs

Three main approaches have been attempted in order to incorporate women in development planning. They are as follows: Women in Development (WID); Women and Development (WAD); Gender and Development (GAD). These paradigms of women and development have different theoretical perspectives. However, in practice, there is considerable interweave among them.

Women in Development (WID)

The concept of Women in Development came into limelight during the Women's decade (1975 – 1985) declared by the United Nations. Women development experts who held the view that the oppression of women by men was compounded by their economic position as dependent housewives initiated it. WID lied within the framework of the liberal feminist theory which attributed women's unequal status and social position to their exclusion from public share. Women's exclusion from the public was said to be largely due to sexual division of labour. To integrate women into the mainstream of economic, political and social life, laws and institutions must be reformed and attitudes changed. Women without the right level of qualifications have to be encouraged and assisted to acquire a higher-level education and training. However, a major shortcoming of the Women in Development paradigm is that it overlooked the fact that women were already engaged in a wide range of activities that contributed to development. The problem was that women's economic contribution to the development process had always been undervalued because the measure of "productive work" was restricted to paid employment. For example, the meal prepared by the housewife is not regarded as a productive or economic activity. If a restaurant renders the same service, it will be considered as a productive work.

Women and Development

The proponents of "Women and Development" argue that the level of women's participation in the process of growth and development is low. Increasing women's participation and improving their shares in resources, land, employment, and income relative to men were seen as both necessary and sufficient to effect dramatic changes in their economic and social development. The WAD approach takes account of the fact that women have always been "in" the development process. It focuses more on the development process itself, emphasizing the way in which it has become a major source of women's poverty, marginalization and inequality.

Gender and Development (GAD)

According to Schuler (1989), women constitute one major social group that is excluded from full economic participation as well as production for development. They are most often the last to benefit from development efforts due to their inferior economic, social and political position, which results in continuous lag in opportunities for them in education and training, employment, health and public life. In spite of the unequal social and economic relationship, The World Bank (1997) showed that African women comprise sixty percent of the informal sector and provide seventy percent of the total agricultural labour. They also head forty percent of African households and supply sixty percent of food processing. Thus, judging from informal sector potentials, the role of women in the development has been significant over the years, but they face obstacles in their development efforts. Unlike both Women in Development, and Women and Development paradigms, the focus of Gender and Development is on both genders. The key propositions of GAD are as follows:

1. A focus on women alone was inadequate to achieve a sustainable development.
2. Women are not a homogeneous category, but rather they are divided by class, color, creed, and so on.
3. Any analysis of a social organization and a social process has to take into account the structure and dynamics of gender relations.
4. The totality of the lives of women and men has to be the focus of analysis, not just their productive or their reproductive activities.
5. The woman is not passive or marginal but an active subject of social processes and recipient of development.
6. Men and women are differently located within the socio-economic structure and as such have different sets of interests and needs.

Obstacles to the Participation of Women in the Development Process

The Nairobi Conference of 1985 identified some obstacles to the effective and full integration of women in development process, some of which include:

1. Lack of awareness of the relationship between development and the advancement of women; therefore, making the formulation of policy, programs, and projects difficult.
2. Inappropriate national machinery for the effective integration of women in the development process.
3. Non-implementation of United Nations treaties.
4. The justification of physiological, social and cultural grounds for the continuation of women's stereotyped reproductive and productive roles.

Gender Mainstreaming in the Nigerian Social Structure

Making organizations gender responsive has continued to be a major dimension since the states, including Nigeria, have ratified many international treaties and conventions on gender equality. In view of this, gender mainstreaming is imperative for social justice since it would utilize the potential of women more efficiently and enhance their contributions to sustainable developments. The work of women was more valued in pre-capitalist and pre-colonial African societies, but the prevailing Victorian concept of the public-private dichotomy has led to the marginalization of women in access to and control over resources such that they constitute the bulk of the poor all over the world. Women constitute 70 % of those living in poverty, hold fewer than half the jobs on the market, and are often paid half as much as men for work of equal value. Globally, only 10 % of all members of legislative bodies and a smaller percent of government ministers are women (Awe, 1992; Parpart and Staudt, 1990:50; CEDPA, 1997:6-8).

Blau and Ferber (1992) noted that differences occur in the distribution of men and women across various occupations (horizontal segregation) and within occupations (vertical segregation). Theoretically, both supply and demand influence occupational gender segregation. Supply side: women may be less motivated to undertake human capital investment decisions in the labour market due to discrimination and gender division of labour in the family. A vicious circle is caused by traditional gender roles, which provides a rationale for labour market discrimination. Other supply side factors are sexism in classroom, gender stereotyping, etc. Demand side influences entail discrimination against equally qualified women in human resources planning (Blau and Ferber, 1992: 197).

Trends in Occupational Segregation in Nigeria

Scarcity of data on horizontal and vertical segregation makes it difficult to determine its extent. Given the large proportion of women engaged in the informal sector, it would be illuminating to highlight trends in occupational gender segregation. However, the FOS Industry Survey excludes enterprises employing less than 10 persons.

Agriculture, Gender, and Development

Agriculture is the major occupation in Nigeria. FOS (1997:51) indicates that 31.6% of all agricultural workers are women compared to 68.55% of men. Men dominated agricultural occupations in all but 4 states (Abia, Akwa-Ibom, Imo and Rivers). Data for female workers were lowest in Jigawa (2.9%), Katsina (6.0%), and Kano (9.5%). Vertical segregation is shown by women's ownership and control of agricultural resources. Women have merely user's right over land owned by their husbands and other male relatives (Adeyeye, 1988; Afonja, 1990; Soetan, 1994; Soetan, 2002). Horizontal segregation exists in terms of crops that are cultivated. Men cultivated higher income earning cash crops, while women utilize marginal and less fertile farms for cultivating subsistence crops like pepper and vegetables for home consumption. Women may be required to help out on their husbands' farms before working on their own plots. However, while women carry out a large share of work including the planting, weeding, harvesting, and food processing, they do not have control over the income from the sale of their husbands. Over 70% of women had farms that were less than one hectare in size. Olurode (1990) supported this view and added that gender segregation is socially conditioned. He further noted that in most Nigerian community's women have no right to land, inheritance of family property, and equal opportunity to education. This means that women would have limited access to credit and other productive assets for which land is usually required as collateral.

Industry, Gender, and Development

Ngeri (1996) noted that Nigerian women are marginalized in the labor force. Women are more likely to concentrate in the trade, agriculture, and services sectors. Women were not found in the mining and utility sectors and were minimally represented in construction. Although there seems to be hardly gender differences in employment in the manufacturing sector, women are often concentrated in small scale manufacturing enterprises, as indicated by the table below:

Table 3.1. Gender Distribution Of Person By Industry

Industry	Male	Female	Both
Agriculture	63.0	47.8	57.4
Mining	0.1	0	0
Manufacturing	4.0	3.7	3.6
Utility	1.0	0	0.4
Construction	1.0	0.1	0.8
Trade	12.0	37.6	21.6
Transport	5.0	2.9	0.1
Finance	0.8	0.3	0.6
Service	14.0	12.4	10.2

Source: FOS, 1997:41: The Statistical profile of Nigerian Women.

Women in the Public Sector

The public sector is the main employer of labour in a developing country like Nigeria. Between 1990 and 1993, consistently less than a quarter of Federal Civil Service employees were women. There are a lower proportion of women in the professional and clerical occupations while a large percentage were in the sales and agricultural sectors. The above could be proved as follows:

Table 3.2. Percentage Distribution of Persons by Occupational Groups (%)

Kinds of Occupation	Male	Female	Both
Professional	7.1	5.9	6.4
Clerks	6.0	3.2	4.7
Sales	12.0	37.8	21.9
Services	2.0	1.3	1.6
Agriculture	63.0	47.6	57.2
Production & related workers	11.0	4.3	8.3

Source: FOS, 1997:40: The Statistical profile of Nigerian Women.

Table 3.3. Federal Civil Service Staff by Gender 1990-1993

Year	Male	%	Female	%
1990	136,553	78.75	36,839	21.25
1991	137,098	75.41	44,700	24.59
1992	145,385	76.02	45,865	23.98
1993	149,712	75.92	47,490	24.08

Source: FOS, 1997:4: The Statistical profile of Nigerian Women.

Gender and the Informal Sector

Although there is hardly any reliable data on the informal sector, most Nigerian women are concentrated in the informal sector as micro entrepreneurs. This arises from low educational status and limited access to productive resources such as land, credit, technology, and agricultural inputs. Low capital requirements, low productivity, and high attrition rate of businesses characterize the informal sector. Most of the businesses in the sector employ less than 10 persons and are constantly overlooked by the FOS census of industrial enterprises. The informal sector provides apprenticeship training for young school leavers who plan to set up their own business upon completing their training. Wages and hours of work are not regulated in the informal sector and there is the potential for exploitation of employees and apprentices. There is evidence of occupational segregation in the sector. Most women are found engaged in occupations such as hairdressing, dressmaking, and food processing which requires low capital and skills and generating low income. On the other hand, more men are found in the relatively more lucrative higher capital, skills and income sub sectors such as the transportation and construction businesses (Soetan, 203:8).

Gender and Medical Practice

In 1984, 14.4 % of all medical practitioners in Nigeria are women. In the ten-year period 1984-1993, there has been a small increase of 3.1% in the percent of females in medical practice. Thus, men are more likely to work as medical practitioners as shown below.

Table 3.4. Medical Practitioners in Nigeria by Sex

Year	Male	Female	Female As % Of Total
1984	8,522	1,436	14.4
1985	10,148	1,760	14.8
1986	10,829	1,965	15.4
1987	11,281	2,051	15.4
1988	12,102	2,262	15.7
1989	12,656	2,419	16.0
1990	13,561	2,653	16.4
1991	14,316	2,929	17.0
1992	15,119	3,211	17.5
1993	15,361	3,258	17.5

Source: FOS, 1997:45: The Statistical Profile Of Nigerian Women.

Gender and Manpower in Educational Institutions

The proportion of male teachers was consistently higher than that of female teachers for all levels of educational institutions, but the gender gap increased more widely from primary schools (5%) to colleges of education, polytechnic and universities (+80%). There is evidence of vertical segregation of gender in the teaching profession in Nigerian universities. By the 1992/1993, sessions among professors and associate professors there were 1,315 males (94.3%) and 80 females (5.7%). For senior lectures and senior research fellows, there were 2141 males (88.1%) and 288 females (11.9%). In addition, the higher the level of educational institutions and cadres (within professions), the less the proportion of females.

Table 3.5. Distribution of Primary School Teachers by Sex

Year	Male	%	Female	%	Total
1995	230,287	52.6	207,332	47.4	437,619
1996	216,950	52.1	199,797	47.9	416,747
1997	227,430	53.0	201,531	47.0	428,961

Source: UNIFEM: Status of Nigerian Women and Men: 1997:30

Table 3.6. Distribution of Teaching Staff by Tertiary Institution by Gender
1980/81-1992/93

Year	University			Polytechnic			Colleges Of Edu		
	Tot	Fem	% Fem	Tot	Fem	% Fem	Tot	Fem	% Fem
1980	-	-	-	-	-	-	-	-	-
1981/82	8470	716	8.5	-	-	-	-	-	-
1982/83	8773	716	8.5	-	-	-	-	-	-
1983/84	9285	1163	12.5	-	-	-	-	-	-
1984/85	10038	1163	11.6	2075	235	11.3	2628	463	17.6
1985/86	11016	1359	12.3	3625	439	12.1	2746	449	16.9
1986/87	11122	1284	11.5	2790	413	14.8	2972	478	16.1
1987/88	11521	1481	12.8	-	-	-	3233	338	10.5
1988/89	9914	1323	13.3	-	-	-	-	-	-
1992/93	8454	1318	15.6	-	-	-	-	-	-

Source: FOS (1997:44) - The Statistical Profile of Nigerian Women

Literacy and Enrollment into Tertiary Education

The male-female literacy in 1995/96 was 56.1% for males and 41.2% for females (FOS: 1997). The enrollment rates for women at the tertiary level in Pharmacy, Science, and Medicine were 25.95%, 26.5% and 22.98% respectively. The enrollment rates for engineering and environmental design were quite low at 6.13% and 13.64% respectively.

Gender and Political Participation

Women lack adequate representation in political and decision-making positions as can be seen here. Agina-Ude (2003:4) noted that out of 49 ministers and Presidential Advisers appointed in 1999, only 6 are women and only 4 of the 52 ambassadors of the Federal Republic of Nigeria were women.

Table 3.7. Distribution of Persons Holding Political Positions (1999-2003) by Gender

Positions	Male	Female	Total	% Female
Ministers/ Special Advisers	35	9	44	20.5
Speakers	35	1	36	2.7
Governors	36	-	36	0
Deputy Governors	35	1	36	2.7
LGA Chairman	765	9	774	1.2
Councilors	8,667	143	8,810	1.6
House of Representatives	978	12	990	1.2
Senate	106	3	109	2.8
State House of Assembly	347	13	360	3.6

Source: UNIFEM, Status of Nigerian Women and Men, Statistical Profile.

Instruments for Gender Mainstreaming in Nigeria

There are several instruments that serve as a basis for gender mainstreaming in the country: National Legislation Concerning Gender Equity: Section 1 of the 1999 Constitution of the Federal Republic of Nigeria. Similarly, section 17, subsection 3 provides that: "all citizens, without discrimination on any grounds whatsoever, have opportunity for securing adequate means of livelihood, as well as adequate opportunity to secure suitable employment." The African Charter on Human Rights or The Banjul Charter (1987) provided for gender equality. Also, other instruments such as the following aim at promoting gender mainstreaming:

- CEDAW or the Bill of Rights of Women (1979)
- Optional Protocol to CEDAW (2000)
- ILO Convention 100 (equal remuneration for work of equal value, 1953)

Conclusion

The chapter has discussed various issues bordering on gender, urbanisation and socio-economic development in Nigeria, and a close review of the paper is necessary to ensure necessary policy implications in line with, among other things, the following suggestions:

1. Incorporation/ Institutionalization of women's issues at local, national, regional, and international levels.
2. Elimination of gender bias and prejudice hindering solution to women's problems.
3. Recognition should be given to the remunerated and un-remunerated contributions of women to all aspects of development.
4. Also, efforts should be made to measure and reflect women contributions in the Gross National Product (GNP).
5. The need should be recognized for the full participation of women in socio-economic and political process.

Notes and References

Agina-Ude, Ada (2003). Strategies for Expanding Female Participation in the 2003 Election and Beyond: SSAN- The Nigerian Social Scientist, 6(1), March 2003: (3-7): 1-55.

Blau Francine and Ferber Marianne (1992). The Economics of Women, Men and Work. New Jersey: Prentice Hall.

.Chinery-Hesse, Mary (1994). "Key Note Address -Poverty Alleviation in Developing Countries with Particular Reference to Africa. Poverty and Development, 10, The Hague, July 1994.

Federal Republic of Nigeria (1999). Constitution of the Federal Republic of Nigeria. Lagos: Federal Government Press.

Igbo, E.U.M (2000). Nigerian Youths and Changing Cultural Values in the Name of Development-The Igbo Case: Journal of Sociology 1 (1) April 2000.

Ngeri, N. (1996). Problems of Gender Disparity: The Guardian, 1/7/96:27.

Nigerian Institute of Social and Economic Research (NISER) (2003). NISER Review of Nigerian Development, 2001/2002. Ibadan: NISER.

Nuhu, Yaqub (2003). Review of the 2001/2002 Nigerian Human Development Reports: SSAN- The Nigerian Social Scientist, 6(1), March 2003: (41-48): 1-55.

Olurode, Lai (1990). Women and Social change in Nigeria. Lagos: Unity Publishing and Research Co. Ltd.

Olutayo, Lanre (2003). History Science and the Dilemma of Sociology in Africa: SSAN- The Nigerian Social Scientist, 6(1), March 2003: (29-31): 1-55.

Omoweh, Daniel A. (2003). The NEPAD: Another False Start? : SSAN the Nigerian Social Scientist, 6(1), March 2003: (31-40): 1-55, ISSN1119-8346.

Soetan Funmi (1994). Technology and Female Owned Businesses in the Urban Informal Sector of Report South West Nigeria. Research Report Submitted to the Carnegie Corporation of New York.

Soetan, Funmi (2002). Gender Mainstreaming in the Work Place: The Nigerian Experience: Economics Dept & Center For Gender Studies, OAU. Paper Presented For The ILO Declaration (A Greater Role For Workers Organisations, A Training Workshop Organized By The Nigerian Declaration Project For The Trade Unions In Nigeria, Lagos, October 9-11 2002.

4

The Impact of Road Transportation

Dipo O. Olubomehin

Introduction

There are two opposing views on the role and impact of road transportation on African colonial economy and development. First, there is an argument, advanced by the dependency school, which says that the colonial road transport system was designed and used for the exploitation of the economic resources of African countries; the transportation system facilitated the carrying from Africa her raw materials for processing in the factories in Europe.[1]

On the other hand, there is another view which says that modern means of communication (road transportation in this case) brought not only wealth to the Africans but also liberty and new and desirable goods among other benefits.[2] Exponents of this view argue that African economies were subsistence when they were opened to international trade. It was the opening up process, according to this school of thought, that led to the expansion of export production of the African countries and this expansion was "facilitated by the improvements in transport and communications brought by western enterprise."[3] It is in line with this view that it has been said that colonial rule offered Africa a development base which in the historical context it is difficult to see any practical alternative.[4]

This chapter examines the impact of colonial road transportation on development in South Western Nigeria. The chapter is situated within the analytical context of the two opposing positions identified above. It attempts to ascertain the validity of the two positions while emphasizing the economy and identifiable physical structures of urban transformation. We shall look at the impact on such areas of the economy as agriculture, internal and external trade, and the local craft industry. The demographic effects of road transportation will also be discussed

The Impact of Road Transportation

Road transportation had a marked impact on the economy and the urban transformation of Southwestern Nigeria. Firstly, it helped in furthering British economic interests in the area. Road transportation created a wide market for

European manufactured goods. The development of roads made it possible for European manufactured goods to reach the markets in the different parts of Southwestern Nigeria. Unlike in the pre-colonial period when European manufactured goods were found mainly in the lagoon and coastal markets, imported goods now found their way in large quantities into the markets in the interior. Some of the markets in the interior that received an increased quantity of European manufactured goods included Oja'ba and other markets in Ibadan; Kajola, Owene, and Ilase markets in Ilesa and Oshogbo districts. Markets in Oyo, Ede, and Ikirun in Oyo province also received great quantities of European manufactured goods. For example, in Ede district, important markets such as Sekona, Olodan, and Sasa received large quantities of imported goods and traders patronized the markets from far and near to buy these goods. In Ondo province, markets, which performed similar function, included Oja Oba, Jankara, Owena, and Mofereyi in Akure, Oshele market in Ikare, Oja Oba market in Owo in addition to numerous other markets located in different parts of the province. As imported goods found their way to these markets, people in Southwestern Nigeria gradually developed a taste for imported goods. In this way, road transportation helped to further British economic interests in Southwestern Nigeria since one of the objectives of the British coming to Nigeria was to find market for their manufactured products.

As a consequence of the opening up process discussed above, road transportation facilitated the exploitation of the indigenous economy by the British. Road transportation made it possible for the colonial authorities to exploit the rich human and material wealth of South Western Nigeria. This exploitation occurred at three principal levels. Firstly, the foreign firms shipped the agricultural resources produced in the region overseas. Sadly, these resources were purchased by the firms under terms not usually set by the producers but by the foreign buying firms, a development that reduced the disposable income of the farmers and hindered their ability to re-invest meaningfully into the agricultural economy. As a result, the economy did not witness any major structural transformation during the colonial period. By 1960 when colonial rule ended, the major weapons of farming in Western Nigeria were still the rudimentary implements such as hoes and cutlasses.

The second level of exploitation took the form of the taxation of indigenous people to finance colonial road development projects. This was done because during the colonial period the government pursued a policy of self-sufficiency that implied that the money for infrastructural development must be sourced within the colonial territory. Hence, the people were made in many cases to fund road development projects themselves.

Thirdly, the exploitation involved the use of forced labor for road construction. For example, in the early years of colonial rule, all able-bodied men were required to supply labor for road construction and similar work up to six days a quarter.[5] Refusal to supply labor was punishable by fine or imprisonment.

As part of its effort in furthering colonial economic interests in South Western Nigeria, road transportation ultimately facilitated the incorporation of the indigenous economy into the world capitalist economy. By opening up the resources of the area to the exploitation of the British and creating markets for European manufactured goods in the area, road transportation did a lot to subordinate the hitherto independent economy of South Western Nigeria to that of the British. This is because as the material resources of South Western Nigeria were taken to Britain, the colonial administration did very little to develop the indigenous economy. Rather, as European manufactured goods were imported into the country, the colonial administration discouraged the development of indigenous industries that could produce goods in competition with the imported ones. This was to provide market for European manufactured goods. Over time, the indigenous economy became dependent on that of Britain not only for the supply of imported goods but also for the sale of her agricultural produce. This condition of dependence subsequently set in motion a process of the underdevelopment of the South Western Nigeria economy, which has persisted till today.

Apart from furthering colonial economic interests and creating a condition for underdevelopment, road transportation had other important impacts on the economy of South Western Nigeria, especially in the agricultural sector. We can look at this from two angles. Firstly, it brought about an expansion in the production of export crops, which was largely for the benefit of Britain. The improvement in transport facilities made the traders offer more attractive terms to the producers which made farmers concentrate their efforts on production thereby leading to an increase in output. Farmers worked with all their strength knowing that at the end of the day their produce would reach the market without much difficulty. Indeed, there was a progressive increase in the output of export produce in South Western Nigeria during the colonial period. For example, the export of cocoa from Nigeria rose from 202 long tons in 1900 to 52,331 long tons in 1930 and 154,176 long tons in 1960. Palm kernels production also increased from 85,624 long tons in 1900 to 260,022 long tons in 1930 and 418,176 long tons in 1960. Likewise, palm oil export rose from 45,508 long tons in 1900 to 135,801 long tons in 1930 and 183,360 long tons in 1960.[6] It should be noted that South Western Nigeria produced over 90% of Nigeria's total cocoa output and a little over 50% of her total palm kernel output.

The second impact of road transportation on the agricultural economy was a shift in the interest of farmers from the production of foodstuffs to the cultivation of cash crops. There are three reasons for this. Firstly, the colonial government's policies were directed mainly at boasting the production of cash crops (raw materials), which the British government needed for her industries at home. Accordingly, the roads that were built were meant to primarily enhance the production of export produce, not foodstuffs.[7] The fact that the government provided on enabling environment for the growth of the cash crop economy made farmers pay more attention to the production of export produce rather than the cultivation of food crops. Secondly, the comparatively higher prices offered for export produce attracted more farmers to cultivate export crops. Thirdly, the problem associated with transporting foodstuffs to the market discouraged farmers from producing food crops. This was particularly so until about 1952 when the indigenous government in South Western Nigeria began to take steps to encourage the production of food crops by building more feeder roads into the farms. Until then, farmers encountered difficulty in transporting large quantities of food crops to the market. Many of the road transporters preferred to carry produce rather than foodstuffs because they made more profit from it. As such, only the big time farmers and traders stood a good chance of getting lorries to transport their goods to the distant market.[8] Of course, it is not being stated that farmers were no longer cultivating food crops. There were still farmers who combined the cultivation of cash crops with that of food crops. However, farmers tended to cultivate more of export produce than foodstuffs because they made more profit from it.

Road transportation also had certain important effects on the development of indigenous trade and markets. Firstly, it became easier and more convenient for traders to move from one market to the other. In this way, it promoted internal trade extensively. Secondly, it facilitated both inter and intra-regional movement of food crops and livestock. Road transportation made it easier for people of South Western Nigeria to supply people outside the region with certain commodities. In return, they received what they needed. For example, kola nut, *gari,* palm oil, and other food items were transported by road to the northern part of the country while the people of South Western Nigeria received in return onions, beans, cattle and other livestock.

Apart from inter-regional trade, road transportation also facilitated intra-regional trade. For example, whereas the people living along the stretch of the lagoon in Ondo and Ijebu provinces supplied their neighbors in the interior with salt and varieties of fish (dried and fresh fish), they received in return yams, maize, cocoyam, beans, and other food items produced in the hinterland. As such, road transportation promoted internal trade.

Road transportation also had a significant impact on the development of internal markets in South Western Nigeria. It led to the expansion of certain internal markets. By virtue of their strategic location, such markets that were well served by the road transport network had their fortunes enhanced. The strategically located markets increased in prosperity, as accessibility to them was made possible by means of modern transportation system. This was the case with the Ejinrin, Epe, and Ikorodu markets. Such was the prosperity of Ejinrin that as early as the first decade of the twentieth century, it was described as "the largest market in the Western province of Southern Nigeria"[9] Other markets in our area of study, which were strategically located and benefited from the road transport system, included Agbabu, Okitipupa, and Igbokoda markets in Ondo province. In the colonial period, Agbabu was important as a port market that traders attended from Ondo, Akure, and Ekiti by road to buy fish and various types of European manufactured goods. On the other hand, Igbakoda was important as a fish market where varieties of fish were sold. It was attended by traders from far and near.

The impact of road transportation on trade and markets was noted by B.W. Hodder in his study of markets in Yorubaland.[10] Firstly, the quantity of goods involved in commercial transactions was increased as road transport made it easier to find markets for surplus production. Secondly, with the availability of road transportation, professional or semi-professional traders now moved goods that were formerly handed along a chain of intermediaries from one market area to the next over much longer distances. Thus, "internal trade and markets were in this way given on important new fillip". [11]

The construction of modern road network also led to an increase in the number of markets in our area of study. Although the actual number of new markets established in South Western Nigeria during the colonial period is not known, there is evidence to show that the inauguration of road transportation brought about an increase in the number of existing markets. B.W. Hodder observes that from the 1920s when the motor transport system became more widespread in South Western Nigeria, "application for the opening of new markets increased."[12] For example, in Abeokuta area, applications were received for the opening of markets at the Arikola station in 1934 and at Opeji in 1935. Applications also came in for the improvement of stalls and sheds in the existing markets as in the case of the Itoku market in Abeokuta province and the Ejinrin market in Ijebu province.

Another effect of road transportation on trade and market was that it stimulated the building of markets at the nearest point on the road from a town or village. This often resulted in a partial movement of settlement from the original site to the market place on the main road. An example of this was in Akinyele (Ibadan). The original site of the parent settlement of Aba Akinyele lay some 500 yards to the west of the present site. After 1905 when the road from Ibadan to Oyo was built, most of the inhabitants moved down to the road to establish a market close to the already existing village of Olosun.[13] Another example was at Ogbomosho where the market was placed by the side of the main road in 1932. Also, in Ode-Remo on the main Lagos to Ibadan road, north of Iperu-Remo, a market was built by the main road in 1954.[14] These examples bring out not only the economic but also the demographic effect of road transportation in South Western Nigeria.

Much as road transportation had a positive impact on the development of markets, it also had a negative effect on their development. In some cases, formerly important trading towns declined as trading centers when modern lines of communication bypassed them. This was what happened to the once important Ejinrin market in Ijebu province and the Agbabu market in Ondo province. Until the opening of the Lagos to Ikorodu road in 1953, traders in Ekiti and Ondo districts took their produce to either Agbabu or Okitipupa for water transportation to Lagos. In like manner, traders in and around Ijebu-Ode took their produce to Ejinrin for water transportation to Lagos. Traders preferred the Ijebu Ode - Ejinrin to Lagos route because the other route, which was by road, was the Abeokuta

- Lagos route and this was a longer route. However, in 1953 when direct road transportation was opened to Lagos through Ikorodu, traders turned from both Agbabu and Ejinrin. They now went to Lagos by road via Ikorodu. This was faster and safer than the water route either through Agbabu or Ejinrin. This caused a decline in the fortunes of the hitherto important markets.

This leads to the next point, which is that road transportation, brought about a decline in the importance and use of waterways as lines of movement. This was so for four main reasons. Firstly, the advent of road transportation made motor transportation available to farmers and traders. Compared to other means of transportation, road transportation was cheaper, faster, and more convenient. Therefore, it drew more passengers and cargoes rather than water transportation and the other means of transportation. The second reason was the insecurity that became associated with water transportation. For example, in March 1930, a passenger canoe named "Iyalode Ikorodu" capsized on its way from Ikorodu to Lagos.[15] Twenty people reportedly died in the mishap. Furthermore, in 1942, there was another disastrous canoe mishap. It involved a passenger motor ferryboat named "Iyalode 4" carrying about 300 passengers from Ikorodu to Lagos. Over one hundred lives were lost in the accident.[16] These mishaps revealed the dangers involved in water transportation. It subsequently made water transportation unattractive particularly as the use of motor transportation was becoming popular in South Western Nigeria.

The third factor responsible for the decline of water transportation was the strict control imposed on lagoon transportation by the government in the 1940s. This followed the disastrous accidents of the 1930s and 1940s. The government made it compulsory for boats to carry life jackets for emergency and safety purposes. Operators of boats were also required to have the necessary experience and to get the license to operate.[17] The effect of these measures was that many operators who found it difficult to meet the required standards were driven out of business. For example, the Owolowo Company, which was one of the companies operating the lagoon transport service "was forced to reduce the number of boats in its fleet".[18] Consequently, the number of boats plying the lagoon reduced which contributed to the decline of water transportation.

The fourth factor that explains the decline of water transportation was the poor maintenance of the waterways by the government. It appears that as the government invested money in the development of roads, there was a relative neglect of the waterways used for transportation. In 1952, for example, the people in the waterside area of Ijebu and Ondo provinces expressed their dissatisfaction over the failure of the government to clear the waterway. In that year, the North Channel near Makun Island was said to have been completely blocked with suds rendering canoe movement almost impossible.[19] The poor maintenance of the waterways by the government reduced the traffic on the lagoon and water routes. Traders sought alternative means of transporting their goods to the market.

Another important impact of road transportation was the employment it provided for many people in South Western Nigeria. Many were employed in the road transport industry as drivers, lorry conductors, panel beaters, vehicle mechanics, vehicle painters, and so on. Others were involved in the transport business as vehicle owners. Some of the notable vehicle owners included Chief Salami Agbaje in Ibadan, Messrs W.A. Dawodu in Osogbo, and Messrs Kasumu Igbin and Kasumu Bada in Abeokuta. Others were Pa Samuel Ayo Olusanya, Alhaji Mayabikan, and Chief Timothy Odutayo Kuti (popularly known as Abusi Odumare) in Ijebu Igbo. In Ijebu Ode, there were Chief T.A Odutola, Alhaji Alatishe, and Pa Saidi Balogun. In the Ijebu Remo area of Ijebu province, Chief Obafemi Awolowo in Ikenne was one of the earliest road transporters. There was also Ile Aje based in Sagamu. In Ondo province, two of the leading transporters were S.A. Oladapo and F.I. Akintoye (who owned Omodunni Transport Service). In Ilesha, in the Oyo province, a notable motor transporter was Chief Lawrence Omole.

These people went into the road transportation business for several reasons. For some, it was because as illiterates they could not do other jobs such as clerks in the offices of the foreign firms or in government establishments. Others simply marveled at the way drivers of government vehicles and foreign firms handled the steering of vehicles, which was a new development at that period.[20] Yet others simply went into the transport business because it was considered a lucrative business.

We do not know the actual number of people employed in the road transport industry in South Western Nigeria during the colonial period, but we know that the number had become large enough to warrant the formation of a union in 1932.[21] This was the Nigerian Motor Transport Union (N. M. T. U). It consisted of owners in the western region and the colony of Lagos. The body had its head office in Lagos and branches in Abeokuta, Ibadan, and about a dozen other towns in the provinces of Oyo, Ondo and Ijebu.[22]

Some of the indigenous road transporters in South Western Nigeria entered into the transport business first as drivers and later became vehicle owners. Others started as owners with only one vehicle, but later they acquired more vehicles. Chief T. O. Kuti is a good example. He entered into the transport business in 1942. The capital he used to buy his first lorry was procured from the sale of a house he had built when he was a teacher. Later on, he bought more lorries, which he used for transporting produce from Ondo to Lagos. Through shrewd management and business acumen, the number of lorries owned by him grew from one to six. When the vehicles became too many for him to manage as an individual, he went into the business of selling vehicles on hire-purchase basis. At one point he was importing up to 6,000 vehicles from Europe, which he sold to other indigenous road transporters.[23]

Many of these indigenous businessmen personally raised the capital to start their businesses, as it was difficult to get loans from the bank in those days. It is necessary to point out that by venturing into a new business under the colonial dispensation, the indigenous road transporters were demonstrating initiative, boldness, and ingenuity, which are often denied by apologists of colonial rule. Many of the African road transporters made a lot of profit from the transport business. Chief T. O. Kuti, for instance, built over a dozen houses from the profit generated from the transport business. Apart from this, many of the transporters sent their children to schools, married more wives, performed their social obligations in the society, and bought some of the best cars available in the society at that time for their personal use.

The involvement of these Nigerians in the road transport business brings out the dimension of indigenous participation in the colonial economy.[24] Whereas the colonial administration was deeply involved in building roads; the indigenous people mainly provided the transport services. Without this, it would have been difficult for road transportation to serve the economy in any significant way. There is, therefore, the possibility of seeing the indigenous road transporters as promoting British economic interests. But this is not exactly so. Although in providing transport services they helped the British to achieve the objective of exploiting the resources of South Western Nigeria, it must be realized that many of the indigenous businessmen did not see the British as imperialists. As far as they were concerned, they simply saw in the road transport business an opportunity to be involved in a lucrative business, and they were quick to take advantage of the opportunity.

Let us now consider the demographic impact of road transportation on the economy of South Western Nigeria. The building of roads and the commercial prosperity that accompanied it encouraged considerable internal migration. There were three major directions of the migration. Firstly, there was the movement of people from the rural areas of less economic activity to those of greater economic activity within South Western Nigeria. For example, a survey of the cocoa-producing areas of South Western Nigeria revealed that people "in the Ekiti district of Ondo province and in the areas between Oshogbo and Offa 'seemed' much disposed to move away from their own places in search of employment on farms" in the more economically advanced cocoa-growing areas of Ondo, Abeokuta, Ibadan, and Ijebu provinces.[25] But as cocoa was planted more extensively in Ondo province in general, and in the Ekiti district in particular from the 1930s, the supply of labor from Ekiti to the cocoa farms in Abeokuta, Ibadan, and Ijebu became reduced.

Secondly, there were movements of migrant peasant farmers across regional frontiers. This involved people moving into different parts of South Western Nigeria from outside the region. The main recipients of such migrant labor were the cocoa-producing areas in the late 1940s and 1950s where there was a remarkable boom in the cocoa business. Apart from the cocoa-producing areas, the flourishing lagoon markets in Agbabu, Igbokoda and Okitipupa in Ondo province as well as Epe, Ejinrin, and Ikorodu in Ijebu and the Colony provinces, also received migrant labor. People migrated from different parts of South Western Nigeria and the Delta province into these markets to work. Many worked as porters carrying loads from one point to another while others engaged in farming as well as oil palm harvesting and processing.[26]

The third line of migration took the form of a drift from the rural areas to the new urban centers of commerce and administration which had developed as a result of the establishment of colonial rule in Nigeria. This included children of peasant farmers looking for better educational opportunities and frustrated peasant farmers and craftsmen looking for wage employment and business advancement. They moved to big towns where they thought their ambitions could be fulfilled. The influx of people into the towns and cities brought with it population increase with consequent rise in the demand for goods and services. Lagos, which was perhaps the greatest recipient of the immigrants, had its population increased from 41,487 in 1901 to 73,766 in 1911. By 1921, the figure had risen to 98,303. Ten years later in 1931, the figure had risen to 126,474, and by 1950, Lagos had a population of 230,256 people. Only three years after independence, in 1963, the population figure stood at 655,246.[27] An important point to note is that the population increase was brought about by immigration rather than the natural process of expansion.[28] It is also necessary to stress that the movement of the people between one town and another was greatly encouraged by motor transportation.

Another important demographic impact of road transportation was that it stimulated the movement of settlements away from former defensive sites, (enclosed by rocky hills or on the tops of rock outcrops) towards sites that were more suitable for trading. The new settlements were usually located on or near the road. For example, old Eruwa gave birth to New Eruwa some 2¼ miles away from the old site in this way. Also the movement of Igbeti in 1905 and Oke Iho in 1917 downhill involved the movement of the market.[29] In this way, road transportation played an important role in the relocation of market sites and settlement.

Furthermore, road transportation injected life back into previously abandoned town sites. This was so in the once deserted town of Ago Owu. In 1943, the Resident, Oyo province noted that the new Apomu-Ago Owu road had inspired new life in the hitherto deserted town of Ago Owu. He remarked that

> the new road is inspiring new life into the place and new houses are being constructed and . . . time will come when this area will in the near future regain most of its former importance . . . [30]

Finally, it must be said that road transportation brought certain benefits to the farmers, traders, and artisans. The society as a whole also benefited from it. To the farmers, part of the labor released from human porterage was channeled into agriculture helping to boost agricultural production. Secondly, road transportation removed the physical tiredness that farmers usually experienced in the course of trekking either to their farms or to the markets. Before the introduction of motor transportation, farmers trekked to the market with loads on their heads. If it involved a long journey, they slept on the way. However, with the introduction of road transportation, this became a thing of the past. Most farmers made use of motor transportation especially for long distance journeys. The existence of motor transportation subsequently encouraged farmers to expand their farms.

Thirdly, road transportation introduced quick and efficient means of transportation. A journey that formerly took days by trekking was now done in a matter of hours with the introduction of road transportation. Farmers were able to move their products to the market quickly. This reduced the problem of crops getting spoilt after harvesting. Perishable goods such as vegetables, onions, pepper, banana, and plantain that used to get spoilt before due to transport constraints were now moved to the market more easily and quickly. This was a great encouragement to farmers and an important boost to the indigenous economy.

Lastly, road transportation benefited both farmers and traders in the sense that they could carry their goods to distant markets without much difficulty in case a good price was not offered at the home market. At such distant markets, goods could then be sold at good prices. This was a further source of encouragement to both traders and farmers.

The artisans also benefited from road transportation. Before the advent of road transportation, production in the local craft industries was at a comparatively low level. For example, the basket makers produced in small quantity. This is because there were no vehicles to convey their products to the market. Also, the pot makers produced comparatively small quantities per time. Since pots were breakable items, there was a limit to the quantity a person could buy at a time because of transport difficulty. However, with the introduction of motor transportation, production was increased. Motor lorries were used for carrying the products to the market and buyers could also buy more as the risk of pots getting broken was reduced. For example, in the Ekiti district of the Ondo province, before the introduction of motor vehicles people used to trek to Ponyon and Arigidi to buy pots. But with the introduction of motor transportation, traders traveled to these towns to buy pots in relatively large quantity. Also, traders traveled by road to Ijero Ekiti to buy sleeping mats. In Oyo province, the calabash makers in Oyo town made use of lorries to take their products to markets in the neighboring towns. In Ijebu and Abeokuta provinces, road transportation contributed to the growth of the mat weaving industry in Omu-Ijebu and the Adire cloth industry in Abeokuta. These products, mats and Adire cloths, were taken by road to Lagos, Ibadan and other towns to sell.

Conclusion

An attempt has been made in this chapter to analyze the impact of road transportation on the colonial economy of South Western Nigeria. Based on our findings, it is wise to exercise some restraint in passing a verdict that colonial road transport system produced "unlimited and wide" beneficial impact on African economy and urbanization as some would want us to believe. Indeed, the evidence tends to support the view that whatever positive impact road transportation had on the economy and urban transformation, was accidental rather than intentional.

Evidently, the primary goal of the colonial administration was the exploitation of the economic resources of the study region for the benefit of Europe. As we have shown, road transportation played a central role in the pursuit of this objective. The pursuit of the goal led to the impoverishment of the people of South Western Nigeria during the colonial period. This, of course is not to deny the fact that road transportation had certain positive and beneficial impact on the lives of the people and the economy of the region. Such benefits and positive impact have been well analyzed in this chapter.

Notes and References

1. For a discussion of the dependency theory especially with reference to Africa, see Walter Rodney, How *Europe Underdeveloped Africa* (London: Bogle-L'oureture, 1972). An analysis of the theory as applicable to Nigeria is HI Tijani, "Political Economy as a tool of historical analysis with reference to Nigeria", in S Johnson (ed.) *Dimensions in Nigeria Foreign Policy* (Lagos, 1989).

2. A. Mcphee, *The Economic Revolution in West Africa* (London, 1926), p.106

3. H. Myint, 'The "Classical Theory" of International Trade and the Underdeveloped Countries' *Economic Journal*, 68, 270, June 1958, p.323.

4. R.A. Austen, "Economic History" *African Studies Review*, Vol XIV, No.3, Dec. 1971, p.431.

5. Daryll Forde, *Yako Studies* (London, 1964), p.199 cited in M. Crowder, *West Africa Under Colonial Rule* (London: Hutchison, 1968), p.208.

6. Carl K. Eicher, "The Dynamics of Long-Term Agricultural Development in Nigeria" in Eicher and Liedholm (eds.), *Growth and Development of the Nigerian Economy* (Michigan, University Press, 1970), p.11.

7. The aspect of this paper especially that dealing with the motives for the development of roads has been well treated by this author in another paper entitled "The Development of Roads and Road Transportation in South Western Nigeria, 1906 – 1920" *Nigerian Journal of Economic History*, No. 4, June 2001, pp.14 - 25.

8. Oral evidence: Chief T.O. Kuti, 89years interviewed in Ijebu Igbo on 19 Dec. 1997.

9. C.O.520 / 74: Report on the Western Province of Southern Nigeria – E.P. Cotton, 19th Feb. 1902, cited in O. O. Ayantuga, "Ijebu and its Neighbours, 1851 – 1914" PhD Thesis, University of London, 1965, p.322.

10. See, B.W. Hodder, "Markets in Yorubaland", PhD Thesis, University of London, 1963.

11. Ibid., p.64.

12. Ibid., p.70.

13. Ibid., p.65.

14. Ibid., p.67.

15. National Archives Ibadan (NAI): Com Col 1 974 Motor Launch Ikorodu Accident, 1930, p.2.

16. Ibid.

17. B.A. Agiri, "Lagos-Ikorodu Relations, 1894 – 1950" in A. Adefuye, B.A. Agiri and Jide Osuntokun (eds.), *History of the People of Lagos State* (Lagos, Lantern Books,1987), p.212.

18. Ibid.

19. NAI: CSO 26/14556 S.1 Annual Report, Ijebu province, 1952, p.27.

20. B. O. Osiyale, "History of Motor Transportation in Ijebuland, 1900 – 1960" M.A. Dissertation, University of Lagos, Nigeria, Dec. 1989.

21. R. O. Ekundare, *An Economic History of Nigeria, 1860 – 1960* (London: Methuen and Co. Limited, 1973), p.146.

22. G. Walker, *Traffic and Transport in Nigeria* (London, 1959), p.115.

23. Oral Evidence: Chief T.O. Kuti, interview earlier cited.

24. The subject of indigenous participation in the colonial economy has been studied by O. C. Adesina, "Indigenous Participation in the Economy of Western Nigeria, 1900 – 1970" PhD Thesis, University of Ife, 1992.

25. Galleti, Baldwin and Dina, *Nigerian Cocoa Farmers* (London: Oxford University Press, 1956), pp.206-209 cited in S.O. Osoba, "The Phenomenon of Labor Migration in the Era of British Colonial Rule: A neglected Aspect of Nigeria's Social History" *Journal of the Historical Society of Nigeria*, Vol. IV, No. 4, June 1969, p.517.

26. H.I. Ajaegbu, "The Impact of Lagos on the Changing Rural Economy of the Creeks and Lagoon areas of Epe and Ikeja Divisions, Western Nigeria" PhD Thesis, University of Ibadan, 1967, pp.77-78.

27. A. Olukoju, "Population Pressure, Housing and Sanitation in Metropolitan Lagos: c.1900 – 1939" in Kunle Lawal (ed.), *Urban Transition in Africa: Aspects of Urbanisation and Change in Lagos* (Lagos: Pumark Nigeria Limited, 1994), p.35.

28. Ajaegbu, "The Impact of Lagos", p.78.

29. Hodder, "Markets", p.67.

30. Oyo Prof 1 1010 Vol. II Roads Leading to Large Cocoa Growing Centers 1943, p.28.

5

Role Of Theater and Drama in Political and Urban Development

Patrick Ebewo

Introduction

Some years ago, it would have been inconceivable to associate Nigerian arts, particularly theater/drama (the Alarinjo[1] art) with the concept of development. With advancement in education and knowledge systems, and experimentation with different methodologies for the betterment of society, theater, which used to be regarded solely as an entertainment industry, has become increasingly relevant considering its contributions towards the development of the community and the individual. Plato's argument against the functionality of art is no longer fashionable as contemporary realities have revealed art as instrument of education and empowerment within any given society.

The relationship between theater and politics is apparent in much of the ensuing literature on the subject. "All theater is necessarily political, because all the activities of man are political and theater is one of them. Those who try to separate theater from politics try to lead us into error – and this is a political attitude" (Boal 2000, ix). Freire (1972), Cabral (1982), and Fanon (1967) have written on the importance of using culture for the purpose of liberation of the underdeveloped nations of the world. South African theater practitioners used theater as a weapon of struggle against the apartheid system. Though some critics oppose the use of theater as a political, "sloganeering" organ, other critics and playwrights have no apologies to offer for using drama as an instrument of propaganda. A South African playwright, Zakes Mda, defends the inclusion of theater in political affairs, thus:

> The separation of art, and specifically of theatre, from politics is an illusive notion; and when one examines the different genres of theatre that exist in South Africa, it certainly has not been a factor in the production and enjoyment of the art in that country. It is generally taken for granted that the creator of theatre selects her or his materials from life, and from his or her society. And of course South Africa is a society characterized by racial segregation, political oppression, and economic exploitation. South African theatre can never be abstracted from this particular context (1996, 195).

In his graduation address on receipt of an Honorary Degree at the University of Witwatersrand, Athol Fugard, widely acknowledged as one of the best dramatists of our time, clarifies the issue further: "When I am asked, for example, outside South Africa, the relationship between politics and my play writing, I answer with total honesty that I don't really give the matter any thought. I point out that, as far as I am concerned, in the South African context the two are inseparable" (1992, 66).

In Nigeria, the creative artist is not divorced from the pressing problems of his society, and politics is one of them in which he participates actively. In fact, Gbilekaa argues that in Africa, there exists a symbiotic relationship between politics and writers. This is not only because African writers incorporate political themes in their creative works, but mainly that the writer and the politician are all rolled into one (Malomo and Gbilekaa 1993, 2). Achebe has vouched for the irrelevant niche an African writer would have carved for himself/herself if matters of politics were ignored. He compares such a writer to the absurd man in the proverb, who leaves his house burning to pursue a rat fleeing from the flames (1975, 78).[2] Ngugi wa Thiong'o (1981, 72-74), an astute African writer and critic, lends a voice to the debate on the relationship between creative writers and politics by postulating that the writer and the politician have many things they share in common. Both use "words" in their dealings with their audiences and are interested in the relationship between human beings in the world around them. Generally, literature, and theater in particular, strives towards expanding human consciousness, including socio-political issues. In this sphere, Ngugi looks at the artist as a politician because in his involvement with human relationships, he is inevitably dealing with the operations of power in society including who controls that power, which maintains it, and the use to which such power is put.

In Nigeria, power, the basic energy to initiative, has been dented beyond recognition. People equate power with might, avarice, force, cruelty, and corruption. The word "power" now carries negative connotations and implications. "With contradictions and polarization of thought and action, power has been sabotaged while a kind of plodding pandemonium surges. Institutions have been rigid, slothful, or mercurial. Supposed leaders seem ignorant and out of touch, insensitive and unresponsive. Worst of all, solutions [to problems] have been jerrybuilt or they have not been built at all" (Bennis and Nanus 1985, 6). This nefarious situation has brought untold suffering on the people and a serious setback to the nation. The development of the nation cannot be divorced from political development, and this is where the creative writers come in. With a deep sense of commitment, playwrights in Nigeria have used their art to chart a path they feel could lead the nation to prosperity. It is not possible for art to contribute to political development in a concrete form. Philosophically, development does not only mean achievements of nations in terms of Gross National Product (GNP). Development of a nation is not only visible in terms of the skyscrapers, Porsche cars, computers, sumptuous meals, and highly advanced technologies available in a nation. There is no doubt that these are indices of development, but creative writers go beyond these in their outlook on development. Committed Nigerian writers, including the playwrights, have given themselves the task of developing the minds of the people, enlightening them on how to take creative control of their destinies. Many studies have revealed that cultural awakening is arguably a crucial stage in the development of a people. "There is little point in introducing high-technology to improve the efficiency of developing economies if one does not stimulate the minds of the people to take creative control of their destinies" (Van Erven 1992, 1). Nigerian playwrights use their plays to awaken the slumbering minds of the people in matters relating to politics as well as to educate, empower, and trans-form the lot of the masses.

Because of the importance attached to politics and good governance in the nation, the Society of Nigerian Theatre Artists (SONTA) organized an interna-tional conference in 1992 at the University of Ibadan. The theme of the confer-ence was "Theatre and Politics in Nigeria." In his Keynote Address, Chief Tola Adeniyi, the Managing Director of Daily Times of Nigeria, Plc, states:

> A theme such as you have chosen offers us a welcome opportunity to take a retrospective and prospective view of the place of theatre and drama in mold-ing the responses of people to the complex changes and challenges they have to face in coming to terms with their environment both as a socio-cultural space as well as an aesthetic-philosophical universe . . . We give allowance for the semantic nuances of theatre as a verbal and symbolic mediation of the reality of life of which politics is part. But from a holistic point of view, all that the artist mediates, reflects or refracts are struggles or conflicts for space, for supremacy of one idea over another, for a choice of what is good from what is bad for society. In general sense, ART is the symbolic expression of the contest for power. Of the three genres into which art is divided, THEATRE OR DRAMA is the most expressive of the essential idea of arts as politics because theatre or drama is the context in which the fundamental forces of life are contested, defined, decided, and analyzed for mankind to see the way through the labyrinth called living (1993, vi).

All through the ages, committed artists have been known to be the conscience of their societies. Sometimes, they proclaim themselves messiahs. Many of them uncover and lash at all sorts of evil and strange conventions. They courageously champion the fight against oppression and injustice in whatever form, and they are restless where tyranny seems to fall astern. Many European and American writers have consistently used their writings to comment on the political atmo-sphere in their countries. During the Peloponnesian War, Aristophanes wrote plays that blasted it. In the middle Ages, Medieval mimes and clerks made theaters of courts and churches to ridicule cruel nobles and corrupt priests. When the old regime was crumbling, Beaumarchais and Gogol helped kick out the pins with their plays. When fascism was breeding in Germany, Bertolt Brecht, the father of the Epic theater tradition, exposed it. During the Richard Nixon years in America, it became fashionable to say, "reality has grown so absurd now, you can't satirize it", but Hollywood proved with *Doctor Strangelove* that the greatest absurdities make the most chilling satire" (Holden 1979, 104).

In Nigeria, one may recognize two schools of playwrights and theater practitioners. The first is the group I have decided to call, the Pioneers[3]. In this group belong artists like Hubert Ogunde, Duro Ladipo, Kola Ogunmola, James Ene Henshaw, Wole Soyinka, Ola Rotimi, J. P. (Bekederemo) Clark, Soni Oti, 'Zulu Sofola, and many others. The second group is a group which, for want of a better tag, I have labeled the Radicals. In this group are writers like Kole Omotosho, Bode Osanyin, Femi Osofisan, Bode Sowande, Olu Obafemi, Tess Onwume and several other budding writers. The first group, the Pioneers, is often regarded as conservative because, as perceived in certain quarters, the pioneering effort of some writers in this group seems to have celebrated fossilized issues in the community. Many have accused some of the practitioners in this class as romantic worshippers of the status quo (the palace poets) who use theater to promote hegemony of the bourgeois class in the society. Most of the plays in this category deal with issues of culture clash, domestic problems, and to some extent, social affairs. The plays employ satire as a modus operandi in mirroring evils in the human society. As is the convention with satire, the attack on society from these plays is not malefic or "murderous shafts", but a gentle ping-pong ridicule, which denounces unwanted behavior in the society in an attempt to help culprits amend their lives in the community. In contrast, the younger generation of theater artists, the Radicals, view the stage as an agent of revolution. Following the footsteps of Brecht, they believe that drama should not only teach and please the audiences, but it should also engage them in a process of critical thinking. This group is anti-establishment; it challenges the status quo and is often regarded by those in authority as "subversive." Though it has become common to criticize the Pioneers for not being forward-thinking in their exposé, many of the plays in this category, especially those of Ogunde and Soyinka, oftentimes express 'revolutionary' sentiments.

The task of this chapter is to illustrate and assess the contributions of theater/drama to the development of political and urban agendas in Nigeria. Because of the numerous webs of plays spun by Nigerian dramatists since the colonial days, it would be impossible to include every dramatist in our discussion. Therefore, this chapter deals with select and prominent Nigerian dramatists whose plays have a bearing on political and urban development of Nigeria. Discussions will be based on the contributions of both the Pioneers and the Radicals, and more weight will be placed on the plays of Wole Soyinka and Femi Osofisan.

The Pioneers and Political Development

The pioneers, or the veterans of Nigerian drama, started their career within a period in Nigerian history that Osofisan has described as, "our nation's Age of Innocence." Concentration was on matters of culture, tradition, and efforts to untie the Eurocentric knot of disbelief that Africa had its authentic theater tradition and was not as dark a continent as some of them labeled it. Writers depicted in their plays domestic situations, infidelity in households, master-servant relationships, traditional religion, marital problems, tribal conflicts. Writers also portrayed amiably the clash of indigenous cultures with those of the European, which became intrusive during the colonial times. This kind of cultural renaissance produced plays such as Clark's *Ozidi* (1966) and Soyinka's *The Strong Breed* (1969) or *Death and the King's Horseman* (1975). Festival and ritual plays, as well as adaptations of European plays, were also popular during this period. The end of colonial rule and the attainment of independence changed a lot of things in Nigeria. Freedom, which the generality of Nigerians clamored for, has become something of a curse as the post colonial period has brought with it a myriad of problems for the nation.

One of the major problems with Nigeria is corruption, which seems to be the handiwork of poor leadership. The main stem-winder in any political organization is the quality of leadership because a nation that is short of good leaders is a nation that is billed to fail since "leadership is what gives an organization its vision and its ability to translate that vision into reality" (Bennis and Nanus, 20). Good leadership is the pivotal force behind successful governments. In order to create a vital, relevant and viable government, leadership is necessary to help political organizations develop a new vision of what they can be, then mobilize the political systems to transform towards the new vision. Nature has endowed Nigeria abundantly in her different spheres of endeavor except leadership. Right from the time of the First Republic, even to the present, Nigeria seems to be a leaderless State. In Nigeria, leadership is synonymous with power and seems to be an exclusive preserve of the privileged, the affluent, and of those who believe they are born with it. Dan Agbese believes that in Nigeria, "power is the ultimate aphrodisiac in both sexual and asexual sense. Power confers enormous privileges on the holder. With power, men play god. They control the lives and times of other people" (2000, 7). A nation with this attribute of leadership can never move forward, and many of the Pioneer Nigerian playwrights have also composed plays to condemn this attitude, thereby promoting what is an ideal path to political development. To understand the pre-occupations of some of the Pioneer Nigerian dramatists in their effort to chart a dynamic path to political development, it is necessary to take a panoramic view of Nigeria's political scenario since independence.

The British colonized Nigeria as they colonized many African countries. A plethora of events led to protests against colonialism and following the 1959 general elections, Nigeria became independent in October 1, 1960. Tafawa Balewa and Nnamdi Azikiwe took over power from the British as Prime Minister and Governor-General, respectively. Shortly after independence, political power plays characterized the reins of government. Politics assumed ethnic dimension as political parties were ethnically conceived. The results of the 1962/63 national censuses were grossly flawed, and many Southerners contested the fact that the Northern region had a larger population than the East and the West combined.

Troubles were brewing in many regional headquarters, particularly in the Western region where Obafemi Awolowo and S.L. Akintola were at each other's throat in a bid to assume leadership. This led to a declaration of a State of Emergency in the West. This and many other crises in the nation prompted the military to step in to restore sanity to the nation in 1966. The Prime Minister and a host of other politicians were killed in a coup that was led by Major Chukwuma Kaduna Nzeogwu, and Major-General Johnson Aguiyi-Ironsi was installed as head of state. In a counter-coup organized by Northern soldiers who saw Ironsi's ascendancy as a ploy to institutionalize Igbo hegemony, the head of state was killed in July 15, 1966, and a pogrom in the North saw the loss of lives of people of Igbo origin. This situation and the attempted secession of the former Eastern region plunged the nation into a civil war that lasted for thirty months.

After the civil war, Major-General Yakubu Gowon took over as head of state, but his regime soon proved to be high-handed and wasteful. On the ninth year of his rule, another coup staged by Brigadier-General Murtala Mohammed removed Gowon from office. Mohammed's reign was short-lived as he was assassinated in an abortive coup in 1976 led by Lieutenant-Colonel B. S. Dimka. General Obasanjo was appointed head of state after the death of Murtala Mohammed, and three years after his rule, Obasanjo returned the country to civilian rule in 1979. After fourteen years of military dictatorship, Shehu Shagari was elected the first Executive President of Nigeria's Second Republic. With malpractices and controversies that surrounded the conduct of the elections and the return of ethnic and regional political parties, Shagari's government was not destined to last. Reports of mismanagement of the economy, squandamania, inefficiency, and unprecedented level of corruption hurried Shagari's government to its demise as the army struck again. Major-General Muhammadu Buhari and his deputy, Major-General Tunde Idiagbon, became the new military leaders with a "messianic mission" to save Nigeria from imminent collapse. As time went by, this regime became a regime of intimidation. "Buhari was a man of speed. He left the nation dizzy by the tempo he adopted, leaping from nation-muzzling decrees to sanitation exercises, introducing record-breaking prison sentences of two or three hundred years [. . .]." He was the man who publicly said, "Yes, I intend to tamper with the press," and promptly introduced the infamous Decree No. 2 which declared any journalist guilty . . . for publishing the truth" (Soyinka 1996, 91). On the 17 August 1985, Major-General Ibrahim Babangida, who was Buhari's Chief of Army Staff, staged a coup against Buhari and pushed him out of office. In his maiden radio broadcast, Babangida told the Nigerian people that his regime was "the midwife nominated by Providence" to salvage Nigeria. With only a matter of time, Babangida became a terror. Of the catalogue of woes he perpetuated in the nation, the worst was the annulment of the June 12, 1993 election that saw M.K.O. Abiola as the President-elect. Babangida, 'Marodonically' retired from the army in 1993 and after a brief interregnum, Sani Abacha took over power in November 1993. When Abacha took over power, many Nigerians, including Soyinka predicted that his regime would "out-Saddam Saddam

Hussein's parting gift to Kuwait" (Soyinka 1996, 13). As rightly predicted, by the time the dictator made his exit, Nigeria was reduced to "rubble" as the nation's treasury was literally empty.

As briefly recounted, Nigeria's leadership crises read like a fairy tale. With this sordid scenario painted of the Nigerian political scene, it is difficult for a committed local playwright to behave like the proverbial ostrich that buries its head in the sand and pretends not to hear the upheavals on the shores. Unlike the Radicals, Nigeria's Pioneer dramatists comment on some of these situations using a playful method with no bitterness in their tone of effort. In their dramatic presentations, they attempt to mirror the bad political behavior amongst the politicians in a bid to emphasize what is tolerable political culture that will enhance development in the country. Besides amusement, these dramatic works serve as effective instruments of criticism.

Some Pioneer Nigerian playwrights have to, to a considerable degree, act both as the consciousness and the conscience of the politically dominant class to which they inevitably belong. They compose plays dealing with politics to attack a specific political evil, and propose or imply that we should not endure such evil. In many of their plays, politicians are presented as usurpers, exploiters, and plunderers of the national resources. Ogunde's play, *Strike and Hunger*, criticized the 1945 general strike in Nigeria, while *Bread and Bullet* condemned police's brutality in the shooting of striking miners in Enugu in 1951. In 1965, *Yoruba Ronu* made public the playwright's disapproval of the late Akintola's usurpation of power from the late popular Yoruba political leader, Chief Awolowo. Ebun Clark (1979) has revealed a range of plays from Ogunde that encompasses political comments. In James Ene Henshaw's *Medicine for Love* (1964), Ewia Ekunyah is a typical Nigerian politician portrayed as cunning and deceptive. In one of the episodes in the play, he orders his partyman to deceive the electorates:

> The road will cost several thousand pounds. But wait . . . tell them that I shall build the road . . . hire about a hundred drums of tar. Line them along the road. . . . Then hire several loads of sand and heap the sand at suitable intervals along the road. An impression must be given that the roadwork is starting any moment now (44).

In his hypocrisy in the religious circle, he gives another instruction to his partyman:

> Don't forget to report in the newspapers the contribution I have made to the church organ fund . . . Think what it will mean when all the women in the church whisper it around that Ewia Ekunyah has paid a hundred and twenty pounds towards the church's new organ fund . . . (45).

These presentations are travesties of the ideal and a subtle appeal for politicians to refrain from deceitfulness and face righteousness for the sake of development. Clark's *The Raft* (1964) is a theatrical metaphor for Nigeria as a country adrift because of political mismanagement. Traces of bad politics and the condemnations of them are present in Rotimi's *Our Husband Has Gone Mad Again*

(1977), and in *Hopes of the Living Dead* (1988). In the former, Rotimi, in his rib-breaking comedy caricatures Lejoka-brown as a typical Nigerian politician who "joins politics with the main intention of enriching himself, acquiring social significance, and becoming famous through the misappropriation of public funds and the wrong application and use of government machinery at the expense of the electorate" (Solomon 2001, 22). As far as this corrupt politician is concerned, politics is "war." "It is war! Politics is war. Oooh – I am taking no chances this time, brother mine [Okonkwo]. Mhm. Last time, I took things slow and easy and what happened? Chuu! I lost a by-election to a . . . a small crab . . . a baby monkey . . . Mhm – This time it is war!" (7). In the opening scene of the play, he makes public his selfish intentions in joining politics:

> Politics is the thing now in Nigeria . . . You want to be famous? Politics. You want to chop life? – No, no – you want to chop a big slice of the national cake? – Na politics. . . . Cakes are too soft, . . . just you wait! Once we get elected to the top, wallahi, we shall stuff ourselves with huge mouthfuls of the national chin-chin . . . something you'll eat and eat, brothers, and you know you've eaten something (4)

Duro Ladipo's *Oba Koso and Oba Waja* (1965) are replete with political messages aimed at persuading the politicians to retrace their footsteps from the path of evil.

Apart from the aforementioned playwrights and their works, Wole Soyinka stands out as a powerful voice crying out against the miscarriage of justice in the Nigerian community by the politicians. As is common in most of his plays, from the sketches in *Before the Blackout* (1971), A *Dance of the Forests* (1963), *Kongi's Harvest* (1967) to *King Baabu* (2001), Soyinka is very skeptical of the political leadership in Africa generally, and in Nigeria in particular. His plays ridicule, mock, and laugh at those who call themselves leaders but lack the qualities of sincere leadership. In his "For Better For Worse" (one of the sketches in Before the Blackout), Soyinka railed at the decadent attitude of the 1963/65 Nigerian politicians. This play is a satire on the period when anything, which did not identify with the ruling party, was "dissolved". We are informed in the short sketch that local government councils, police stations, schools, markets, bars, and other similar institutions were all closed down. In the foreword accompanying the play, Soyinka, hints sarcastically that "that period in politics, a poultry could be ordered dissolved for not laying eggs already stamped with the symbol of their party" (22). One institution, which the majority of people pressed that it should be dissolved, the House of Assembly, is not dissolved. Rather, one of the politicians (Politician B), in the ironic voice of Brecht calls for: " . . . DISSOLVE THE PEOPLE" (25). "For Better For Worse" is Soyinka's satire of infusion on the "Akintola–Fani Kayode affair" of the mid-sixties. The play also mirrors the doings of the corrupt politicians of Nigeria's First Republic.

"Symbolic Peace, Symbolic Gifts" is another sketch, which deals with the wiles and deceits of 'regionalized' political leaders. This play employs satiric irony and humor to demonstrate how politicians fool not only the electorates, but also their colleague- politicians. Two politicians, Away Politician (A) and Home Politician (B) are touring B's region. In this region there is no sign of meaningful democracy and the common people are rioting because of joblessness. Missiles are hurled at the two politicians, but Politician B out of shame, deceives A that the missiles are not "stones": "Maybe kolanuts. They probably think you'd like kola-nuts" (225). This explanation may invoke a comic laugh from the audience, but the visiting politician knows that all is not well with the city except for the Home Politician who is still enjoying some amenities in the region including absolute safety, " . . . the windows barred. Twelve night guards and twenty police dogs plus an electric fence" (27). A real comedy and satire emerges from this sketch through the satirist's use of verbal wit and humor to expose the politician's wick-edness and dubious disposition in his explanation of the state of unemployment in the city.

> A: (in a sudden frustration) But there is no one about. Windows shut, Shops closed . . . what is going on here?
>
> B: They've all gone to sleep.
>
> A: Sleep! At four in the afternoon?
>
> B: It's the new prosperity. There is no more work for anyone.
>
> A: You mean you've abolished work?
>
> B: Completely.
>
> A: (very confidently, and somewhat embarrassed.) Er . . . it isn't . . . I mean . . . er, what I am trying to ask is . . . the region is not bankrupt or anything like that, is it? We may be able to help, you know.
>
> B: Oh that stuff you read in the papers, unemployment and all that rubbish. Not at all. Just plain good prosperity. When there is money why should people work? (28).

This sort of clever verbal witticism and argument is pathetic when weighed against the sordid condition of the suffering people. It may compel a laugh from the audience, but the laugh is not the type of laughter one would expect from pure comedy. It is a sort of laughter that suddenly fades to leave only darkness and gloom. The audience may be forced to react the way Pushkin reacted after reading *Gogol's Dead Souls,* he laughed, but suddenly fell silent and remarked: "Oh God, how sad our Russia is" (Andrew 1980, 80-81).

In many of his plays, Soyinka blames political dictators he regards as inimical to political progress in the community. Tyrants and military dictators are not also spared in his dramatic works. Soyinka has recognized that in Nigeria, while some seek power by 'noble' democratic means, others seek it through the muzzle of the gun. In Kongi's *Harvest* (1967), totalitarianism is debunked. In *Opera Wonyosi* (1981), the evil acts of military men in Nigeria are exposed and taunted, and the playwright sympathizes with the defenseless civilians for their suffering in the hands of irate soldiers. The play, in a journalistic mode, catalogues instances of civilian molestation by "unknown soldiers": "Mushin Riots, 1970; Ugep Village, 1975; Epe Riots, 1975; Orile-Agege, January 1976; Kalakuta, February 1977; Shendan, Plateau State, June 1977; Enugu, September 1977." (72).

From Zia With Love (1999) ridicules   the high-handed government of Buhari and Idiagbon military regime, 1984-1985. The play opens with a mock cabinet of the "Eternal Ruling Council"(Supreme Military Council) in session. The major deliberation by this council is how to quell civilian uprising against the military, especially the activities of the "radicals" who simply demand of the soldiers to hand over power to a democratically elected government. A character in the play, the Education Minister, warns: "This is a military regime, so don't mess about" (98). Another character, Wing Commander, supports him:

> Don't mess with the military
>
> Or we'll write your obituary
>
> Underworld or over-brass
>
> No one dare embarrass
>
> Power, the pure commodity
>
> To which our little ditty
>
> Is forever consecrated
>
> Don't ignore or underrate it (156).

Buhari/Idiagbon's War Against Indiscipline (WAI) is pilloried in the play, as the acronym BAI (Battle Against Indiscipline) functions against the background of people being manhandled, tortured, and detained without trial. In the play, the regime's WAI is referred to as "obscene litany," and somewhere else, Soyinka attests that this was a slogan inserted into the Nigerian dictionary of mayhem for there was "never war seen to be waged with such consistent virulence against the disciplined and progressive" (1996, 88). In the play, the government that preaches discipline vandalizes the citizens' property, nurtures crooks and swindlers, encourages police corruption, promotes arson and belief in superstition and other callous rituals. Top military officers, exemplified by Wing-Commander, use civilians as conduit pipes for their crimes. Major Awam, the Director of Security, is the only member of the Eternal Ruling Council with a resenting voice who supports the civilians. As would be expected, other members abhor his presence. Even though Major Awam speaks the truth about the delicate security situation in the country, he is not seen to be doing the work of a Security Minister because security to the military dictators means surveillance and the hunting down of subversives. To the dramatist, military people are "*sebe irawe*", deadly snakes on the innocent grass; their patron god is Eshu, the Yoruba god of mischief. In essence, the playwright presents this situation for the audience to watch and spit at. A call for a change, albeit in a subtle form, has been uttered.

The Radicals and Political Development

The Radicals, like the Pioneers, are not different from each other in terms of commitment to the society. What makes them different is their mode of operation; for while the Pioneers are reactionary in their method and employ tact and attempt to appeal to the consciences of the ruling elites, the Radicals are revolutionary and rebellious in their fight against corrupt officials who draw society backwards through their retrogressive behavior in office. What the Radicals fight against is the prevailing 'terrorism' in contemporary Nigerian politics. To Osofisan, "terror" means: This atmosphere of continuously polluting crisis, of fear and insecurity, the suppression of freedom and the gradual imposition of a closed and unrelenting police state. Politics has been mostly a game of musical chairs among a greedy, parasitic elite, from both the civilian and military sectors, who have grown increasingly vicious against one another, while they exploit the common people as mere fodder in their power-grabbing tussle (1998, 14).

The exploitation of the common people is what these writers protest in their writings. They revolt and protest against the system; they are the "angry young men" of the Nigerian stage that have chosen an ideological stance, which they hope, will benefit the masses. Unlike the Pioneers, who are rather compassionate and passive in their approach and believe that people cannot do much to effect change in the face of fate; the Radicals believe that with unity, the yoke of oppression can be broken and the common man can be liberated in the process. This lot believes that man is capable of changing his fate in the face of tyranny. Gbilekaa states that these younger generations of writers compose works that re-examine the socio-political and economic structures of Nigeria and their implications for those below the breadline. These new plays differ remarkably from the committed plays of the Pioneers because they unambiguously articulate the aspirations and yearnings of the working class and the peasants (1993, 8-9). These innovative plays, like those of the Pioneers, are critical of the socio-political situation in Nigeria, but unlike those of the Pioneers, they go further to point the way forward, or direct the way society should follow in order to achieve a level of success. These playwrights write to wound, maim, and dislocate the joints of corrupt politicians. Their art is malefic in nature.

Bode Sowande's *Farewell to Babylon* (1979) and *Afamako* (1986) emphasize the role the peasants could play to bring about a revolution. Kole Omotosho's *Shadows in the Horizon* (1977) shows the class structures of a capitalist state. Politicians and army officers are portrayed as the affluent in society, while the intellectuals are the impoverished lot. A corpus of plays has dealt with military and civilian corruption and the commoner's response to such situations. Georgina Alaukwu's *The Longest Rope* (1983) brings to justice a corrupt Owerri politician who thought the villagers were illiterates and will not see through his crimes.

Ogbuago, the village representative in the regional assembly, is forced to confess his crimes for according to one of the elders, "We may be illiterate villagers but we cannot rear a bird and let it shit on us simply because it has grown wings overnight."[4] Many of these playwrights present dramas that focus on communal action for change. In Esiaba Irobi's *Nwokedi* (1991), unemployed youth organize themselves to fight against corrupt politicians. Akanji Nasiru's *Our Survival* (1985) deals with the revolt of the masses against the undemocratic rule of the self-appointed ruler, Jagun. A character called, Our Son, in Chimalum Nwankwo's *The Trumpet Parable* (1987) is ostracized by the people for being instrumental to the anguish and suffering of the community.

Amongst playwrights of the radical school, Osofisan is the most eloquent. With a Marxist's slant in his theater orientation, he creates plays that carry the ideology of resistance and confrontation of the bourgeois class in the Nigerian society. As he stated in an Inaugural Lecture delivered at the University of Ibadan in 1997:

> In the plays, which I have written onto the bleeding pages of this troubled age, I have sought, advisedly by suggestive tropes, to deny consolation to the manu-facturers of our nation's anomy, and at the same time, to stir our people out of passivity and evasion. Thus far, indeed, I can say that there is no aspect of our present incoherence that one or other of my plays has not addressed, always from a conscious ambition to deconstruct it, heal it, and lessen its sting. Furthermore, by constantly entering the camp of the dispossessed, I am able to identify, and bring to public attention, areas of injustice, of gathering anger in the land. Al-ways I insist on unpacking the sweet and anodyne versions of official accounts, on looking at history "from the lower side", that is, from the perspective of its victims, such as women and the common folk (1998, 30).

Osofisan has written over twenty-five plays and most of them fall in line with his theater philosophy and ideology. In *Who's Afraid of Solarin* (1978), *The Chattering and the Song* (1977), *Aringindin and the Nightwatchmen* (1991), and *Yungba Yungba and the Dance Contest* (1993), Osofisan brilliantly makes wry comments on Nigeria's decadent political arena. Even in his celebratory drama, *Birthdays are not for Dying* (1990), echoes of the extermination of corruption in society reverberate. His *Once Upon Four Robbers* (1991) takes a cursory but leftist look at the practice of killing armed robbers in stadia all over Nigeria. While one who cannot discern into the bizarre nature of the practice may accept it as worthwhile, Osofisan shows us another side of the coin. He is strongly opposed to the killing of robbers (after all, most of the rulers are robbers themselves). While he does not approve of their activities, he believes that external circumstances force individuals to respond in their separate ways, and they react to one another only in relation to these external circumstances. To Osofisan, the unfortunate armed robbers are only victims of circumstance because corrupt society nurtures her citizens to become criminals and the only way to eradicate criminals is for the leaders to lead by good example.

Of greater importance is Osofisan's radicalization of J. P. Clark's play, *The Raft* (1964). Clark's play presents four innocent lumbermen (Olotu, Kengide, Ogro, and Ibobo) taking a raft down the river Niger (the name Nigeria is derived from this river). The four characters are trapped in a situation from which they cannot rescue themselves. In fact, they are adrift and believe this to be an ancient mariner's curse that is irremediable. This seems to be the only significant action in the play, but its connotations are complex. The play is indeed a metaphor for a nation that is directionless and without hope, and the lumbermen represent the downtrodden citizens caught in the middle of the crisis. Osofisan's *Another Raft* (1988) is a representation of an ideological front that is different from Clark's. The play is a reaction to *The Raft*, using a revolutionary esthetics. The helpless and ignorant characters presented by Clark are transformed into activists in Osofisan's version of the play. He attempts to "update the story of a nation adrift" and put in perspective reasons why people are sometimes traumatized in their society. In *Another Raft*, the theme of socio-political and economic turmoil assumes a special historical analysis and attempts to proffer reasons why its society is adrift and identifies morbid corruption as the ubiquitous syndrome that characterizes this society. This syndrome is shown to be predicated on individualism (Uji 1993, 74). In Osofisan's play, hope is not lost; man is capable of redeeming his fate if grabbed by greedy lions in the guise of politicians.

Theater and Urban Development

Our discussions in this section are premised on the understanding that "urban" means the opposite of rustic village life; in other words, something to do with town or city life and consequently, modernity. In those days, Nigerians were basically village dwellers, but as modernism penetrates the cultural fabric of the nation, many Nigerians have migrated to the cities while some of the villages are fast becoming town centers. The hunt for white- collar jobs, availability of social amenities, and sophistication brought about by 'civilization' has compelled many Nigerians to leave their ancestral homes to the metropolitan cities. Many Nigerians who crave for town life do so with the belief that the village is home for witches and old illiterate folks. For people who are not progressive in outlook, they believe the city is where one goes to make a fortune, a place for progress and peace of mind. Our ancestors who lived in villages must have dwelt under the illusion that life would be much more enjoyable if they had decent houses, enough food, and health care facilities. But modernity has brought skyscrapers with digital airconditioning units, buffet meals, hospitals with modern equipment to transplant even the human heart, and other technological developments that have beaten the human imagination; yet, the modern man's life is a void, a nightmare, a life packed with frustrations and disillusionment. While some Nigerian playwrights have portrayed in their plays the bliss of village life and the need for adaptation to modern trend of events, others have shown the sense of loss experienced by some Nigerians who flee the village to live in urban areas. These plays are meant to serve as mirror images of village life and urban environments and criticisms of some ugly situations associated with village and town life in Nigeria.

With the understanding that culture is dynamic, some Nigerian playwrights compose plays that dramatize the need for the Nigerian villagers to adapt and respond to innovative changes in the world, which are likely to bring about development and enlightenment in the society. To a reasonable extent, Soyinka's *The Lion and the Jewel* (1963) illustrates this point. The play is a reflection of the contending cultural values in an African village, Ilujinle, which is facing the challenge of modern civilization. Two characters stand out in the play, Baroka, a village Bale and Lakunle, a teacher (symbol of modernism). The trick of the situation is an innocent village beauty, Sidi, who is saddled with the responsibility of choosing either Baroka or Lakunle as husband.

The Bale is regarded as a force behind the people's tradition, but his attitude to traditional power and progress in the community is highly questionable. Soyinka exposes Baroka's greatest weakness to be women. The indiscriminate manner in which he takes young and tender girls in the community as wives is severely derided in the play because he uses them as mere property; for the purpose of their being is his "sole out-puller of my sweat bathed hairs." Baroka typifies some traditional rulers in Yorubaland and Soyinka is probably attacking the traditional institution in this regard (Ebewo 2002, 36). He is presented as a ruler who is not committed to progress in his community. Lakunle narrates an instance when the wily Bale bribed the white surveyor in an effort to foil the Public Work's attempt to build a railway through Ilujinle. Many critics have stated that his reason for this action was to protect his land from cultural invaders, but he was myopic not to know that unnecessary resistance to change may lead to a stagnation of the human potentials. Lakunle epitomizes modernism: he teaches his pupils well in the school, and instructs Sidi on how to carry herself like a modern girl. He promises to be a husband who will marry out of love, and share equality with the wife. Lakunle proposes to transform the village by abolishing bride price, promoting equality in marital matters, building roads, introducing saucepans to replace clay pots, discouraging polygamy, building modern parks to serve as recreation centers. He concludes his plans with: "We must be modern with the rest/ or live forgotten by the world." Unfortunately, this community refuses to embrace Lakunle's propositions. He is regarded as a "madman" who chokes the villagers with "big loud words." That Sidi has chosen Baroka for a husband instead of Lakunle is a tragedy we must contemplate because the lion has no value for a jewel except to destroy it.

Another good example of a play that stresses adaptation in cultural matters is Tunde Aiyegbusi's *Ladipo's Last Stand* (1965), which "deals with the collision of old and new priorities in social organization." In the play, the administrators of a local government want to purchase Ladipo's house and earmark it for destruction in order to commence construction work on the community's sanitation project. Ladipo sees the plan as a move to destroy his ancestral heritage, and therefore, resists eviction. As the action of the play unfolds, Ladipo's son benefited from the project by being offered a position in Town Planning. Dunton notes that the title of the play suggests that change is inevitable in a progressive society (1998, 27).

Our next focus in this section is to deliberate on plays which express disillusionment in the Nigerian cities. In 1956, Henshaw published *This is Our Chance*, a volume that contained a play titled, *A Man of Character.* This two-act play is set in an unspecified Nigerian town during the last years of colonial rule. Kobina, the lead character, a one-time village dweller moved to the town in search of European job and finds himself in a dilemma as he cannot cope with life in the city and is too ashamed to return to the village empty-handed. Because Kobina's legitimate salary cannot match the demands of city life, his wife, his daughter, and sister-in-law and her husband encourage him to collect bribes. In this play, Henshaw is trying to highlight how hardships experienced by people in the cities could pave way for corruption. Greed and exhibitionism of wealth associated with the town are assiduously mirrored in the play when the sister-in-law continuously boasts of her trip to foreign countries: "it was simply wonderful; Las Palmas, London, and Paris. Very expensive, but it was worth it." Dunton states that the emphasis in this is to show the corrupting effect of exaggerated materialism, and that Henshaw implies that the colonial/western/modernizing order both enhances and corrupts traditional forms of social organization (1998, 91). In his *Dinner for Promotion* (1967), two low-income tenants, Tikku and Seyil, who share a rented room, suffer the threats of ejection from their capitalist landlord. In order to avoid disgrace, a decision to pawn their integrity is contemplated as they plan to cheat and deceive in order to win promotion. The play contains a range of comical satire on materialism, marriage of convenience, and genteel expectations of behavior in the cities, which are nothing short of disguises. Ken Saro-Wiwa, the murdered Ogoni activist, composed a play entitled *The Transistor Radio* (1973) that also touches on the theme of the harassment of tenants in Lagos by landlords (landlady in the play), and the tenants trying to find their way around by becoming con men in order to make money. Naiwu Osahon's *The Destitutes* (1980?), which is set in a Lagos slum, portrays an Igbo man, Ada, who has left his village to settle in Lagos and search for a job. Ada and other characters in the play experience nothing but utter poverty that has driven them to armed robbery. Ada is arrested for robbery and shot; this serves as a warning to others to refrain from such evil act.

The last play to discuss in this section is Soyinka's *The Beatification of Area Boys* (1999). This is a kaleidoscope of Lagos life as it exposes the marauding activities of township touts known as "Area Boys." In the play, there are hints on unemployment, armed robbery, food and petrol scarcity, poor sanitation, drug trafficking, police corruption, profiteering, unreliable transport system, and money-ritual superstition. This city is full of greedy people and devil incarnates. People go to dangerous extremes in order to become "overnight millionaires":

BARBER: . . . and the things people have to do to get such money, it's terrible business. Sometimes they have to sacrifice their near relation, even children.

It's a pact with the devil but they do it . . . these things happen. . . .You see all
those corpses with their vital organs missing – breast in the case of women, the
entire region of the vagina scooped out. And sometimes just the pubic hair is
shaved off for their devilish mixture. And pregnant ones with the foetus ripped
out. Male corpses without their genitals or eyes. Sometimes they cut out the liver
(239-240).

According to Sanda, a character in the play, many of the get-rich-quick swine
are involved in some other illegal practices like "cocaine" and "419 swindle",
"Godfathering or mothering armed robbers." In the play, Soyinka makes reference to the forceful eviction of civilians from their homes in the Maroko area of
Lagos during the military rule of Babangida. They were relocated in a swampy,
isolated area without any infrastructure. As law-abiding citizens, this lot went
to court and though judgment was in their favor, the military dictators ignored
court's injunction and drove the people to the streets. What do we expect homeless people to become? As we saw earlier, the "Area Boys'" involvement in crime
spells the rhythm of the society in general. If the leaders become heartless in their
dealings with the common people and exhibit wealth in Lagos through corruption,
the subjects (call them whatever name) must follow suit. In fact, corruption is
a cyclical affair as the Minstrel in the play quips: "You tink one chop, de other
siddon look?" Soyinka piles up these evils in Lagos city in order to expose them to
ridicule and subsequent condemnation. Soyinka seems to say that there is nothing
wrong in transforming a place into a town, but for the purposes of urban development, the people must be transformed too. In order to reap the fruits of town life,
the inhabitants must be disciplined and law-abiding citizens.

Conclusion

Many have been known to doubt the efficacy and potential of theater in its
role as contributor to national development because the by-products of its contribution are not visible in terms of concrete and immediate financial or other material gains. This view is not only limiting in scope, but it is also one that should be
discouraged judging from the committed stand and risk which some playwrights
have taken to act as the conscience of their nation. A play, a creative work using
words and action, cannot perform the miracle of transforming words into food for
the body (the major concern of poverty-stricken Nigerians), but it can transform
words into food for thought. Conversely, when food for thought materializes, it
becomes an ingredient that nourishes the body.

Throughout the discourse in this chapter, an attempt has been made to establish the enviable position Nigerian artists occupy in the political and urban development of their nation. These playwrights have attempted to expose the meanness
and drabness of so much of the political and urban crimes they see in their environment. As the vox populi and self-proclaimed watchdogs in the society, they are the
concerned observers of the corruption, oppression, hypocrisy, injustice, and other
political absurdities in the Nigerian society, especially during the postcolonial

era. These playwrights do not simply hate politicians, and therefore, they write to abuse them. They are philanthropists who love politicians and people, but think that they are sometimes blind and unpatriotic. They write plays not to repel them but to rescue them from ignorance. They attack behaviors that are conventionally respected, but these behaviors are really absurdities or vices blindly accepted by society. Most of the plays discussed arise out of specific political and urban conditions in Nigeria and reflect the profound tensions which have marked the Nigerian society since independence. Therefore, Nigerian theater has become not only a critique of prevailing society, but also an attempt to change it, by contributing as realistically as art can ever allow, to a meaningful co-existence in society. Theater's participation in matters of politics and urbanization in Nigeria is indeed a patriotic front towards development and the "formulation of a progressive ideology." It is indeed, a kind of "playful revolution."

Notes and References

1. Alarinjo is the name for one of the Yoruba Traveling theaters in Nigeria. Some people have made fun of this name by using it as a derogatory term for theater performers.
2. I gratefully acknowledge Saint E. T. Gbilekaa for drawing my attention to this quotation in his article, "Theatre and Political Change in Nigeria Since Independence." See Theatre and Politics in Nigeria, pp. 1-11.
3. My choice for this label may be influenced by my undergraduate exposure to Professor J. A. Adedeji (late), the first African Professor of Theater Arts, who was very fond of using this term to refer to the earlier generation of playwrights and theater practitioners in Nigeria.
4. This is quoted in Chris Dunton's Nigerian Theatre in English: A Critical Bibliography, p. 31 (see bibliography).

Further Bibliography

Achebe, Chinua. "The African Writer and the Biafran Cause." in *Morning Yet on Creation Day*. London: Heinemann, 1975.

Adeniyi, Tola. "Theatre and Politics in Nigeria." in *Theatre and Politics in Nigeria*, edited by Jide Malomo and Saint Gbilekaa, v-x. Ibadan: Caltop Publications (Nigeria) Ltd., 1993.

Agbese, Dan. "The World is a Stage." *Newswatch*, 31, no. 1 (2000): 7.

Alaukwu, Georgina. "The Longest Rope – A Playlet." *The Muse*, 15 (1983): 38-44.

Bennis, Warren, and Burt Nanus. *Leaders: The Strategies for Taking Charge*. New York: Harper Perennial, 1985.

Boal, Augusto. *Theater of the Oppressed.* New edition. Translated by A. Charles, Maria-Odilia Leal McBride and Emily Fryer. London: Pluto Press, 2000.

Cabral, Amilcar. "On Culture and the New Man." in *The African Liberation Reader: Documents of the National Liberation Movements, Vol. 3: The Strategy of Liberation*, edited by Acquino deBragannca and Immanuel Wallerstein. London: Zed Books, 1982.

Clark, Ebun. *Hubert Ogunde: The Making of Nigerian Theatre*. London: Oxford University Press, 1979.

Dunton, Chris. *Nigerian Theatre in English: A Critical Bibliography*. London: Hans Zell Publishers, 1998.

Ebewo, Patrick. *Barbs: A Study of Satire in the Plays of Wole Soyinka*. Kampala, Uganda: Janyeko Publishing Centre, Ltd., 2002.

Fanon, Frantz. *The Wretched of the Earth*, translated by Constance Farrington. London: Penguin, 1967.

Freire, Paulo. *Pedagogy of the Oppressed*. London: Writers and Readers Publishing Cooperative, 1978.

Fugard, Athol. Playland. Johannesburg: Witwatersrand University Press, 1992.

Gbilekaa, Saint E. T. "Theatre and Political Change in Nigeria Since Independence." in *Theatre and Politics in Nigeria*, edited by Jide Malomo and Saint Gbilekaa, 1-11. Ibadan: Caltop Publications (Nigeria) Ltd., 1993.

Henshaw, James E. *Medicine For Love*. London: University of London Press, 1964.

Holden, Joan. "Satire and Politics in America." *Theatre*, 10, no. 2 (1979): 104-107.

Mda, Zakes. "Politics and the Theatre: Current Trends in South Africa." in *Theatre and Change in South Africa*, edited by Geoffrey V. Davis and Anne Fuchs, 192-218. Netherlands: Harwood Academic Publishers, 1996.

Osofisan, Femi. *Playing Dangerously: Drama at the Frontiers of Terror in a "Postcolonial" State* (An Inaugural Lecture 1997). Ibadan: University of Ibadan, 1998.

--------.*Once Upon Four Robbers*. 1980. Reprint. Ibadan: Heinemann, 1991.

--------.*Another Raft*. Lagos: Malthouse, 1988.

Rotimi, Ola. *Our Husband Has Gone Mad Again*. Ibadan: Oxford University Press, 1977.

Solomon, Ejeke Odiri. "Ola Rotimi's Drama and the Democratic Quest in Nigeria." *Nigerian Theatre Journal*, 6, no. 1 (2001): 22-27.

Soyinka, Wole. *The Beatification of Area Boy in Plays: 2*. London: Methuen, 1999.

--------.*From Zia, With Love in Plays: 2*. London: Methuen, 1999.

--------.*The Open Sore of a Continent: A Personal Narrative of the Nigerian Crisis*. London: Oxford University Press, 1996.

-------.*Opera Wonyosi*. London: Rex Collings, 1981.

--------.*Before the Blackout*. Ibadan: Orisun Acting Editions, 1971.

--------.*The Lion and the Jewel*. London: Oxford University Press, 1963.

Uji, Charles. "Ideologico-Political Persuasions in the Theatre of Clark and Osofisan." in *Theatre and Politics in Nigeria*, edited by Jide Malomo and Saint Gbilekaa, 67-79. Ibadan: Caltop Publications, 1993.

Van Erven, Eugene. *The Playful Revolution: Theatre and Liberation in Asia. Bloomington*: Indiana University Press, 1992.

Wa Thiong'o, Ngugi. *Writers in Politics*. London: Heinemann, 1981.

6

Prostitution and Urban Social Relations

Saheed Aderinto

Introduction

Discourses on prostitution either in Africa or in any other part of the world must commence from some conceptual clarifications. The need for conceptual clarification stems from the fact that prostitution has been viewed from different perspectives. The conceptualizations of prostitution also vary from culture to culture and time to time. This is presumably why it has been regarded as the "oldest profession" amongst mankind. The major limitation of this universal assertion is that it does not differentiate between the definition of prostitution as a professional identity or role, or rather, of a female that earn her livelihood through the sale of sexual relations on one hand, and different forms of extra marital or multiple sexual practices prevalent amongst all mankind and dated back into antiquity on the other hand.[1] For instance, multiple sexual practices such ritual sex, exchange of wives, concubines, courtesans, etc., where were prevalent amongst groups that would later became Nigeria in pre-colonial times, have been misconceived as prostitution. It is inappropriate to identify the above-mentioned cultural practices as prostitution because they neither involved a professional identity nor were carried out solely for material gratification. The historical moments that gave birth to the new forms of stigmatization were from the period of colonial urban transformation, and they were the product of social, economic, and political changes during the first have of the twentieth century.[2] There was a "cultural uncertainty" as a result of mix ethnicity and gender relations in urban areas during the period. Suffice it to say that the ambiguity of this situation-enabled people to borrow selectively from both indigenous culture and foreign norms of behavior associated with modernity in order to produce cultural hybridity.[3]

Prostitution in the context of this study is defined as a professional identity or role of female who earned her livelihood through the sale of sexual favor in urban colonial centers.[4] How can a literature like this establish the difference between sexual relations carried out solely for material gratification and those carried out not chiefly for material gratification? Kenneth Little has provided comprehensive detail of the difficulty which one could face in trying to discuss prostitution as a

professional identity that involves exchange of sexual favor for material gratification and extra marital/multiple sexual practices in urban Africa.[5] While it might
be difficult to identify prostitution as a professional identity, which involved sale
of sexual services in some parts of African during colonial period, the Nigeria
situation provides a different picture. This is because the *modus operandi* of prostitution which includes the method and places where prostitutes solicited, demand
and supply of prostitutes, procurement, laws, reformist arguments, etc. which are
well documented. Colonial documents, in spite of their fragmented nature, include
much information about prostitution as a "deviant career". Meanwhile, newspaper
reports and oral history remain the most veritable genre of data for the reconstruction of the history of prostitution in colonial Nigeria. The vast materials related to
prostitution in newspapers and magazines spanned from the late 1920s to the late
1960s. With a substantial number of newspaper reports coupled with archival and
oral history, it is not difficult to say in concrete terms that the category of females
under consideration were those who professionally provided sexual services for
material gratification. What is known about prostitution in colonial Nigeria is the
information supplied chiefly by those who felt that it was a social problem.

Colonial documents and newspapers generally labeled prostitutes as "undesirables."[6] The condemnation which prostitution received in the world of public
opinions was akin to the one related to nationalism, a phenomenon that took a
dynamic dimension after the Second World War (1939-1945). The intensity and
manner in which the print media reported prostitution between the late 1930s and
the closing years of the 1950 show how very alien it was to the people as is was
cynically described by one observer as "a shock".[7] This chapter will thematically
discuss prostitution as one of the social legacies of urban transformation during
the colonial period. The emergence of prostitution is discussed as the aftermath of
some socio cultural and economic changes ushered in by the incorporation of the
various groups in the Nigerian geographical area into the vortex of colonialism.
Prostitution in Nigeria, just as it is in most parts of Africa, is basically an urban
phenomenon and a relationship between rural/urban socio-cultural, political, and
economic relations.[8] The origin of prostitution is therefore located within a lot of
extremities. None of the factors, vis-à-vis economic, social, cultural, etc., which
allowed prostitution to emerge, can be understood in isolation. The best way of
appropriately locating the impact of colonial rule in the emergence of prostitution is by treating all the factors as working and complimenting one another. The
impact of colonialism on the ways of lives of the colonized can only be judi-
ciously examined through a survey of pre-colonial social formation. It is in the
light of this that this study is going to take a look at some sexual practices that
were misinterpreted as "prostitution" and the transformation they took during the
colonial era. The work also takes a cursory look at some machinery put in place
to "regulate sexual behavior" and limit the incidence of "deviant sexual behavior"
amongst selected groups in the Nigerian geographical area before the advent of

colonialism. This will lead us to a general survey of some socio cultural and economic changes that allowed prostitution to emerge in colonial Nigeria.

Theoretical Framework

Modern academic research on prostitution started in the 19th century with the influential work of Alexander Parent-Duchatelet, a Parisian Public Health Officer.[9] In his study of prostitution in France, he had access to police records which enabled him to categorize prostitution based on weight, eye color, place of origin, years of schooling, etc. After a judicious appraisal of data, he concluded that prostitutes are not biologically different from other women, and that they were driven into prostitution for economic reasons.[10] Parent-Duchatelet's work did not only become influential but also motivated academic research on prostitution in Europe and America. By the first half of the 19th century academic research on prostitution had occupied the attention of scholars from diverse intellectual persuasions. Prostitution also attracted the attention of criminological research of Lombroso and Ferrero,[11] W.I Thomas,[12] Otto Pollak,[13] etc. As diverse as prostitution related theories are, they can be broadly divided into biological, pathological, economic, social, and psychological categories.[14]

Significant factors, which make the adoption of theories of prostitution difficult, are that social and sexual characters of human beings vary from one part of the world to another. Also, time, socio- cultural, economic, political, etc. circumstances have to be considered. While social scientists have the opportunity of carrying out research on prostitution and adopting theories "freely", a historian's task of reconstructing the past would constitute problems. How does a historian determine the socio-cultural, economic, psychological, biological, etc. factors which made some female to take up prostitution as a career in the past? For instance, the access, which Parent-Duchatelet had to document sources about biological and life history of prostitutes in 19th century, France allowed him to propound theories related to biological and economic status of prostitutes. This type of opportunity is absent in Nigeria. Colonial documents related to prostitution are fragmented. Prostitution and human trafficking in Nigeria were politicized. The politicization of prostitution is exemplified in the refusal of the colonial government to provide credible data on the nature of Traffic in Women and Children to the League of Nations and later United Nations. Questions related to the origin or causes of prostitution were not contained in the questionnaires of the Economic and Social Council of the United Nations on Traffic in Women and Children. The questionnaires, as great as they were, were targeted towards knowing the efforts made by individual countries of the world in prohibiting the trafficking of women and children for prostitution along international and national borders[15]. Such information, if available, would have paved the way for critical insight into the origin or causes of prostitution and human trafficking in Nigeria.

Also, the use of police records is made impossible because prostitution was not an illegal offence in colonial Nigeria. Even when prostitutes were arrested for breaking anti-prostitution laws such as loitering, brothel keeping, procuring, living on immoral earnings, etc., information related to their place of origin, family background/life history, age, etc were not collected.[16] The Venereal Diseases Ordinance was passed in 1943 to combat the unprecedented upsurge in the incidence of venereal diseases in the country.[17] However, reports stated that unattached women who had venereal diseases did not patronize government hospitals so that they would not be branded as "prostitutes."[18] Medical reports from the Federal Ministry of Health throughout the colonial period did not provide the number of cases related to venereal diseases and the contributions of prostitutes in its spread.[19] Therefore, the assertion that prostitutes were responsible for the spread of venereal diseases through their "repatriation" from one part of the country to another remained an assumption during the period under consideration. Materials are not available to justify the presumed biological/pathological mutation inherent in the career of prostitutes. So what is known about prostitution is the information about their work i.e. provision of sexual services, places where they solicited, and their relationship with the government and the people who collectively branded them as "undesirables". There is no access to credible sources such as the family background of prostitutes, ethnic origin, life history, and other models that include biological/pathological and psychological motivations. The unavailability of the above mentioned models constitute a serious problem in the reconstruction of the history of prostitution in Nigeria. However, the socio-cultural and economic theories remain the only formidable theories in the analysis of the origin of prostitution in colonial Nigeria. Meanwhile, the fact that prostitution is more rampant amongst some tribes in colonial Nigeria makes its discussion as a product of colonial rule to be probable.[20] Nevertheless, this limitation does not nullify or undermine the historical fact that prostitution is a social legacy of colonialism in Nigeria. It only calls for research on the factors responsible for the preponderance of prostitution amongst some ethnic groups and to look at cases from individual prostitutes' perspective.

Conceptualizing and Clarifying the Pre-colonial Situation

As pointed out earlier, there are a lot of cultural practices, which have been wrongly interpreted as "prostitution" in the Euro-American sense. One such cultural institution is *Karuwanci*. Dated back into the pre-Islamic Hausa socio-cultural history and with its own organizational hierarchy and paraphernalia of authority, *Karuwanci* thrived in the society that witnessed a high rate of divorce, early widowhood, post-partum taboo, etc. Also, it gave women a substantial degree of social and economic independence while serving as a link between the period of divorce and re-integration into the household.[21] Scholars over the years have tried to discuss *Karuwanci* either as "prostitution" in the sense of sexual relations for material gratification or as "courtesanship". Jerome Barkow[22] and Barbara Cooper[23] demonstrate the complexity behind a discussion of *Karuwanci* as prostitution by looking at the similarities and differences between it and courtesanship.

Therefore, they resolve to identify *Karuwanci* as "courtesanship" by exploring its social and sexual features, which are similar to coutesanship. M G Smith[24], Renee Pittin,[25] and Abner Cohen[26] discuss *Karuwanci* as "prostitution" and a "*Karuwa*" (a female who practice *Karuwanci*, plural *Karuwai*) as a prostitute without exploring the differences and similarities between it and courtesanship. They analyze all the social and sexual attributes of *Karuwanci* which are similar to the western understanding of prostitution i.e. provision of sexual services for material returns. Of equal importance is Renee Pittin's[27], and John Iliffe's[28] categorization of some divorcees as "independent women" because they were not economically dependent on men and did not have to live on earnings from prostitution. This categorization therefore limited *Karuwanci* to a practice of mainly poor divorced Hausa women who had to sleep with men for survival. The data, which earlier authors used in writing about Karuwanci, was either collected towards the end of the colonial period or a few years after the demise of colonial rule in Nigeria.[29] Time is a very important factor in the discussion of social behavior amongst all mankind. A major limitation of all the attempts that have been made over the years to discuss *Karuwanci* either as "prostitution" or as "courtesanship" is the inability of earlier authors to identify the differences in the social and/or sexual character of the *Karuwa* during the pre-colonial, colonial, and post independent periods. The argument here is that the institution of *Karuwanci* was basically a form of courtesanship in pre-Islamic and pre-colonial Hausaland.[30] The circumstances that led to its transition from a form to courtesanship to "prostitution" can best be appreciated within the framework of the socio-cultural and economic dislocations brought about by colonialism. There is much evidence that suggests that during the colonial period, there were *Karuwa* who retained the identity of *Karuwanci* and therefore could be categorized as courtesans; this is similar to what was practiced in pre-colonial period when there were a lot who carried out the task of providing sexual services solely for material gratification and could be called prostitutes.[31] My fieldwork in Katsina, Kano, Sokoto, Kaduna, and Zaria demonstrate that in colonial Hausaland, there was no demarcation between these two categories of free or unattached women. Divorcees who lived in *gidajen mata* (houses or compounds where *Karuwai* lives) and required a specific period of relationship with men, who in most cases end up marrying them, and the peripatetic one who moves from one place or *gidan mata* to another soliciting/seducing and providing sexual services mainly for material purposes were generally called *Karuwai.*[32] A major flaw in Jerome's work is, therefore, a generalization that all *Karuwai* were courtesans in spite of the fact she discussed some aspects of the features of a *Karuwa* that are completely similar to provision of sexual services for material gains alone. M.G Smith's classification of *Karuwai* on the basis of access to resources is a strong indication of how greater economic opportunities provided in colonial urban centers allowed *Karuwanci* to undergo corruption. *Karuwanci* is therefore one of the socio cultural ways of life of the Hausa that underwent continuity and change during colonial period of Nigerian history.

Before the conquest of the Sokoto Caliphate in 1903, there existed a form of concubinage, which involved sexual relations between slaves and their masters. Their masters for sexual attractiveness chose female slaves, and they had rights which were denied other slaves.[33] Islamic law makes a rigid distinction between slave wives and free ones. Slave wives can only be free at the death of their masters while their children enjoy freedom upon birth.[34] In spite of the deprivation which concubines had, they belong to a category of privileged female slaves because they are important members of the household at least by bearing children for their masters. Several cultural exigencies were responsible for the entrenchment of this form of concubinage in Sokoto Caliphate. Prominent amongst these were the need to increase the size of the aristocratic class and consolidate the Caliphate's dominant culture.[35] One of the major concerns of Lugard after the conquest of the Sokoto Caliphate was the social problem which were capable of following the emancipation of slaves most especially female slaves. The reason for this was that the British were interested in avoiding insurgency by making a final pronouncement against slavery, which was a very prominent culture of the Caliphate. In the first instance, the British feared that escaped female slaves would become prostitutes and thereby contribute to the criminal class.[36] To avoid such an eventuality, Lugard wanted all unattached slave girls and freed women to be placed under guardianship "as it minimizes the chances of prostitution."[37] Girouard also believed that women slaves who had ran away tended to "drift into prostitution," and this was tendency that had to be checked.[38] In another report, he confessed that:" continual reports are reaching me as to constant desertions of domestic slaves, who often become banded together as robbers and malefactors when men, or drifted into prostitution when women".[39] What was the outcome of the fear of British Administrators about the custody of female slaves? Oral history in Kano recalled the story of one Mai Kano Agogo who built houses where fugitive female slaves resided and lived on the proceeds of prostitution. Mai Agogo's was reported to have introduced broth keeping and prostitution into Kano.[40] By the early 1920s, fugitive female slaves had formed a very important class of *Karuwai.*[41] Redemption of female slaves was difficult since it was relatively hard to identify a freeborn *Karuwa* who was hitherto married and the ones who ran away from their masters. As previously identified, all "free or unattached women", irrespective on their economic, legal, or political status in colonial Hausaland, are called *Karuwai.* Tasks that remain difficult are the ones which involved the identification of the percentage or number of *Karuwa* who were prostitutes and the ones who did not live on proceeds from prostitution[42]

Similarly, amongst the *Igbo* of Southeastern Nigeria, a form of concubinage known locally as *Iko mbara, uga,* or *enyi* took the dimension of the exchange of wives and husbands. A man who is interested in contracting *iko mbara* required the knowledge and approval of the wife and vice versa. In this manner, the husband and wife have the right to contract *Iko mbara.* Traditionally, the husband got the wife's paramour to promise under oath that the woman should be given no injurious medicine which night turns her attention and devotion from her husband. This cultural practice provided sexual adjustment required in an andocentric *Igbo* culture in which the marriage of a woman and a child, long post-partum taboo, early widowhood, relative equality between the sex, etc. were the characteristic traits.[43]

Points that have to be understood about the above-mentioned sexual practices are that they were rooted in people's cultures and carried no stigma at all in the pre-colonial period. Similarly, they present an antithesis of the stigma, which a female carried because of her job of providing sexual services under the condition of which she must be compulsorily remunerated.

Household and "Deviant Sexual Behavior" – Pre-colonial Phase

It can be argued that the emergence of prostitution in Nigeria is a product of disintegration of the household and weakened socio-cultural and traditional ties set in motion by colonial rule. Females who were prostitutes and men who patronized prostitutes were products of social dislocations. Prostitution as a "deviant career" had no place in pre-colonial societies where customs and tradition of individual communities were built around the stability of the household. Marriage was a normal rite of passage that was conducted at the traditionally accepted period.[44] Conditions, which were capable of preventing someone from not undergoing the rite of passage at the traditionally accepted time, is considered abnormal and therefore uncommon. Polygamy and woman-to-woman marriage are practices that must have contributed in reducing 'free or unattached women' in pre-colonial societies[45]. Divorcees and new brides were readily absolved into large households that formed a basis of production units. Except amongst some tribes such as the Hausa of Northern Nigeria divorce, this was rare amongst the groups that later became Nigeria. Women throughout their lifetime were either daughters in their father's houses or wives in their husbands' homes.[46] To a very reasonable extent, this made the availability of 'free women' or women who refused to marry to be uncommon in pre-colonial period. Below is the observation of Basden about the disposition of women to divorce in pre-colonial Igboland:

> Then no Ibo woman dares to charge her husband with bigamy is the case ever so scandalous. For one thing she does not seriously resent the introduction of another wife, but a more potent reason by far is that she is not prepared to risk losing home and in practice, though not legally, her children. She is fully aware that she would deprive herself of any further chance of marrying again.[47]

Amongst the Yoruba of southwestern Nigeria, divorce, to use the word of Samuel Johnson, was "so rare to be practically considered as non-existing."[48] When married, women, were forever attached to the house and family of their husbands. The fear of divorce is rooted in the possibility that a divorced woman might not be taken up legally by another man.[49] "Free women", or better put, women who decided not to marry after divorce or widowhood, were very uncommon. As it will be seen later, a major factor that led to migration of female who went to urban centers to work as prostitutes was the commercialization of marriage and the introduction of British laws that provided 'unlimited access' to divorce.

P.A. Talbot provides a detailed appraisal of all taboos related to extra-marital sexual practices.[50] What this suggests is that there were some forms of extra-marital or multiple sexual practices that the society treated as "deviant behavior." Some of these multiple sexual practices included adultery that is committed if a man sleeps with a woman other than his wife and vice versa. *Ale yiyan* is a form of adultery, which was prevalent amongst the Yoruba in pre-colonial times. *Ale yiyan* is, therefore, a "deviant sexual practice" which was curtailed through a lot of religious and customary sanctions. In Appiapum and Ediba, for instance, oral tradition recalled the presence of a traditional council of elders called the *Ogua* society.[51] This society was used to prevent women from living and having sexual relationships with men who did not pay their dowry. A fine of six bar imposed on such women was said to have gone a long way to prevent promiscuity.[52] In other parts of Cross-River it was a heinous crime for a woman to sleep with somebody who was not her husband. Such women otherwise called *Akunakuna* were sold away as slaves, exchanged for canoes, or killed.[53] The preponderance of prostitution amongst the people of rivers and cross rivers during the colonial period was attributed to the refusal of the colonial government to allow the people to make use of customary laws which were believed to have gone a long way in ameliorating marital problems before the imposition of colonial rule and the introduction of several British Laws related to marriage.[54]

Betrothal was a common practice in pre-colonial Nigerian societies. In fact, it was an important preliminary stage of marriage that occurred before the final marriage rites were completed. Amongst virtually all groups in the Nigerian geographical area, undue contact between a betrothed girl and her husband to be was prevented. The social and economic changes brought about by colonial rule and the emergence of urban centers provided situations whereby the betrothal of children became used as a popular means of procuring girls for prostitution in urban centers.

Some feminist augments about the transformation of pre-colonial Nigerian societies from the type which entailed equal rights of males and females in the realm of social, political, economic, etc. responsibility to a masculine one under colonial rule are significant.[55] The male-dominated nature of the society under colonial rule, a product of the imported socially constructed sexual dichotomy, allowed females to be alienated in the colonial capitalist space, and, as shall be demonstrated later, provided a condition for the emergence of prostitution.

Colonial Urban Development and Emergent Prostitution

Prostitution in Nigeria is a product of two major and closely connected phenomena; these included urbanization as exemplified in the unprecedented growth of cities, a reflection of the new capitalist edifice put in place by alien rule, and new pattern of social outlook or behavior that emerged. The imposition of colonial rule enhanced tranquility and facilitated the movement of people from one part of the country to another. The Pax Britannica imposed by the British was further promoted by the commencement of rail lines which opened up communities and the development of port facilities in Lagos, Warri and Port Harcourt.[58] Succinctly, all these led to the rise of urban centers such as Lagos, Ibadan, Kano, Port Harcourt, Kaduna, Kano etc. While some of these urban centers, as seen in the case of Kano, developed partly as a result of ancient economic activities, the British deliberately established others like Port Harcourt and Kaduna as administrative centers in 1912[59] and 1914[60] respectively. Whether in the first, second, or third category of township, urban centers generally attracted a lot of people due to the availability of infrastructural facilities which included electricity, pipe born water, tarred roads, and greater economic opportunities.[61] The second phase of urbanization that can be described as social is the aftermath of the first type was namely the new pattern of social behavior and a product of the cultural heterogeneity of cities.[62] As a melting pot of cultures, the cosmopolitan/heterogeneous nature of urban centers that emerged during the colonial period paved the way for the emergence of social vices prominent amongst which were prostitution, child labor and new forms of criminal behavior, etc. Numerous beer parlors, cinema houses and several places that were stigmatized as "red light district"[63] all over the country are known for "urbanized behavior" and "deviant characters." "As a container and transmitter of culture,"[64] Nigerian cities are characterized by dual role as solvent; i.e. "weakening traditional social ties and loosening the hold of traditional beliefs and values."[65]

A distinctive aspect of urbanization is, therefore, rural-urban migration. Migration of male and female into urban centers is multifaceted in nature. There is no gainsaying the fact that the principal reason for migration of men; categorically the first to migrate into urban centers was the need to partake in the new economic opportunity put in place by colonial rule. Female migration into urban centers continued in spite of several attempts by traditional authorities to restrict female mobility for economic and social reasons. Patterns of female migration had a more multifarious outlook. In the first category of women that migrated into urban centers were those who went to join their husbands to live permanently in the city but went home occasionally. Also were those whose interests were akin to those of men, namely to seek greener pastures. Some women were induced to migrate to look for husbands while a sizeable number left the countryside after a marital breakdown. This last category belonged to women who migrated to the city for the purpose of being "urbanized," socially.[66] In all, female migration into urban centers enhanced greater degree of economic and social independence, both of which were, absent in most rural areas. Out of the aforementioned categories of female migrants into urban centers, the first category appeared to be more economically empowered and secured. This is because they enjoyed a relatively stable social and economic status, which can readily be provided for by their husbands. Frequent visits to the countryside could also generate resources that might be used to augment the fluctuating economy of the colonial state of Nigeria. The economic and social prosperity of the other categories were closely tied to the deplorable and unpredictable economic condition of the urban centers. This is because the colonial capitalist structure was male-centered. Nigeria's urban centers, like those of her other African counterparts, were designed (sometimes years after their foundation) to contain and maintain pools of competitively cheap male laborers, who in theory would return to their rural families. Wage labor was introduced for men in urban centers of Lagos, Ibadan, Kano, Kaduna, Port Harcourt, etc. Colonial capitalist structures such as the mines of Jos and Enugu and the railway were male dominated. While wage labor was introduced for men, female migrants in cities were restricted largely to the off-the-book economy. Urban economy did not provide women with the social and economic security traditionally obtainable in the countryside. The alienation of female migrant within the urban capitalist space placed some of them in the very precarious situation of providing sexual services for their male counterparts, majority of who migrated into the city as bachelors or as husbands with wives and children remaining in the villages. The effect of colonialism on the socio-economic lives of the people of Kano is best illustrated from the following extract:

> The breakdown of the household also led to the release of women some of whom migrated to the *Birnin* Kano to stay as independent women, as *Mata Masu Zaman Kan su* (free women) practicing prostitution, making themselves available to the increasing number of urban laborers who had left their wives in their localities. Prostitution as an institution was said to be unknown in the pre-colonial Kano, but with the consolidation of colonial economy and the resultant penetration of capitalist values into the society, the phenomenon of sex as a commodity began to appear.[67]

By the early 1930s, strains of unemployment were apparent in some Nigerian cities, the most important of these cities being Lagos.[68] The situation uncontrollable during the Second World War when more people migrated from the provinces as a result of pauperization caused by wartime exigencies and emergencies. The integration of female migrants into the vortex of a male dominated colonial capitalist economy was hindered by the nature of colonial cities that could not provide employment for the teeming male migrants, and their female counterparts.

The question of employing women into government services was first broached in the early 1920s. It was decided that women who were to be recruited to the services should have passed the Clerical Service Examination as their male counterparts. None was forthcoming. Subsequently, women were appointed to such posts as teaching, nursing and such other fitting posts, but none were appointed to the clerical grade. However, in 1945, due to the growing drive for female education and influx of women into the service, the government appointed a Committee to inquire whether women possessing the prescribed educational qualification should be admitted to the standard scale with particular reference to the Clerical grade. The recommendations of the Committee was that the clerical grade should not be thrown open to women but that in special cases "women of marked ability" may be admitted. In 1949, just one woman was able to satisfy the provision of the "women of marked ability".[69] A significant factor that jeopardized the employment of females in government jobs was the poor attitude of the colonial government to female education. Had adequate attention been given towards the education of females, it would not have been difficult for them to be employed into the clerical grade, which absorbed most females in colonial Africa. As little emphasis was placed on female employment, the few lucky ones who were able to work with the government faced a lot of discriminations in terms of remuneration and emolument. This was because the government felt that most men have dependants and most women have none. It was not until 1956 when females who were recruited to government departments with the West African School Certificate got the same salary as their male counterparts.[70] The table below shows the statistics of female employees in all the government departments from some urban centers by 1950:

City	Number
Lagos	920
Kaduna	158
Ibadan	252
Enugu	56
Port Harcourt	3
Kano	3

Source: Computed from NAI, CS0 26/035171 Vol II *Employment of African Women in Government Services*

Some economically underpowered female migrants were not lax in adjusting to the economic realities obtainable within the colonial capitalist space. There is an ample amount of evidence of how women migrated to the cities to become prostitutes due to economic hardships caused by the large-scale recruitment of men for wage labor.[71] The compromised nature of female employment in colonial Nigeria must have informed the thinking of the editorial comments of the *Southern Nigeria Defender* of 5 April, 1944. After a careful observation of the ostracized nature of female employment and the role it played in the emergence of prostitution, the editor made these recommendations:

> As men in lower classes are generally seen in mean walks of life, prostitutes should also be employed by both government and mercantile houses to work as laborers, trade callers, shop girls, messengers, gate women and if possible be recruited for services elsewhere, where they could be in position to earn a more decent livelihood.

Of unimaginable importance is Alexander Paterson's observation about the technological backwardness of colonial Nigeria and the absence of industries. He

located the preponderance of prostitution as a product of the lack of industrialization in the country. In his monumental 1944 report of the Social Welfare in the
Colony and Protectorate of Nigeria, he opined:

> In many countries, two major occupations absorb the labour of the unmarried
> girl. One is factory work and the other is domestic service. Both of these are de-
> nied to the Nigerian girl, and if she wants to escape from close grip of the family,
> prostitution is almost the only alternative open to her.[72]

Another imperative colonial structure that allowed prostitution to flourish was mines. Mines all over Africa were known to attract 'free or unattached
women' who provided casual sexual service for miners. Despite the absence of
official recognition, the presence of women who provided casual sexual services
for miners was a popular scene in the mines. Burkar has this to say about the
conduct of prostitutes at Jos mines:

> The harlots were associated more intimately with the immigrants' mines labor-
> ers, who as a rule, left their families behind when coming to the mines. In this
> connection, some of these harlots cooked for the immigrant mine laborers, giv-
> ing them a semblance of the comforts of a home.[73]

Burkar's observation in Jos is similar to the account recorded Bill about the presence and conduct of prostitutes in Nigerian mining camps:

> Independent women came to the camps along with the rest of the floaters; they
> included prostitutes as well as traders and farmers. It was characteristics of cap-
> ital's need for a semi-stable but still migrant labour force that prostitutes were
> encouraged by the management to settle in the camps. They cooked for the men,
> fulfilling some of the necessary functions of a household at a very cheap cost[74]

Also, the sexual and domestic importance of prostitutes in the mines attracted
the concern of delegates from Zaria at the Conference of Chiefs and Emirs of
the Northern Provinces in 1942. The delegates suggested that prostitutes should
be sent to Jos 'where they could cook for mines laborers.'[75] Mine laborers, in
spite of the severity of their job, had money to patronize prostitutes who were
always at their beck and call. Prostitution, gambling and drunkenness provided
good opportunities for the proletariat to ease the stress of their deplorable working
condition.

A significant indicator in the connection between prostitution and the rise of
urban centers in the colonial period is the origin and geographical distribution of
the brothels in major cities of the country. Brothels and/or places where prostitutes were seen in large numbers are culturally heterogeneous parts of the cities.
In Ibadan, for instance, 90-95 percent of brothels that emerged after the colonial
rule could be found in culturally heterogeneous parts of the city like Ekotedo,
Ojoo, Mokola, Sabo, etc.[76] These areas, most importantly Ekotedo and Dugbe,
developed due to colonial economic activities such as the extension of railway to
Ibadan in 1901 and the concentration of colonial economic structures such as banks,
mercantile houses, etc. The British first introduced stranger quarters to separate

strangers from the natives in Kano in 1913.[77] Between 1913 and 1960 virtually all the major urban centers in the country had their own stranger's quarters otherwise called *Sabon gari*.[78] (Hausa word that can be translated as new town). *Sabon gari* encouraged a large influx of strangers, a majority of which were men and women looking for greener pastures in urban centers all over the country. While non-Hausa densely populated *Sabo garis* in the north, their counterparts in the south were predominantly Hausa in ethnic composition.[79] Prostitution flourished within the conditions of weakened social ties and cultural heterogeneity characterized by stranger quarters of *Sabon garis* most importantly the southern ones. In a study of Hausa migrant's settlement of Ibadan, Abner Cohen has demonstrated that out of 1753 females in *Sabo gari* in Ibadan in 1963, 250 were prostitutes. Only 2 out the 250 were born in *Sabo gari* while the remaining migrated from the northern part of the country.[80] Renee Pittin's survey shows that of 123 *gidajen mata* (compounds occupied wholly or in part by Hausa women living away from kin, and available for sexual liaisons) in Katsina, seventy three are located in *Sabon Layi*. In a short, detailed description of these strangers' quarters, she wrote:

Sabon Layi within which are also found the majority of inexpensive hotels, beer parlours and restaurants. Katsina's two cinemas are sited on one side of Sabon Layi, and such night- life as there is, is centred in this section of town. Newcomers to the city, transients, newly arrived women on their own and men looking for women tend to gravitate to Sabon Layi[81]

The situation in Ibadan and Katsina are similar to what was obtainable in Kano about two major culturally heterogeneous part of the city; Fagge and *Sabon gari*:

In fact as early as 1920, one of Kano's famous attajirai, Maikano Agogo, had built some lodgings at Fagge rented mostly by these "free women". From the 1940s, the Fagge quarters became a well-known abode of prostitutes. It is true that it was not everywhere in the settlement that was occupied by these prostitutes. The point being made is that some parts and streets of the settlement became the "red light district" of urban Kano. Certain locations such as Tudun Lawarudu, lay in Jalannawa, lugun ruwa etc were known areas of prostitutes business. Most of these prostitutes that were residing at Fagge were either Hausa or Northern Nigerian origin. The ones that mostly from Southern Nigeria and some West Africa countries lived at Sabon gari which from 1950 when the impact of import-substitution-industrialization began to be felt in the society of Kano came to surpass Fagge in the prostitution business. In fact, even in the old city where the Native Authority was very strict in eradicating this deviant behavior, prostitution houses began to mushroom during the period[82]

Socio-Cultural Dislocations

One of the most potent aspects of colonial rule was its effect on several aspects of the socio-cultural ways of life of the people. The widened differentials between the income of rural dwellers and their urban counterparts led to many changes in aspects of customary marriage, most importantly of bride price. Parents became more interested in giving out their daughters to wealthy urban migrant workers. This type of outlook developed out of the countryside's gradual absorption into the urban system, which made the possession of money increasingly essential for local needs. The result was a circular process because there was a demand for consumption goods that, in turn, could only be met by earning money abroad. Thus, this withdrawal of male labor disturbed the rural subsistence economy making the village more and more dependent upon the remittances as well as the goods and cash brought back by returning migrants.[83] The monetization of the economy, to a very reasonable extent, led to the "commercialization" of marriage phenomenon, which undoubtedly affected the whole country with little or no variance. One of the major problems that occupied the attention of the Conference of Yoruba Chiefs in 1937 was the need to fix a certain amount to be paid as bride price due to the notoriety that occasioned the unprecedented increase in bride price.[84] In Hausaland, the new economic structure made cash and marital gift to become important in all aspects of marriage. Thus, the *Mirmushin Chiromas Maikano Agogos*[85] and the *Kaima tsaya ka samu naka*[86] were introduced as *Kayan zance*.[87]

The Igbo were certainly the most badly hit by the high bride price demanded by families of brides in the villages. P.C. Lloyd pointed out that sixty percent of the Igbo in Lagos with age ranging from 15 to 34 were young men in search of the high bride price demanded in their various communities.[88] Men from the Mbaise clan, Owerri district, resided in Lagos in 1953 and had to save for eight years before they could raise two hundred-pounds demanded by their clan as bride price.[89] *The Nigerian Spokesman* reported in 1948 that the Youth of Awo-Omama (Lagos Branch) threatened not to marry from their community if the bride price was not reduced. The youth advocated for the reduction of bride price to twenty five- pounds for illiterate and fifteen- pounds for literate brides.[90] Arguably, the role which unprecedented increase in bride price played in promoting prostitution is that men who could not raise the required amount needed as bride price remained in the city and lusted after prostitutes who they could always pay for providing the needed sexual labor. There is much evidence that suggested the influx of women who after years of living in the villages without husbands migrated to become prostitutes in the cities.[91] The following extract from 12 December 1951 issue of *Nigerian Spokesman* comprehensively describes the connection between high bride price and prostitution:

> Much has been said and written about the sky-rocketting bride price which seems to have been prevailing in Iboland since the past two decades and barring two or three towns, all other places in the East are still encouraging the seeming "slave traffic" in marriage. Many writers have aired their views on the situation but yesterday an Okija indigene went all out x-raying the Okija's plight. A girl is to be priced from €90 to €300 in part of this rural district. Today, when we look around, we notice prostitutes in great multitude swarming into cities from various villages. This is one result of the high bride price permeating the Iboland. Many young girls have found marriage in their towns unaccomplished, because they are unable to meet the high demand of bride-price from parents who want

"money at all costs" by demanding much, they have demoralized Nigeria boys and girls

A contributor to the 20 January 1948 issue of the *Eastern Nigeria Newspaper* on the problems and causes of prostitution also wrote:

> The exorbitant bride price is therefore one of the greatest if not the greatest cause of prostitution in our clan today. A clan that regarded marriage as a holy institution has lost the dignity of this institution in pursuance of unholy wealth.

The *Daily Comet*, a newspaper published in Kano, has this to say about the deleterious effect of high bride price and the trafficking of girls for the purpose of prostitution:

> Everyone is surprised nowadays at the astonishing development and spread of prostitution and the emulation of foreign and indecent ways of living quite un-africa. In some districts of this country, parents traffic in their daughters by as much as 80 to 100 pounds from young men".[92]

The extract below is part of the communiqué issued by the Committee on Prostitution in Northern Nigeria about the causes of prostitution:

> Parents should be made to realize that it is not the amount of money paid for their daughters that leads to a successful marriage. Highly- paid-for wives are ill treated and become unhappy and therefore do not stay long with their husbands.[93]

The fragile nature of customary marriage in colonial Nigeria, partly a product of monetized economy, is the root of the contemporary problems of the trafficking of girls for the purpose of prostitution. Betrothal, a very significant aspect of customary marriage that in pre-colonial and colonial periods sometimes took place even before the bride or the bridegroom or both were born, came under heavy abuse. By the late the 1930s, child betrothal had became a very important means by which young girls below the age of 15 were trafficked for the purpose of prostitution in urban centers, most importantly Lagos and Ibadan. The *modus operandi* was for a trafficker to secure or lure girls from parents under the pretense of training them and getting husbands for them in the city. The parents did not release such girls until the traffickers, who in most cases were retired or adult prostitutes, had paid a dowry ranging from 8 to 10 pounds to marry an anonymous man in Lagos. In a letter to the Welfare Officer, a child prostitute narrated her ordeal in the hand of her procurer:

> In the year 1945, she asked me to follow her to Ikeja where I shall be better trained. We arrived in Ikeja early in 1945 when I was given to a certain army who took my virgin and he paid 3 pounds to this woman, from there I was forced by her to become a harlot. Sir, all the money that I have been gathering from this harlot trade from 1945 is with this woman.[94]

The above information is similar to a letter written by a petitioner to the District Officer about child prostitution in Ibadan:

> I beg to report to your necessary information about the following Urhobo women
> in this town who keep their houses and premises for brothels. The following
> are the experienced leaders of harlots in Ibadan. Madam Isobo: a well-known
> woman in the town as the leader of all Urhobo harlots. She occupies large prem-
> ises in a compound very close to high class Hotel of Urhobo Union. She has
> some set of young Isobo girls of about 12 years old upwards about 12 in number,
> and some old women with her. If one goes to her compound to look for harlot,
> verbal application will be made to Madam Isobo who will decide the charge and
> supply any one that will serve the purpose. All harlots usually hold meetings in
> her house to decide about their prostitution charges for a trip or for sleeping with
> a man till day break.[95]

One of the most important factors that increased the demand for child prostitutes
was that men preferred them to adults who were conventionally difficult to deal
with. Similarly, there was an assumption common amongst male migrants from
the Eastern Region that sexual intercourse with virgin could cure certain ailments.
Traffickers, therefore, earned better pay when they produced girls who were still
virgins.[96] Closely connected to the problem of high bride price were divorce. As
earlier mentioned, before the imposition of colonial rule, divorce amongst many
groups that later became Nigeria was rare. Therefore, this made the presence of
"free or unattached women" in pre-colonial times rare. Amongst the Hausa where
the incidence of divorce was highest, the institution of *Karuwanci,* as previously
pointed out provided an opportunity for a divorcee to be reintegrated back into
household. The imposition of colonial rule and the introduction of British Law
eroded some of the virtue of customary marriage that made women a very important member of an indissoluble household. While the introduction of colonial
courts empowered women by allowing them to be "liberated" from unhappy marriages through divorce, it nevertheless contributed immensely in the production
of large number of "free or unattached women." Discourses on divorce and other
processes that produced free or unattached females can best be appreciated against
the background of the fact that prostitution as a professional career, both on long
or short basis, thrived amongst the unmarried and divorced in colonial Nigeria.

By 1929, cases of divorce and legal separation instituted by women had
become common according to the records of the Supreme Court at Lagos. The
rate of divorce in Lagos alone was estimated to about 20% in 1958-59.[97] Records
have been found containing stories about women who after having divorced their
husbands by merely putting up an appearance in the court and paying necessary
charges to the court and the divorced husband migrated to the city to become prostitutes.[98] P.A. Talbot has this to say about marital breakdown during the colonial
period:

> It would appear that the standard of morality has been lowered since the arrival
> of European and the establishment of a government, which does not encourage
> the treatment of adultery as a criminal offence, while it forbids the cruelties,
> which were amongst some peoples practiced on an erring wife, and the exacting
> of personal vengeance on an offender. Matrimonial "palavers" form by far the

greatest proportion of civil cases heard in the courts to day, and it will be found that the vast majority of these is due to the desire of the women for new husbands; a man will usually submit to almost anything in order to keep his wife[99]

In the colonial society, which had little economic opportunity for economically un-empowered women in the cities, divorce did nothing but increase the number of women who fled to the cities and lived on earnings from prostitution. A major problem encountered by the police during the period of arrest and repatriation of prostitutes was how to differentiate between a divorced woman who left on her own "legitimate/moral earning" and the ones who went outside in the night to solicit and bring men into her room. The *Southern Nigeria Defender* reported in 1946, "If demobilization must be carried out, all divorced and unmarried must be demobilized for they are all birds of the same feathers."[100] While it is inappropriate to identify all unmarried women as prostitutes, the fact that "free women" were highly susceptible to prostitution must have influenced some of the comments made in the print media about "free women".

Conclusion

The origin of prostitution in Nigeria has been discussed against the backdrop of socio cultural and economic changes brought about by colonial rule. The major indices for the measurement of the role that colonialism played in the emergence of prostitution are the rise of colonial urban centers, colonial capitalist structure, and attendant social milieu.

Prostitution attracted the concern of many people majority of who were urban dwellers. It was regarded as a "deviant career" because the society was not in support of it. The history of the public condemnation of prostitution can be dated back in the 1930s and 1950s when newspaper reports carried stories related to what can summarily be called "public pollution" caused by prostitutes. "Public pollution" signified the preposition that prostitution lead to an increase in crime rate, venereal diseases, reduction of access which people who engaged in "legitimate work" had decent accommodations and a generally high rate of immorality. Pages of the *Southern Nigeria Defender, Eastern Nigeria Guardian, Nigerian Tribune, Nigerian Observer, Nigerian Guide, West African Pilot, Nigeria Spokesman,* etc. in the late 1930s, 1940s, and the 1950s are replete with a lot of stories which signify that prostitution was not only a societal problem but a product of colonial urbanization. The point being made here is that a very good percentage of what we know about prostitution in Nigeria during the colonial era is information supplied by the print media about the societal implications of commercial sex labor. It was also in the late 1940s that prostitution became known as commercial sex working.[101] This is contrary to the general conception that the word "commercial sex working" is a new way of euphemistically describing prostitution in contemporary Nigeria. The major factor that molded the public stigmatization of prostitution was that people recounted the state of things before colonial rule and were able to trace the origin of the problem to "westernization." So, what we consistently read in colonial newspapers in the 1930 and 1940s are 'during our father days', 'in the olden days', 'in those days', 'in our days' etc. All these were words used to describe the situation of things before colonial rule and to demonstrate that the deplorable situation was a development occasioned by colonialism.

Amazingly, right from the opening years of the 1960s down to 2005, the level at which we read stories about prostitution reduced. Whereas, stories on prostitution were reported at least four times in a week during the late 30s, 40s and early 50s, post independence reports in the print media reduced to a very unimaginable degree. This development is explicable partly in what can be called the "institutionalization of prostitution." The "institutionalization of prostitution" signifies the extent or degree at which the society began to see prostitution as an inevitable aspect of life.

The response of the colonial government to the problems of prostitution took the dimension of the enactment of ordinances to regulate or prohibit activities such as loitering, soliciting, procuring, brothel keeping, etc., which are connected to prostitution. Throughout the colonial period, the arrest and prosecution of prostitutes continued without a major breakthrough in the reduction of their numbers. This called for a consideration of the lopsidedness in the government's disposition towards the administration of justice between the two sexes. Categorically, between 1944, when the prosecution and repatriation of prostitutes started, to 1960, there is no record that showed the prosecution of male solicitors.[102] The relevant section of the criminal code which made it illegal for men to publicly solicit and traffic women and girls are 225A (b) 224(1). [103] The fact that prostitution in colonial Nigeria is a female offence made the exclusion of men who broke anti-prostitution laws easy.[104] The practice of excluding one sex from legal sanctions or applying different legal categories according to sex is highly suspect to charge of sexual discrimination.[105] Men, who throughout the colonial period patronized prostitution, were not brought to book. A major flaw in the government and people's perception of prostitution is its treatment as the degradation of females without recognition that prostitution thrives because of the patronage received from men.

Notes and References

1. Saheed Aderinto, "Colonialism and Prostitution in Africa", in Melissa Ditmore (ed.) *Historical Encyclopedia of Prostitution*, (Westport, CT; Greenwood Press) forthcoming.
2. See Nakanyike B Musisi, "Gender and the Cultural Construction of "Bad Women" in the Development of Kampala-Kibuga, 1900-1962" in Dorothy L. Hodgson and Sheryl A McCurdy (eds.) *"Wicked" Women and the Reconfiguration of Gender in Africa*, (Portsmouth, Heinemann, 2001) pp. 171-187
3. Nakanyike, "Gender and the cultural Construction," pp. 172

4.   In this conceptualization of prostitution, two things are cardinal. The first is that the female is providing sexual services, for which she must be compulsorily paid or remunerated. The female is providing sexual services for men who paid for it.

5.   Kenneth Little, *African Women in Towns: An Aspect of Africa's Social Revolution* (Cambridge University Press, London 1972) pp. 76-218

6.   National Archives Ibadan (NAI), COMCOL, 1 1016 Vol III, "Undesirables in the Lagos Township and Suburbs, Repatriation of", Eastern Nigeria Guardian, (ENG), "Undesirable Women", 7 September 1947, p 3, *West African Pilot* (WAP), "Undesirable Women to Get Uneasy Time," 21 January 1955, p. 1, *Southern Nigeria Defender* (SND), "Ekotedo Undesirables", 21 September 1946 p. 3

7.   *The Comet* (Nigeria) "Smoke Out the Prostitutes," 24 June 1944 p. 2

8.   Luise White's work is one of the excellent works on prostitution in Africa. See Luise White, *The Comfort of Home: Prostitution in Colonial Nairobi*, The (Illinois, University of Chicago Press Ltd, 1990).

9.   Charles Bernheimer "Of Whores and Sewers: Parent-Duchatelet, Engineer of Abjection" Raritan 6,3 (Winter 1987), pp. 84

10. Charles Bernheimer, p. 84

11. C Lombroso and W Ferrero, *The Female Offender,* (London, Fisher Unwin 1895)

12. W.I Thomas, *The Unadjusted Girl,* (NewYork, Harper and Row, 1967)

13. O Pollak, *The Criminality of Women* (NewYork, A.S Barnes, 1961)

14. For a general survey of history of prostitution see, S Williams *The History of Prostitution: Its Effect, Causes and Throughout the World.* (NewYork, Eugenics Publishing Co 1937)

15. Saheed Aderinto, "Journey to Work: Nigerian Prostitutes in the Gold Coast," 1935-1955, unpublished manuscript, 2005. See also, National NAI CSO 26/03338 Vol II *International Convention for the Suppression of White Slave Traffic and Traffic in Women and Children,* 1913-1925, 1936-1956, NAI, CSO, 27837 Vol I and II *Annual Report on the Traffic in Women and Children and Obscene Language Publication,* NAI, Oyo Prof 1, 1373 *Traffic in Women and Children, Obscene Language etc, Report for the League of Nations,* NAI, CSO 36005 Vol II *Traffic in Girls From Nigeria to the Gold Coast etc*

16. NAI, A Special List of Records on the Police Force, *Annual Report of Police* 11814 vol I-XII, 1905-1960

17. Saheed Aderinto, *Urban Threat: Prostitutes and Venereal Diseases in Colonial Nigeria,* Paper presented at the African Health and Illness Conference, University of Texas at Austin March 25-27 2005.

18. Saheed Aderinto, *Urban Threat,* See also all the annual reports of the Medical Services between 1930 and 1960 in NAI, CSO *Simple List of Federal Ministry of Health,* Venereal Diseases Ordinance 1943in NAI, *Annual Volume of the Laws of Nigeria, Legislation enacted during 1943*

19. Saheed Aderinto, "*Urban Threat*"

20. One of the most indisputable facts about prostitution in colonial Nigeria is that apart from Northern Nigeria, chiefly female who migrated into urban center carried out prostitution. The phenomenon was not well pronounced amongst the indigenes apart from in the Northern Region. The names given to prostitutes by the host community sometimes signify their place of origin. For instance, prostitutes from Idoma were

called *Akwato* by Easterners see, Jerome Barkow, "The Institution of Courtesanship in the Northern States of Nigeria," *Geneva Afrique* X, 1 (1971), pp 59-73. In Ibadan most of the migrant's women who practices prostitution were from Warri, see NAI, Oyo Prof 1,3562 *Measures Against Prostitutes 1942-1944*. In Lagos women from Calabar were chiefly accused of prostitution. See NAI, COMCOL 1 248, *Calabar Improvement League, Minutes of Meetings*. While the Traffic in women to the Gold Coast was rampant amongst women from Obubra Division of Ogoja Province, see Public Record and Archives Administration Department, (PRAAD) National Archives, Accra, CSO 15/2/2222 *Traffic in Women and Children,* 1940-1948, see also Saheed Aderinto, *"Journey to Work".*

21. Jerome pp 59-73

22. Ibid

23. Barbara Cooper, "The Politics of Difference and Women's Association in Niger: of "Prostitutes" the Public and Politics" in Dorothy and Sheryl (eds.) *"Wicked," Women, p 257-260.*

24. M.G Smith, "The Hausa System of Social Status" *Africa,* 29 (1959) pp 239-253

25. Renee Pittin, "Houses of Women: a Focus on Alternative Life-Styles in Katsina City" in Christine Oppong (ed) *Female and Male in West Africa* (London, George Allen and Unwin, 1983) pp 291-301

26. Abner Cohen, *Custom and Politics in Urban Africa: A Study of Hausa Migrants in Yoruba Town* (London, Routledge and Kegan Paul. 1969) pp 51-71

27. Renee, "Houses of women," p 294

28. John Iliffe, *The African Poor, A History* (Cambridge: Cambridge University Press, 1987) p34,

29. Cohen carried out his survey in 1963, Pittin, 1971-72, Smith, 1957-58, Jerome, 1968-70. All these authors are either sociologist or anthropologist.

30. I call it "a form of Courtesanship" because *Karuwanci* is one of the numerous African cultural institutions that cannot be rendered directly in English. *Karuwanci* is therefore discussed here as a practice similar to Courtesanship.

31. Oral evidences, Mallam Yaro Ahmed, N0 14, Emir Yahya Road, Sokoto age 90+, 10/10/2004, Alhaji Barau Haroun, Gausau Road, Sokoto, age 80+ 21/10/2004. Mahdi Adamu who carried out very extensive fieldwork on pre-colonial ways of life of the Hausa asserted that there is no evidence of the presence of prostitution in Hausaland before the imposition of colonial rule. Mahdi Adamu, *The Hausa Factor in West African History* (Zaria/Ibadan, Ahmadu Bello University Press and Oxford University Press, 1978), pp 171-172. For a categorical expression about the absence of prostitution in Hausaland before colonial urbanization see, Tahir, *Scholars Sufis, Saints and Capitalist in Kano, 1904-1974, The Pattern of Bourgeois Revolution in an Islamic Society* unpublished PhD Dissertation Cambridge University, 1975

32. Oral interview with Hajia Awau Kashim, Zamaru, Zaria, age 90+, 21/10/2004; and Hajia Fatima Fatiu, Kawo, Kaduna, age 80+, 07/11/2004. All my informants made it clear that the major problems which the Emirs and local authorities faced during the enforcement of anti-prostitution laws in the 1940s and 50s was that it was difficult to identify the *Karuwa* who went out to seduce men for sexual intercourse in their rented homes and those living on "legitimate earning".

33. Paul Lovejoy, "Concubinage and the Status of Slaves in Early Colonial Northern Nigeria" *Journal of African History*, 29 (1988) p 246

34. Paul E Lovejoy and Jan S Hogendorn *"Slow Death for Slavery: The Course of Abolition in Northern Nigeria, 1897-1936.* (New York, Cambridge University Press, 1993) p 112

35. Paul, "Concubinage," pp 245-248

36. Paul and Hogendorn, *Slow Death,* p 117

37. Ibid. p 117

38. Paul, "Concubinage," p 249

39. Paul and Hogendorn *"Slow Death,"* p 63

40. Oral evidence, Mallam Sherif, Agwarimi, Kano, 22/10/2004 age 90+. For some documented accounts related to this man, see National Archives Kaduna (NAK) Secretary of Northern Provinces (SNP) 7, "Kano City Assessment," 1921-1922

41. Oral evidence, Mallam Sherif

42. Catherine and Mack asserted that *Karuwanci* is an occupation amongst Hausa women, which is yet to be systematically studied. Catherine Coles and Beverly Mack "Introduction" in Catherine Coles and Beverly Mack (eds) *Hausa Women in the Twentieth Century* (Madison Wisconsin, University of Wisconsin Press, 1991) p18

43. Victor Uchendu "Concubinage Amongst Ngwa Igbo of Southern Nigeria", *Africa,* 35 (1965) pp187-197

44. Published works on traditional custom related to marriage are numerous. For a general survey see P.A Talbot *The Peoples of Southern Nigeria, Vol II* (London Longman 1926).

45. This practice does not have any resemblance with North American and Western understanding of lesbian marriage or homosexuality. For a very interesting account of this type of marriage, see, Ifi Amdiume *Male Daughters, Female Husbands: Gender and Sex in an Africa Society* (London, Zed Books Ltd, 1987)

46. La Ray Denzer, "Yoruba Women, A Historiographical Study", a paper presented as a lead paper at the Congress of the Historical Society of Nigeria, University of Calabar 18-23 May 1992 pp4-5

47. G T Basden, *Amongst the Ibo of Nigeria,* (Ibadan, University Press Publishers 1921) p 102

48. Samuel Johnson, *The History of the Yoruba* (Lagos CSS 1921) p116. Amongst the Esan, what was obtainable was what Igbafe called theoretical divorce because it never took place. For further readings see, P.A Igbafe, "Tradition and Change in Benin Marriage System," *Journal of Economic and Social Studies* 1970 p 76

49. Samuel *The History* p 116

50. P.A Talbot, *The People of Southern* pp 425-467

51. National Archives, Enugu (NAE) Obubdist 4.1.71, *Prostitution in Obubra Division,* 1939-1944

52. NAE Obubdist

53. The Nigerian Observer, *Is Prostitution a Trade,* 19 July, 1930 p3. This word must have been corrupted over time. This is because, there is a town in Obubra called Akunakuna.

54. NAE, Obubdist

55. For instance, Ifi *Male Daughters,* Oyeronke Oyewumi, *The Invention of Women: Making An African Sense of Western Gender Discourses* (Minneapolis University

of Minnesota Press, 1997), Oniagwu Ogbomo, *When Men and Women Mattered: A History of Gender Relations amongst the Owan of Nigeria* (Rochester NY University of Rochester Press 1997), Gloria Chuku "Women and the Complexity of Gender Relations" in Toyin Falola (ed) *Nigeria in the 20th Century* (Durham Carolina Academic Press 2002) etc

56. E.G Ravenstein "The Laws of Migration", *Journal of the Royal Statistical Society,* 48, 2 1885

57. Akin Mabogunje, *Urbanization in Nigeria* (London, Longman 1968)

58. For a comprehensive discussion of the origin and development of railway transport in Nigeria see Wale Oyemakinde, *A History* of *Indigenous Labour on the Nigerian Railway*, 1895-1945 unpublished PhD thesis, University of Ibadan (1970)

59. C.N Anyanwu, *Port Harcourt, 1912-1955; The Development of A Nigerian Municipality,* unpublished PhD thesis, University of Ibadan (1971)

60. Oyewole Enoch *Colonial Urbanization in Northern Nigeria: Kaduna, 1913 1960*, unpublished Ph.D thesis, Northern Historical Research Scheme, Department of History, Ahmadu Bello University, Zaria, 1987

61. Akin Mabogunje, *Urbanization in p112*

62. Kenneth Little, *Urbanization as a Social Process: An African Case Study* (London, Routledge and Kegan Paul, 1973)

63. Most "red light districts" are found in culturally heterogeneous parts of the cities. In Kano such places include the *Fagge* quarters and *Sabongari*. Such places in Ibadan can be found in Dugbe, Ekotedo, Mokola etc.

64. Lewis Munford use this statement to depict the character of cities, see Lewis Munford "City" in David I, Sills (ed) *International Encyclopaedia of the Social Sciences Vol II* (New York, Heinemann 1968)

65. Thomas Hodgkin, *Nationalism in Colonial Africa* (New York, 1962)

66. Kenneth, *African Women,* chapter one. See also S. O Osoba, "The Phenomenon of Labour Migration in the Era of British Colonial Rule: A Neglected Aspect of Nigeria's Social History", *JHSN* 4, 4 (1969)

67. Ado Muhammed Yahuza, *Pattern of Urbanization in Colonial Kano, 1903-1960* Unpublished M.A thesis, University of Ibadan p148

68. NAI, CSO *26/38322/S.193, Unemployment Movement, Petition by*

69. NAI, CSO 26/03571/S, *Employment of Africa Women in Government Services-Emolument,* For materials in the Impact of Colonialism on women in Nigeria, see Women Research and Documentation Centre (WORDOC) Institute of African Studies University of Ibadan *Symposium on "The Impact of Colonialism on Nigeria Women, 16-19 October, 1989.*

70. *Evening Times* (Nigeria), *"Women To Get Same Salaries As Men,"* 9 June 1956, p 1

71. NAI, COMCOL 1, 2844: *Child Prostitution In Lagos,* 1943-1946

72. NAI, Ondo Prof 1, *Social Welfare in the Colony and Protectorate of Nigeria* 1940-1954

73. Burkar Dan Azumi, *Tin Mining and Peasants Impoverishment in Jos Division, 1900 1950* M.A thesis, NHRS, Department of History, Ahmadu Bello University, Zaria (1986)

74. Bill Freud, *Capital and Labour in The Nigerian Mines,* (London Longman 1981), p 98

75. NAK (SNP) 8, 4575 *Northern Chief's Conference, 1942*

76. Saheed Aderinto, "My Office is My Home: Prostitutes and Brothel Keeping in Ibadan", unpublished manuscript, 2005

77. Olawale Albert *Urban Migrant Settlements in Nigeria: A Historical Comparison of the Sabon Garis in Kano and Ibadan, 1893-1991*, unpublished Ph.D thesis, University of Ibadan, 1994.

78. Some of these *Sabon gari* have been studied in detail see for instance Arthur Vukile Dhliwajo, *A History of Sabo Gari, Zaria, 1911-1950: A Study of Colonial Urban Administration,* unpublished Ph.D thesis, NHRS, Department of History, Ahmadu Bello University, Zaria 1986, Olawale, *Urban Migrant*

79. Olawale, *Urban* chapter three

80. Abner, *Custom and Politics, p 54*

81. Renee, *Alternative* p292. *Sabon gari* might be given other appellation, such as *Sabon Layi, m*eaning (new lane),

82. Ado *Pattern,* chapter 2

83. Kenneth Little, *African Women,* p18. See also Saheed Aderinto, I Need to Work Hard for Marriage: Masculinity and "Bride Price Hysteria" in Colonial Nigeria, a working paper

84. N.A Fadipe, *The Sociology of the Yoruba* (Ibadan, University of Ibadan Press, 1970) pp 91-93

85. The name of a popular trading agent given to a brand of imported cloth

86. A statement which means you should get your own

87. Meaning, courtship. In all, these three Hausa statements were popularly and summarily used to jokingly describe the magnetization of marriage or how great emphasis was placed on expensive gift as a prerequisite for marriage. For further readings, see Mansur Ibrahim Mukhtar, *The Impact of British Colonial Domination on the Social and Economic Structures of the Society of Kano, 1903-1950* unpublished M.A thesis, NHRS, Department of History, Ahmadu Bello University, Zaria, 1983

88. P.C Lloyd, *Africa in Social Change: Changing Traditional Societies in the Modern* (USA, Penguin Books 1967), p 123

89. WAP *Bride Price in Mbaise* September 1 1953, p 2

90. Nigerian Spokesman, *Youth of Awo-Omama Will Boycott Their Girls, Want Bride Price be Reduced* 8 January, 1948, p 1

91. Nigerian Tribune, *Prostitutes in Ibadan* 21 July, 1952, p 3

92. Daily Comet, *Bride Price in Iboland* 7 July, 1949, p 3

93. NAK, Ministry of Local Government (MLG/S/RGA) *Committee on Problems of Prostitution in Northern Nigeria,* 1950-1965

94. NAI, COMCOL 1, 2844 *Child Prostitution.*

95. NAI, Oyo Prof 1, File No 3562 *Measures,* the letter is dated 16 March, 1944.

96. NAI, COMCOL 1, 2844 *Child Prostitution.*

97. John, *The African Poor,* p. 183. For a detail discussion of other causes of high rate of divorce, see Damachi Ukandi Gowin, *The Nigerian Modernization: The Colonial Legacy* (New York The Press 1977) p. 110

98. NAE, Obubdist, 4.1.71.

99. Talbot, *Peoples* p. 430.

100. SND *Demobilization of Prostitutes*, 3 October, 1946 p3
101. See SND Ekotedo, September 26, 1946. See also WAP in the late 1940s.
102. NAI, CSO 26/27837 *Annual Report on*
103. NAI, *Annual Volume of the Laws of Nigeria, Legislation enacted during 1944*
104. NAI, COMCOL1, 2600 *Social Welfare, General Questions, Establishment of Welfare Department*, 1942-1945 Vol II
105. Carol Smart, *Women, Crime and Criminology: A Feminist Critique,* London Routledge and Kegan Paul, 1976, pp 77-93.

7

Policing Urban Prostitution: Prostitutes, Crimes, Law, and Reformers

Saheed Aderinto

It is a plain truth and well-known fact that prostitutes and criminals go together. Without the prostitutes, there can be no home for those who live solely on crime. The two are a disgraceful pair and in order to clear any community of the menace of the one the other also must be given similar attention[1]

Introduction

In chapter six, we analyzed the history of urban prostitution during the terminal colonial period. This chapter is a follow up as it describes how the colonial state dealt with the problem of urban prostitution during the period under review. "Demobilization and Repatriation" was the popular slogan that summarized the reaction of the government and the public to the activities of prostitutes who were labeled "undesirables" during the period.[2] The "reformers" was the public who agitated for the introduction of laws to abolish/regulate prostitution. The slogan "DR" entered official lexicon because it was the most popular statement made in the print media and in petitions sent to the government by the reformists. "Demobilization," therefore, does not have any resemblance with the ones carried out amongst the soldiers after the First and Second World War. In addition, "Repatriation" is not akin to the government's official regulation of controlling lepers, beggars, criminals, lunatics etc whose public presence constituted serious health and security threats.[3] The "Repatriation and Demobilization" of undesirables (prostitutes), therefore, found solace in the presupposition that the activities or conditions of prostitutes was akin to those of fugitives, criminals, lunatics, lepers and other categories of people who were officially called undesirables and who required repatriation to their home towns.

Prostitution in colonial Nigeria was not a criminal offense.[4] However some activities such as public soliciting, brothel keeping, living on immoral earnings, procuring, etc. that are connected to it were all criminal offenses. Three major presuppositions facilitated the process of criminalizing of prostitution. The first was that prostitution is a "deviant career", that owned its origin to emergence of urban centers and the search for white-collar jobs. The second was the moral and health considerations that allowed them to be seen as a class of people who constituted "public pollution", through their roles in the spread of venereal diseases and general "immorality."[5] Lastly, there were the assumptions, as the epigraphs above indicates, that prostitutes were responsible for increase in crime rate and limiting the access that people who engaged in "legitimate jobs" had to decent accommodation. The process of criminalizing prostitution, which was initiated by the reformers through the print media and in the petitions sent to the government, had its root in the labeling of prostitutes as "undesirables" and the presupposition that they encouraged the entrenchment of some new forms of criminal and "deviant behavior". The colonial state's institutional responses were, therefore, inherent in the social, economic, and moral contradictions. As a female specific crime,[6] the male dominated colonial society provided an easy condition for all forms of condemnation that prostitution received; this was a situation that introduced new dynamics to the exacerbated nature of gender disequilibria in colonial Nigeria. Thus, this chapter focuses on the process of criminalizing prostitution, a product of the labeling of prostitutes as "undesirables" and the colonial state responses that took the dimension of the promulgation and enforcement of anti-prostitution laws. The limitations of the government policing of urban prostitution, which we called "demobilization without rehabilitation", are also analyzed.

A Theoretical Overview

The study of female criminality in colonial Nigeria is still in its infancy. In the first instance, criminology as a field of academic inquiry did not emerge in Nigeria until end of colonial rule in 1960. The first major attempt at developing criminology started in 1964 with the inauguration of the Nigerian Society of Criminology.[7] Also, the critical academic study of female criminality only emerged in 1982 through the pioneering efforts of Olufunmilayo Oloruntimehin.[8] The colonial government commissioned Alexander Paterson to carry out a survey of the crime and prisons administration in Nigeria. His report entitled *CRIME AND ITS TREATMENT IN NIGERIA*, the first of its kind was presented in 1944.[9] Unlike the "Lombrosian" biological positivist school of criminology, which attributed female criminality to biological or pathological mutation,[10] Alexander Paterson made no attempt at locating crime in the light of any male or female primitivism. Instead, he identifies the impact of the Second World War in the rise of new forms of criminal behavior in the major cities of Lagos, Ibadan, and Kano in Nigeria. While admitting that professional criminals are few, he pointed to unemployment, idleness and economic implications of the war-time-exigencies as factors that allowed crime rate to increase. His discussion of crime is, therefore, akin to the W.I Thomas and Otto Polak Liberal School of Criminology, which identifies crime and "deviant behavior" to attendant social problems.[11] Just like many works on criminology in the West, Paterson's depicted violent crime as a male dominated and made no comment about female or prostitutes' criminality.[12]

A major problem that one encounters in reconstructing the history of prostitutes' criminality is the nature of sources available and the methods used by the police in the enforcement of anti-prostitution laws. The police did not keep records related to personal data of prostitutes from the early 1940s, when arrests and prosecution started, to 1960.[13] Prostitution related offenses such as brothel keeping, procuring, living on immoral earnings, etc. are not computed separately in the annual crime statistics of the police. The usual practice was that prostitutes were presented to the Magistrate after the raiding of places where they solicited had been conducted. They were readily released after they must have paid the imposed fines.[14] There is no record that a prostitute was jailed because of her inability to pay the imposed fines. Availability of data related to place of origin of arrested prostitutes, age, tribe, family background, and the general life history would have assisted in providing materials for propounding relevant theories related to prostitutes' criminality. The only data available is the number of prosecutions contained in the Annual Questionnaire on the trafficking of women and Children which Nigeria and other countries in the world were enjoined to fill and submit to the League of Nations and later the Economic and Social Council of the United Nations.[15] The Inspector general of Police of Nigeria did not provide credible and reliable information related to the arrest and prosecution of people that broke anti-prostitution laws. For instance, while the government reported that five people were arrested for breaking anti-prostitution laws in her annual report submitted to the United Nation's Economic and Social Council in 1958,[16] the *West African Pilot* of January 20th of the same year reported that 40 were arrested in one single story. Going through other newspaper reports during the same year, it is abundantly clear that more prosecutions were made during that particular year.[17]

In addition, while the government reported that 71 Nigerian prostitutes were deported from the Gold Coast in 1944,[18] other sources from Nigeria and the Gold coast show that more prostitutes were repatriated during the same year.[19] Significantly, there is no question related to prostitutes' criminality or the role played by prostitutes in crime in the questionnaire. The information, which was expected to be supplied in the questionnaires, was restricted solely to how prostitution and the trafficking of women and children across international borders were carried out and individual countries in stemming the tide.[20] Prostitution and human trafficking were some of the social issues that were "politicized" in colonial Nigeria adopted approaches. The "Politicization of prostitution" took the dimension of the government's desire to prevent international surveillance from knowing about social problems in the British colonies. This was the principal reason why Nigeria did not accede to all the International Conventions on the trafficking of women and children throughout the colonial period.[21] This was also the reason why the Inspector general of Police presented doctored information related to figures of people arrested for breaking anti-prostitution laws and declared that there wasn't any international traffic at a period when the traffic in girls and women to the Gold Coast for the purpose of prostitution had reached a pinnacle. Admitting the prevalence of prostitution and human trafficking will provide the protagonist of nationalism, which grew drastically after the Second World War, the instrument of campaigning against British rule.

From the foregoing, it is apparent that the knowledge of the relationship between prostitution and crime is limited because it is necessary to depend on sources provided by the reformists who condemned prostitution and the activities connected to it. The conventional historical approach of the cross-examination of sources without any doubt remains the most veritable tool for studying the connection between prostitution and crime in colonial Nigeria. In this regard, newspapers as well as archival and oral history stand out. While a sizeable percentage of what is read about the role of prostitutes in crime blamed them for allowing the perpetration of crime, there is still the opportunity of reading stories from some reformists who argued contrarily.[22] Three major variables are nevertheless discernable in the discourse of the relationship between crime and prostitution. These prostitutes are criminals because they broke anti-prostitution laws, and they are catalysts and victims of crime due to environment and activities related to their career.

Prostitutes and Crime in Colonial Urban Centers

In looking at the relationship between prostitution and crime in Nigeria, it is imperative to understand that prostitution grew within the framework of the social and economic circumstances obtainable within the colonial urban and capitalist domain. It is basically an urban phenomenon not only in Nigeria but also in most parts of the world. Nigerian urban centers are known for an assortment of crimes, a majority of which were not obtainable or rare before the establishment of colonial rule. Geographically, high crime rates were to be found in most part of urban centers that were culturally heterogeneous or that developed as a result of the new economic opportunities put in place by colonial rule.[23] Such places were also contained many beer parlors, brothels, cinema houses, and areas stigmatized as "red light district," which attracted "urbanized people". I have in another work demonstrate how migrant settlements and culturally heterogeneous parts of urban centers allowed prostitution to thrive.[24] Prostitution and other social problems such as juvenile delinquency, vagrancy, unemployment, child labor, etc. were incorporated into the framework of social urbanization and economic pauperization, which reached a peak during the Second World War (1939-1945).

Another very important way of looking at prostitution and crime is that it involved a group of females who were not only labeled "undesirable" but also had to survive economically within a space that was male–dominated. Also, since a very sizeable percentage of what we know about their activities were provided by those who felt that it was bad in the society, there were tendencies for prostitutes to have been accused of crimes which they did not commit. So, economic, social, and moral/behavioral tendencies loomed large in the analysis of the connection between prostitution and crime in colonial Nigeria. Categorically, most of the reformists who wrote about prostitution in newspapers were men who detested the casual sexual labor provided by prostitutes. While it was plausible for the hatred to be rooted in some "moral or ethical considerations," the access that prostitutes have to "quick resources" must have been the motives behind the hatred. In a petition to the District Officer of Obubra Division, the executives of Egbisim Improvement wrote:

> We beg to state that the chief reason why our women refused to stop harloting is because it is usual for the women to go out harloting, while there, they will collect money in all sort of immoral ways. When they come home, they take upon themselves to marry Ibo, Ibibio and any other tribe in the eastern provinces. After doing so, they will send these so-called wives to the Gold Coast and other places for harloting and thus increases the population of harlots. And because of these immoral practices, our women look low on us (men) because these so-called wives help to increase our women pockets. . . . Because our women cannot marry or live at home to produce children, the shortage of labor is acute in our town so much that we are compelled to employ labor from other villages. It is practically impossible to count all the havoc done to any village, town, tribe or nation in which harlotism prevails.[25]

The content of this letter and other related sources demonstrated the gendered nature of issues related to prostitution and female mobility in general. Mobile women were accused of allowing local agricultural production to drop due to their absence from home. The undue control which men and traditional authorities tried to impose on women led to serious agitation by women in Agwagwune and Ugep in Obubra Division of Ogoja province on May 26, 1948.[26]

Child prostitution was one of the most criminalized prostitution related activity. The fragile nature of customary marriage, partly a product of magnetized economy is the root of the contemporary problems of the trafficking of girls for the purpose of prostitution. Betrothal was a significant aspect of customary marriage that, in pre-colonial and colonial period, sometimes took place even before the bride or the bridegroom or both were born, came under heavy abuse. By the late the 1930s, child betrothal had became a very important means by which young girls below the age of 15 were trafficked for the purpose of prostitution in urban centers, most importantly Lagos and Ibadan.[27] The *modus operandi* was for a trafficker to secure or lure girls from parents under the pretense of training them and getting husband for them at the city. Such girls were not released by the parents until the traffickers who in most cases were retired or adult prostitutes had paid a dowry ranging from 8 to 10 pounds to marry an anonymous man in Lagos.[28] This is what a newspaper report had to say about the phenomenon:

> A practice exists whereby girls of tender age are given away in "marriage" with the consent of their parents for a monetary consideration. These children are virtually sold into slavery . . . The attention of the Native Authorities and Government is called to the above and it is urged that steps be taken to prevent girls under sixteen years of age leaving the Divisions on the pretext of marriage. The chief or head of compound are in a measure responsible for giving away of the

girls in the compound in "marriage" and are the people to whom money is being paid. It is to them we look for a stoppage of this practice of slave trade and
prostitution, which passes under the guise of marriage.[29]

Another very important condition which placed prostitution on a criminal
agenda was the activities of touts who acted as "consultants" to prostitutes. These
touts, who were fondly called *boma boys,* sometimes acted as guides to seamen
and foreigners who visited important ports like Lagos and Port Harcourt.[30] The
insecurity of public soliciting and living in brothels might have forced prostitutes to make use of *boma boys* whose responsibility was to connect male solicitors with prostitutes. *Boma boys* often receive between 25 and 33 percent of the
amount charged by the prostitutes in addition to the fees that they must have
charged male solicitors.[31] Apart from consulting for prostitutes, *boma boys* were
known for crimes such as pickpockets, burglary, and other criminal activities.
Prostitution received greater concern because it was seen as a major promoter of
crimes perpetrated by *boma boys.* A contributor to September 7, 1947 issue of the
Eastern Nigeria Guardian reported the activities of prostitutes and crime in this
manner:

> I feel to call the attention of the moral public of Port Harcourt and the Press to
> the evils being practiced by prostitutes and seamen guides in this township. They
> have made it a habit of drugging the seamen they may harbour in their rooms,
> while drinking wine or beer, thereby rendering them temporarily unconscious
> while they dip hands into the pockets of the poor fellows and rob them of any
> money they may have brought ashore. This is a usual practice amongst the pros-
> titutes. The sooner they are sent out of the township, the better it will be for Port
> Harcourt.[32]

Another contributor to the June 12, 1944 issue of the *Southern Nigeria
Defender* after considering the historical origin of prostitution and the role played
by colonialism described the connection between prostitution and *boma boys*
thus:

> There is another great evil of prostitution. Prostitutes are the roots of boma boys.
> They feed and clothe the boma boys who conduct customers to them. It has
> been discovered that given the condition in which prostitutes and boma boys can
> thrive, you cannot induce a boma to obtain a regular job at four pounds a month.
> Remove the prostitutes and the boma boys are no more[33]

The need to curtail the excesses of *boma boys* led to the enactment of the
"Unlicensed Guide Ordinance" in March 1941 and the prosecution of 1,050
unlicensed guides and touts in December 1943.[34] By 1946, the effectiveness of
the enforcement of the ordinance and the contributions of the "Licensed Guides
Union" might have been responsible for the reduction of the numbers of persecu-
tion to 242.[35]

Another significant presupposition that allowed prostitution to come under
legal sanctions was the moral and health considerations. Prostitutes were accused
of being responsible for the high mortality rate through their roles in the spread of

venereal diseases. In a letter to the Emir of Kano, the Senior Medical Officer wrote, "Your Highness: several death occur in this City Hospital due to very serious cases of venereal diseases, the unhealthy prostitutes in this township cause these. What should be done to lessen these complaints?"[36] While reformists' arguments about venereal diseases might be from a health perspective, the government's position looks economic. The government felt that the preponderance of venereal diseases among its workers, most importantly the military and police, led to low productivity.[37]

Of immeasurable significance was the hatred that prostitutes received because they had access to better accommodations. All over the major urban centers, activities of prostitutes were sometimes condemned because people felt they had access to better accommodation because their profession gave them "quick access" to resources. Landlords were also accused of always ready to provide accommodation for prostitutes who had the resources to pay for it.[38] Going through documents related to prostitution and accommodation, one will discover that men who wrote about prostitution and agitated for the introduction of laws to regulate it were disgruntled because of access which "free or unattached women" had to better accommodations. Therefore, attempts were made to brand all urban women who lived alone and had access to better accommodation as "prostitutes". While it was plausible for prostitutes to have had better access to accommodation, the unscrupulous generalization that all women who were not living with their family and could afford better accommodation were "prostitutes," left little to be appreciated.[39] The magnitude of this issue is best summed in an article published in the Eastern Nigeria Guardian about the accommodation problems in Port Harcourt. This article read, "The prostitutes have deprived workers of decent houses. They are in a way responsible for high cost of living and high rentage."[40] The situation in Port Harcourt was similar to what was experienced in Northern Nigeria. The following is an extract from the report complied by the Secretary of the Ministry of Social Welfare and Cooperatives:

It is now considered necessary to draw the attention of all Native Authorities in the region to some provisions of the Law in order that some more effective efforts to reduce the problem could be made. Action on these measures could only be effective if action is taken first with the landlords who in many cases refuse to let their premises to men (sometimes with families) in favour of loose women who form the large army of prostitutes all over the country. Accommodation in places like Kaduna, Jos, Sabon Gari and Tudun Wada of Zaria, Kano, Maiduguri, Gasu, Sokoto and many others is so difficult for the male population who are strangers to these places, but a prostitute can easily find one. There is a great deal of hardship suffered by men with families in finding accommodation in the places mentioned, simply because of the prostitutes have the better ones. The rents too are made too high due to the fact that the prostitutes are prepared to pay much higher and would not make demands for better conditions knowing that their trade is illegal and undesirables[41]

Policing, Law, Reformers and the Society

Prostitution related offenses come under Chapter 21 (Offenses against Morality) of the criminal code of Nigeria. Section 1 of this criminal code defines prostitution "with its grammatical variations and cognate expressions include the offering by a female of her body commonly for acts of lewdness for payment although there is no act or offer of an act of ordinary sexual connection."[42] Apart from this, the definition made prostitution a female-specific offense and also as previously mentioned several offences such as public soliciting, loitering, trafficking/procuring, unlawful guardianship, brothel keeping, etc. were illegal. The first criminal code related to prostitution was passed in 1916.[43] This law appeared in the criminal code not because there were cases or evidences of procurement of girls for the purpose of prostitution but because the International Conventions on The trafficking of women and Children enjoyed all countries of the world to enact laws related to female mobility across international borders. Most of the prostitution related ordinances passed between 1916 and 1920 were, therefore, meant to allow Nigeria to be in consonant with what was obtainable in other parts of the world.[44]

Section 224 (1) of the criminal code ordinance makes it illegal for a person to "by threat or intimidation of any kind procure a woman or girl to have unlawful carnal connection with a man, either in Nigeria or elsewhere." Chapter (2) of the same criminal code made the trafficking of women who was not a prostitute for the purpose of prostitution illegal. The maximum penalty for these two major offences was one-year imprisonment.[45] 1944 signified a very important year in the history of prostitution and human trafficking in Nigeria. Between 1916 and 1944, the criminal code on human trafficking did not undergo any meaningful amendment. The revolution which the criminal code related to prostitution took in 1944 can be appreciated against the backdrop of the fact that the problems related to prostitution had reached a very serious dimension. Wartime emergencies led to the neglect of social responsibilities on one hand, and the increase in many social problems including vagrancy, unemployment, child labor, and general pauperization on the other hand. The late 1930s and the early 1940s were characterized by a lot petitions and reports in newspapers about the activities of prostitutes and the role which they played in increasing "public immorality" and crime. The criminal code amendment of 1944, apart from officially defining prostitution, involved men in its related offenses in a manner that was hitherto unobtainable. This was because section 225A (b) of the criminal code made it illegal for men to solicit for sex in public while sections 225B (a), (b), and (c) spelled out the illegality of brothel keeping. The maximum penalties for these two offences are one and two month's imprisonment, respectively. Before the criminal code 225A (b), 1944 amendment, there was no provision for the punishment of males who publicly solicited for sex.[46]

Prostitution belonged to the "off the book sector" of the colonial economy. Nevertheless, there were attempts by Traditional/Native Authorities to incorporate it into the national income of the country. This incorporation reflected in the decision by Emirs in the north and traditional chiefs in the east to make prostitutes to pay tax. The idea of "prostitute's taxation," as it was called, was conspicuously a scheme meant to swell the pockets of traditional authorities. The chiefs who introduced "prostitute's tax" in their locality argued that the payment of such tax would prohibit prostitution while others felt that prostitutes should be taxed because they allow the local treasury to be depleted. As enunciated by the Chiefs of Agwagwune in Cross-River, "because of harlotism, the population of our village is diminishing. Our taxable males are few and for that sake our taxation money is no little that it does not suffice for use for general improvement of the town."[47] One of the most hotly debated agenda at the 1942 Conference of Chiefs of the Northern Provinces was whether prostitutes should be taxed or not. While the Emir of Gwandu noted that prostitutes had increased after he had stopped taxing them, the Emir of Gumel felt that "to tax them is to give them a license for their trade."[48] As controversial as "prostitutes' tax" was, the practice in some places was for prostitutes to be allowed to publicly solicit and carry out other activities after they had paid certain amount to local authorities.[49]

Reference has already been made to the procurement of girls below the age of 15 through fictitious betrothal for the purpose prostitution. After consultation with many native authorities in the provinces where girls were recruited, a proposal for the regulation of native laws on marriage, most importantly betrothal was made. The proposal suggested that the age of consent be fixed at 18 and that betrothal below this age should be disallowed. This proposal was greeted with a lot of opposition from native authorities who felt that such orders would aggravate the poor state of customary marriage that had degenerated seriously as a result of social and economic changes ushered in by colonial rule. In Ibadan, for instance, the Olubadan Council felt that the recruitment of young girls for the purpose of prostitution was not prominent amongst the Yoruba because the betrothed girls continued to leave with their parents until the full dowry and marriage arrangements were carried out. The council felt that the ordinance should be made to operate in parts of the country where the incidence of procurement of girls through fictitious betrothal were must rampant.[50] The Emirs of the Northern provinces were also divided about the introduction of this law. In Islam, a girl could be married to a man after her first menstruation.[51] The passing of laws to fix the age of consent was going to alter the tradition and custom of child marriage. Also, it was seen that "child marriage, as of "purdah", is the only way to prevent a girl's chastity in the present atmosphere of sexual promiscuity."[52] In the Eastern provinces, the intended law was frowned upon because it was felt that not all girls given out for the purpose of training or marriage were used for prostitution in urban centers. The resolution made by some native authorities in the Eastern provinces was that the government should keep close look at what young girls were used for in the urban centers of Lagos, Ibadan, and Port Harcourt where the incidence of child prostitution was the highest. They also advocated for the "repatriation" of girls used as prostitutes back to the provinces.[53]

In spite of the divergent view and opposition to the regulation of traditional marriage custom, must importantly the ones related to child betrothal, The Native Authority (Child Betrothal) Order was passed in 1943. The order made the betrothal of girls below the age of seventeen illegal and made provision for the registration of all betrothal.[54] The Eastern Region took a giant stride in 1956 by legally abolishing child marriage.[55] Just like several laws with good intention, this ordinance could not ameliorate the problems of the trafficking of girls for the purpose of prostitution because public opinion in the villages were not too strong against it. This partly explains the reasons why the recruitment of girls for the purpose of prostitution continued throughout the colonial period. Also, the widened gap between the economic opportunities of rural and urban workers, which was the major contributing factor, continued unabated. Since the economic and social differentials between the countryside and the urban centers could not be bridged by the government, the latter continued to demonstrate its interest in partaking from the greater economic opportunities obtainable from the residents of the latter by increasing bride price or giving out daughters genuinely for the purpose of training and or for prostitution.

Before the outbreak of the Second World War in 1939, there was no government social welfare organization in Nigeria.[56] The debate for the establishment of social welfare department started in 1940. The debate dragged for a long time because some government officers felt that social welfare related activities were part of the responsibilities of the department of education. In another category were British officers who felt that social problems caused by the war would disappear after the war, and that the missionaries and other voluntary organization that had been helping the government should continue with their philanthropic gesture.[57] The debate, however, did not prevent Alexander Paterson from carrying out a national tour of social problems in Nigeria in 1942. In the same year, a member of the prison service with a Borstal and Social Welfare experience in the United Kingdom was appointed as Social Welfare Officer and was stationed in Lagos. Based on the recommendations contained in Alexander Peterson's 1944 report entitled: *SOCIAL WELFARE IN THE COLONY AND PROTECTORATE OF NIGERIA*, a Social Welfare Department was established in Lagos and gradually introduced to the protectorate.[58] The role played by the Colony Welfare Service in the reduction of the problems of child prostitution cannot be over-emphasized. A laudable activity of the department at its inception was tour of parts of the country were traffickers capitalized on the ancient traditional custom of child betrothal to recruit girls for prostitution in Lagos. The colony welfare department was also instrumental to the passing of several ordinances, which assisted in the protection of children and juvenile from the activities of trafficker. The most significant of these ordinances was the Children and Young Person Ordinance. This law was made to protect children from maltreatment by adults. The establishment of girls' hostels assisted in removing young girls who would have been used for prostitution from streets.[59]

The table below indicates the admission of pupils into the girl's hostel in Lagos in 1946:

Cases	No of victims	Remarks
Raped	1	
Unlawfully carnally known	2	One of them, age 5 had venereal disease
Child Prostitutes	34	Formally in custody of adult prostitutes
Runs away from maltreatment by guardian	13	9 of them had venereal disease
Beyond parental control	3	One of them age 13 had venereal disease
Girls in moral danger	2	One of them, age 13 was found pregnant
Girl Hawkers	1	Age 11, found not to be virgin
Total	56	

Source: Computed from NAI, COMCOL 1, 2600 Vol II, Social Welfare, General Questions, Establishment of Social Welfare Department, 1942-1945

The roles played by tribal unions in the enforcement of prostitution related laws are bifurcated into two. Firstly, they provided the government with information related to the activities of their members who were accused of the trafficking of young girls through petitions. There were occasions when they sent a list of members of their union who were prostitutes to District Officers. Also, they sent reports to their towns about the activities of their members who were accused of prostitution. Tribal unions felt that they were carrying out one of their important manifestoes of overseeing the welfare of their people. The usual practice after petitions have been sent was that the government will sermon important members of the tribal unions to meetings.[60] While it was obvious that tribal unions were against the activities of prostitutes from their tribes, the problems related to the cost of "repatriating" arrested prostitutes constituted problem between the unions and the government. The government was obliged to ask tribal unions who collect yearly and monthly dues from members of their tribes accused of prostitution to pay for the cost of "repatriation." Members of tribal unions felt that prostitutes made a lot of resources, which should be able to take care of their transport back home whenever they were arrested for breaking anti-prostitution laws. Obviously, the problems related to "repatriation" were not the cost of "repatriation" but rather the readiness of the prostitutes to leave the town.[61] Throughout the colonial period, the problems of who was to pay for the cost of "repatriation" remained between the government, the tribal unions, and accused prostitutes.

One of the most important debates in the 1940s and 1950s were the ones related to licensing of brothels and prostitutes. Many reformists felt that the licensing of prostitutes would allow the government to recognize adult prostitutes and regulate their activities, the most important of these being public soliciting which encouraged the activities of the *boma boys* and trafficking of girls below the age of consent.[62] As there exists no evidence that the enactment of the "Venereal Disease Ordinance" in 1943 was motivated by the increase in venereal diseases spread by prostitutes, the issuing of certificate of fitness according to some observers was the best way of ensuring that prostitutes are prevented from spreading diseases.[63] There was also a proposal that prostitutes be provided with separate quarters. The government turned down the proposal for the licensing of prostitutes and the creation of separate quarters on the grounds that these two steps were responsible for the entrenchment of prostitution in Great Britain in the 19th century.[64] Significant debates on the need to regulate the activities of owners of nightclubs were also made. Nightclub owners were seen as the bane behind the recruitment of girls for prostitution. Employing women also accused them of generally providing the enabling environment for the flourishing of prostitution as staffs.[65]

The enforcement of anti-prostitution laws was left in the hands of police who embarked on the raiding of streets, houses, or brothels that harbor prostitutes. It was in 1944 that the government started serious convictions of prostitutes. Convicted prostitutes were accused of breaking anti-prostitution laws. In that year, 53 and 5 people were convicted for keeping of brothel and living on immoral earnings respectively.[66] On July 1, 1944, the responsibility of raiding brothels and bringing prostitutes and traffickers to book was removed from the regular police and an "anti vice squad", a specially trained personnel drawn from the Police, was inaugurated.[67]

Women Police had its origin in the need to enforce anti-prostitution laws. The Women's Party first made the proposal for the employment of female police in December 1944. They advocated for the employment of women from between the ages of 40 and 50 years as constables "because they would be better able than men to prevent prostitution and to deal with female criminals."[68] The proposal was turned down for several years because it was felt that women police would not be able to deal with "screaming and swearing prostitutes, drunken merchant seamen of all nationalities, pimps, *boma boys*, touts and the rest of the unsavory fraternity"[69] The Commissioner of Police in his disapproval for the appointment of Women Police noted that:

> Women Police will not by itself solve the problem. We must in the main rely upon the influence of parents, teachers and ministers of religion, together with a sound public opinion, if we are to deal successfully with the social mischief created by the war emergency.[70]

The opposition to the enrolment of women as police took a different turn with the amendment by the Economic and Social Council of the United Nations of the Annual Questionnaires on the trafficking of women and Children in 1953.

Question No 7 of the new questionnaires wanted information related to "the extent to which women police and public services are engaged in the prevention of prostitution and it assisting its victim."[71] Just like other laws and regulations related to prostitution, Nigeria became interested in enrolling women as police to satisfy the requirement of the United Nations. The international pressure was collaborated by local nationalist agitation by Nnamdi Azikiwe and A.O. Ogedengbe. By 1951, Dr. Nnamdi Azikiwe had urged the Nigerian Police Force to employ policewomen to deal with "the growing number of female offenders."[72] The proposal for the enrolment of females, as constables did not see the light of the day until 1954, when the House of Representatives announced the establishment of the "Women's Police Branch."[73] At its inception, the "Women Police Branch" activities were limited to the Juvenile Welfare Center, motor traffic duties, and control of street hawking. With just about 172 policewomen and three from Northern Nigeria in 1962, and the fact that they chiefly carried out responsibilities which were not directly connected with the enforcement of anti-prostitution laws, the role of policewomen in the incidence of anti-prostitution laws were grossly undermined.

How did prostitutes react to the laws and reformists prohibition of their activities? The best way of appreciating the responses of prostitutes to the regulation and prohibition of their activities is by recognizing that prostitution was a career that gave a substantial degree of economic and social independence to females that practiced it. So, when government made laws that affected the activities of prostitutes, they were trying to destroy the social and economic existence of a class of people in the society. Also, they were trying to reduce the access that men who patronized prostitutes had to frequent supply of females who provided them with the needed sexual services. A major flaw in the government and reformists' arguments about prostitution was shrouded in hypocrisy. As identified by the Committee on Prostitution in Northern Nigeria: "both government and Native Authority officials do go on tour with prostitute."[75] Prostitution thrived because there were men who demanded the sexual services provided by prostitutes. It was only on occasional basis that the government and the reformists, majority of who were men acknowledged this fact. So when prostitutes were asked not to publicly solicit in one particular part of the city, men who patronized them also have to look for other places where they could find them or provide avenues that will protect them from legal sanctions.

Pimping was a prostitution-related activity that incorporated men into the vortex of the career. Aside that they could be accused of "living on immoral earnings" pimp's activities received a high level of protection against the law. In many ways, prostitutes made use of pimps to avoid arrest by the police. As earlier mentioned, the *boma boys,* who also acted as pimps, served as consultants in parts of the country or city where frequent arrests were rampant. The responsibilities of pimps vary from one part of the country to another. In the southern cities, most importantly Ibadan, Port Harcourt and Lagos, pimps acted as consultants by linking prostitutes with men majority of, who were foreigners in areas where

government control of their activities were stringent. In the North, the responsibilities of pimps took another coloration. This was because the regular legislation
was that prostitutes should get married or leave the town. It was not too difficult
for prostitutes to make arrangements with men, a majority of whom were trans-
vestites and normally acted as husbands to prevent them from being arrested. Men
who in most cases did not know them before arrest sometimes claimed prostitutes
who did not have pimps before arrest as "wives." A newspaper report describes
the limitation of this measure thus:

> The present system is to be married to an old friend with little or no income. The
> lady only houses the man and of course feeds him. The conditions are that the
> "husband" should leave the house whenever, a "client" comes. He must not seek
> the aid of the court for a divorce and should pass the night out of doors if and
> when a friend wishes the company of the lady. [76]

The ease at which prostitutes and pimps circumvent the law must have
made some Emirs in the north to introduce the payment of dowry before a man
could claim an arrested prostitute as "wife". As reported by the *Southern Nigeria
Defender* of June 12, 1948:

> The Emir ordered that the dowry must not exceed five shillings cash and three
> kola nuts totaling eight shillings. And that any man who married a prostitute
> must go to Birni (Kano City Palace) and sign an agreement, before His highness.
> If not they must not be allowed to stay here. Ever since, prostitutes have been
> running helter skelter in search of husbands. Some people have already started
> to engage them and those who are unfortunate to find emergent husbands are
> quietly moving to other places. [77]

This regulation introduced some forms of social and geographical segregation to prostitution in the north. While it was possible for Hausa prostitutes to get
a Hausa pimp, it was relatively difficult for non-Hausa prostitute to get pimps who
were Hausa men. This was one of the reasons why the population of non-Hausa
prostitutes swells up in *Sabon Gari* and other stranger quarters in the North. The
cultural heterogeneity of *Sabon Gari* provided a good cover from the non-Hausa
prostitutes who can always claim to be traders. [78]

The most important aspects of the government's and reformists' anti-prostitution campaign, which aroused questions about gender inequality, was the
distinction between who were prostitutes and other women who lived on "legitimate earnings." There were attempts by reformists and the state to derogatorily
categorize all sprinters and "unattached women" as "prostitutes." This development introduced new dynamics to the established economic, political, and social
magnetization of female under colonial rule. The situation was, however, worse
in Northern Nigeria Provinces where all unmarried women were derogatorily
categorized as *Karuwa*i, i.e. "prostitutes." The public stigmatization of all "free
women" as "prostitutes" was easily absolved by the state that was persuaded to
pass laws related to the access of all "free women" to basic facilities such as

accommodations. For instance, the reformers through the print media made recommendations to the government to pass laws related to female mobility.[79] A proposal for the introduction of laws that will make it an offense for landlords to give
accommodations to "free or unattached women" was examined by the Northern
Nigerian Committee for the reduction of prostitution.[80] A contributor to October
3, 1946 issues of the *Southern Nigeria Defender* argues, "if really, demobilization
will be carried out, all divorced and unmarried women must demobilized for they
are all birds of the same feather."[81] This extract from the Eastern Nigeria Guardian
best depict the situation:

> Every tribal union should take census of their female elements in the community,
> sort the married from the lot and hand over the surplus ones to the police. Every
> landlord, landlady and caretaker should give the names of all unmarried women
> in their plots to the police.[82]

The most popular method adopted by prostitutes to avoid the rot of law was
fleeing from one place to another. They tended to move to places where enforcement of anti-prostitution laws was less stringent. In the category of places where
the enforcement of anti-prostitution laws were high are Lagos, Ibadan, and northern Nigeria.[83] Although there is no record that show that prostitutes were jailed,
the usual practice of fining them coupled with molestation must have encouraged
some of them to move before the police conduct raids. As reported by *The Daily
Service* of June 27, 1944:

> One of other complaint concerns the steady influx of prostitutes into the town,
> especially from Lagos, where they find the vigilance of the police too uncomfort-
> able. Their presence in increasing number has caused serious misapprehension
> in the minds of thoughtful members of the community. They are looked upon a
> potential danger to public health. We feel that who engaged in this trade must
> have no asylum in any town whatever. If the evil of prostitution must be stamped
> out, the Police should constantly be on the heels of the traffickers wherever they
> are found. They should have no peace and no breathing space whatever until they
> retrace their footsteps and return to a decent life. We hope the police authorities
> at Ibadan will take steps at once and given the new "arrival as hot as a reception
> as they deserve[84]

Conclusion

A very apparent fact about the enforcement of anti-prostitution laws was the
exclusion of men who patronized prostitutes from its legal sanctions. While prostitutes were busy responding to laws by adopting methods to avoid arrests and
prosecution, men who patronized them had only to respond to laws by serving
as pimps and living on the proceeds of prostitution. Men through some colonial
administrative and economic structures allowed prostitution to thrive in places
were it was hitherto unknown. The question is thus: How undesirable were prostitutes who provided men with the needed sexual services in colonial Nigeria?
Although the colonial government of Nigeria identifies prostitution as one of the

problems accelerated by wartime exigencies,[85] adequate steps to regulate/abolish prostitution only reflected in the passing and enforcement of anti-prostitution laws. Attempts were not made to improve the standard of living of prostitutes after "demobilization" and "repatriation" had been carried out. The government refused to increase the chances of female migrants to education and economic opportunities in spite of the fact that the reports commissioned to look into social problems identify prostitution as a product of the deplorable situation of female employment.[86] What were the effects of "demobilization without rehabilitation?" "Demobilization and "repatriation" without rehabilitation" did nothing but to facilitate the spread of prostitution to places where it was hitherto unknown. Evidently, prostitutes tended to move from places where reformists' and government's opposition was high to places where it was weak. It became apparent that when prostitutes were "repatriated" from the north, they found refuge in Lagos and when raided in Lagos they flee to Ibadan and other towns in the Western Region. All over the country, the situation was that of "prostitutes are now leaving the town to [. . .] Prostitutes now have a new haven in [. . .]."[87] A contributor to June 27 issue of *Southern Nigeria Defender* pointed out:

> Where do you want the prostitutes to go? Everywhere they are sent, strong objection is raised. What is to be done with them? Are they to be shot or drown? If they are sent to their respective homes will that prevent them from continuing to be prostitutes" will their homes give them money to care for themselves?[88]

Of equal important was the international the trafficking of women and girls to the Gold Coast for the purpose of prostitution. This international traffic, the first of its kind in Nigeria, did not start until the late 1930s and blossomed into a veritable enterprise during the war years. "Repatriated" prostitutes found their ways into the Gold Coast "exodus."[89] By 1947, when the concerted efforts of the Government of Nigeria and the Gold Coast had been able to stem the tide through mass deportation of Nigeria prostitutes in the Gold coast, the deportees readily joined their local colleagues who had been involved in vicious movement since the early 1940s when mass arrest and prosecution of prostitutes began in the major Nigerian cities of Lagos, Kano, Ibadan and Port Harcourt etc.[90]

A very noticeable flaw in government and reformists' arguments about prostitution was, therefore, the exclusion of men from the legal sanctions of prostitution and "demobilization and repatriation without rehabilitation". In stead of putting in place adequate mechanism to reduce the alienation of female in the colonial capitalist and social structure, the government was busy trying the reduce the spirit of nationalism which took an outstanding dimension during and after the Second World War. Some steps put in place to reduce crime and other social problems could not achieve the desired result because of its origin as well as the need to reduce agitation of independence and divert the attention of the people.

Notes and References

1. *Southern Nigeria Defender* (SND) "Prostitutes and Criminals" 29 November, 1950, p 2

2. See, *West African Pilot*, (WAP), "Undesirable Women to Get Uneasy Time" 21 January 1955 p1, (SND), "Ekotedo Undesirables", 21 September 1946 p3, SND, "Demobilization of Prostitutes" 3 October, 1946 p3, SND, "Repatriation of Prostitute" 22 May, 1944 p2, SND, "J.E Osoroh Feels That Repatriating Prostitutes is Not The Right Thing" 4 May, 1944 p2, Eastern Nigeria Guardian, (ENG), *"Undesirable Women"*, 7 September 1947 p3, National Archives Ibadan (NAI), COMCOL 1, 1016 Vol III, *Undesirables in the Lagos Township and Suburbs, Repatriation of,* 1937-47, 1947-1952.

3. For some materials related to government official of controlling some of these categories of people, see (NAI), COMCOL 1, 1016 Vol. files related to these categories of people can be found in the Class List of Papers from the Federal Ministry of Health, Lagos.

4. NAI, CSO 26/27837 Vol I and II *Annual Report on the traffic in women and Children and Obscene Language Publication.*

5. Saheed Aderinto, *Urban Threat: Prostitutes and Venereal Diseases in Colonial Nigeria*, Paper presented at the African Health and Illness Conference, University of Texas at Austin March 25-27 2005.

6. See the definition of prostitution in NAI, *Annual Volume of the Laws of Nigeria, Legislation enacted during 1944*, Government Printer, 1945

7. National Archives, Kaduna (NAK) Simple List of Documents removed from the Ministry of Social Welfare and Community Development, Kaduna Second Group, MSWC 1908/S.1 *Nigeria Society of Criminology*, 1964

8. See, Olufunmilayo Oloruntimehin "A Preliminary Study of Female Criminality in Nigeria" in Adler Freda (ed) *Incidence of Female Criminality in Contemporary World* (New York: New York University Press, 1982). One of the best works on female criminality is Carol Smart, *Women, Crime and Criminology: A Feminist Critique.* (London Routledge and Kegan Paul, 1976). For general discussion of female criminality in Nigerian see Proceedings of the Symposium on Women and Crime organized by the Women in Uniform Forum at Nigerian Institute if International Affairs Lagos, 25 June, 1992.

9. NAI, Oyo Prof 1, 4113, *Crime and Its Treatment in Nigeria*, 1944-1946

10. C Lombroso and W Ferrero, *The Female Offender,* (London: Fisher Unwin 1895)

11. W.I Thomas, *The Unadjusted Girl,* (New York: Harper and Row, 1967), O Pollak, *The Criminality of Women* (New York, A.S Barnes, 1961).

12. NAI, Oyo Prof 1, 4113, *"Crime and Its,*

13. See NAI, Simple Annual Report of Police Department in the Simple List of Police.

14. NAI, Simple List of Police

15. NAI, CSO/26 27837 Vol I and II *Annual Report,* see also, CSO26/03338 Vol II *International Convention for the Suppression of White Slave Traffic and The trafficking of women and Children,*1913-1925, 1936-1956,

16. NAI, CSO 26/27837 Vol I and II,

17. See ENG, SND between January and August, 1958

18. NAI, CSO26/ 27837 Vol I and II,

19. Saheed Aderinto, "Journey to Work: Nigerian Prostitutes in the Gold Coast", 1935-1955, unpublished manuscript 2005 p5 see also Public Record and Archives Administration Department, (PRAAD) National Archives, Accra, CSO 15/2/2222 *The trafficking of women and Children*, 1940-1948.

20. NAI, CSO 26/27837, Vol I and II, and NAI CSO 26/03338 Vol II,

21. This is contrary to the general assertion that Nigerian acceded to international conventions related to traffic in children and women during the colonial period. It is a truism that the Northern Protectorate acceded to the 1903 and 1910 Convention on The trafficking of women and Children while the Southern Protectorate refused to accede to the conventions. But between 1914 and 1960, Nigerian did not accede to all conventions on the trafficking of women and children spearheaded either by the League of Nations or the United Nations.

22. ENG, "Problem of Prostitution" 19 February, 1951 p4, ENG, "Problem of Prostitution" 27 February, 1951 p4, SND "That Prostitution Problem" 17 April, 1946 p3, SND "This Prostitution Problem" 26 June 1944p3, The Comet "Re: Irresponsible Women" 31 May, 1944 p3, ENG "Are Prostitutes Harmless in Community or Do They Ruin in Their Trial?" 22 January, 1947 p3, ENG "Women are Equal of Men" 22 July, 1946 p4, etc

23. See NAI COMCOL 1, 2403, *Pickpockets and Kidnapping in the Township of Lagos*, for Kano see NAK Supplementary Simple List of Confidential Files from Provincial Office Kano, C104 *Robbers/Thieves*, 1933-1945, for Onitsha see, National Archives Enugu (NAE), Onitsha Prof op2944-12/1/2030 *Burglaries- Measures against*, 1940-1950.

24. Saheed Aderinto, *"Prostitution: A Social Legacy of Colonialism in Nigeria"*.

25. NAE, Obubdist 4.1.71, *Prostitution in Obubra Division*, 1939-1944.

26. ENG, "Demonstration by Women of Agwagwune" 30 June, 1948 p1

27. Saheed Aderinto "Prostitution: A Social,

28. Ibid.

29. The Nigerian Observer, "Child Stealing and 'Marriage" 10 August, 1940 p11

30. NAI, COMCOL 1, 248/S.173 *Licensed Guides Union*

31. SND, "Prostitution and Boma Boys" 12 June, 1944 pp3 and 4

32. ENG Undesirables Women,

33. SND "Prostitution and Boma Boys",

34. See NAI *Annual Volume of the Laws of Nigeria, Legislation enacted during 1941*, Government Printer, 1942.

35. NAI, COMCOL 1, 248/s.173,

36. SND "No Prostitutes to Stay in Kano City" 12 June, 1948 p1

37. NAI, Class List of Papers from The Federal Ministry of Health Lagos,92/22 *Venereal Diseases (1) Treatment of Seamen, Circular re (2) Center at Which Treatment could be given*, 1921-1958

38. SND "Landlords and Agents and Prostitutes" 11 March, 1944 p2 ENG "Commercial and House Owners Urged to Help Purge Prostitutes" 11 February, 1947 pp 1, 2 and 4, ENG, "Women Indict Landlords and Non Africans for Given Protection to Prostitutes" 20 February, 1947 pp1 and 4, ENG "Refuge for Prostitutes" 8 April, 1947 p3, The Comet "Re: Irresponsible Women" 31 July, 1944 p2 etc

39. SND *Demobilization of Prostitutes*,

40. ENG, "Problem of Prostitution" 8 August, 1951 p3, see also, ENG "Repatriation of Courtesan: A way of Solving Housing Problems in Port Harcourt" 20 January, 1947 p2

41. NAK, MSWC 301/86 *Prostitution*, 1955-1965

42. NAI, *Annual Volume of Laws 1944*, see also, Criminal Code Cap 77 Laws of the Federation of Nigeria, 1990

43. NAI, *Annual Volume of the Laws of Nigeria, Legislation enacted during 1916*

44. See, for instance, section 217 of the criminal code ordinance.

45. NAI, *Annual Volume of Laws 1944,*

46. NAI, *Annual Volume of Laws 1944,*

47. NAE, Obubdist 4.1.71,

48. NAK (SNP) 8, 4575 *Northern Chief's Conference, 1942* see also, NAI, Oyo Prof 1,3562 *Measures Against Prostitutes 1942-1944.*

49. See petitions in NAE, Onitsha Prof OP2297 *Measures Against Prostitution* 1942-1944

50. NAI, Oyo Prof 1,3562 *Measures,*

51. See Mammudah 'Abd al 'Ati *The Family Structure in Islam* (Lagos Islamic Publication Bureau, 1982) chapter three.

52. NAK Supplementary Simple List of Confidential Files from C186 *Prostitution, Juvenile Delinquency"* 1940-1956

53. NAE, Obubdist 4.1.71, *Prostitution,*

54. NAI, *Annual Volume of the Laws of Nigeria, Legislation enacted during 1943,* Government Printer, 1944

55. The Eastern Region of Nigeria, *House of Assembly Debates, 1956, Vol II*

56. See Mr. Chinn's report in NAI, Ondo Prof D.13 *Social Welfare in the Colony and Protectorate of Nigeria, 1945-1955*

57. Some government officers continued to see the need for a government department of social welfare as unnecessary after a very comprehensive report of situation of social welfare had been submitted by Alexander Patterson see NAI, COMCOL 1, 2600 Vol II, Social Welfare, General Questions, Establishment of, Social Welfare Department, 1942-1945

58. NAI, COMCOL 1, 2600 Vol II,

59. Ibid.

60. See the minutes of meetings of some of these tribal unions in NAI, COMCOL 1, 248/1-30

61. NAI, COMCOL1 248, *Calabar Improvement League, Minutes of Meetings*

62. See The Daily Comet "Oged Maculay Suggestion Licensing of Prostitution" 30 November, 1944 p1 and 4. The debates continued after the demise of colonial rule, The Comet Midwest Champion "Government and Prostitution" 11, November 1964 p3, Daily Times "Judge Calls For Licensed Brothels" 11 March, 1969 p1,

63. Saheed Aderinto, *Urban Threat: Prostitutes,*

64. NAI CSO 26/27837/S.I,

65. WAP "Night Club Glamour" 23 February, 1957 p1

66. NAI, CSO 26/27837 Vol I and II,

67. Ibid.

68. NAI, COMCOL 1, 43399 *Employment of Women in the Police Force,* 1944
69. Ibid.
70. Ibid.
71. NAI, CSO 26/27837 Vol I and II,
72. Tekena Tamuno, *The Police in Modern Nigeria,* 1861-1965 (Ibadan, Ibadan University Press 1970) pp136-138
73. Ibid. pp 136-138
74. Ibid.
75. NAK, Ministry of Local Government (MLG/S/RGA) *Committee on Problems of Prostitution in Northern Nigeria,* 1950-1965
76. SND "More About Prostitutes" 5 August, 1948, p 13
77. SND "No Prostitutes, p 1
78. NAK, Simple List of Records Removed from Kano Provincial office "Second Collection" Kano Prof 2nd Collection, 6115 *Sabon Gari Administration* 1938-1945
79. SND "Landlords and,
80. NAK, Ministry of Local Government (MLG/S/RGA) *Committee,*
81. SND *Demobilization of Prostitutes,* 3 October,
82. ENG, "Men, Women and Prostitution" 6 June, 1950, p3
83. SND, "Some Prostitutes Now Leaving Town" 3 May, 1948
84. The Daily Service, "Prostitution" 27 June, 1944 p 2
85. NAI, Oyo Prof 1, 4113
86. Ibid.
87. See ENG, SND, WAP, The Comet etc in the 1940s
88. SND "The Prostitution Problem (4) 27 June, 1944 p3
89. Saheed Aderinto, "Journey to Work," p 4
90. Ibid. p 4

8

Urban Neglect and Underdevelopment of a Border Town

Abolade Adeniji & Hakeem I. Tijani

Introduction

Generally speaking, a common feature of a border town is its abject poverty, neglect by government, and underdevelopment. One explanation for this is the historical identification of border towns as a non-central place, not worthy of government developmental projects. It, however, serves as the gateway to other parts of the country. Policing, rather than developmental programs are common features in border towns without an exception. In Africa, international boundaries were created by colonial administrations to accommodate exploitation rather than development. Boundaries are defined arbitrarily in terms of latitudes, longitudes, and other geometric lines which bear very little or no relevance to the pre-colonial history and character of the societies.[1] The resultant effect of this was that coherent cultural areas were fragmented and border communities were neglected. All border communities shared these characteristics whether in America, Asia or Europe up to 1945. From 1945 however, the character of European border regions began to change from fragmentation and neglect to integration. African border regions have, on the other hand, retained the earlier characteristics despite the changes that have taken place in Europe since 1945. While border towns in Europe are merging and forming conurbations, African border towns are decreasing in population and forming "frontier marchlands."[2] Therefore, it is hardly surprising that what has characterized African border towns is neglect, especially in the provision of communication facilities, industries, road networks and other physical infrastructures. The absence of these facilities has affected population growth along the border regions.

It is within the framework of the foregoing that the case of Badagry, a border town between Nigeria and the Republic of Benin, would be examined. It will be demonstrated presently that while border towns in Africa generally experience neglect, the case of Badagry has been especially traumatic. This is indicated by the fact that Badagry, which before the colonial era over a century ago had an estimated population of over 12,000 and was a booming trade center, has not only suffered population reduction, but it has been reduced to a neglected market town outside the main stream of development. This chapter has therefore set for itself the task of examining how and why Badagry came to find itself in such a pitiable state and what can be done to reverse this unfortunate occurrence.

Location and People

Badagry is located in the extreme southwest part of the Nigerian border with Benin Republic. It is located precisely between latitude 6.5° north of the Equator and longitude 3.25° east of the Greenwich Meridian.[3] Today, Badagry is bounded on the west by Porto Novo and Weme, on the North by Ilugbo, Ipokia; on the south by the Osa lagoon and the Atlantic Ocean and on the east by the Awori settlements of Ojo and Lagos (Ibid). The territory is comprised of several villages and hamlets such as Ape, Gbaji, Gberefu, Topo, Igbogbele, Ajo Vetho, Ajara Gamathen, Ajara Topa, Alathagun, Muwo, Iworo, Erekiti, Ajido, to name a few. In this chapter, therefore, the name "Badagry" refers to these towns and villages.

Like most pre-historic societies that rely on oral traditions to reconstruct the past, Badagry has a history of controversy regarding which the original founders of the town are.[4] There is no doubting the fact that the people of Badagry are not strangers to one another. They had interacted in various ways before the modern European administrative system was set up during the nineteenth century. Before its formal establishment as an international boundary, the location of Badagry had made it a peripheral and strategic location. It was a key market between the Aja and Yoruba countries. Such was the strategic significance of Badagry that at various times in the 1830s through 1840, there was a fierce struggle for the control of the Badagry port among its strong neighbors, especially the Egba and the Egbado states. Badagry also attracted the focused attention of neighboring states of Lagos, Porto Novo and Dahomey.

We have already alluded to the mixed population of the Yoruba and Aja speaking peoples of Badagry. What remains to be done is a brief survey of migration and settlement with a view to establishing the interlocking cultures that were arbitrarily severed by the creation of the international boundary. First, there was the Yoruba migration led by an Ife prince, Aheshe, who eventually established Apa (west of Badagry) and a line of Kings (Oba) called "Alapa."[5] It was under Aheshe, the eleventh Alapa of Apa that Hontokunu, a Dutch trader, who influenced the growth of Badagry, was granted land for trade on the present site of Badagry. Meanwhile, another branch of the Ife migration established the Akoro (Aklon) and Ija Osa (Jasin) quarters of Porto Novo .[6]

It is instructive to note that at about the same time that the Yoruba settlements were being established, Agaja Trudo, King of Dahomey 1708–1740 decided to take control of the coast of southern Dahomey. His subsequent assault on such states as Whydah, Hueda, Weme, Allada, and Jakin led to a widespread population dislocation. The waves of migration occasioned by these wars laid the foundation for the large-scale Aja presence in Badagry. The Aja migrations seem to have had more enduring impact on the demographic pattern of Badagry. Thus,

Aja refugees formed the eight wards of Badagry and others settled in scattered villages beyond the town. But the Yoruba of an earlier migration had occupied parts of Badagry. The two groups came together and formed a mixed community. The Aja of Badagry in particular was historically and culturally linked with the Aja of Porto Novo, a link that has remained sustained till date. When Badagry was eventually established as an international boundary, it was on these mixed communities with interlocking cultures extending to Porto Novo that the international boundary was imposed.

Evolution of International Boundary

The demarcation and establishment of Badagry as a frontier state predated the imposition of international boundary by over a century. It would be recalled that Badagry had, from its early history, been a frontier state and the struggle for its control had affected the relations between old Oyo and Dahomey. Between 1726 and 1747, Oyo had waged wars against Dahomey and successfully imposed tributary obligations on her that was to last for over a century. The wars had also led to the demarcation of territory between Badagry and Oyo with Badagry falling within Oyo's sphere of influence.[7]

In concrete terms however, the occupation of Lagos in 1861 and the cession of Badagry in 1863 were the first major steps in the evolution of the boundary. The presence of the French in Porto Novo and the British in Lagos and Badagry generated an intense rivalry that resulted in the acquisition of protectorates by the belligerent imperial powers. With the declaration of protectorate by the French over Porto Novo, Ipokia, and Okeoda, most of which were close to the bank of the Yewa River (which entered the Lagos Lagoon through a deep estuary in Badagry), it was only natural for the British to react to this challenge by acquiring Badagry. The continued tension generated by this crave for territories necessitated the signing of a convention between the representatives of the two countries (Glover and Didelot) in Porto Novo in 1863. The provisions of this convention were not ratified. It was not until 1899 that a proper boundary treaty was signed between the countries.[8]

Socio-Economic Development of Badagry in the Pre-boundary Era

Before it metamorphosed into an international boundary, Badagry had tremendously enjoyed the advantage of its strategic location. The slave trade linked Badagry with Europe and America while the Trans-Saharan trade linked Badagry with North Africa. The land routes also linked Oyo and Hausa land in the North with Badagry. Indeed, Richard and John Lander used one of the trans-Atlantic routes from England to Badagry. They set out from Portsmouth in England to Madeira, to Cape Coast, then to Cape Verde Island to Freetown in Sierra Leone, then to Whydah and Badagry. Badagry was, therefore, an international route terminal and a number of routes from France, England, Portugal, Brazil, and America converged there. Traders from these countries came to Badagry to transact business.[9]

Land routes, although mostly made up of footpaths and often marshy during the rainy season, were nevertheless well developed.[10] The land route that linked Badagry with old Oyo also passed through Owo, Ipokia, Ilaro, Ijana, Ilogun, Iseyin, Shaki, and Kisi. From Oyo, the route passed through Kaba on the Niger, then to Kano and ultimately to Bornu. The route also went across the Sahara Desert to North Africa. Richard Lander confirmed the existence of this route during his last journey from Badagry to Sokoto. From these various routes, contact was maintained between Badagry and the North African cities of Tripoli and Tunis. From North Africa, interested travelers made their way to Europe.

Pre-boundary routes in Badagry also included a network of lagoons, creeks and rivers that criss-crossed the whole area. Badagry creeks link both Porto Novo and Lagos lagoons. Also, canoe services were maintained between these areas to ferry people across from one end to the other.

Though crude by modern standards, the means of communication in pre-boundary Badagry was well maintained and thoroughly organized. Ajayi Crowther, for example, described the Badagry-Ipokia road as a fine road that would "admit four persons ridding abreast."[11] Caravans and tollgates were also another prominent feature of the roads. Some of the routes had natural obstacles such as the rivers mentioned earlier. In such cases, bridges were erected to overcome such obstacles. Gollmar gave a detailed description of one of such bridges across the Yewa river when he noted that the bridge was about 100 feet long, 3 feet above water at flood and consisting of about 500 sticks in two rows and one stick opposite each other.[12]

The elaborate development of communication in the pre-boundary period was undoubtedly designed to foster trade. Trade in Badagry at this period could be classified into long distance and local trade. The long distance trade, which linked Badagry and the outside world, enabled such European goods as gin, rum, iron-bars, swords, muskets, cutlasses, glass, Manchester plates, jugs, and dishes to find their way into Badagry markets through the European traders. Aside from these European goods, Badagry was also the distribution center, for such goods as palm kernel, palm oil, kola, local cloth, and salt. Salt was produced at Ajido while kola came from Ikorodu, Abeokuta, and other parts of Yorubaland.[13] The water-borne routes formed the major routes for local trade. Thus, these water routes linked the surrounding Yoruba district to Badagry. On a field visit to Badagry recently, this writer could hardly believe that the forlorn looking river along the Marina in Badagry had served as the route through which slaves were transported to Europe and North America.

Beside trade, population was another index by which the vibrancy of the pre-boundary economy of Badagry can be measured. Whatever the weakness of figures provided by European travelers, missionaries, and administrative officers, what appears certain is that the population of the town was much higher before effective British occupation.

Table 8.1. Badagry Population 1846 – 1890

Date	Population	Source
1846	5 – 6,000	Gollmer
1864	3,000	Freeman
1890	5,000	Moloney

Source: Mabogunje, A.L. *Urbanization in Nigeria*, London, 1968, p. 91

Table 8.2. Badagry Population 1890 – 1911

Date	Population
1890	4,000
1911	6,000

Source: *Hodder, B.W. "Badagry: One Hundred Years of Change" Nigeria Geographical Journal* 6(1) 1963.

These figures in Tables 8.1 & 2 above are mere estimates and at times estimates for the same date conflicted as illustrated in Table 8.2.

By 1890, there was a sharp drop in both Tables above. This contrasts somewhat with the figures for 1848 and 1864. The growth of population before the establishment of the boundary in the area was influenced by a number of factors. The Yoruba civil wars, which began following the fall of Old Oyo, bought about instability and disrupted the demographic balance in Yorubaland. Thus, Badagry served as a center of inward migration; when Okeodan was sacked 1851, Badagry was one of the recipients of its scattered population. The strategic location of Badagry at this time, especially for international trade, served as an attraction for returned Africans from either Sierra Leone or Brazil who chose to settle in Badagry. Its urban setting (before it was later overtaken by Lagos) made it an ideal settlement for refugees fleeing from the Yoruba hinterland.

Post-boundary Economic Development or Under-development?

The annexation of Badagry in 1863 brought immediate changes to the fortunes of the town. The first casualty can be located in the violent contraction in trading activities that took place since Badagry could no longer continue with its exportation of slaves. The geographical factors of location and topography, which had been an advantage in earlier times, had been neutralized by the harbor improvement, which took place in the 20th century. Thus, Badagry, which had continued exporting slaves in defiance of the British anti-slavery naval squadrons due to its peculiarity of being separated from the open sea by a sand pit, now came within the range of the operation of the British naval vessels. Subsequently, the neighboring port of Lagos then displaced Badagry as the premier port of the region; a reversal of their respective positions in 1815[14] captures the tribulations of Badagry thus:

Everything was against Badagry. Trade had shifted from west to east and centered on Lagos, and generally from the lagoon side to the seaside. What is more,
through the modern route development Lagos port had stretched its tentacles into
the interior and had captured what used to be the hinterland of Badagry prior to
the establishment of British administration.[15]

With the establishment of the boundary in 1889, restrictions on trade and
the movement of people commenced. The trade route, which linked Badagry and
North Africa through Hausa land, could no longer operate. While the Yoruba civil
wars may have aided this trend, a major contributory factor must be located in the
determination of rival European powers to carve out territories for themselves;
this was a practice which led to the elimination of erstwhile trade routes that
passed through Badagry. The borderland location of Badagry, couple with British
colonial policy to divert trade away from the border ushered in a period of rapid
decline for Badagry. In 1876, Badagry ceased to be an international port of entry,
though customs duties continued to be collected on merchandise from Porto
Novo in transit. It then became a lagoon port of some significance in southwestern Nigeria, but it was no more than a mere satellite of Lagos in the subsequent
period.[16]

The large number of Europeans who transacted business in Badagry shifted to
Lagos with the exception of Miller and Bothers, African Oil Nut Company. Messrs
W.B. MacIver and Co. Ltd., and Hutton Trading Company. Whatever remained of
Badagry local trade was equally stunted by the unsettled situation in Yorubaland
and the restrictions by the French in Porto Novo. It is within this context that
one can appreciate the low population figure of 3,000 estimated by Moloney for
the town in 1890, compared to the high of 12,500 in 1800.[18] Despite the efforts
of African agents such as Seriki Abass Faremi Williams, Badagry remained an
underdeveloped frontier of Lagos and the hinterland Yoruba country. Thus, it can
be submitted that the emergence of Badagry as a border town eliminated both land
and sea routes to Badagry, removed its port, destroyed its trade, and diminished
the population.[17]

The depression that devastated the world economy between 1929 and 1934
had a profound impact on Badagry. The annual report on the area in 1931, at the
height of the economic adversity, noted "a good deal of poverty" there since the
people did not produce the foodstuffs they consumed. Rather, they were "dependent on the sale of palm produce which cannot be exchanged from the protectorate
because the farmers themselves have ample supplies of oil,"[19] which they could
not sell.

The ensuing economic hardship in Badagry created a great demand for coins
of lower denomination than the half penny. This was because such coins were
required in the purchase of small quantities of goods. To be noted here is the
fact that in more prosperous times the people of Badagry never demanded for
the denomination. But even when between October and December 1931 when
tenths of penny were put into circulation in the Badagry area, by the end of the

year practically all the tenths had disappeared; they had been used to purchase foodstuffs from the Ilaro Division.[20] The annual report for 1932 captured the grim picture of human existence in the Badagry area thus:

> The people of this District have suffered considerably owing to the fact that the soil is extremely poor, except near the northern boundary, where sand gives place to laterite . . . Very little farinaceous foodstuff is grown and the majority of the population must purchase this from other districts. In order to pay for this imported food the people are largely dependent on Nigeria's export trade on palm oil and palm kernels, although there is a considerably demand for edible palm oil and died fish from Badagry for local consumption in Lagos.[21]

In the face of the deprivation noted above, the people of Badagry embarked on various strategies for survival, one of which was the establishment of border markets. The border markets were undoubtedly a response to the presence of the international boundary. In the face of the severance of the international links of the people, coupled with the restriction of movement occasioned by the fragmentation of coherent culture areas, border markets sprung up which did not conform to the traditional market system in Yorubaland. The people bought, sold, and used various currencies interchangeably in apparent defiance of the arbitrary separation imposed by the boundary. Unfortunately, the colonial authorities labeled these markets illegal and accused the people of "smuggling". These "smugglers" were subjected to severe beatings, their goods were seized and they we made to pay exorbitant fines, and in most cases were convicted. In spite of these, cross-border trade (smuggling) continued.[22]

Road network in Badagry at this period also left much to be desired. Even by the 1930 it was said that:

> There are no roads, unless Badagry marina is counted as such. The usual paths run everywhere. They are all sand, more or less soft, except just on the Protectorate boundary where laterite is found. In fact, with the exception of the sea-beach and the lagoon side path from Badagry to Iworo, it may be said that no journey can be made from any village to the next one without having to wade somewhere, except for a part of the dry season.[23]

In effect, by the 1930s, the need for effective all-season land communication between Badagry District and the outside world had become imperative. Badagry did not get its first all-season road until 1958, which was about ninety-five years after the cession of the town.

Another area in which Badagry was neglected was in the sitting of industries. In 1966, an attempt was made to site a fiber-bag industry in Badagry, but this drew a spate of protests from individuals. A leading article in the journal entitled *West Africa* carried the caption "What future for fibre?" Industries were sited away from Badagry because as a border town, it was regarded as unstable and unsafe for the establishment of industries.[24]

One other feature of the boundary phenomenon that has affected the people of Badagry was the constant harassment of the indigenes on the pretext that they are

illegal immigrants. At various checkpoints, security officials subject the people
to untold humiliation, asking them to provide evidence that they were Nigerians.
Such was the degree of hardship and ridicule experienced by the people of the
town that at a point, the *Oba* of the town had to issue identity cards to his people
to reduce the harassment.[25] The siege, no doubt, must have constituted a psychological disorientation. We can therefore affirm that the creation of the border in
Badagry led among other things to the elimination of the hitherto functional trade
routes, the disappearance of the pre-colonial international prestige of the town,
the sitting of industries away from the border, the colonial policy which made
roads run parallel to the town instead of crossing it, and above all, an almost
unconscionable degree of official neglect.

While the reasons identified above must have constituted a hindrance to
Badagry development, Ayo Omotayo has, however, identified yet another factor
which is worth noting. According to him, in its quest for development Badagry has
been poorly serviced by a wretched hinterland. Omotayo posits that while Lagos
enjoyed the resourcefulness and vibrancy of the people of the interior, especially
the Ijebu traders, Badagry suffered from its association with hinterland towns
populated by the Aworis and Dahomeans, "whose ambition as far as legitimate
trade was concerned especially in the 19th century is debatable."[26] In a nutshell,
Omotayo submits,

> Badagry's lack of growth can be attributed to the fact that it lacked the men
> with sufficient knowledge of modern day economic tools needed to advance their
> society at a time in history when various societies were jostling for economic
> advantages . . . that modernized their societies[27].

The problem with the analysis provided above is that it fails to put the blame
for Badagry's relative lack of growth where it truly belongs. Are the people of
Badagry being blamed for the refusal of government to site industries in the
town? Should they be held responsible for the fragmentation of coherent culture
areas, which resulted from colonialism and subsequently grounded the erstwhile
booming pre-boundary trade? What could the people have done in the face of the
determination of government to accentuate the development of Lagos, relative to
surrounding towns? It is instructive to note that Omotayo himself admits that his
proposition is not based on any empirical study;[28] hence, his submission could be
said to exist only at the realm of speculation.

Attempts at Urban Development and Socio-economic Development Since 1950

With the advent of partial self-government in Nigeria in 1953, the Badagry
division became a part of the Western Region. At independence, it was envisaged that the long neglect of Badagry would come to an end. To be sure, post-
1950 Badagry did witness some form of renaissance. The first secondary school
was established in 1955 (after 110 years of the establishment of the first primary

school), to be followed by ten others by 1985, primary and secondary school enrolment increased at an astronomic rate, the popular Lagos Badagry expressway was successfully completed in 1976, the coconut fibre industry was established in 1980, the Administrative Staff College of Nigeria (ASCON) was established in 1978, a General Hospital and some maternity home and Health Centers were constructed by the government, and the Federal Government of Nigeria's Directorate of Food, Road, and Rural Infrastructure commenced the extensive construction of feeder roads which linked various communities and helped to facilitate trading activities, especially in agricultural produce. Altogether, DFRRI was said to have constructed 154 kilometers of rural roads to link 120 communities in the area. The Table below indicates this.

S/N	Cleared/Graded Feeder Roads	Kilometers
1.	Enuko – Yetekeme – Pashi	4.00 km
2.	Itoko – Aradagun	7.00 km
3.	Imeke – Igbanko	6.10 km
4.	Agalsaso – Agbovipe – Erekiti – Iragbo – Ikoga	10.00 km
5.	Aivoji – Gberefu – Yowgan – Topo Island – Central Road	26.00 km
6.	Epe – Ago-Ajo	4.00 km
7.	Esepe – Mushin – Obele – Magbon – Ibiye Road	10.00 km
8.	Abia – Ilogbo	6.00 km
	All Season Roads	
1.	Oke-Afo – Kogbo – Pota	10.03 km
2.	Iworo – Epe	5.03 km
3.	Akarakumo – Ajido	7.06 km
4.	Ajara – Agric Farm Road	3.00 km

Adapted from: Lagos State Government "Border Developments, Current Efforts and Future Programmes". Paper presented at the Conference on Accelerated Development of Nigeria Border Regions: Durbar Hotel, Lagos, 1989, p 3.

Two major steps taken to jump start development in Badagry are worthy of mention. One is the establishment of a model secondary school in Kakon, which is about five kilometers from the border. It is the nearest secondary school to the border along Nigeria's western boundary. It has full boarding facilities and has indeed developed into one of the most remarkable centers of learning in West Africa. The other step involves the establishment of the "French Village" in Badagry. The Nigeria French Language Village in Ajara, Badagry represents a bold attempt by the Federal Government of Nigeria to encourage the study of French language especially since Nigeria is surrounded by French speaking African nations.

But as Dioka noted, the large number of both primary and secondary schools established in Badagry convey a wrong impression of the actual situation on the ground.[29] A distinction must be made between Badagry town and the Badagry District and later Badagry Local Government. When Lagos State was created in 1967, Badagry became a divisional headquarters. By 1976, its importance as a growth pole was diminished when it changed to become the headquarters of Badagry Local Government. By 1989, the Local Government, which hitherto extended to Apapa and Orile Iganmu industrial areas as well as Festac and Satellite towns, including the Volkswagen Assembly Plant was divided into two. With the excision of the rich part of Ojo area, what were left were Badagry town and the largely poor rural environment. Thus, Badagry was deprived of the high tenement rates formerly collected from these areas.[30]

It is necessary to mention here that the Lagos State Government has over time taken steps to improve the quality of life in the border town of Badagry. Attention can here be drawn to the supply of electricity to Gbaji, Gayingbo Apa, Igbogbele, Konkon, Iragbo, Erekiti, Itoga-Zenmu, and Ibiye at the estimated cost of N7.5m (at 1989 Naira value). Jetties have also been constructed to facilitate water transport.

As laudable as these projects could be said to have been, they no doubt represent a belated attempt to remedy some of the glaring injustice of the past. After all, it was the same town that a hundred and fifty yeas earlier had boasted of a densely settled population engaged in agriculture and food production of various types.[31] European explorers had testified to the fact that Badagry was so economically vibrant in those days that the struggle for its control had elicited fierce conflict among its powerful neighbors.

One potential developmental attribute of Badagry, which has not been fully harnessed, is its tourist attraction. The lagoons and sea fronts offer excellent opportunities for sea cruising, nature watching, hotel development, and other tourism related activities. In terms of water quality, the waters of Badagry beach are relatively cleaner and certainly less polluted than those of the Victoria Island beach, which by virtue of its urban location is more prone to environmental abuse.[32] Equally significant is the calm tropical weather of Badagry which serves as an additional incentive to visitors especially foreign tourists from the temperate regions. It should be stressed that the relative quiet that usually prevails in Badagry presents a sharp contrast to the hustle and bustle of the Lagos metropolis thus providing a special attraction for those who long for a temporary break from city life and its associated problems.

Aside from the attractive beaches, other tourist sites in Badagry include the Badagry Museum that houses the relics of the slave trade. Some of these relics include the neck chain, hip clap and baby link for child slaves, the site of the fallen Agia tree, where Christianity was first preached in September 1842 by the Rev. Thomas Birch Freeman of the Wesleyan (now Methodist) Mission, the first-story building in Nigeria completed in June 1845 by the CMS Missionaries, a number of cemeteries, graves and tombs which contain the remains of a good number of early missionaries, the Ogu Toplisen Shine where Badagry monarchs are crowned, etc.[33] Unfortunately, only feeble attempts have been made by governments at various levels to harness the tourism potentials of Badagry.

As regard road construction, while the kilometers covered on paper appear impressive, in reality, many of the roads do not survive the rains. On a recent field trip, this writer noticed that many of the roads have fallen into disuse and are dilapidated due to lack of maintenance. While a total of eight roads covering a distance of 72 kilometers were rural roads, only four roads of 25 kilometers were all-season roads[34].

Again, it is now clear that much as the establishment of the Kankon Model Secondary School and the "French Village" has impacted their host communities, the schools have full boarding facilities and only a negligible number of indigenes have access to them. Indeed it is possible for a child to spend six years in the secondary school and not recognize the town's main market.

Badagry is a border area and border areas present peculiar developmental challenges and therefore deserve special attention. Some of the problems presented by border regions indeed go beyond what states or local governments can tackle; they require the Federal Government attention. How, for example, does a local government tackle the issue of harassment of indigenes on the pretext that they are aliens? When the nation experienced persistent scarcity of fuel in the early 1990s, the Federal Government took the panicky step of closing down all the petrol stations along the border. The people of Badagry suffered untold hardship as a result of this ill-advised and ultimately ineffectual measure.

For example, for tourism to be successful, experts have suggested that there must be, among other things, banking services and a free use of convertible currencies. This goes beyond what a local or state government can provide. The point being stressed here is that there is a need for the Federal Government to formulate consistent and imaginative policies towards border regions in the country. For this to be effective there must be cooperation with neighboring governments.

It is being suggested here that Badagry must be treated as a growth center and governments at all levels should move beyond lip service and make their practice felt. Mabogunje has noted the importance of accessibility in his study of urban centers in Nigeria.[35] Badagry requires more than its present level of accessibility to enhance its growth. Perhaps a line of the railway linking not only Lagos but also other areas like Idi-Iroko, Owode Egbado, and Ilaro will be a useful experiment. Its port could also be developed to serve the western corridor. Above all, the government should seriously consider implementing the creation of an export-processing zone in the area.

One area that is yet to be addressed by both the Federal and State Government is the issue of trans-border cooperation at the local level. The communities aside the border are often culturally, historically, linguistically, and economically linked. It is, therefore, futile to attempt to severe them. There is need for a policy that will positively harness this affinity for the development of these communities. Dioka, for example, has suggested that the Fishing Cooperatives already existing in Badagry could cooperate with similar societies in Porto Novo to boost food production since their combined resources would enable them to buy more modern fishing equipment and generally profit from the resulting economy of scale.[36]

Border markets have evolved into an indispensable phenomenon of border communities. Instead of expending so many resources on combating "smuggling" (trans-border trade), government would be better advised to streamline this trade by ratifying the relevant protocols aimed at strengthening the free movement of goods and services. The recent innovation of the National Identity Card Scheme is a welcomed development. Certainly, the issuance of identity cards is far beyond what the *Akran* and his subject or the State government, for that matter, can do. The plan for the issuance of identity cards to all Nigerians should be seen to its logical conclusion by the Federal government. It is hoped that the issuance of these identity cards would go a long way in fostering a sense of belonging to Badagry indigenes that have been at the receiving end when it comes to proving their nationality.

Conclusion

This chapter has focused on some aspect of the multi-dimensional nature of urbanization in Nigeria. The narratives have shown the fluctuating fortunes of Badagry largely because of its borderland status. We can conclude that our understanding of the fluctuating fortunes of Badagry would help bring to the foreground the dilemma confronted by most border communities worldwide. We have shown that before the evolution of Badagry into a border town, it had served as a strategic location for the conduct of international trade, and it was generally densely populated and had a vibrant economy. With the boundary, however, came stagnation, a phenomenon made worse by the shift of attention to Lagos, which had by this time become the seat of the colonial government. The people of the town have suffered deprivations for which they could hardly be held responsible.

Notes and References

1. I. James "The Nigeria-Chad Border Conflicts", *Nigeria Journal of International Affairs* Vol. 10 Nos. 1984, p 83.
2. See L.C. Dioka "The International Boundary and Under-development in Badagry in (eds.) G.O. Ogunremi, M.O. Opeloye and Siyan Oyeweso *Badagry: A Study in History, Culture and Traditions of an Ancient City* Ibadan, Rex Charles, 1994, p 90; and L.R. Mills "The Development of a Frontier Zone and Border Landscape along the Dahomey-Nigeria Boundary" *Journal of Tropical Geography* Vol. 36. 1983, p 44.
3. V.S. Akran "The Founding of Badagry Reconsidered" *Lagos Historical Review* Vol. 1 2001 p.32.
4. For the Various Views on the Origin and Establishment of Badagry Town, See T.O. Avoseh *History of Badagry*, Lagos. Ife Olu Press, 1938, I.A. Akinjogbin, *Dahomey and its Neighbours 1708 – 1818*. London: Cambridge University Press, 1967, A.I. Asiwaju "The Aja Speaking Peoples of Nigeria. A Note on their Origins, Settlement and Cultural Adaptation up to 1945" *Africa A.J.A.T.*, Vol. 49 No. 1, 1975, and Kunle

Lawal, "The Ogu – Awori Peoples of Badagry Before 1950: A General Historical Survey" in (eds.) G.O. Ogunremi et al *Badagry: A Study in History Culture.*

5. See Dioka "The International Boundary" p.92.

6. Igue and Adams, "Porto Novo and Cotonou Hinterlands" in (ed) D. Aradeon "The Role of Small and Intermediate Settlement in the Development Process: The Badagry Porto Novo Region, Human Settlement Programme 1 Faculty of Environment Science, University of Lagos, 1986.

7. R. Norris *The Memoirs of the Reign of Bossa Ahadee, King of Dahomey* London 1789, cited in L.C. Dioka "The International Boundary" p.93.

8. L.C. Dioka "The International boundaries" p.93.

9. R. Lander *Record of Captain Clapperton's Last Expedition to Africa.* London Frank Cass, 1966, pp 16-17.

10. J.H. Kopytoft, *A Preface to Modern Nigeria: The Sierra Leonians in Yorubaland 1830 – 1890,* London: OUP 1965, p 58.

11. T. Falola "The Yoruba Toll System: Its Operation and Abolition", *Journal of African History* Vol. 30 1989 p.62.

12. Cited in K. Folayan "Trade Routes in Egbado in the Eighteenth Century" in A.I. Akinjogbin and S. Osoba (eds.) *Topics on Nigeria Economic History,* Ile-Ife: University of Ife Press, 1980, p 65.

13. L.C. Dioka "The International Boundary" p.96.

14. See B.W. Hodder "Badagry: One Hundred Years of Change" *Nigeria Geographical Journal* 6(1) 1963.

15. G.A. Fadeyi "The Growth and Decline of Badagry: A Geographical Analysis," Unpublished M.A. Thesis (Geography) University of Lagos, 1969 pp 128-129.

16. A. Olukoju "Ecology and Economic Development, Agriculture, Trade and Transportation in Badagry C.1880-1950," in G.O. Ogunremi, M.O. Opeloye and Siyan Oyeweso (eds.) *Badagry: A Study in History,* p.76.

17. J.F. Ade-Ajayi, *Christian Missions in Nigeria* 1841 – 1891. London: Longman 1974, p 155. For details about Seriki Abass, see HI Tijani, "The Career of Seriki Faremi Abass Williams in Badagry, 1870-1919," in GO Ogunremi et. al (eds.) *Badagry: A Study in History.*

18. K. Faluyi "The Fluctuating Economic Fortunes of a Nigerian Sea Port: Economy and Trade in Badagry up to 1900" in G.O. Ogunremi, M.O. Opeloye and Siyan Oyeweso, (eds.) *Badagry: A Study in History,* p.66.

19. Quoted in A. Olukoju, "Ecology and Economic" p.78.

20. Ibid.

21. Ibid. p.94.

22. L.C. Dioka, "Badagry since 1842, Urbanization in a Nigerian Border Region," MPhil. History Thesis, University of Lagos.

23. Quoted in Olukoju "Ecology and Economic" p 81.

24. L.C. Dioka, "The Coconut in Badagry: A Trans-border Economic Crop" *Lagos Historical Review* Vol. 1, 2001, pp 59-67.

25. L.C. Dioka, "The International Boundary" p 103.

26. A. Omotayo, "The Physical Fabrics of Badagry: A Developmental Discourse in (eds.) G.O. Ogunremi, M.O. Opeloye and Siyan Oyeweso, *Badagry: A Study in History,* p.253.

27. Ibid. 256.

28. Ibid. 257.

29. L.C. Dioka, "The International Boundary" p. 97.

30. T. Odumosu, "Problems of Urbanization and Development in Coastal Towns: The Case of Badagry in G.O. Ogunremi, M.O. Opeloye and Siyan Oyeweso, (eds.) *Badagry: A Study in History,* p.267.

31. A.L. Mabogunje *Cities and Social Order.* An Inaugural Lecture, University of Ibadan 1974.

32. A. Omotayo, A.O. Ojo and T. Odumosu, "The Rural Environment of Lagos State: The Problem and Prospects for Rural Development," in *Perspective on Integrated Rural Development in Lagos State.* Lagos: The Office of the Military Governor of Lagos State, 1987.

33. O.Ojo "Tourism Potentials in Badagry Area: Opportunities and Challenges" in (eds.) G.O. Ogunremi, M.O. Opeloye and Siyan Oyeweso *Badagry: A Study in History,* p 299.

34. S. Amosu *"Coming of the 'Stallion'* "Lagos State: Badagry Local Government 1996, p.16.

35. Mabogunje, *Cities and Social Order.*

36. Dioka, "The International Boundary" p 105.

9

Transformation of the Sabon Gari

Rasheed Olaniyi

Introduction

Across Northern Nigeria, Sabongari became transformed from migrant enclaves to merchant cities. Culturally, the significance of Sabongari became even more profound because of the unrestricted nature of inter-ethnic social interaction. Sabongari is a pre-eminent site for re-socialization processes. To a greater degree, layers of social networks in the workplace, neighborhood, religious, and relaxation centers produce a crosscutting solidarity structure. This chapter argues that Sabongari system was one the many unrecorded resistance against colonial segregation policies. For many communities such as Hausa, Nupe, and Yoruba that had a long history of interactions, it became difficult for the British to effectively segregate them. The establishment of Sabongari system was a central thrust of the British divide and rule system constructed to make colonial rule flourish on ethnic divisions, the creation and recreation of identities and enforcement of segregation. In its transformation, however, Sabongari developed into a cosmopolitan entity incorporating both the migrant and hosts elements. From the 1940s, Sabongari became the seething base and political fortress of the nationalist movement. It was indeed the terminus of collaboration between the northern and southern Nigerian elite of radical persuasion. The chapter concludes that in the post-independence era, Sabongari became more cosmopolitan and Nigerian in its ethnic composition, but witnessed exclusion in terms of social development when compared to the Government Reserved Areas (GRA) now inherited by the ruling elites.

Segregation Policy in the Colonial Context

Residential segregation was a principal feature of the British urban policy in Nigeria. Academic debates on the Sabongari system emphasizes health security, religious and cultural differences, sanitation, and racial factors for the segregation policy, but it did not examine the aftermath in terms of ethnic relations, nationalist movement, and the politics of urban development. It was argued that the British purposely created Sabongari as Christian settlements in Muslim cities to encourage prostitution, drinking of alcohol, and gambling, in order to corrupt the social morality of the Muslim society within the walled city.[1] This argument is, however, baseless since the British outlawed liquor trade and consumption within the precincts of the Muslim Emirates.[2] Fika opines that Sabongari were created because most of the southerners who migrated to Kano and other towns of Northern Nigeria were undesirable people who were fraudulent in their dealings with their Hausa and Fulani hosts.[3] However, inter-ethnic and commercial relations between Hausa and Yoruba, for example, from the pre-colonial era indicated a mutual understanding that led to the integration of the immigrants into the host community. Olukoju argued that an inimitable indication of institutionalized racism was the segregation of Europeans and Africans in colonial cities.[4] In 1916, Lugard had asserted that since his return to Nigeria in 1912, he had "given continuous attention to the question of Segregation of Europeans and Natives in the various towns of Nigeria." He directed that plans of virtually every station where Europeans resided be made and a "European Reservation" indicated on each plan.[5] The "European Reservation" would be surrounded by a 440-yard wide Non-Residential Zone. Beyond this neutral zone was the Native Reservation. Wherever possible, indigenes that "had no reason for living within the township" were "encouraged" to leave it for a purely indigenous settlement beyond the limits of the Government Station. The wholesale enforcement of this model was the practice in Northern Nigeria. Segregation equally became expedient in order to ensure the health security of Europeans against malaria, yellow fever, and sleeping sickness that was prevalent amongst Africans. Unlike the Europeans, Africans had immunity against the diseases. However, the policy of segregation was reviewed under Hugh Clifford who argued that in Northern Nigeria, free interactions by Europeans and Africans were being impeded by the practice of residential segregation.[6] For example in 1921, African traders in Lokoja who were long established in a place considered too close to the new European Reservation, were asked to evacuate their plots once their leases expired. This was in spite of the fact that they had invested considerable sums of money in erecting buildings on the plots assigned to them two decades earlier. Clifford felt that since the government allocated plots to Europeans in the neighborhood where the indigenous traders were already established, it was the former that should have been relocated. The inexpediency of the wholesale disturbance of the entire native population became intolerable for Clifford considering that Lokoja was, in his view, the only place that had a semblance of commercial viability in the entire Northern provinces. Therefore, he argued that if the development of the region by the expansion of trade and the encouragement of immigration was to be pursued by the administration, greater security of tenure of business premises must be granted to both Europeans and Africans alike.[7]

Clifford observed that colonial officials in the Northern Provinces had exploited the 440yard rule to serve political rather than a sanitary end.[8] They had served quit notices to European missionaries who had earlier been allowed to establish missions in African settlements as soon as the terms of their occupancy expired. If this was in the emirates, it would have been tolerable; however, this was in the so-called "pagan" areas where such a restriction was unwarranted. The presence of European missionaries in "pagan" towns was "regarded by the Political Officers of the Northern Provinces with a rather jealous eyes, as they are apprehensive lest they should acquire too much influence over the people and be tempted to interfere in their local and political affairs.[9] Clifford administration concluded that in new Townships such as Kano (Category B), there would be a European Residential and Segregation Area surrounded by a building-free-zone 440 yards wide. In the Residential Area the buildings were for the exclusive residence of Europeans and their personal servants. Contiguous to this zone on one side, and located between it and the neutral zone, was the European Business and Residential Segregation Area, containing shops, offices and business premises. Finally, there was the Native Reservation in which Europeans were not permitted to reside. Other Townships in Northern Nigeria such as Minna belonged to Category C in which a neutral zone as in the case of Class B Townships did not separate the European Residential and the European Trading Areas. While racism and health security may justify the segregation of Africans and Europeans, the segregation of Nigerian immigrants and their hosts was carried out for administrative expediency. Thus, Olusanya maintained that it was paternalism and unwarranted fear of the of the penetration of Western ideas in Northern Nigeria that made the British created Sabongari in the north.[10]

In Northern Nigeria, the establishment of Sabongari between 1911 and 1913 was a central thrust of the British divide and rule system constructed to make colonial rule flourish on ethnic division and enforcement of segregation. In the colonial era, Yoruba immigrants in Northern Nigeria were British citizens and the hosts were subjects. The dichotomy in the realm of culture and rights was completed with spatial division, the segregation of the two social groups (hosts and immigrants) in different areas of the cities. Despite the imposition of £5 on defaulters of the Cantonment Proclamation, the attempt by the British to segregate the Yoruba from the natives failed in Kano and Zaria due to historical relationships that had existed between them before the British conquest. In Kano, despite restrictions, Yoruba Muslims whose parents had been born there and who agreed to abide by Sharia laws were allowed to continue to live within Kano old city (birni) while some Hausa lived in Sabongari. In July 1914, Yoruba traders in Zaria who had lived with the hosts since the 18th century were relocated to the newly created Sabongari.[11] The policy was short-lived as some Yoruba continued to live within the old city while some Hausa hosts relocated to Sabongari.

Colonization by an alien, with an already developed urban culture, promotes urbanization in at least two ways: a) by bringing into a town new settlers and b) an urban-focused economic system and the preservation of pre-colonial settlement system.[12] Even though the basic ideology for the establishment of Sabongari was commercial, cultural, and administrative, it was difficult to control the influx of both the indigenous population and immigrants in the settlements. The socio-economic development and the strategic commercial location of Sabongari near the railroads attracted traders of northern Nigeria origin. For example, the 1913 population statistics of Sabongari, Zaria estimated a total of 750 male residents, out of which 693 persons were of Northern Nigeria origin. The following chart shows the population distribution.

Table 9.1. Persons of Northern Nigerian Origins, Sabongari, Zaria 1913

S/N	Place of Origin/Tribe	Number of Persons
1.	227	Kano
2.	66	Beri-Beri
3.	65	Zaria
4.	53	Ilorin
5.	44	Nupe
6.	24	Katsina
7.	16	Sokoto
8.	12	Yoruba
9.	7	Yola
10.	3	Bauchi

Source: A.D. Edley (1976) Cited in A. Bako " Colonial Rule and Residential Segregation in the Muslim Emirates: The Creation of the Sabongari Settlements Reconsidered" p. 12 paper presented at the International Conference on the Transformation of Northern Nigeria at Arewa House, Kaduna, 25th –27th March, 2003.

For the Yoruba and Hausa, the colonial segregation was ineffective due to historical relations that had existed between the two groups, five hundred years before the British rule. In Sabongari, Kaduna, the earliest settlers were Hausa, Nupe and Yoruba.[13] The idea of segregation was in some way resisted by the two ethnic groups. For example, the establishments of the Townships of Sabongari created some problems for the British in Kano. In 1914, northerners who were not from Kano were relocated from Sabongari, Kano and resettled in Tudun Wada. According to C. L. Temple:

Non-native Africans and such natives as might cause trouble if they lived in Kano city should occupy the Sabongari in Kano. On the whole, natives should not be encouraged to live in the Sabongari.[14]

In 1915, the British found it difficult to keep out "Emirate natives" who "were not either employees of Government, Trading Firms or other Residents in the Township" from Sabongari. Hence the British resorted to the system of issuing "permits" to all residents of Sabongari. 1,355 permits were issued: 885 to "non Government" and 470 to "Government" residents.[15]

By 1917, Sabongari was constituted under the Township Ordinance into the Second Class Township of Kano that is second to the Government Reservation Area and not to the Kano city which it superseded within the British arrangement.[16] Simultaneously, the Township Area comprising of Europeans and Non-natives was severed from the Kano Divisional Administration and placed under an officer who discharged functions analogous to those of Cantonment Magistrate and who was directly responsible to the resident. Sabongari was therefore granted autonomy in the Emirate system apparently for tax and fiscal purposes. Taxes paid by Sabongari residents and or European employees of the British went directly to the colonial treasury rather than the Native Authority.

The residential segregation between the migrants and the host communities sowed the seed of xenophobia, contempt, and communal conflicts. Equally, the British policy of Liaise faire placed the bulk of security provisioning on the community and subsequently the Native Authority (N.A.). Through several policy shifts government expenditure on police was drastically reduced. In a cosmopolitan community, this created a fertile ground for crime and criminals. In its formative stage, Sabongari, Kano, its security, market and land tenure administration were placed under the Township Administration outside the Native Authority headed by the Emir.

By the end of July 1915, pockets of serious crimes had been recorded in Sabongari.[17] The settlement had attracted a considerable influx of a criminal element of both males and females. This was allegedly attributed to the freedom they enjoyed in the British law from the restraints and discipline of organized native society. However, the government police exhibited levity in combating crime in the Township areas particularly Sabongari.

The growth of Sabongari Kaduna from 1917 to 1929 shows its cosmopolitan character. For example, in 1920, of the 37 plots auctioned in Sabongari, twenty-four were bought by Hausa, nine by Yoruba, three by Nupe, and one by Ghanaian.[18] In the 1922 auction of plots, forty-seven out of seventy-nine were bought by Hausa, ten by Yoruba, three each by Nupe and Fulani, and one by Edo.[19] However, the social and ethnic background of those who bought the remaining twelve plots was not indicated.

In Tudunwada, southern Nigerian immigrants occupied Kaduna, which was a settlement primarily created by the British for Northern Nigerian immigrants as well. Economic reasons forced non-Northerners to relocate to Tundunwada. For example, between 1926 and 1927, a large group of artisans and traders of Southern Nigeria origin left Sabongari for Tundunwada.[20] This trend disrupted the basis of segregation policy in Kaduna, by dislocating the ethnic, administrative, and religious basis of the policy.

Many of the migrants in Sabongari could not secure desirable jobs they had anticipated, particularly during the Great Depression of the 1930s. Unemployment created criminal tendencies such as petty theft and burglary, and it also created a dependence on ethnic and town unions in the cities.[21] Property crime, as gangs of burglars and armed robbers made of migrants of Southern and Northern Nigerian origins, carried out business. The major rendezvous for the criminal gangs were bars, off licenses, hotels, cinema halls and clubs in Sabongari. The joint Native Authority and Nigeria Police Suspect Squad that, in view of the corrupt practices, which criminals employed to keep out of trouble, maintained a very high standard of integrity frequently arrested these criminals and their patrons. Criminals were let off with light fines or bail and their cases "put on ice". [22] During the Second World War, the British made a major policy shift in the administration of Sabongari Kano to expend resources (human and material) on the war efforts. Equally, the security lapses in Sabongari had forced the British to compromise the theory that the Native Authority should be aloof from administering Sabongari. In April of 1940, Sabongari administration was transferred to the Kano Native Authority under the control of Wakilin Waje. [23]

In Kano, despite the British insistence, Yoruba Muslims were allowed by Emir to either live in the native area or in Sabongari. By 1937, the population statistics of Kano Township showed that there were 1,903 Hausa residents in Sabongari as against 1,547 Yoruba. [24] In 1938, there were 2,040 Hausa (26 %) of the population in Sabongari, Kano. [25] In 1939, the population of the Hausa in Sabongari Kaduna was 1,568 while Yoruba population was 1,093. [26]

Sabongari in northern Nigeria equally possessed religious diversity. Southern Nigerian immigrants established Christian and Muslim religious centers and schools. In Sabongari, Kano, Yoruba Central Mosque (Samori-Adeen) was built in 1925, Ahmadiyya Mosque in 1930, and Ansar-ud-deen in 1936. In the 1930s, Sabongari, Sokoto had a large population of Muslims. [27]

The following chart shows the number of Muslims and Christians in Sabongari, Kano in 1939.

Table 9.2. Population of Muslims and Christians in Sabongari, Kano 1939

S/N	Religious Denomination	Number
1.	Orthodox Muslims	3, 000
2.	Church Mission Society (Holy Trinity)	1,096
3.	Roman Catholic Mission	1,082
4.	Baptist Mission	156
5.	Ansar-Ud-Deen	120
6.	African Church	90
7.	Sudan Interior Mission	84
8.	Ahmadiyya Movement	74
9.	Methodist Church	71
10.	Faith Tolerance	21

A. Bako, 2003, "Colonial Rule and Residential Segregation in the Muslim Emirates" p. 11.

Transformation of Sabongari

After the Second World War, one of the problems Sabongari faced was the influx of immigrants, high cost of living, and pressure on land. In Kano, for example, because there were far more migrants than Sabongari could accommodate, the area developed as an overcrowded and haphazard urban slum. [28] The development of Sabongari was considered as a Southern Nigerian outpost in Northern Nigeria, a facsimile of Lagos. This perception and demarcation between the traditional city (birni) and Sabongari was a locus of friction. In Kano, since 1953, Sabongari residents and the host community engaged in conflicts. Meanwhile, the conflicts encouraged population redistribution in Kano metropolis by which many of the southern Nigeria immigrants tried as much as possible to live within the confines of Sabongari. In recent time, this pattern has been intensified by internecine ethno-religious conflicts in Northern Nigeria.

The British had created Sabongari as a device to drive a wedge between Nigerians and forestall the emergence of a united front in the anti-colonial struggle. In the 1940s, Sabongari Kano witnessed a major political transformation that increased the formative process of development and ethnically based associations. During the Second World War, the British made a major policy shift in the administration of Sabongari Kano in order to expend resources (human and material) on the war effort. Equally, the security lapses in Sabongari had forced the British to compromise the theory that the Native Authority should be aloof from administering Sabongari. In April 1940, Sabongari administration was transferred to the Kano Native Authority under the control of Wakilin Waje.[29]

The colonial policy shift and incorporation Sabongari into the Indirect Rule of the N.A. marked the beginning of the demise of British rule in the area. It set in motion identity reformation leading to the fusion of hitherto separate interests. Sabongari residents began to identify themselves as a community in the context of the colonial state. Indeed, the establishments of centralized ethnic and cultural associations were partly expressions of nationalist feelings and resistance against the British rule. Ethnic identity turned out to be a strategic phenomenon linked with a territorial, economic niche and differential access to state resources. Ethnic identity constituted a major stake in the negotiations between the emerging community and the colonial state. The driving forces of these negotiations were the subalterns: workers, migrant artisans and the urban poor posing poignant questions about their social, cultural and political place in the colonial state.

In Kano, Sabongari became the republican zone of the radical nationalists. The Zikists, particularly Raji Abdallah and Osita Agwuna, were vanguards of anti-racism, pan-Nigerian nationalism, inter-ethnic unity and cooperation in Sabongari Kano. For example, in 1945, Agwuna founded the African Anti-Colour Bar Movement (AACBM). In August 1950, a coalition of radical elite of diverse ethnic backgrounds formed the Northern Elements Progressive Union (NEPU) with its base in Fagge and Sabongari, Kano. NEPU represented the most vibrant anti-colonial and feudal movement, which equally championed the cause of the working class.[30]

By 1960, while the European Reservation passed into the hands of the Nigerian elites under the name Government Reservation Area, the Sabongari collapsed into an urban slum. The physical development in Sabongari reflects the over-crowded and poverty stricken ghettos. The process has led to the realization of Sabongari as a site for the massive transfer of rural standards taken place in a crowded setting for which they were disastrously inappropriate.

The problems of urban centers in Nigeria arose in response to the processes of development. They reflect a growing disequilibria between these processes and our capacity to manage.[31] Immigrants often live in groupings and ethnic enclaves with different social subsystems through which they obtained information, contacts, employment and access to schools and social groupings.[32] Sabongari ethnic enclaves attracted immigrants who often found their first foothold in the cities. Since ethnicity affects where one lives, with whom one associates and at what occupation one works, the cities are partly overlapping ethnic enclaves.[33] Sabongari witnessed rapid growth without a sufficient infrastructural base. It experienced problems of unemployment, underemployment, poverty and overcrowding. Hawkers, peddlers, artisans, and government employees proliferation of Sabongari. In most of the Sabongari, there are strong functional and ecological links with between immigrants, unemployment, overcrowding, segregation, and discrimination.[34]

From the middle of the 1980s, the withdrawal of governments from social provision was strikingly present in Sabongari. Provision of municipal facilities such as electricity, piped water, and main drainage were neglected. Entrepreneurs and families purchased electrical generators to carry out their businesses. In 2000, in Sabongari Kano, an average person spent at least N50.00 to buy water supplied daily by the Nigerian vendors. As urbanization expands, its disutility becomes more manifest. The crisis created by its expansion becomes more focused and translated into practical problems, especially those of uncontrolled and unplanned growth including overcrowding, poor and substandard housing, environmental pollution, open spaces, traffic paralysis.[35]

Indeed, suburban migration is predicated on the level of expenditure and social security. Increased mobility and rising standard of living paved way for many immigrants to move out of Sabongari. Deterioration of the social facilities, over-crowding and crime pushed many immigrant families out of Sabongari to other parts of the metropolis. But this process has equally encouraged the movement of young Hausa artisans, traders and commercial sex workers into Sabongari. Indeed, from 2000, the launching of the Sharia law in Kano gave a boost to this process. Mobility in the post-independence era brought about a degree of dispersal of work, residence, and leisure activities. In Northern Nigeria, the units of socioeconomic space have become more complex and extensive but governments have been inertia in responding to the changes. The Cities have become contiguous and overlapping. This is the essence of the Sabongari that has emerged in which the segregation between the old city (birni) and Sabongari lose their meaning. In Kaduna, the essence of Sabongari has virtually diminished.

The concept of urban responsibilities became a crucial factor in Sabongari. These responsibilities related to the capacity to support community services. Sabongari as immigrant precinct or territorial unit formed the basis of social solidarity, which creates an interest unit. The immigrant community's ecological base serves broad range of valuable functions that are related to its existential needs. These include the development of ethnically based institutions, such as schools, religious establishments and social clubs that generate capital as well as provide employment, education, and loyalty. For example, by 1930 in Sabongari Kano, four Christian organisations established by migrant communities had built primary schools with total enrolment of over 1,990 pupils of diverse ethnic backgrounds in 1939. These included the following: Church Mission Society Primary School, Holy Trinity Primary School and Baptist Primary School. During this period, there was not a single government school in Sabongari, Kano.[36] In the 1970catalogue of schools in Sabongari, Kano shows that they were owned by religious and ethnically based organisations.

Table 9.3. Schools in Sabongari, Kano, 1925-1973

S/N	Name of School	Year of Establishment	Agency
1.	Holy Trinity	1925	C. M. S. Anglican Church
2.	U.N.A.	1929	African Church
3.	Baptist	1929	Baptist Church
4.	St. Thomas	1930	Roman Catholic Mission
5.	Ansar-ud-deen	1944	Ansar-ud-deen Society
6.	S. I. M.	1945	S. I. M. / ECWA
7.	Igbo Union	1945	The Igbo State Union
8.	Methodist	1947	Methodist Church
9.	Ahmadiyya	1970	Ahmadiyya Muslim Mission
10.	Council of Muslim Community	1973	Council of Muslim Community

Source: Fieldwork in Sabongari, Kano and A. Bako, 1990, A Socio-Economic History of
    Sabongari, Kano p. 298.

In 1986, the Kano State government took control and renamed most of the mission schools. Since the economic crisis in the 1980s, governments in Sabongari neglected the provision and maintenance of social infrastructure as well as security. The government's departure from social provisioning has ushered in a medley of multi-ethnic civil society such as the Non-indigene Consultative Committee was formed to protect the lives and property of Sabongari residents in the period of violent riots and development purposes. Representatives from centralized ethnic associations in Sabongari, Kano constituted the committee. Its major achievement included the demand for the compensation of riot victims and organizing vigilante activities to defend Sabongari during riots.[37]

Other multi-ethnic civil societies included the Sabongari Development Association, Sabongari Elders Forum and neighbourhood associations which provide social security by repairing bad roads, clear refuse, provide security barricades/gates and organize vigilante groups through funds contributed by residents. In June 1996, the representatives of Sabongari Leaders Associations, Kano presented five-point developmental proposals to the Chairman of the Nassarawa Local Government, Kano State that administratively controlled Sabongari.

a. Refuse Disposal in Sabongari: poor sanitary condition in Sabongari should be fully addressed.

b. Streets in Sabongari: priority attention should be given to streets in Sabongari to allow free flow of traffic devoid of accidents.

c. Tenement Rate and Operational Fees: Payment of various taxes in Sabongari to both the State and Local Government by residents are duplicated and required critical review.

d. Health Inspection in Sabongari: both the Environmental and Occupational Health Unit of Nassarawa Local Government Health Department claim authority over Sabongari residents in terms of collection of various fees, particularly from hotels.

e. Drainages and Shortages of Water Supply in Sabongari: good water supply, good drainage and others are some of the teething problems, which should be seriously addressed.

It was in the context of this agitation for development that the Movement for the Creation of Sabongari Local Government, Kano State was formed and led by the Non-Indigenes Community Leaders Association (NICOLA). In its Charter of Demand submitted to the Speaker, Kano State House of Assembly on 28th February, 2002, NICOLA argued that despite an estimated population of over a million, a vibrant commercial nerve centre contributing about N200million per year as shop tax, land tax, levies, and other forms of taxation to the governments' treasury, the area was neglected in terms of developmental projects. Consequently, roads in Sabongari became unmemorable and sometimes completely washed away by erosion due to lack of proper drainages or blocking the existing drainages.[38] In 2004, the new administration of Governor Ibrahim Shekarau embarked upon road rehabilitation in Sabongari.[39]

Conclusion

In terms of ethnic relations between diverse cultural groups, colonial rule was something of a paradox. Through its socio-economic and political institutions, it brought peoples together in new integrating forces. In its transformation, Sabongari developed into a cosmopolitan entity incorporating both the migrant and hosts elements. From the 1940s, Sabongari became the seething base and political fortress of the nationalist movement. It was indeed the terminus of collaboration between the northern and southern Nigerian elite of radical persuasion. In a generic sense, the policy of residential segregation was ruined by the growing wave of nationalism and urbanization processes. However, the withering away of urban development policies of governments has led to the environmental deterioration, overcrowding and realization of Sabongari within the urban space in northern Nigeria. New actors particularly ethnic and communal associations are taking keen interest in the security, sanitation and social provisioning in Sabongari. Sabongari has equally become the flashpoint of confrontation between northerners and southerners as witnessed in Kano and Kaduna.

Notes and References

1. G Basri, Nigeria and Sharia: Aspirations and Apprehension (London: Islamic Foundation, 1994), p. 12.

2. A Olukoju, "Prohibition and Paternalism: The State and the Clandestine Liquor Traffic in Northern Nigeria, c. 1898-1918" in The International Journal of African Historical Studies, Vol. 24, No.2, (1991); pp. 349-368 and A. Olukoju, "Race and Access to Liquor: Prohibition as Colonial Policy in Northern Nigeria, 1919-1945" in Journal of Imperial and Commonwealth History, Vol. 24, No. 2, (1996); pp. 218-243.

3. A. M. Fika, The Political and Economic re-orientation of Kano Emirate, Northern Nigeria, 1882-1940, 1973, Ph.D. Thesis, University of London, pp. 414-415.

4. A Olukoju, "The Segregation of Europeans and Africans in Colonial Nigeria" in L. Fourchard and I. O. Albert, (eds.), Security, Crime and Segregation in West African Cities since the 19th Century, Paris: Karthala-IFRA, 2003, p 264.

5. A Olukoju, "The Segregation of Europeans and Africans" p.265.

6. Ibid. p 268.

7. Ibid. p 269.

8. Ibid. p 271.

9. Ibid. pp 271-274.

10. GO Olusanya, "The Sabongari System in Northern Nigeria," Nigeria Magazine, No. 94, (Sept. 1967); p. 244.

11. R Jones, "Factors Promoting Urbanisation" in R. Jones, Essays on World Urbanisation, London: Butler and Tanner Limited, 1975, p. 19.

12. E Oyedele, Colonial Urbanisation in Northern Nigeria: Kaduna 1913-1960, 1987, Ph.D Thesis, Zaria, Ahmadu Bello University, p. 227.

13. E Oyedele, Colonial Urbanisation in Northern Nigeria, pp. 239-242.

14. EE Osaghae, Trends in Migrant Political Organisations in Nigeria: The Igbo in Kano, IFRA: Ibadan, 1994, p 32.

15. MM Tukur, "The Nature, Extent and Essence of British Social Policy in the Emirates 1900-1914,' in T. Abubakr, (ed.), The Essential Mahmud: Selected Writings of Mahmud Moddibo Tukur, Zaria: ABU Press, 1990, p.144

16. Ibid. p 141.

17. Ibid. pp 144-145.

18. E Oyedele, Colonial Urbanisation in Northern Nigeria, p. 282.

19. Ibid. p 282.

20. Ibid. pp 282-293.

21. A Olukoju, "Nigerian Cities in Historical Perspectives" in T. Falola and S. J. Salm, (eds.) Nigerian Cities (Trenton: African World Press, 2004), pp 32-33.

22. NAK/Kanoprof/R/258: Sabongari Mixed Court.

23. M. M. Tukur, "The Nature, Extent and Essence of British Social Policy in the Emirates" pp 144-145.

24. A Bako, "Ethnic Relations in a Colonial Setting: The Settlement of Sabongari Kano, 1913-1960" FAIS Journal of Humanities, Vol. 1, No. 2, (2000), p 67

25. IA Frishman, The Spatial Growth and Residential Location Pattern of Kano Nigeria, Ph.D Thesis, Northwestern University, USA, 1977, p. 134

26. O Oshin, "Railways and Urbanization" in T. Falola and S. J. Salm, Nigerian Cities, Trenton: Africa World Press, (2004), p.114.

27. R Mohammed, The Rise of Sabongari Settlement in Sokoto Town: Its Socio-Economic Impact, B.A. Project, University of Sokoto, 1986, p 32.

28. EE Osaghae, Trends in Migrant Political Organisations in Nigeria: The Igbo in Kano – IFRA: Ibadan, 1994, p. 32.

29. RO Olaniyi, "Nationalist Movement in a Multi-Ethnic Community of Sabongari Kano" in M.O. Hambolu, (ed.), Perspectives on Kano-British Relations, Kano: Gidan Makama Museum, (2003), p. 226

30. A Abba, The Politics of Mallam Aminu Kano: Documents from the Independence Struggle 1945-1960 (Kaduna: Vanguard Printers and Publishers Ltd., 1993, p. 18

31. A Mabogunje, " Towards an Urban Policy in Nigeria" in P. O. Sanda and J. S. Oguntoyinbo, Urbanisation Process and Problems in Nigeria (Ibadan: University of Ibadan Press, 1980, p. 8.

32. P Scholler, "The Problems and Consequences of Urbanisation" in R. Jones, Essays on World Urbanisation, London: Butler and Tanner Ltd, (1975); pp. 42-43

33. G Brejen, 1985, Migration to Shashemene: Ethnicity, Gender and Occupation in Urban Ethiopia, Uppsala: Scandinavian Institute of African Studies, 1985, p. 114.

34. AE Smailes, "The Definition and Measurement of Urbanisation" in R. Jones, Essays on World Urbanisation, London: Butler and Tanner Limited, 1975, p. 3).

35. GJA Ojo, "Action-Oriented Observaries for Urban Development" in P. O. Sanda and J. S. Oguntoyinbo, Urbanisation Process and Problems in Nigeria, Ibadan: University of Ibadan Press, 1980, p. 24.

36. A Bako, 1990: 295-296 A Socio-Economic History of Sabongari, Kano, PhD. Thesis, 1990, Kano, Bayero University, pp. 295-296. An earlier thesis is that of David Allyn, The Sabon Gari System in Northern Nigeria, 1911-1940", PhD Thesis, 1976, University of California.

37. EE Osaghae, Trends in Migrant Political Organisations, p.35.

38. A Mamaiyetan, "Movement for Creation of Sabongari Local Government Takes off" in Civil Society Newsletter, pp. 1-2; "Sabongari Demands Local Government" in Civil Society Newsletter, May/ June 2002, pp. 1 and 5; "New Local Government Agitators Form Body" in Civil Society Newsletter, pp.1 and 5; and "Assembly Verification Exercise: Proposed Sabongari Local Government Scales First Hurdle" in Civil Society Newsletter, February, 2003, p 1.

39. Yusha'u Adamu Ibrahim, "Changing Faces of Sabongari, Kano" in Daily Trust Newspaper (Nigeria) April 9, 2004, p 13.

10

Colonial and Postcolonial Architecture and Urbanism

Seyi Fabiyi

Introduction

This chapter presents historical overview of Nigerian arch-type and urbanism. Every urban area in Nigeria has its unique history and architectural experience, which make generalization difficult, therefore the chapter present epitome panoramic view of urban archetypes and urbanism in Nigerian. Nigeria is a highly urbanized nation with three of her cities listed among the first one hundred most urbanized cities in the world. In 2004, World Gazetteer ranked Lagos, Ibadan and Kano as 27th, 78th and 88th respectively among the world most urbanized cities. In population sizes Lagos ranked 15th Kano 53rd and Ibadan 54th. Nigeria has a long history of urbanization with as many as 100,000 populations congregating in cities as early as early 1900 (Mabogunje, 1968). Three epochs of architectural forms and urbanism could be identified in Nigerian history. These are pre-European era, the colonial period, and the post independence period till date. The emphasis of this chapter is on the colonial and postcolonial periods, which are succinctly examined.

Pre Colonial Architecture – The Yoruba Example

The arch-type of most Yoruba pre-colonial urban buildings could be classified into three, the King palace, the chief and nobles houses and the houses of the commoners. The palace performed numerous functions for which it was initially designed - to provide apartment and space for leisure, entertainment, and receiving dignitaries. The following spaces were provided in the Traditional Yoruba palace:

- *Apartment for religious functions*, this apartment accommodate the ancestral shrine(s) of the dynasty and some time communal shrines. Yoruba kings occupy political and spiritual positions in most kingdoms. The king therefore performed two types of rituals, one that is private to his ancestors and other on behalf of the communities/kingdoms. These types of deities (Orishas, gods and goddesses) differed in importance, ceremony and shrines from one city to the others. Spaces were provided within or outside the kings compounds

- *The throne room*. This is where the king meets important subjects and his chiefs. The throne room is different from the Aganju (the open place where public meetings and ceremonies took place). The throne room is usually the judgment room or the court room for difficult cases
- The harem apartment –Within the palace is a secluded apartment where the king's wives have separate rooms. In some cities it has its own wall or fence.
- The prices and princess apartments: the royal seeds stays in the princes quarters
  Other apartments within the palace include:
- Apartment for the palace eunuchs
- Apartment for the Servants
- Apartment for the drummers
- Apartment for the staff bearer
- Apartment for the king trumpeter
- Apartment for the slaves
- Apartment for the previous kings wives

These groups of people that lived in the palace required large compound and many rooms to house them. This explains why most traditional palace was very large. According to Clapperton as quoted by Dmochowski the king palace of Old Oyo before it was destroyed was about 160 acres. The Oba's palace was surrounded by high walls, as described by Frobenius (1913) and Mabogunje (1968). The palace walls could be visible from every parts of the city. Usually the King palace was located at the centre of the city or the highest point in the city (Mabogunje 1968).

The chief's houses: The houses of chiefs and nobility were similar to the king except in size and elegance. Their sizes and designs were equivalent to the status and ranks. The Chief houses were also surrounded by high walls; based on their status. Most chief have quarters, which housed patrilinear extended family and may be enclosed in form of square or rectangle bounded by mud wall. There was only one entrance, however for the houses of high chiefs and nobles the entrances were topped by a gable roof to allow entry of horses.

The commoners' houses are smaller and rectangular or square in shape housing extended family along patriarch lineage. The rooms open into the court-yard and linear veranda. The entrance opened into the courtyard where all rooms could be accessed through a common corridor or veranda.

Building Process in Pre-colonial Yoruba Towns

The buildings of most traditional Yoruba towns were made of Mud walls before the arrival of the Portuguese the fist European to arrive in Yoruba areas. The building process involved a large number of people usually the mason (Omole) and arrays of laborers. The laborers were sourced from the community through the popular free service called (*Aro*). The laborers in *Aro* were drawn from family members, friend neighbors and other well wishers they offered free services in anticipation for their turns. The local mason some times was paid fees, which varies from one place to another and sometimes depend on the relationships with the house owner.

The local mason is a professional in some sort and knew what type of laterite soil will be good building material. The laborers organized in groups, one group excavated the earth laterite usually from deep pit located by the mason, the earth is conveyed to the building site, another group processed the laterite by pouring water and pounding the earth by legs or pestle until it becomes malleable to the gauge ready for building. Another group of the same group kneaded the processed laterite into sizeable *clay balls*, which were thrown to the mason who picked the clay ball in a characteristic expertise manner and is positioned on the building sites. There were no real foundation, the builder/ mason clear the ground, remove the topsoil and pour water to allow the clay to stick. He collected the clay balls to mould the building.

The building wall was built in layers, each layer reaching about 30 – 50 centimeters, the layer was allowed to dry for about three to four days before the second layer commenced. The walls usually reached the height of 4 to 6 meters. The upper parts of the walls were built either through scaffolding or the mason sat on the wall and mould as he moved backward the laborers threw the clay balls to him.

The earth materials used to build the walls required that building project had to be done only during the dry seasons. The late December or early January are the usual period of building project in traditional Yoruba settlement. Before the introduction of Corrugated iron sheet for roof, which was introduced by the European traders, thatch was the prominent roofing material. The same set of communal laborers was used in the roofing stage of building project, which was done about a month after the wall was finished. Different workers/ professionals were engaged during the roofing stage. These professionals specialize in thatch roof but free service providing laborers were used in the procurement of leaves, grass or palm fronds used in the roofing material.

The popular leaves used for roofing was *Gbodogi,* (a shrub plant having very wide leave), or *bere* grass or palm frond. The materials were specially woven to be waterproof and to withstand strong wind. The truss and beams were made from planks and bamboo or coconut plank, these were securely knitted with special rope and the leaves or grass were straddled to the planks and truss.

Usually on an average of once in three to five years the roof had to be replaced. Dmochowski (1990) described the common house of pre-colonial times as follows

> The house is usually a rectangular or square plan, A single entrance gate gave access to a number of inner courtyard the formed a series of separate apartments

occupied by closely and usually patrilinear related families. Verandas surrounded the courtyards, with doors to they different rooms.

The structure described above prevailed in major urban centers before the arrival
Europeans in Nigeria.

Colonial Urban Centers and Urbanism

The abolition of slave trade encouraged a new form of trade relations with the
Europeans and the subsequent industrial revolution in Europe brought a number
of changes to Nigerian cities. The emphases in trade changed from slaves to agricultural produce such as cocoa, palm, rubber, kolanuts, cotton and groundnuts.
The locations of these agricultural products and cities around the coasts or major
estuaries were used as depots. The depots became popular because of the demand
for the bulky agricultural produce and the need to transport them to the coast for
exports and grew to large urban areas. Later settlements around railway stations
became prominent in the early parts of 1900s when railway was constructed to
link south to the north The British rule was fully established in Nigeria in 1914
with the amalgamation of the Northern and southern Protectorates. The British
rule in Nigeria lasted between 50 to 60 years and brought a number of transformations to Nigeria urban layout and pattern and building architecture. The colonial
administration discontinued traditional pattern and introduced European ideal to
urban forms and townscape in all urban centers where they had officers. However
traditional pattern still located side by side with the implant from Europe.

During the colonial periods Nigerian cities went through tremendous changes
in every aspect of their construction and physical organizations many of these
changes had origin in Lagos (Mabogunje, 1968). Significant of this transformation process was the enactment of Township ordinance in 1917. The act provided
for the creation, constitution and the administration of all towns and municipali-
ties in Nigeria. The act also classified cities in Nigeria into three, which were
First class towns, second-class towns and third class towns. The criteria for this
classification were not explained in the act. Lagos was the only first class town
by the classification though Lagos (derived from Portuguese *Lagoon de Curamo*
was initially known by the Awori as Eko (farm), it was made popular by the colonial administration, being the seat of government and a port city. It was not as
important as many other Yoruba settlements both in term of population size or
area extent during the pre colonial era. Lagos became the seat of Colonial government and the earliest dispersion point of modern urban style and architecture
in Nigeria. The first class town was administered by a Town council while the
second and third class towns had appointed officers. The second class towns were
mainly trade centers where there were European depots. In 1919, they were 18 in
numbers.

The town council in Lagos had a ten - man board members charged with
the responsibility of urban planning and redevelopment. The Creation of Lagos
Executive Development Board in 1927 marked the beginning of direct govern-

ment intervention in urban physical form and architecture in Nigeria. In the native towns and third class settlements the traditional apparatus were used in urban management because the Colonial government saw in them cheaper means to administer the towns through their retune of administrative staff.

Many towns sprung up as break of bulk points for agricultural produce, especially where Europeans had stores and around railway stations. The Railway project began in 1904 and link towns not on the basis of their pre-colonial importance but their closeness to raw materials for exports. Smaller towns around railway lines or stations started growing in importance and sizes.

Most towns developed or parts of the existing cities that developed during the colonial rule were patterned according to the planning concepts prevalent in UK at the time. Many of the road layouts at that time were criss- cross pattern (gridiron) Segregation in term of income were fashionable at that time. The European reservation areas (ERAs) were residential schemes developed to house the colonial rulers and their enclaves. There were marked differences between the European settlements and the Nigerian or African settlements in term of quality of housing and urban infrastructures. While the layout in the ERAs had adequate accessibility, the African settlements especially the traditional parts of the city were in the process of fragmentations of the large compound into smaller units to house successful single or two family members. The consequence was that the accessibility into the traditional part of the city was mainly narrow lanes or footpaths. The hygiene condition of the traditional parts of the city became worse, while housing amenities were either inadequate or absent. The main toilet facility in the traditional core at the tine was bucket system, which the soil man evacuated for disposal at night.

The pre-colonial urban centre had concentric pattern radiating around the King's palace and central market. Two major centers were noticeable during the colonial period, these were; the traditional centers where the Obas palace and the traditional market were and the commercial/ administrative centers where the District officer (DO) office was or the new commercial or industrial areas. Shortly the new centers replaced the traditional centers in Importance and relevance. The traditional markets in front of king's palaces were waning in importance, as imported goods and other household items became available at the new commercial centers.

Most importantly, the contribution of the Colonial government to urbanism apart from influencing the layout design is the introduction of direction of Migration from rural areas and suburban areas to newly created urban lands. Jobs were available at the designated areas by the Colonial government, therefore migration from different parts of Nigeria to Lagos started during the colonial regime. Places like Kano; Enugu; Ibadan also experienced massive rural- urban migration. Young school levers moved to the cities, to benefit from the developed economy of the cities where the British presence was. Urban areas in the colonial period therefore have the following sectors: Residential precinct, Commercial areas, Administrative area and Industrial areas.

Nature and Types of Urban Architecture - Colonial Period

Though the pattern and forms of traditional areas became increasingly disorganized, the building structure and architectural pattern borrowed from European design. The changes in building materials, pattern, architecture and engineering manifested in the replacement of the mud walls (that characterized the older building) with baked bricks and later cement blocks. The baked brick was introduced in the last segment of the 1800, it was however more pronounced in Lagos and major cities shortly after the colonial rule began. The brick wall eventually gave way for the cement blocks. Cement was used to mould blocks and to plaster houses, though storey building was common among the nobles and prominent chief even with the mud and brick walls. The introduction of cement blocks allowed a number of adaptations and different styles in buildings. Though many Europeans living in the ERA did not build above one floor for residential purposes, Some Nigerians as a display of social symbols and affluence built lofts. King palaces also began to change forms along this lines. The roof materials at this time were corrugated iron sheets and windows were much bigger and airy. The doors made from wood artistically carved.

Despite the abundance of cement and brick housing in most urban centers mud wall, brick wall could be found in most Nigerian centers during this period. Residential areas also change significantly in pattern architecture. The new building materials used at that time (cement and corrugated iron sheets) were imported and required substantial capital to purchase. Prior to the time of the colonial administration, thatch roof and mud were easily available and communal\labor was often used to build houses, all these made housing development cheaper during the pre colonial period. The high cost of imported building materials and of hiring more specialized professionals was out of reach of many people, except big time farmers and business men whose thriving business especially the exports of agricultural products allowed them to have sufficient money to purchase the building materials and hire semi skilled professional to build. The building profession became more specialized and huge sum of money was required to build than it was previously.

The large compound that initially housed patrilinear extended family was broken and fragmented to house successful smaller family units. The fragmentation had significant impact on the urban landscape. Modern housing stood side by side with old derelict buildings. The walkway was narrow and building stand roof to roof that one can exchange handshake with a friend in the adjacent building. The fragmentation of large compounds into smaller family units was accompanied by emergence of an architectural design known as Brazilian style brought by ex-slave returnees from Brazil.

Broad categories or architectural forms could be identified in colonial urban centers as reflected in residential buildings, departmental /shopping malls, large stores and ware houses and public building and corporate headquarters and religious buildings such as Churches and mosques

Arch-Types in Residential Precincts

The colonial period manifested three district residential precincts in most urban centers in Nigeria. These are:

Older low quality residential precincts, which are usually located within the traditional core of the city. A mentioned earlier the pre colonial traditional quarters and compound of Yoruba urban centers were fragmented to house younger up coming family units. The break up of the old traditional compound into smaller dwelling units also went side by side with the development of new housing units by immigrants who secured spaces adjacent to the traditional core. The building in these areas was typically Brazilian type, which were rectangular or square in shape. The Brazilian housing types were extensively modified in most of the core area but basically were mainly bungalow except for few storey buildings. The Brazilian design had 4 to 6 rooms in a bungalow and storey buildings had between 12 to 20 rooms. All rooms face a common corridor with two entrances the main door facing the street while the other entrance door faced the backyard where there were kitchen, toilet and common bathroom. The Brazilian design was given different modification based on the financial resources of the house owner. Building at this time became a conduit to display affluence and wealth in the Yoruba Urban centers. With the breakdown of traditional hierarchy and roles of chiefs, the societal importance was no longer based on hereditary but affluence and wealth. The affluence was extensively displayed in the quality and modernity of housing types and design.

New low quality - residential district: Immediately outside the boundary of traditional older residential districts are the new low quality newer residential areas. The location of this type of housing was not necessarily concentric. These buildings were on separate plots as opposed to the traditional building where old traditional quarters were fragmented. In some government residential scheme especially in the Lagos and some second-class towns, plots were allocated to Natives to build upon. The layout scheme was designed after the gridiron pattern. The plots were linearly arranged along streets, backing each other and facing the streets. The street at the time were just marked with beacons, they were not developed. Consequently the private developers developed beyond the boundaries of their plots leaving narrow lane in most of these precincts that were hardly passable for delivery vehicles. The houses in this precinct housed young families for whom there was no longer land within the family compound and those who wanted to escape the burden of traditional ties of extended family relations.

Majority of these houses were built with mud but a sizeable number of them were built with bricks plastered with cement and some were built with cement blocks. This type of building marked the obvious beginning of tenement building in Nigeria urban centers. The tenement buildings house the migrants to the city especially the school leavers and young professionals in the industrial or business and civil service.

At this time most urban dwellers aspire to build houses to live in and to let out as income generating ventures. The delight for quick financial returns from properties and the fact that majority of developers in this area are predominantly low and middle income earners; the quality of houses in these area are generally low but significantly different from buildings in the traditional core area in term of spaces and building materials. Most of these settlements quickly became squalid and manifested slum condition.

Government housing schemes

The outbreak of bubonic plagues in central Lagos moved the colonial government to directly intervene in the building process and urban layout of the indigenous settlers in a more meaningful way. The slum clearance program in central Lagos and the resettlement scheme at Surulere are some of the earliest direct intervention of the colonial government in the layout and the building pattern of the indigenous African settlements.

The colonial government moved beyond provision of site and services to the direct construction of housing and transfers to African urban residents either as outright sale or bond payment. For example Surulere housing estate was originally designed to house the large number of people displaced in the 1956 slum clearance and provided them with relatively cheap and affordable housing. The allocates were to pay rent of 25 shillings per month, which was considered too high by most residents who let out their houses and moved to cheaper residences. In addition the resettlement moves many too far from their work places, shortly afterwards the middle income earner gradually displaced the original low income earners in Surulere Housing scheme. The government housing scheme had prototype buildings of flats of various types and sizes. These designs of housing were quite different from the local Brazilian types that were popular among the Africans. Most of these houses were built for single family and not designed for multi-tenanted purposes, which was the main attractive attribute of the Brazilian types especially to the low-income earners. The result of these is that most of these houses were occupied by the middle -income earners especially those that are in the white-collar employment.

European reservation areas (ERA)

There was significant influx of the British into the country during the colonial rules most of who are businessmen, professionals such as Doctors, Nurses Engineers and Missionaries. They were accommodated in a well laid out high quality residential area popularly known as European reservation areas (ERA) exclusively for the European settlers. The ERA was usually the residency of the district officers and other European settlers and in most cases housed the seat of provincial government in the second-class settlements. The design of the houses in the ERA was typical of English equivalent at that time. They depicted a typical country house, some of them include chimney and fire place despite the fact that Nigeria has a tropical climate. A number of the houses in the ERA were bungalow but some were storey buildings placed centrally in large plot. Most of the colonial houses were painted white or white washed with wide balconies and large windows. The roof was made of clay or concrete tiles and the internal paneling were generous in timber carefully laid in a modern fashionable way. The European houses were well ventilated with more windows than could be found in other houses of Africans. The houses have large verandas and play areas either as courtyard or sit out in front of the house. The plots boundary of the plots was demarcated by vegetal hedges -both ornamental and fruit trees.

High Quality African Residential Areas

Towards the end of the colonial rules in Nigeria especially during the self-rule period a number of private residential schemes were embarked upon by the government especially to house the high-income African urban population. The government prepared planning schemes and site and services programs which people were to buy into and build their different designs. Different architectural master piece were displayed in such residential estate the occupants were among high level professionals, emerging politicians, business tycoons and highly placed civil servants.

The Architecture of Central Areas

The central areas during the colonial period comprised of commercial or business areas, the warehouses, factories, religious buildings and administrative offices.

Business or Commercial districts: These areas are characterized by active commercial activities. The main buildings in the CBD during the colonial periods include ware houses for big multinational like John Holt, UAC among others. There were retail and departmental stores usually more than one storey. There are a number of British and America companies, banks insurance firms and public buildings. Some packaging factories also located within the central areas. The buildings for ware houses were usually large single bungalow built with few or no windows. Such ware houses were used to store imported goods before distributions and to store farm produces before export. The departmental stores and corporate offices could reach several floors of sky crappers. Some of these reach as much as 12 floors and had offices and shops.

Administrative areas: The secretariat and the government offices are located in the administrative areas. The administrative areas are closely linked with the central areas business areas though there were few exceptions. The building in this area housed the civil servants and the colonial administrators. It also had town halls, courts major secondary health facility and several other public's uses.

Factory or Industrial areas: At this time most packaging business were referred to as factories. They are located in the industrial zones or away from the CBD. The most important industries at that time were food and drinks, motor assembly and repair and metal industries

Transportation played dominant rows in urban development especially to link the industrial areas with other parts of the city for the movement of goods and employee. Many middle class families in the smaller towns make monthly trips or quarterly to bigger cities for their shopping (Mabogunje, 1968).

Postcolonial Urban Forms and Urbanism

The Nigerian independence was followed by a four-year civil war, which could be referred to as interregnum period in urban planning and development. However shortly after the civil war, the peaceful atmosphere and the sudden wealth that came with the discovery of crude oil in Nigeria popularly referred to as *Oil Boom* had significant effect on the urban forms and urbanism. The economic revolution that was brought about by the new fiscal policy and indigenization decree of early seventies transformed the cities or major urban centre to job haven for young men who wanted to escape from the energy sapping farm work and young school leavers. The resulting massive rural urban migration was unprecedented and the receiving urban centers were not equipped to accommodate such influx of rural unskilled migrants. The population explosion in major urban centers therefore resulted in overstretched facilities, inadequate housing and development of shanties and slum in most urban centers in Nigeria. Lagos was the worst hit by this pressure for space in urban areas. Other major towns like Ibadan, Abeokuta, Aba, Onitsha, Calabar, Kano, Kaduna, Sokoto, Jos and Maiduguri among other urban centers were also receiving influx or rural migrants.

By the early eighties Nigeria has over 42 cities with very high population (Abumere 1986). Only few of these cities have comprehensive master plans and the Land reforms of 1978 were purely implemented. Therefore the invisible hand of price mechanism and the communal land ownership systems define the direction of growth and pattern of many urban settlements in Nigeria.

On the other hand the buoyant economy in the seventies and early eighties put a lot of money in individual hands and these wealth were utilized for developments. Different private building projects sprung up in most cities and the private development efforts quickly supposed the government efforts in housing delivery. The rate of private developments outstretched the poorly staffed and inadequately equipped local planning authority. The consequence is spread of unplanned developments in Nigerian cities. Along side of the developments by the wealthy were also the building of shanty structures and squatter settlements to house the increasing urban population whose income could not afford the developments in the cities. The rural urban migrants had no sufficient income to secure themselves decent accommodation found themselves places in squatter settlements and shanty structures. Some of the shanty structures initially emerged as make- shift shops, which later became place of abode for the tenants who converted and extend the shanty shops to living place.

The Planning authorities in most Nigerian urban centers failed to chart a particular course for planning development especially in forms and design or comprehensive structural plan for future developments. Most planning authorities merely serve as coordinating and approving agencies to ratify private plans and scheme in building and rebuilding operations. Theoretically urban land is vested in the State government; the governor gives certificate of occupancy, at the state levels and Local councils or authorities give statutory right on rural lands. In reality however lands are still in the hands of individuals and families.

The planning schools and professional bodies concerned with urban planning and architectural forms could not do much to promote orderliness and proper arrangement of spaces and structures due to poor legislative environment. Private layouts and schemes are many and the government residential schemes are few. Except some planted towns like Abuja, Ajoda and some big residential estates there were few large-scale preconceived planned developments in Nigeria. What obtain since independence is pockets of narrowly conceived planning schemes in form of housing schemes site and services urban renewal program, township improvement project and urban basic services projects.

It is noteworthy however that after independence there were marked private involvements and in the development of architectural forms and urban patterns in Nigeria. The large number of professionals in the built industry; Urban planners, Architects, Developers, surveyors, Civil engineer are performing important roles though under trying legislative conditions to force order and shape in Nigerian city space. Unfortunately however these efforts and initiatives were not properly coordinated by appropriate legislation therefore design conflicts and forms abound in most Nigerian cities.

The economic landscape and the absence of any serious governmental control on development resulted in a redistribution and realignments, regrouping of people across urban space. Though some traditional urban centre still has core areas where old buildings that best fit for antiquity could still be found; new entrants have built upon most of them. The traditional core areas still housed the indigenous population especially the low economic class and the very aged.

The low involvement of government in residential housing and urban planning in cities generally resulted in spatial segregation of people in space based on social, economic, tribal or other affiliations. Fabiyi (2004) has classified the forces of agglomeration or segregation in Nigerian urban areas in what follows:

Ethno-cultural Enclaves

Agglomeration and segregation refer to a process of clustering wherein individuals and groups shifted and sorted out in space based on their sharing certain traits or activities in common or equal status. (Van der Zandern 1996, Fabiyi 2004). The segregation or grouping factor can be based on ethnicity; wherein members of the same ethnic group, finding themselves in a foreign land, could choose to live in close proximity to one another, this arrangement is also called 'ethnic enclaves' (Boracich and Model 1980, Aldrich et al 1989, Adeboye 2003). Ethnic enclaves exist in most Nigeria organic cities

It is also noticeable in most Nigeria cities that in-migration into the city has specific preference for location in some places. It is common to see small agglomeration of immigrants on the basis of tribal line or national line. When people are migrating from their villages of neighboring countries they often found places where relatives and friends have settled. Though the place is meant to be a transit camp, it often becomes permanent abode. There are some neighborhoods that are dominated by particular nationals such as migrants from Ghana, Togo, Liberia, Benin Republic, and Cameroon among others. Some of these international immigrants have ownership status of properties.

Land Use and Housing Policy Factor

Another is the legislative policy of the government by which certain groups are separated spatially from others through some form of policy such as land use scheme or Master plan when land is allocated on the basis of income or race through government policy, it can encourage segregation and corresponding social exclusion to non members of the neighborhoods. Private and public organizations do have housing schemes or development where people of different occupational and professional status are grouped together in different parts of the urban areas. There may be junior staff estate, senior staff estate or managerial staff estate. This procedure can also be found in government or institutional housing programs such as barracks, Universities and other public agencies. When government prepare residential housing scheme, the price placed on the plot determines the income class that is naturally attracted to the scheme.

Socio-Temporal Class Agglomeration

Different parts of the city develop at different times. Residential mobility is also associated with the income mobility of urban residents. When people of equal economic class migrate to a part of the city based on the facility available and the ability to pay for the service. With time age and reduction in economic capacity as the economically active households retires and the children move out of the neighborhoods, the area becomes residential enclaves of retirees and old people. There is generation-shift of residential neighborhoods as land price determines the economic status of people that are attracted to particular neighborhoods. There can also be succession of residential neighborhoods when a given social class is partly or completely replaced by another social class who are stronger economically and buys over the properties thus displacing the existing class who have hitherto moved down economic ladder.

Mixed Neighborhood Agglomeration

Apart from the agglomeration factors identified above there are a number of mixed neighbourhoods socially and development wise. With only few exceptions of planted towns like Abuja, poor neighbourhoods often intermix with good neighbourhoods or lie side by side. People of different social, economic, ethnic, educational and occupational status live together in the same or adjacent neighbourhoods. Nigeria is not a segregated community and there are few towns with master plans therefore the land prices and land tenure systems often determine residential location, distribution and pattern. The resultant effect of these agglomeration forces in Most Nigeria organic settlements is that it is difficult to classify Nigeria cities on the continuum of models of urban structures as most towns do not have a clear cut single centre or discrete boundaries of land use. The location of rich class and the poor do not necessarily based on distance to the CBD.

Urban Spatial Growth After Independence

The unprecedented growth that followed the 1970s economic revolution explained the rapid explosion of most cities in Nigeria. Shortly after independence most cities in Nigeria exerted high centripetal forces to surrounding hinterlands. The consequence is rapid expansion of most towns. Some of the towns earlier classified as third class town grew astronomically. The successive creation of states and local governments created more growth poles for urban expansion. The expansion of Nigerian cities after independence have been documented by a number of authors for instance Lagos (Adeniyi) Ibadan (Areola 1980, Fabiyi 1999) Ilorin (Ozo). In this chapter we briefly examined the expansion of Ogbomosho, a town that did not enter the first and second class list of the colonial administration classification of townships. The city grew from about 1.3 km square in 1914 to 2.07 Km square in 1949. This is a growth of 0.69 km square in 35 years. In 1978 the city has grown to 9.6 km square an increase of 4.7 kilometer square in 29 years. In 1995 it grew to 19-kilometer square and in 2003 the city has grown to 27-kilometer square. These figures show that remarkable growth was observable as from 1978.

The growth rate of urban areas in Nigeria has been estimated as 3.5 %by the National population commission in 1991 census but it was estimated that Lagos grows at the rate of 9% per annum. (Lagos 1980). This growth rate is a challenge to urban planning and housing supply in the cities. The growth of urban area was enhanced by the provision of infrastructure such as roads, pipe born water, and health facilities educational institutions among others. These further served as pull factors of rural dwellers to urban areas.

Infiltration of Foreign Design in Urban Architecture and Structural Forms

Professional in the building industry such as Architects Land surveyors Planners, Civil engineers were actively involved in building activities right from the colonial days. However most of these were foreign trained or they were associates of foreign experts. The establishment of town planning and architecture and engineering departments in tertiary institutions such as Yaba College of technology and Ibadan polytechnic was the earliest attempt on indigenous training in urban and building forms. Most of the teachers in these institutions were foreign trained; they therefore introduced foreign concepts of design and forms in the training and perspective of urbanism and architecture. Quite active at this time were also the artisans who assisted the professionals during the colonial period such as Architect and Surveyors and engineers. The high demand for the services of these professional after independence pushed up the relevance and patronage of these artisans. The artisans who masquerade as professionals and offer cheap services became prominent especially in housing the urban poor. Consequently these artisans secured high patronage in subdivision layout, building designs and building constructions.

The building designs that prevailed in the early first decade of independence were mainly imported designs or their adaptations copied by the local professionals from their foreign masters and from existing buildings. The submission of building plans were a necessary requirement for building and rebuilding operation had been adopted by the Town council at this time Town and country planning act of the Western Nigeria CHAP 123 and CHAP 146 in northern Nigeria, which were patterned according to the 1946 town and country planning act of Great Britain. Unfortunately the town council staff saddled with the responsibility of implementing the law was principally unenlightened in the rudiment of town planning and urban forms, consequently, the building plans were basically to satisfy the demand of the law and most plans were not followed in the implementation. Most buildings were designed for functionality and not for forms and aesthetics. However with increasing number of indigenous trained professionals in the building industry, a new form of local ingenuity and aesthetically pleasing architecture evolved especially in major urban centers. The new architectures and forms were initially introduced in Public buildings, corporate headquarters of major companies, Shopping arcade and some private residential houses of the affluent. As early as 1970s a number of privately owned housing estates emerged in Nigerian urban centers such as such as Lagos, Ibadan, Kano, Jos Kaduna Aba, Port Harcourt, Enugu Sokot and Abeokuta.. Industries and major companies built residential quarters with prototype architectural designs.

European Reservation areas were changed to Government reservation areas and housed indigenous population. The GRA later have new forms and design pattern as more changes were introduced by new occupants. All these changes and development consciously introduced new forms and fashion to urban architecture as local professionals have somewhat to copy from.

Gradually the Brazilian types became less popular especially in the new urban centers and in urban peripheries. The land reforms of 1978 were designed to make land available to urban dwellers by removing the bottle neck of customary land holdings that have existed in the past. After about three decades of Land use decree family lands are still privately surveyed, subdivided and sold to individual property developers who built on those lands with the approval of the government. Land is still subject of much litigation till today in Nigerian urban areas. The private subdivision affected urban development in the following ways:

- The land subdivisions were done with principal focus on profit maximization of land speculator interest; therefore there were no provisions for recreation or other public uses in most of the privately subdivided residential schemes.
- Some families allocate plots for members of the family who could decide to sell or build on. This encourages intermix of poor and good housing especially where middle class family members decided to build on their allotment. The roads in the private schemes were windy and narrow sometimes only providing minimum accessibility to residents within the neighborhoods.
- A number of vacant plots exist within built up areas as a result of waiting game of land speculators who expect land value to appreciate before disposing lands
- Discrete residential precincts of different social status and quality exist in a disjointed sectoral pattern as opposed to a continuum of high quality to low quality residential neighborhoods.

The Rise of Modern Architecture in Urban Nigeria

Modern arch types in Nigeria urban centers are influenced by some dominant actors/factors, which are enumerated as follows:

The Public Housing Programs and Policies

In the late seventies and early eighties there was the emergence of amalgam of new architectural designs featuring prominently in the public buildings a number of urban development project were embarked upon by both the federal government and the state governments. The vogue them were high rise building and the extensive splash of aesthetics on public buildings.

Government also embarked on a number of housing related urban development programs such as site and services, schemes where government prepared planning schemes and developed infrastructure and allocate the plots to private individual to build. The government especially the federal government embarked on n a number of housing project where proto type housing were built by the government and transfer to private individual for outright purchase or bond payment by installment. Significant was the housing program of the National government during the second republic. The central government planned to build low cost housing in all major urban centers in the country. The design of the low cost housing some of which are one bedroom, two bedroom and three bedroom were designed without specific assessment of the site characteristics this account for the mass failure of most of these housing projects. However the prototypes became models from where other mass produced building project could learn from.

Investment in urban infrastructure was very prominent road construction linking settlements and regions were prominent in the country until the mid eighties when the economies of Nigeria nosedive. During this epoch of rapid investment in urban infrastructure many urban settlements were provided with electricity and pipe borne water. Urban amenities were provided in many towns such as pipe born water, electricity and road construction.

These notwithstanding the policies of the government in urban structure and architecture are not only inconsistent but sometimes contradictory. Some specific interventions of the government in housing and urban forms in Nigeria are Creation of Federal housing Authority in 1973; Establishment of Federal Mortgage bank of Nigeria in 1977; the Land use decree in 1978, National Housing policy in 1991, Establishment of Urban development bank in 1992, national Housing Fund 1992 Formulation of National urban development policy in 1992, Urban and Regional Planning Law in 1992 provision of low cost housing, site and services, Infrastructural developments fund (IDF) program initiated in 1986 to assist 14 selected states. The goals and the mechanism of implementations of these arrays of policies among others contribute to the quality and structure of urban architecture that can be found in Nigerian cities today. Despite the laudable ideals and intents of these policies, they were poorly implemented as most past government lack sufficient enthusiasm to see to the implementation of these policies and programs. They have thus not achieved much in urban form, structure and architecture.

Private Corporate Bodies

Corporate organizations also took after the public sector and construction of tall storey buildings in the business districts became noticeable. The company profile and strength were openly displayed by the type and the structure of their head or corporate offices. The central business districts/ commercial centers of major urban centers have several dominant landmarks of massive archetypes. Banks, Hotels, large multinationals sought to display their achievement and dominance in the market through architectural design of their premises. The trend of the invasion of these super structure in major urban centers was enhanced by the engagement of indigenous professionals which helped to reduce the cost of building operation Though some corporate bodies embarked on housing program basically for their staff members the input of corporate bodies in private housing was very marginal. The banks do not show appreciable interest in building project and this has stifle the ability of most individual urban dwellers to own properties., the high interest on bank loans does not make investment in private residential properties very attractive.

Legislative Environment:

Prior to the 1992 Urban and regional planning decree, the only legislative apparatus guiding building and rebuilding operation sin the urban centers was the town and country-planning act of 1956. The requirements and the specifications of the laws could not cope with the urban challenges of post independence era. The implementations of the planning regulations were largely left to the discretion of the planning authorities, which encourage corruption among planning officials.

One of the requirements for building project is the submission of building drawings and structural details to the planning authority and secures approvals before such building project commenced. Unfortunately inadequate logistics resources for development control and monitoring, coupled with massive corruption among staff failed to tame the influx of unwholesome developments in most urban centers. Consequently most urban centers have pockets of blighted structures in different parts of the city.

The government housing policies are disjointed and haphazard and successive government appears to have different foci and strategies to tackle housing problems. In the mid nineties the government embarked on housing program tagged housing for all by the year 2000. The main strategy of this policy was to build cheap and affordable housing for urban dwellers. The strategy though was pursued with little enthusiasm by the government it however encouraged the development of informal housing in urban areas.

The Rise in Crime

The late seventies and especially early eighties witnessed a sudden rise in the rate of violent crime in many urban centers socially Lagos, Aba, Onisha. Urban residents consequently responded to the crime wave through target hardening. The reaction to crime manifest in the type of windows and doors used building. The windows were installed with iron burglary proof a tall fences and iron gates replaced ornamental edges that were the vogue in the earlier days. The affluent urban residents increasingly live in a jail-like houses and the aesthetic quality of most buildings were obscured by the tall fences and massive iron gates around the houses. The houses were more economical in the openings and openings are well protected by iron bars. Therefore the emphasis of building design shifted from display of forms and aesthetic to safety and security. The reaction to crime is extended beyond the dwellings to the streets. There a number of gated neighborhoods in urban centers where residential streets are boomed and sometimes non resident's passer by are closely monitored within the neighborhoods. Some neighborhoods streets are permanently closed or restricted to neighborhood residents only in urban areas. This has significant effect on urban imageability and traffic managements.

Emergence of New Professionals in Building Industry

By the mid eighties Nigeria has quite a number of qualified professionals in the building industries both in the public and the private sectors. The experience in the earlier period of independence was that most professionals in the building industry sought employment in the public sector, but with time a number of private architectural, land surveying, Urban planning Quantity surveying Civil engineering, property development/ Valuation and building construction firms emerged on the scene of urban property businesses. Consequently the competition improved quality of service delivery, design and implementations of building and urban developments programs. The designs are tailored to the taste of clients and sometimes new discoveries or archetypes were introduced. The tertiary training institutions and research institutes develop new approaches and new design concepts to urban architecture and management. However in the absence of strict legislative control, Nigerian urban areas became the laboratory to test new ideas and concepts, which often lead to visual chaos in urban landscape.

Income Disparities

The steady increase cost of living readily increased the inequality between the urban high class and the urban poor. The early eighties saw a significant proportion of urban residents below poverty levels and the effects were manifested in building and housing condition. The old buildings are not maintained leading to deterioration in visual quality and structure while some new ones are best described as shacks. Every available cheap lands such as water logged areas, abandoned mine sites, right of ways for electricity power lines among other unusable lands are colonized by urban poor to build shacks around the urban areas without adequate provision for facilities and orderliness. These shanties are a challenge to urban management and emergency services in most urban areas.

As income of indigenous urban resident increase they migrate from the core to other parts of the city, leaving the hopelessly poor and the aged in the traditional core. The indigenous cities have till date traditional core that have buildings that are more than hundred years old. Most of these building are in derelict condition and housed the poorest of the urban population. Most indigenous urban dwellers have family house at the core and their personal house somewhere within the city. The old commercial core however had different experience, while the owner of businesses and apartments grow old and moved down economic ladder, there is invasion of new interest that renovates or demolishes old structures and rebuild. There is greater attention to urban renewal in the commercial core compare to the traditional core of the cities. Therefore while the property values of the commercial core appreciate because of upgrades and improvement of adjacent properties and the environment generally the property value in the traditional core steadily slide downward.

Spatial Pattern of Nigerian Urban Archetype Today

In the introduction of Lagos state regional plan of 1980-2000, the governor of Lagos state acknowledge the planlessness of Lagos urban centers as follows: "A notorious feature of the territories now comprising Lagos states over the years has been haphazard development. Many of the popular towns and districts in the state –particularly metropolitan Lagos – were unplanned."

This is true of most urban centers in Nigeria even till the present times, there are no formal regional or structure plan to holistically guide developments therefore as mentioned by the then governor of Lagos state Lateef Jakande, Development in Lagos ". . . sprung up as contraventions and the government is, . . . rendered helpless by the sheer quantity of the contraventions, eventually accepted them as de facto townships . . . new ones are springing up." While some cities like Lagos, Bida, Minna, Kaduna Jos Kotangora have Master plans at some times in the past, the plans were poorly implemented and sometime after the expiration of the planning year no reviews were made for planning. Despite these we could still find pockets of homogenous classes of land use in the urban settlements. Such as high-density residential, Medium density residential Low density residential. Separate pockets of administrative units commercial precinct, industrial and institutional use. Each urban area in Nigeria has peculiar history and the morphology of the city clearly provides picture of the historical background of the cities.

Five broad types of housing could be found in contemporary Nigerian urban centers: these include: Informal dwellings and shanty structures, Derelict old buildings especially at the core of old traditional cities, Low income planned housing, Middle income planned Housing and Multi tenanted housing High income planned housing.

Informal Dwellings and Shanty Structures

These are dwellings built with wood and corrugated iron sheets to house one or two family in slum areas. It started as make shift shops and workshops on vacant lands or useable lands like water fronts, abandoned sand mines and water logged area. With times these shanties become living places. There are concerted efforts from the government to rid the cities of this urban visual menace.

Derelict Old Buildings Especially at the Core of Old Traditional Cities

The old urban areas still have remnants of the old building structure especially in the traditional core area. These buildings have not been renovated for years and thus are in derelict condition. The walls are standing but most fixtures are in disrepair while building facilities such as toilet, bathroom are either non existent or in deplorable condition. It is possible to find some pre-colonial design in some of these core areas.

Low Income Planned Housing

The low-income earners housing are often builds with brick or cement blocks and plastered, the windows and doors are made of wood and they have corrugated iron sheet as roof cover. The walls and floors are plastered with no fanciful designs. They could be found immediately after the traditional core or at the periphery. The land value in most urban centers in Nigeria is not proportional to the distance from the Central Business District (CBD), rather available infrastructural development and the direct government policy such as planning scheme which suggest government plans for future site improvement are the primary determinants of land value in the city. Private planning schemes are common in different parts of the city for poor and middle income family to buy. The plot lay out in this zone are usually 18 x 30 meters or 15 x 30 meters. (about 540 meters square).

The middle income earners housing/ Multi tenanted housing are also build with cement blocks. The roofs are made of corrugated iron sheet, asbestos or clay tiles. The windows and doors made up wood or louver glass windows with or without burglary proof.. They can be found in different areas within city. Most building in these areas is occupied by owners and few renters.

High-income earners housing: The high-income earners housing types is the most varied architecture in urban areas. They are built in different designs and forms. Though there is a ban on the importation of some building materials, imported building materials could be found in these zones. The building materials include cements, aluminum, and glass, highly refined wood and sophisticated internal building amenities.

Institutional Buildings

The public institutional buildings are built with different material quality depending on the budget available for the project and the prevailing circumstances. In all cases public and institutional building display the latest architecture prevailing at the time it was built. Institutions like secretariat, tertiary education institute, Commission head office, Hospitals, Courts among others carried different designs forms and building materials.

Conclusion

Nigeria is urbanizing at a very high rate. It is estimated that urban population in the last three decades has been growing close to about 5.8% per annum.(Federal Ministry of Housing And Development 2003). This is among the highest in the world. It is further estimated that by the year 2010 more than half of the country's population will be living in urban centers. The Explosive growth of the cities has consequences on the quality urban housing and infrastructures and generally on cityscape. The government needs more committed interventions to rescue urban areas from decay and blight. Suffice it to say that par capital income of urban residents has high influence in the archetype and urban forms. The specific intervention that can rise the per capital income of urban dwellers will inevitably help in improving urban quality and forms.

Notes and References

Adeboye, O, A, (2003), "Intra-ethnic segregation in colonial Ibadan: The case of Ijebu settlers," in *Security, Crime and Segregation in West African Cities Since the 19th century*, L. Fourchard and I.O. Albert eds. IFRA Publication.

Aldrich, H.Zimmer, C&D, McElroy (1989), "Continuities in the Study of Ecological Succession: Asian Businesses in three English cities," *Social Forces* Vol. 67.

Clapperton, H. Journal *of a Second Expedition into the Interior of Africa*, London, 1829, p 147.

Dmochowski, Z.R (1990*) An Introduction to Nigerian Traditional Architecture - South-West and Central Nigeria*, **Vol. 2**, Ethnographical London.

Fabiyi O,.2004, *Gated Neighborhoods and Privatization of urban security in Ibadan Metropolis*. Occasional Publication No 16 IFRA, Ibadan.

Federal Ministry of Housing and Urban Development (2003), *Sustainable Human Settlements and Development in Nigeria: National Urban strategies.*

Lagos State Regional Master Plan 1980-200. Lagos State Government.

Mabogunje, A, (1968), *Urbanisation in Nigeria*, University of London Press Ltd (1968).

Talbot, P A. *The People of Southern Nigeria*, Oxford University Press, London 1924, p 885.

World Gazetteer (Access 2005), World Urban Area Rank. http//:www.mongabay.com.

11

Legal Aspect of Urban Development

Mosope Fagbongbe & Hakeem I. Tijani

Introduction

Under the Nigerian legal system, a combination of legislation impact on urbanization and development, some of which does not have any linkages or cross-reference. This situation is also compounded by the dual system of law – whereby both State and Federal government of Nigeria can make laws.[1] This chapter critiques some of the laws relevant to urbanization and physical development in Nigeria. The existing legislative framework will be examined in order to determine it's adequacy. Our emphasis is on Lagos State being the political cockpit and economic center of modern Nigeria.[2]

The chapter is divided into eight parts. While Part I is the introduction, Part II defines the terms used throughout the chapter in order to delimit the scope. Part III discusses the existing urban situation in Nigeria while Part IV gives the historical perspective of physical development and urbanization. Part V then highlights relevant legislation on the subject. In part IV issues relevant to physical development, urbanization and the federal system of government with regards to law is examined with particular emphasis on Lagos State, the economic nerve center of Nigeria. In addition, we assess the adequacy of law and regulations and made necessary recommendations in Part VII.

Definition of Terms

While Tijani has provided a useable definition of urbanization in chapter one, we further elaborate on the term as it relates to our theme in this chapter. Urbanization refers to the process by which a population becomes concentrated in cities or "urban places." The process may be through an increase in the number of urban places or through an increase in the size of the population resident in each urban place. An urban place is generally described in demographic terms - on the basis of the minimum number of inhabitants. To urbanize therefore means to alter, modify, make a change or cause a transformation to an urban place.[3]

Development in the sense of this paper will be construed in the narrower aspect of physical planning[4]. According to the Nigerian Urban and Regional Planning Act,[5] development is defined as:

> the carrying out of any building, engineering, mining or other operations in, on, over or under any land, or the making of any environmental significant change in the use of any kind or demolition of building of free standing erections used for the display of advertisements on the land and the expression 'development' with its grammatical variations shall be construed accordingly.

From the above definitions it is apparent that land is indeed basic to how physical development activities are organized in any society. The land tenure system and associated legislation set out the rights, obligations and methods of administration with regard to acquisition, exploitation, and use of specific portions of land. Past and existing patterns of development in Nigeria are a function of the laws that regulate land use and land control in the society. Land use process must be able to deal with new necessities like the emergence of vast industrialization process, population growth and urban concentrations. Indeed, modern usage of development leans towards sustainable development, which implies development that meets the needs and aspirations of the current generation without compromising the ability to meet those of the future generations.[6] Under the Nigerian legal process a number of laws are relevant to the process of urbanization in Nigeria; however, the extent of the efficacy of the existing framework is to be ascertained.

Existing Urban Situation

Rapid urban growth concomitant with continued poverty and economic stagnation is a major problem in developing countries, Nigeria inclusive. The population of some cities is increasingly beyond the capacity of the society to cope with the human influx. The political forces and elite continue to funnel resources towards cities to the neglect of the impoverished rural areas. The depletion on the quality of life in the rural areas leads to the congestion of the urban centers thereby making them socially unhealthy. The poverty stricken condition of our rural areas is an elective mechanism, which motivates urban migration. The urban centers are mainly incapable of absorbing the rural migrants who are usually lacking in any essential training to make them employable.[7] Accordingly, the inevitable consequences of these vicious circles are universal poverty, housing shortage, urban slum, environmental squalor and a host of other environmental and human problems.[8]

Suffice it to say that informal settlements outnumber legally planned developments and are increasing more rapidly. Demand for land, services and housing as a result of high rates of urbanization overwhelm urban authorities.   The situation is not made better by the fact that planning and building standards, regulations and procedures are based on European norms rather than local circumstances. Attempts at a Victorian model of physical urban development in Nigeria, as in other non-English areas under the British, did not help matter. Rather, it creates other problems such as maintenance, life span, and suitability to the environment.

The Nigerian legal system derives its sources from customary law, received English laws and local statutes.[9] The tenure system reflects this pluralistic nature of the legal system. In the South, the growth of traditional societies into urban centers did not abolish the pre-existing customary land tenure, characterized by individual, family and communal land holding.[10] This exists alongside the introduced English forms of estates and interest such as the fee tail and fee simple. In the North, following the English conquest and colonial administration, the land had been reduced into public ownership and subsequently declared to be "native land" under the Land Tenure Law 1962.[11] The individual interest in the "native land was designated as rights of occupancy which was either statutory or customary.[12] The Land Use Act has extended the main principles of the Land Tenure Law to the rest of the country. The Act provides the basic tenural design for urban land throughout the country with the land in public ownership under the relevant state land law. It is thus necessary to examine the antecedence of land use and control in order to put the paper in proper perspective.

Historical Perspective

Fabiyi, Olaniyi, Olubomehin, and Tijani discuss detailed historical narratives about pre-colonial transformations in the preceding chapters. This section focuses on modern historical antecedents buttressing our focus in this chapter. We emphasize pre-colonial land use patterns, with its varieties from one locality to another, and how the colonial administration used it as foundation for continuous urban transformation. The customary and the Islamic or Moslem land law systems operated in Nigeria. On the other hand, corporate land ownership seems to be the norm in the southern parts. According to Lord Haldane in "Amodu Tijani v. The Secretary, Southern Nigeria,"[13] the head or the chief of the community has the concurrent power to control the use of land and may make allocations or grants to needing members of the group or strangers. Where a particular parcel of land belonged to an individual, its use would usually respond to the general land use pattern of the location concerned. The individual land use was thus influenced by corporate land use practices. In the North, the traditional approaches in the Moslem settlement were modified by the principles of Moslem land law under which land was regarded as a gift of God. The Emir merely held land in trust for the purpose of its allocation for private emirate uses.[14]

The cession of Lagos in 1861 brought about British role in the transformation of what later became Nigeria in 1914.[15] The British Crown acquired limited rights of administrative interference over land, first over the Colony of Lagos and later extended hinterland to cover all territories comprised in the Southern Protectorate.[16] In the Northern Protectorate, the colonial administration had obtained the control of the land from the Fulani's under the Proclamation of 1900, culminating in the Proclamation Acts of 1910 and 1916. British suzerainty over the territory comprising modern Nigeria became com_____ _ith the 1914 amalgamation of Lagos colony with the Northern and South____ ___tectorate. The colonial administration embarked on systematic control of la__d use by series of statutory measures on adhoc basis having established political and administrative control over the land.[17]

The British policy on urban planning and development was contained in the Township Act 1917. The Act empowered the Governor General to declare and administer any place or area as first, second or third class Township.[18] Pursuant to this provision, the Lagos colony was declared as First Class Township. According to Mabogunje,[19] the selection and classification of townships did not depend on the size of the population or the traditional importance of these towns; rather it was based on the level of the presence of colonial activities of one form or the other in the area. The local authority was established to undertake urban administration and empowered to make and administer by by-law, matters relating to conservancy, sanitation and building regulations in the designated townships throughout the country.

The British adopted an urban policy of segregation and separation in Nigeria. The Governor-General is empowered to zone each of the townships into "European", "Non-European" Reservations and open spaces for the urban physical development.[20] Mixed racial residences were rendered unlawful in a reservation area under the Act.[21]

The Lagos Town Planning Act, 1924 was enacted to deal with the problem of overpopulation related epidemic leading to a threat to public health as colonial socio-economic activities in the colony had intensified, transforming Lagos into a modern city. The segregation policy resulted in the virtual non-existence of infrastructural support in the settlements occupied by natives, urban development activities having been restricted to European Reservation areas.

In 1946, the Nigeria Town and Country Planning Act, was enacted, fashioned after the English Town and Country Planning Act, 1932. The law had a nation wide application. The title of the Act is misleading. It gives the impression that the Act is a unified federal code covering all aspects of land usage within the federation of Nigeria, and covering the utilization of land by local Town Planning Authorities. However, the provision of the Act do not seek to regulate and control the use of land, but rather they spell out the type of interest obtainable in land, the mode of acquisition and the quantum of rights exercisable therein.

By virtue of section 4 of the Act, the governor-general was empowered to appoint a Planning Authority in any part of the country that in his opinion required a scheme. An example of such planning authority was the Lagos Executive Development Board made up of the chairman and members appointed by the governor-general.[22] The authority was the executive organ for the planning and carrying out of any scheme on the area to which it was applied. The Lagos Central Town Planning Scheme (Approved) Order-in-Council 1952 attempted to apply the 1946 Act but failed woefully.[w]

Although town planning had been conceived as a central matter at the initial stage, with the adoption of the federal constitution in 1954, it became regionalized. The emergent regions thereafter reenacted the 1946 Act as their respective regional law. The Lagos Planning (Miscellaneous Provisions) Act 1967 introduced the medium of 'master plan' as a means of securing the orderly development of the Lagos metropolis.[24] The Act was hardly implemented presumably due partly to the on-going civil war in the then Eastern states, and the constitution of the Metropolis as part of Lagos State. The problem of land use became intensified by the paradoxes of urban prosperity while indiscriminate land development characterized the development of Lagos Metropolis.

In 1972, Lagos State enacted the Town and Country Planning law, which repealed the 1967 Act though retaining the concept of "Master plan" as an instrument of physical planning throughout the state. Again, the 1972 law was found to be a less responsive and inadequate for dealing with the problem of urban sprawl and uncontrolled development. The Town and Country Planning Edict, 1985 was enacted and it maintained the Master Plan concept[25].

The slow pace of project implementation made the resultant physical development unsatisfactory. The Second National Development Plan 1970-74 identified the difficulties of land acquisition as one of the main causes of poor performance in town and country planning sector. In dealing with these problems, the Federal Government enacted the Land Use Act, 1978.[26]

The Act does not provide for direct land use planning and control.[27] According to its preamble, the intendment of the Act is to assure and preserve the rights of all Nigerians to use and enjoy land in Nigeria and natural fruits thereof in sufficient quantity to sustain themselves and their family. The Federal Government to control planning in Nigeria thereafter enacted the Nigerian Urban and Regional Planning Decree.

Laws Relevant to Urbanization and Development

As earlier noted a combination of legislation affects land use and control in Nigeria, setting out the background for physical planning and development. The relevant provisions in some of such laws will be considered. A veritable starting point for any discussion on legislation in Nigeria is the Constitution.

The Nigerian Constitution[28]

The Fundamental Objectives and Directive Principles of State Policy of the government of Nigeria contained in the Constitution include political objectives, economic objectives and social objectives, among other objectives. All these objectives are geared toward the primary purpose of moving the nation forward in terms of development.[29] The Constitutional ideals contained therein are not justifiable,[30] but are required to guide the actions of all persons and authorities in Nigeria.

The inclusion of the Land Use Act in section 315(5) (d) of the Constitution elicits controversies as to the status of the Act.[31]

The Section provides that "Nothing in this Constitution shall invalidate the following enactment, That is to say-the Land Use Act, and the provision of those enactment shall continue to apply and have full effect in accordance with their tenor and to the like extent as any other provision forming part of this Constitution and shall not be altered or repealed except in accordance with the provision of 9(2) of this Constitution".

The most acceptable interpretation by the Court appear to be that the Land Use Act is a Federal Act made extra ordinary by virtue of its enactment in the Constitution, but this does not make it an integral part of the Constitution. Moreover, by virtue of Section 4 of the Constitution, legislative power is vested in the Federal and State legislatures. The National Assembly has power to make laws in respect of matters in the Exclusive and the Concurrent legislative lists while the State House of Assembly can make laws on the Concurrent Legislative list as well as exercising residual power outside these lists. The effects of these constitutional provisions will be examined in relation to other laws subsequently.

The Land Use Act

The Land tenure system, particularly in the southern states of Nigeria, prior to 1978 undermined the effective control of land use by the government in the public interest. Due to the rapid rate of urbanization in the country and the increasing demand for the use of land both in cities and rural areas for physical development and necessary infrastructures, land was highly valued and a scarce commodity to the government for development projects and for the private sector. Though existing legislation provide for the government to acquire land compulsorily for public purposes, it became very difficult if not impossible for government to do this at reasonable cost. This problem was very pronounced in Lagos, then Federal Capital, as families and individuals held tight to land and landed properties.[32]

The Land Use Act was enacted by the Federal Military Government to address the problems of scarcity of land in the cities per se rather than for the purpose of ensuring orderly development and harmonious use of land. Section 1 of the Land Use Act vests all lands in each state of the Federation in the Governor of that State, to be held in trust and administered for the use and common benefit of all Nigerians. This provision has been the subject of interpretation by the Court.[33] The Supreme Court in Madam Salami v. Oke[34] held that "absolute ownership of land is no longer possible.[35] The Court also held that the Land Use Act has removed radical title from individual Nigerians and has vested the control and management of the land in urban areas in each State on the Military Governor.[36] The Governor creates a "bare trust"[37] in the sense of alluvial rights over land.

Section 2(1) (a) vest the control and management of all urban areas on the Governor of each State and section 2 (2) establishes for each State the Land Use and Allocation Committee as an advisory body to the Governor. Land is categorized into urban and rural areas for the purpose of development control and management. The purport of section 3 of the Act is to give the Governor an unquestionable power to designate by order published in the State Gazette parts of non- urban areas of the State to constitute an urban area, and thereby enlarge the extent of urban area. Pursuant to this provision, Lagos State has, for instance, declared almost every part of the State as urban area by virtue of the Designation of Urban Area Order, 1982.

The Governor is also empowered to grant statutory right of occupancy (i.e. Certificate of Occupancy (C of O) to any person (not under the age of twenty-one years) in respect of land, in urban area, for all purposes.[38] On the other hand, the local government may grant customary rights of occupancy for the use of land not in an urban area for agricultural, residential and other purposes for a definite term.[39] The Act vests all lands in the State in the Governor and not to the Local government, applying the maxim "nemo dat quod non habet," a local government does not have the power to grant customary right of occupancy.

JO Omotola[40] rightly states one of the objectives for which the Land Use Act was enacted is to enable the government to bring under control the use to which land can be put and thus facilitate planning and zoning programs for particular uses. The extent to which this objective has been met is not within the purview of this paper however; it is necessary to examine the Nigerian Urban and Regional Planning Act.

Nigerian Urban and Regional Planning Act[41]

The primary concern of planning is the control of the use of land and development through the instrumentality of legislation. The main objective of every landowner is 'development,' therefore to ensure the best utilization of land in the national interest; the planning laws and regulations ought to prevent individual landowners from using their land to the detriment of the body politic. Rather, control development should be for the benefit of people and the country at large.

The major legislation on planning in Nigeria is the Nigerian Urban and Regional Planning Act and the Regulations made there under. The Act was not aimed at ensuring orderly development, health and aesthetic environment and functionally effective urban and rural societies in Nigeria. Rather, it was intended to provide sufficient quantity of land for Nigerians to use for whatever purpose. It provides for the establishment of the Commission, Board or Authority responsible for physical planning at the federal, state and local Government levels respectively[42]. Each of which shall establish a Development Control Department charged with the responsibility for matters relating to development control and implementation of physical development plans.

The Act provides that the conditions for grant of development permit by a Control Department must conform to condition of issue of certificate of occupancy or a customary right of occupancy as provided by the Land Use Act.[43] It is provided further that the Control Department in approving or rejecting development permit as provided under section 34 of the LUA shall take into account matters of overriding public interest. The Act states further that, "condition for

compensation for revocation shall be only if the application had complied with
the requirement of the Act with respect to right of occupancy of the land on which
a development was to take place."[44] The successful implementation of the planning legislation in Nigeria depends on the workability of the Land Use Act. Thus,
the Act provides that all matters connected with the payment of compensation
for the revocation of right of occupancy under Part IV (Acquisition of Land and
Compensation) of the Act shall be governed in accordance with the relevant provisions of the Land Use Act.[45]

The Constitutionality of the Planning Decree has been questioned in view
of its inconsistency with section 4 of the 1999 Constitution. In the originating
summons filed by the Attorney General of Lagos State in Attorney General, Lagos
State v. A.G. Federation & Ors,[a] the plaintiff contended that urban and regional
planning as well as physical development is a residual matter within the exclusive
legislative and executive competence of the State. Thus, challenging the power of
the Federal Government over land in its territory. The Court was invited to declare
the Decree unconstitutional, null and void to the extent of its inconsistency with
section 4 of the 1999 Constitution.

Arguments were made both ways with decided cases to support each view.
The plaintiff relied on both A.G. Ogun State v. Aberuagba[47] and Attorney General,
Ondo State v. Attorney General of the Federation[48] to support the argument that
planning matter not being exclusively mentioned in the Exclusive and Concurrent
Lists, is a residual matter for which the state should legislate. The defendant
relied on the decision of the Supreme Court in Attorney-General of Ondo State
v. Attorney General of the Federation, argued that the National Assembly had
Incidental powers under item 60(a) and 68 of the second schedule, part 1 of the
1999 Constitution, and could therefore legislate on the matter in contention.

Attorney General, Lagos v. Attorney General of the Federation was decided
in favor on the plaintiff. The Court declared that the power to make Town
Planning Laws should be the exclusive preserve of the State House of Assembly.
This position has been found unacceptable considering the complementary nature
of planning control and environmental law. According to I. O. Smith,[49] "Land use
has a critical impact on the environment and sustainable development." He noted
further "planning is a veritable instrument for achieving a healthy environment
and sustainable development." Planning without environmental consideration
may result in environmental and human problems as exemplified by the existing
situation in Lagos. The link between planning has hitherto been recognized by
legislation such as the Environmental Impact Assessment Decree.[50]

The Environmental Impact Assessment (EIA) Decree

The International Community in Agenda 21 recognized the role and relevance
of physical planning as a tool for sustainable development.[51] Like feasibility
studies, E1A is a planning and management tool for officials and managers who
formulate policies and make important decisions about development projects.[52]
It is a formal study of the effects of a proposed development action on the envi-

ronment.[53] The primary aim is to ensure that the possible negative impacts of development projects are predicted and addressed prior to project take off.[54]

Industrialization, which is the primary vehicle for economic development, rapid population growth and rapid urban growth, has led to increase in environmental degradation. Recognizing the relevance of EIA to sustainable development, the Environmental Impact Assessment Decree was promulgated in 1992. The Decree made it mandatory for developers to apply the EIA for all major development projects. Section 2(1) of the Decree provides that:

> the public or private sector of the economy shall not undertake or embark or authorize projects or activities without prior consideration, at an early stage of their environmental effects.

The purpose of the Decree is to aid the process of decision making by planning authority and to advise the developer and public of the environmental consequence of the planned development activity. Furthermore, the schedule to the Decree lists 19 development activities for which EIA studies are mandatory in Nigeria while Section 62 prescribes a penalty of a fine for failure to comply with the provision of the Decree.

Federal Environmental Protection Agency (FEPA) Decree

The FEPA Decree is vested with statutory responsibility for overall protection of the environment. It establishes the Federal Environmental Protection Agency (FEPA) to serve as the basic institutional machinery for environmental management in Nigeria while also providing a legal foundation essential for the realization of the National Policy on the Environment. Part 1 of the Decree establishes the Federal Environmental Protection Agency, its function and powers. FEPA is at the core of the Federal Government's determination to stem the tide of increased environmental degradation in the country. Part II provides for the setting of national standards applicable to the respective environmental media, viz.: water, land, air, noise and hazardous substance. Of relevance to urbanization and development are sections relating to land. Section 20(1) of the FEPA Decree prohibits the discharge of harmful substances upon the nation's land.

The EIA Decree empowers the Federal Environmental Protection Agency (FEPA) to facilitate and supervise the EIA projects. The FEPA Act serves as a consolidating legislation to the extent that it covers sectors whose laws were to be found in scattered enactment.[55] The review of the above laws makes no claim to being exhaustive. Many other laws have some relevance to the subject matter. These include statutory provisions found in the Petroleum Act,[56] the Harmful Waste Act,[57] the National Housing Fund[58] and the Federal Mortgage Act.[59] However, despite this and other laws, conflicts still arise between some states and the federal government over the power to regulate the environment, physical development, urbanization and enforcement of relevant laws. Attention will be focused on Lagos State because of its peculiarity.

Federalism, Urbanization and Development – The Lagos Example

Lagos State stands out in terms of urbanization in view of its former status as capital of Nigeria and having remained the commercial nerve center of Nigeria. Rural - urban migration to Lagos and its environs still continues in spite of the movement of the nation's capital to the Federal Capital Territory, Abuja. Lagos State continues to expand absorbing most of its sub-urban areas while the unabated development within the city center put it's at the level of the world's great cities of New York, Paris, Tokyo, London, etc.[60]

Due to rapid urbanization and population growth in Lagos, severe pressure is placed on existing infrastructures and services such as housing, roads, portable water, electricity, telecommunication, solid and water waste among others. Commenting on the problems of Lagos and the need for the relocation of Nigeria's capital, the late General Murtala Mohammed stated that;

> you are no doubt aware of the many problems that have arisen from the city of Lagos serving as the dual capital of both the Federal Government and the Lagos State Government. Some of these problems have proved intractable and there have been persistent suggestions that, as Lagos seem unable to accommodate both Governments, either the Lagos State government or for Federal Government should move its capital elsewhere.[61] The nation's capital was then relocated to the Federal Capital Territory, Abuja. The problems of urbanization in Lagos have however remained and have been exacerbated by the conflict arising between the State and the Federal government over planning control.

The Nigerian Urban and Regional Planning Act existed along side with the Lagos State Laws on planning prior to 2003.[62] The operation of federalism in Nigeria has often led to conflicts within the polity. Nwabueze defines Federalism as:

> an arrangement whereby the power of government within a country are shared between a national, countrywide government and a number of regional (i.e. territorially localized) governments in such way that each exist as a government separately and independently from the others operating directly on persons and property within its territorial area, with a will of its own its apparatus for the conduct of its affairs, and with an authority in some matters exclusive of all the others.[63]

The Constitution of the Federal Republic of Nigeria determines the extent of legislative power exercisable by the component parts of the Federation.[64] Conflicts as to the extent of these powers exercisable appear as a reoccurring decimal.[65] In relation to physical development, the recent Supreme Court decision in Attorney Government of Lagos State v. Attorney General of the Federation and 35 others[66] reflect the problem inherent in Nigerian Federation.

Commenting on hypothetical ways of resolving the case prior to its determination, Amokaye, proposed three hypotheses.[67] The simple approach applied in Attorney General, Ogun State v. Aberuagba[68] whereby the Court may rule that planning matter not being listed in the Constitution is a residual matter for which the state could legislate. The second hypothesis by which the Court may apply the principle of covering the field enunciated and applied in Attorney General Ogun State v. Attorney General Federation.[69] The Court ruled that since the Federal Government has evidenced an intention to cover subject area, state laws, which are inconsistent with such law, are null and void in accordance with section 4(5) of the 1999 Constitution.

The final approach is the holistic and purposive approach applied in Attorney General Ondo v Attorney General of the Federation.[70] Here, examining the provisions of section 4, item 60 of the Exclusive Legislative list vis-à-vis the Fundamental Principles and Directive Policy of the State expands the legislative competence of the National Assembly. Suffice it to say that this invalidated the Federal Law. The Supreme Court by a majority of 4 to 3 applied the first hypothetical approach and held that Urban and Regional Planning is a residual matter in respect of which only the State House of Assembly can legislate.

This decision has not resolved the friction between the State and Federal authorities on the legislative powers. In this particular case, the Nigerian Urban and Regional Planning Decree which sought to cure the underlying mischief of lopsided and inconsistency in physical development was struck down. Indeed the decree was an attempt to lie the "floor standard" the framework of which state government can build.[71]

Adequacy of the Law and Recommendations

The Land Use Act is characterized by deficiencies in several respects. The power of the Military Governor to grant a statutory right of occupancy has not been exercised to give equal access to all urban dwellers.[72] The operation of the consent provisions has neither enhanced security of title nor facilitated the conveyance process of right of occupancy; rather they have been operated to increase insecurity of tenure and made the conveyance processing more expensive and difficult.[73]

The mechanisms of judicial resolution of land dispute that are contained in Sections 39 and 41 of the Act have not aided the speedy and cheap settlement of disputes over land. The power of revocation has also been abusively exercised so as to engender insecurity of title to land.[74] The centralization of grant of land in the Governor has made urban land less affordable. The denial of title to land to local government within the urban centers by the Act is regarded as objectionable.[75] The history of the statutory land use control process has not been effective in integrating the urban poor into urban socio-economic opportunity. Rather in most cases, it has been used to dispossess the class of their homes and land.

The shortcomings of the Land Use Act not withstanding, its relevance to land use and control cannot be overemphasized. The case is being made, not for the repeal of the Act, but for amendment for improvement taking cognizance of the inadequacies. The planning powers of the federal and state governments are nowhere expressly enumerated. Both tiers of government continue to exercise their respective powers in conflict with each other. Due to deficiencies in the existing tenure and planning framework for urban land management, the needs of urban residents in the provision for employment facilities and basic services such as decent housing, portable water supply, uninterrupted electricity supply, good road network, transportation, communication, etc have not been met. Land redistribution to vital economic and social sectors where urban land is most needed has been impossible.

The fact that land has remained unaffordable to majority of Nigerians contributes to the problem of slums and shanties. Provision of land to the less privilege members of the society should be seen as a social service and not a revenue generating enterprise for the government. The three tiers of government must be involved in the land use and control process of urban land, with an agency for coordinating these activities.

Improper enforcement of laws as well as the inadequacy of the existing legal framework and lack of a comprehensive legislation on urbanization to take care of the whole country has contributed to the present urban crisis in our country. The ineffectiveness of the law is compounded by the apparent confusion arising from the federal system of government. The individualistic application of relevant laws exclusive of each other makes coordination of urbanization and related matters difficult. A holistic application of these the goal, different governmental agencies involved in these issues must work together for better results. With due respect, the judicial interpretation of the position of the Planning law have failed in laying to rest the existing confusion as to who has planning power, Attorney General Lagos v. Attorney General of the Federation has to be revisited.

Conclusion

The legal framework for urbanization and development in Nigeria reveals a cacophony of statutes that are disjointed but related. Suffice it to say that the blind acquaintance to English legal system in land tenure and planning need to be changed. The position stated by Mabogunje,[76] that the urban crisis of underdevelopment is not so much unemployment, poor housing and social delinquency but how to integrate the indigenous solution to these problems within, an overall strategy of development still rings true. The need to harmonize the different laws cannot be over emphasized for proper and even development and urbanization to take place. The Constitution of the Federal Republic of Nigeria enumerates lofty ideals, goals and objectives. For the realization of these ideals, there must be commitment on the part of the government, planning authorities and every citizen to achieve the goals. The Court in favor of the development of the country must review the subsisting problem of legislative power in matters of urban planning. A consistent and integrated physical planning with the supervision of the Federal Government is necessary for uniformity in urban development and sustainability.

Notes and References

1. See section 4 of the Constitution of the Federal Republic of Nigeria 1999.
2. Lagos is the former capital of Nigeria and has remained it commercial nerve center. The cities over the years have continued to experience influx of large number of people from other cities and the rural areas. See, HI Tijani, "A history of Lagos State", in Odumosu, T. (ed.) *Lagos State in Maps* (Rex Charles Publication: Ibadan, 1999), p. 7-9.
3. See www.thefreedictionary.com/urbanise. Visited on 29/6/2004.
4. The dictionary meaning of development is "growth; land or property that has been improved". See English Dictionary, Geddes & Grosset, 2000, p. 91
5. See section 91 of No.88 of 1992, (Hereinafter Planning Act). This definition is similar to Section 3 of the Federal Housing Authority Act; See also Section 96 of the Lagos State Urban and Regional Planning Board Law Cap L.52 vol.14 Laws of Lagos State of Nigeria 2003.
6. Global Biodiversity Strategy, 1992, p 230.
7. Adigun, O. *The Problem of Housing in Nigeria* in Obilade A. O., (ed.) A Blueprint for Nigerian Law (Faculty of Law, University of Lagos 1995) p.155
8. Onibokun, P. (ed.), *Housing in Nigeria* (A Book of Reading) (Nigerian Institute of Social and Economic Research (NISER, Ibadan, 1985) p. 8.
9. Park A.E. *Sources of Nigerian Law* (Lagos African Universities Press, 1963); Obilade A. O. *The Nigerian Legal System,* (London, Sweet & Maxwell 1972).
10. See *Amodu Tijani v. The Secretary of Southern Nigeria* (1921) A.C 399.
11. See section 4 of the Law.
12. See sections 6 and 7 *ibid.*
13. Ibid.
14. Ibid.,
15. Lagos became a British colony with the signing of the treaty in 1861.
16. See, for instance, Town Improvement Act (1863); Swamp Improvement Act; 1877, Criminal Code Act 1916; Public Health Act, 1917.See, A Olukoju, "Nigerian Cities in Historical perspective;" HI Tijani, "The New Lagos Town Council and Urban Administration, 1950-1953," T Falola & S Salm (eds.) Nigerian Cities (Trenton: Africa World Press, 2003), pp 8-46; 255-269 respectively.
17. See, the Preamble, Township Order-in-Council No.8 of 1923.
18. See section 3 of the Act.
19. Mabogunje, A.L,. *Urbanization in Nigeria* (London, 1968), p.12.
20. Olukoju, "Nigerian Cities in Historical Perspective", p 29-31
21. See section 66 of the Act.
22. See section 4(2).
23. HI Tijani, "The New Lagos Town Council and Urban Administration", p 260-267.
24. See section 1 of the 1967 Act.
25. In response to the Nigerian Urban and Regional Planning Decree 88 of 1992, Lagos State Urban and Regional Planning Board Edict 1997 was enacted.
26. See Decree No.6 of 1978 (now Act) (Hereinafter 'LUA').

27. See, Utuama A. A., *Nigerian Law of Real Property: An Introduction*, (Shaneson C.I Ltd, 1989) p.118.

28. See Constitution of the Federal Republic of Nigeria (Promulgation) Decree No.24 of 1999.

29. See Sections14,15,16 and 20 of the Constitution.

30. See Section 6 (6) (c) of the Constitution.

31. The Section was first inserted in Section 274(5) of the 1979 Constitution. In *Aina and Company Ltd v Commissioner of Lands and Housing Oyo State of Nigeria* [1983] 4NCLR 571, the Court held that the Land Use Act is part and parcel of the Constitution while other decided cases such as *Chief Nkwocha v Governor of Anambra State* [1983] 4 NCLR 719; and *Alhaji Adisa v Oyinwola* [2000] 10 NWLR (Pt 614) 114 hold that the Land Use Act is itself an existing law with its validity and its continued existence assured by the Constitution, but it is not an integral part of the Constitution.

32. This was stressed in the National Development Plan, Federal Republic of Nigeria 1970 – 74, 1975 – 1980 (Lagos, 1975)

33. See Part 1, second schedule and Part II second schedule to the Constitution 1999.

34. [1987] 4 NWLR (Pt 63) p 7.

35. Ibid.

36. The Supreme Court in *Abioye v Yakubu* [1991] 5 NW:LR (Pt190) at 130; See Section 3 of the LUA

37. *Nnadi v Okoro* [1998] 1 NWLR (Pt 535) 573.

38. Section 5(a) of the LUA.

39. See section 6(1) *ibid*

40. Omotola J. O., *Essays on the Nigerian Land Use Act, 1978* (Faculty of Law publication, University of Lagos, 1980).

41. Decree No.88 of 1992. Now Act (Hereinafter "Planning Act"). This is a Federal legislation now adopted in some states. See for example Lagos State Urban and Regional Planning Board Law Cap L.52, Vol.4, Law of Lagos State of Nigeria, 2003.

42. See section 5(a), (b) and (c) of the Planning Act.

43. See section 36 of the LUA.

44. See section 43(2) (a) and (b) of the Planning Act.

45. See Section 76(1), *ibid.,*

46. [2003] 12 NWLR (pt 833) supra.

47. [1985] 1 NWLR (pt. 3) 395.

48. [2002] 9 NWLR (pt 772) 222 at 308

49. Smith I.O., *Power to make Town Planning Laws in a Federation: The Nigerian Experience*, J.P.P.L vol. 24 January 2004 p.24; See also Amokaye.O.G., *The Struggle for Legislative Supremacy by the Federal and State Governments over Physical Planning Matters: The need for Judicial Caution* JPPL vol. 23, July 2003, p 66

50. Decree No 86 of 1992 (Now Act)

51. The United Nations General Assembly by its resolution 44/228 of 22 December 1989 decided to hold the United Nations Conference on Environment and Development in June 1992 in Riode Janeira, Brazil. The Conference was an international forum where strategies to fully integrate relationship between the environment and development into every aspect of economic life was agreed upon. One of the significant develop-

ments that occurred at the conference was the Agenda 21 whereby program of work was agreed on by the international community to address major environment and development priorities for the initial period of 1993 2000 and leading into the 21st century was adopted.

52. Ivbijaro, M.I. *Environmental Impact Assessment/Environmental Audit Report in Nigeria: An Overview* in Ajomo M. A.& Adewale O. (eds.) *Law and Sustainable Development in Nigeria* (NIALS, Lagos & The British Council 1994) p.150.

53. *ibid.*

54. *ibid.*

55. Adewale O. *"An Examination of Federal Environmental Laws in Nigeria"*, in Ajomo M.A. & Adewale O. *Law and Sustainable Development in Nigeria.*

56. Cap. 350 LFN 1990.

57. Cap. 165 LFN 1990.

58. Decree No. 3 of 1992.

59. Cap 138 LFN 1990.

60. Ojo T. I. *Management of Domestic Wastewater: Focus on Lagos Metropolis* in Ajomo M. A. & Adewale O.

61. See Federal Ministry of Information, A Time for Action – A collection of speeches of late Government Murtala Mohammed p.10

62. This is the Town and Country Planning Law Cap 188, Laws of Lagos State 1994 that was repealed by the Lagos State Urban and Regional Planning Law Cap L.52, vol.4 Laws of Lagos State of Nigeria 2003.

63. Nwabueze B. O., *Federalism in Nigeria under the Presidential Constitution* (Sweet & Maxwell London) 1983 p.170.

64. See the *Constitution of the Federation Republic of Nigeria*, 1999.

65. See *AG Ogun State v. AG Federation* [1982] 1 – 2 SC 13, *AG. Ogun State v. Aberuaga* (1985) 1 NWLR (pt 3) 395. *AG Abia State v. AG Federation* [2003] 4 NWLR (pt 8090 124 at 179, 202.

66. See [2002] 12 NWLR (pt 833). See also supra p.14.

67. Amokaye, *The Struggle for Legislative Supremacy*, p 66.

68. The issue was the determination of the Rights to charge tax on goods.

69. This was the sharing of Federal Revenue case.

70. The case on the regulation of corrupt practices (i.e. the ICPC Act)

71. Amokaye, *The Struggle for Legislative Supremacy*, p 66.

72. See Omotola, J. A. *Law and Land Rights: Whither Nigeria*, in Utuama, A.A. *An Evaluation of Tenural System*, p. 219

73. See *Savannah Bank of Nigeria Ltd v. Ajilo* (1989) I NWLR (pt. 97) 305 at 324.

74. *Nwocha v. Governor of Anambra State* (1984) 6 SC 362.

75. Utuama, p.220.

76. Mabogunje, A.L., *The Development Process: A Spatial Perspective.* (London, 1980).

12

Industries as Catalyst of Urban Development: A Microanalysis

Hakeem I. Tijani

Introduction

This chapter suggests that sustained industrial estates in a central place are important in understanding development and urbanization in both developed and developing economies. The creation of industrial estates did not only create more jobs and spurred population increase, but affects cosmopolitan nature of the area.[1] An exposition of industrial development with its resultant effect of population increase, among others, would elucidate our understanding of urban politics[2] and development in contemporary Nigeria. We have chosen Mushin as the micro litmus test for our proposition partly because of its central proximity to Lagos (the cockpit of development in Nigeria).[3] Mushin is a suburb of Lagos metropolis, which fits into the "central place theory." The theory posits that, "below an urban centre are regions which depend on it for specialized goods and services."[4]

Urbanization and Development

Between 1950 and 1966 the population growth of Lagos increased from 3.4% to 18.6%.[5] This was partly due to the development of Lagos with the clearing of the slums, ii, harbors, building of ports and increased commercial activities that provide job opportunities for the people. Urban development during this period has been described as unprecedented. In fact, government sponsored separate researches were conducted towards solving the problem of urban centers such as Lagos metropolis.[6] The acute has been aptly described thus: problem of Lagos metropolis by Akin Mabogunje the rapid industrial development which took place in Lagos after 1950 resulted not only in an unprecedented rate of growth, but also in the spectacular spatial expansion of continuous built-up area beyond the legal confines of the municipality.[7]

Thus, on assumption of office, the then Military Governor of the newly created Lagos State, Colonel Mobolaji Johnson,[8] found it expedient to find solutions to the urban problems of Lagos Island as well as develop the mostly rural parts of the state.[9] With the pronouncement of the Lagos State Industrial Policy, followed by an articulated rural development program, the State was launched on the path to development and industrialization.[10]

The official objectives of the Industrial policy were:

(i)   A business climate that attracts promotes and sustains private sector invest-
      ment in the State, especially in the preferred sectors as determined from time
      to time by Government.
(ii) Integrated rural development and the balanced economic growth and devel-
      opment of the State.
(iii) The sustenance of the State's premier position as the centre of industrial and
      commercial activities in the country.[11]

Towards the realization of these goals, the various governments (Military and Civilian) embarked on the review of existing legal and administrative practices and procedures that might hitherto have hindered private sectoral investments in the various Local Government Areas within the State.[12] The State Government excelled in the area of Land Policy and Industrial Estates. Hence, in order to curtail the continuous drift of people to Lagos metropolis for job opportunities, certain portions of Mushin area, such as Isolo, Ilasamaja and Matori were ear-marked as commercial and industrial centers. The Government provided encour-agement in these areas by deliberately charging Ground Rents well below that of Lagos metropolis.[13]

In fact, the Decree No. 22 of 1971 which amended the provisions of the 1958 Income Tax Relief Act, encouraged private pioneer industries to set up industries beyond - Lagos. It would seem plausible that the geographical location of Mushin favored it, as three distinct industrial estates were sited there. Moreso, the 'Tax Relief for Investments in Economically Disadvantaged Local Government Areas' made Mushin most favorably disposed in view of its geographical contiguity to Lagos metropolis. The policy formulation stated that entrepreneurs who invest in economically disadvantaged Local Government Areas are entitled to 'special income tax and other concessions'.[14] These include:

(a)   Seven years income tax concessions under the pioneer status scheme;
(b)   Special concessions by relevant State Governments;
(c)   Additional 5% over and above the initial capital depreciation allowance under
      Company Income Tax.[15]

In fact, Mushin was seen both by the colonial and post-independence Governments as one of the least industrially and economically developed Local Government Areas.[16] Suffice it to say that the development of such areas as industrial Estates, i.e. Isolo, Ilasamaja, Matori, Oshodi and Ilupeju are landmarks in the urban devel-opment of Mushin and the State as a whole. Despite its turbulent political culture in the late 1950s and early 1960s, Mushin was the second area to have industrial estate after Apapa in 1958;[17] Ikeja followed this in 1959. Table 12.1 below shows some of the industries established within Mushin Area.

Table 12.1. List of Some Industries within Mushin Area

S/No.	Companies	Locations
1.	Berec Batteries	Mile 2/Oshodi Expressway
2.	Aswani Textiles	Mile 2/Oshodi Expressway
3.	Five Stars Industries	Mile 2/Oshodi Expressway
4.	Sawyerr Bottling	Mile 2/Oshodi Expressway
5.	Bowak	Mile 2/Oshodi Expressway
6.	Henkel	Mile 2/Oshodi Expressway
7.	Daltex Tergal	Mile 2/Oshodi Expressway
8.	Swenig	Ladipo/Matori
9.	Super Ceramics	Lapido/Matori
10.	Daily Needs	Lapido/Matori
11.	Ducat	Lapido/Matori
12.	Firestone	Lapido/Matori
13.	Architecural Metal Products	Lapido/Matori
14.	Barklay Clothings	Lapido/Matori
15.	Cinsere Sewing Machines	Lapido/Matori
16.	Ambaco Industries	Lapido/Matori
17.	Johnson Wax Nig. Ltd.	Isolo
18.	Afro-Tech Services	Isolo
19.	Lanre Commercial Industry	Isolo
20.	Intra-Fisheries Nig. Ltd.	Isolo
21.	Vitalink Pharmaceutical	Isolo
22.	Bewac	Isolo
23.	Enpee Industries	Ilupeju
24.	Macmillan Publishers	Ilupeju
25.	Food Specialities Nig. Ltd.	Ilupeju

Source: Lagos State Ministry of Commerce and Industry, Ikeja, Lagos

Table 12.2. Industrial Estates in Lagos State

S/No.	Location	Year of Establishment	Size of Hectares
1.	Apapa	1957	100
2.	Matori[1*]	1958	120
3.	Ikeja	1959	180
4.	Ilupeju*	1962	110
5.	Ijora	1965	160
6.	Iganmu	1965	80
7.	Oshodi/Isolo*	1968	120
8.	Amuwo-Odofin	1969	200
9.	Ogba	1969	150
10.	Oregun	1981	100
11.	Agidingbi (CBD)	1969	97
12.	Gbagada	1958	50
13.	Ikorodu	1976	1582.27

14.	Surulere	1981	20
15.	Badiya	1958	15
16.	Oyadiran/Yaba	1970	20
17.	Ilasamaja*	1971	60
18.	Lagos South West	1972	317.04
19.	Kirikiri	1981	30
20.	Abesan/Ipaja	1981	100
21.	Akowonjo	1976	50

1.   Industrial estates in Mushin local government area.

The mathematical exposition of Table 12.2 above shows that Mushin was not doing badly amongst the big four industrial areas within the State. Total area for industrial estate as of 1981 stood at 3,661.31 hectares. Lagos South-west; Mushin; Ikeja; and Ikorodu areas had 317.04; 410; 527; and 1,582.27 hectares respectively. They thus have the following percentages: 8.66%; 11.20%; 14.39% and 41.74% respectively. Despite the fact that Ikorodu has the highest percentage, it cannot however compete with Ikeja and Mushin in term of visible industrial layouts. Mushin without mincing words is more developed and urbanized than Ikorodu. Notable features of these industrial estates are the provision of good access roads, electricity and water supply; telephone facilities, post offices and banks.[18]

In some instances, housing schemes, hospitals and recreational facilities are often provided to meet the needs of the workers and other populace. As part of its continuous efforts at industrial development, the State Government embarked on the extension of the Ilasamaja Industrial Estate, and concentrated small-scale industries at the Matori Estate.[19] The efforts of the Mudasiru administration 1984/85 are remarkable here. The Government posits that, "the building of industrial estates was designed to solve the teething problems of small scale industrialists with regard to factory accommodation and infrastructural facilities".[20] It was in realization of this policy statement that the Matori and Oyadiran/Yaba small-scale industrial estates were developed. The Matori small-scale industry is an extension of the old Matori Industrial Estate. It has, unlike its Oyadiran/Yaba counterpart, thirty-two units of various sizes and a large canteen to serve the food needs of the customers and sellers therein.

Perhaps, more important is the fact that it serves as the meeting point for most of the populace within Mushin and beyond. Interactions within these estates might not necessarily have been solely economic, but also political. This writer's experience during the fieldworks show that politics and public affairs were freely discussed, and opinions aired. It should be noted that continual urban growth in terms of sustained gross output by the various firms within the various Industrial Estates in Mushin Local Government Area, as well as, urban development in terms of sustained physical infrastructural facilities depends on maintenance. For the maximization of total costs there must be good roads for easy transportation of raw materials and finished goods to the markets.

Apart from the Oshodi Expressway, Ikorodu Expressway and Agege Motorway built by the Federal Government, such access roads as Isolo Road, Osolo Way, Itire Road and Ireakari/Okota Road, link the various industrial sites and housing units. The Osolo way on its part was constructed in 1986 as leverage to the old Isolo Road constructed in the late seventies. This, no doubt, has aided gradual transformation of Isolo and its environs. The Ireakari/Okota road was constructed at Isolo and Ireakari/Okota areas. Furthermore, access in 1985/86 to cater for the development of housing estates roads along Ilupeju Bye-pass, Fatai Atere Road Matori) and Oshodi have enhanced industrial development and growth.[21]

The place of the market place and market women has been well analyzed.[22] It should be noted however that markets were the most vulnerable centers of political turbulence during the 'Wild Wild West' episode in Mushin in the 1960s.[23] Apart from the Odi-Olowo, Ojuwoye and Awolowo markets, such markets as Majolate-Oshodi, Daleko modern market, and Oja-Oba at Itire, among others have emerged in recent times as important political centers for market women activities within Mushin. In fact, by 1987, about thirty-five markets were identified by the Mushin Local Government Council.[24] However, non-availability of records made further discussion on the maintenance culture difficult. Contemporary records show nonetheless, the Council's (Mushin's) effort at maintaining and refurbishing the industrial and other facilities in its urban area. Moreso, efforts are also being made to uplift such rural parts as Ejigbo and Ewu-Titun into the orbit of urban development.[25]

In 1981 for instance, a total sum of N26, 616.00 was spent on the construction of motor parks at Matori, Idi-Oro and Mushin.[26] On re-activation of roads, the Council spent N59,508.50.[27] Moreover, culverts and drainages were also constructed in the same year at a N75,883.32 on the various estates within the area. 29 cost of N370,340.00.[28] Records for 1981 financial year explicitly how that the Council spent the sum of N370,340.00.[29] Although the breakdown of how this was expended was not available, we could proffer that, there was, and still is, the urge for the maintenance of the facilities within the urban area.

In fact, the 1983 Financial Statement of the Council shows a considerable increase in amount spent on the maintenance of these facilities. The table below shows this clearly:

Table 12.3. Works Department Capital Projects 1983

Head	Details of Expenditure	Actual Amount (N)
C200	1 Construction of drains and Culverts	362,208.41
	2 Roads	383,519.00
C400	Construction of Motor Parks	100,712.40
	Construction of Markets	219,952.60
C200	11 Provision of Street Lights	8,649.16
	Total	N 1,075,141.57

Source: Mushin Local Government Financial Statement January 1, 1983 - December 31, 1983.

The efforts of the Local Government and the State Government might have been responsible for the World Bank assisted project on the provision of modern drainage system in recent times. These drainages on completion are expected to stop annual flooding situation in Mushin area. Moreso, it would serve as avenue for disposing liquid industrial bye-products in the industrial estates.[30] The Isolo mini-waterworks has 93.3% capacity usage was the construction of the Isolo mini-waterworks compared with the Agege mini-waterworks that has 61.3%.[31]

It is relevant to state here that sample interviews carried out during the field-work with workers in some of the industries, particularly those resident within Mushin Local Government Area, show that interactions with their colleagues in the factories, offices and canteens have changed their attitudes towards politics. Between 1979 and 1987, what obtained were urban politics and not communal politics of the 1950s and 1960s based on patron/client syndrome.[32] To some appreciable degree therefore, the cosmopolitan and urban nature of Mushin during the period under review, has changed the political attitudes of the people.[33] Another noticeable feature of this industrial upsurge was the development of housing units. The increase in population gave rise to the development of housing units at Ikate, Itire, Idi-Oro, Oshodi/Isolo, Ijeshatedo and Mushin. In fact, the population of Mushin was said to have been increasing by 13% annually during the 60s compared to Lagos, which has a rate of 5%.[34]

In recent times, Mushin's population is estimated at 1.46 million, which is presumed to be the highest of all the Local Government Areas in the State.[35] Consequently, by 1978, the total number of housing units developed by private individuals and the Lagos State Development and Planning Corporation (LSDPC) to meet the growing urban shelter needs in Mushin Area has increased to 58.7%.[36] Thus, the Isolo Low-Cost Housing Unit was completed in 1983 by the Jakande administration to meet the housing needs of Mushin Populace. One consequence of this phenomenal growth in Mushin's population is its heterogeneous composition, which led to gradual displacement of the Awori value system and the upsurge in crime and insecurity within the area.[37] It was in view of this that the Government constructed the Olosan, Alakara and Zone "D" Police Stations in Mushin area. In fact, there are other police stations/posts at Isolo, Ilupeju, Ejigbo and Oshodi, to maintain security and order in the area.[38]

Conclusion

In the final analysis, we could say that while the industrial development was planned to offset the problem of urban Lagos metropolis, the emergence of housing units is largely the reverse. Nonetheless, the development of industries has influenced the pattern of housing units in recent times. This partly explains why the early private housing units in Mushin, like most urban frontiers in Africa, lacked any aesthetic value. The cosmopolitan nature of the Mushin populace and the interactions between the component ethnic groups thesis here therefore is that industrialism transcends the patron/client dimension and is therefore relevant in understanding urban politics and development in contemporary Mushin.

Notes and References

1. Professor Sandra Barnes in *Patrons and Power* (Berkeley, 1986) affirmed that politics in Mushin was (is) based on patron/client syndrome. This however should be seen as a proposition that does not adequately explain the cosmopolitan politics of Mushin. While this could be true of the 1950s and 1960s, the emerging results from our field-work, shows that politics in Mushin has moved beyond that axis.

2. Tijani, H.I. "Urban Politics in a Yoruba Frontier - Mushin," in Falola, T. and Genova, A. (eds.) *The Yoruba in Transition: History, Values, and Modernity,* (Durham: Carolina Academic Press, 2005).

3. Such works include: Lineberry R.L. and Sharkansky I: *Urban Politics and Public Policy,* Harper and Row Publishers, New York, 1971. Bellush and Hausknecht (eds.) *Urban Renewal: People, Politics and Planning,* Garden City, New York, 1967. Martin Meyerson and Edward Banfield, *Politics, Planning and the Public Interest,* New York, 1955. Williams B.A. and Walsh A.H. *Urban Government for Metropolitan Lagos,* Praeger Publishers, New York, 1968. Mabogunje A. L. *Urbanization in Nigeria,* New York, 1968. Sada P.O. and Adefolalu A.A. "*Urbanization and Problems of Urban Development,*" in Aderibigbe A.A. (ed.) *Lagos: the Development of an African City,* Longman, 1975. And Aboyade O. *Issues in the Development of Tropical Africa,* Ibadan University Press, 1976.

4. See Ukwu, I. Ukwu, "*Urbanization and Socio-Economic Development*" in Adebayo A. and Rowland L. (eds.) *Management Problems of Rapid Urbanization in Nigeria,* Ife Press, 1973.

5. Ayo Omotayo, "Flooding as a Consequence of Urban Growth in Lagos Metropolis" in Kunle Lawal (edited), *Lagos Society in Transition: Aspects of Urbanization and Change,* Pumark Publishers, Lagos, 1994

6. These are: Jones, G.C., and Lucas, B.K. *Report of the Administration of the Lagos Town Council,* Lagos, 1963. Koenigsberger O. et al. *Metropolitan Lagos* (Prepared for the Government of Nigeria), New York, 1964. And, Williams, B.A. and Walsh, A.H. *Urban Government for Metropolitan Lagos,* New York, 1968.

7. Akin Mabogunje *Urbanization in Nigeria,* London, 1968. This remains the most authoritative research effort on urban growth and development in Nigeria up to the late 1960s.

8. General Yakubu Gowon created Lagos State in May 1967 along with seven other states. With this, the then Major Mobolaji Johnson as the Administrator of Lagos became the first Military Governor of the State.

9. These divisions are: Ikeja, Badagry, Epe, Ikorodu and Lagos Island. Within the divisions there were local administrative districts, notably, Mushin Local District was under Ikeja Division.

10. See, "Lagos State Directory of Manufacturing Companies," Ministry of Commerce and Industry, Lagos, 1989 for details.

11. Ibid, page 4.

12. See, Brigadier M.O. Johnson, "Budget Speech," Ministry of Information, Ikeja 1971; Also, Jakande, L.K. "The New Order Budget," 1979, Lagos.

13. See, "Lagos State Handbook," Ministry of Information, Ikeja, 1988.

14. For details see, Lagos State Ministry of Commerce and Industry Publication, 1989, page 16.

15. Ibid.

16. See, "Industrial Development (Income Tax) Act 1971, No. 22," Government Publications, Lagos.

17. Matori Industrial Estate was the first of such estates in Mushin Area built in 1958.

18. Mushin area is no exception. See Tijani, "Urban Politics" op. cit;

19. See, Lagos State Facts and Figures, No. 3, Ministry of Information, Lagos.

20. Ibid.

21. Lagos State Handbook, Ministry of Information, page 116. The total road length (km) has increased considerably as against 1963, 18.9 km.

22. See, Mba, N.E. *Nigerian Women Mobilized: Women's Political Activities in Southern Nigeria, 1900-1965*; Berkeley, 1982, particularly chapters 7 and 8.

23. See Barnes, *Patrons and Power.*

24. *"Handbook,"* op. cit. page 148; 172-173.

25. The activities of the DFFRI agency and other government agencies is discussed by Onoja in this book.

26. Mushin Local Government Annual Financial Statement January 1 to December 31, 1981, p 40.

27. Ibid.

28. Ibid.

29. Ibid.

30. "Facts and figures No. 6," Ministry of Information, Lagos.

31. "Handbook" op. cit; p 162f.

32. Tijani, "Urban Politics" for details.

33. Ibid.

34. Oluwa and Talabi "Tribunal of Inquiry into the Re-organization of Local Governments in Lagos State" (Minority Report, 1970).

35. "Facts and Figures" op. cit., Professor Barnes also provides an account of housing units in Mushin up to 1975, which her study covers.

36. See, "LSDPC 50Th YEAR ANNIVERSARY" Pamphlet, Lagos, 1987.

37. Efforts at getting police reports on these incidents over the years proved abortive, as the officers claimed they could not get past Records/Files. However, for brief exposition, see, Akintola-Arikawe J.O. "The Rise of Industrialism in Lagos State," in Adefuye et. al. (eds.) *History of the People of Lagos State*; Lantern Books, 1987.

38. Interview with Mrs. Kassim (30 June 1990) at 10A, Bamgbose Street, Off Alafia, Mushin. She is one of the first sets of women police recruited in 1955, but resigned in 1963.

13

Urbanism and Traditional Religion

Danoye Oguntola-Laguda

Introduction

The belief and practice of African traditional religion appears to be bleak in a world that has become highly secularized. In the main, the religion has witnessed a decline in the continent (in influence and practice) due to factors such as westernization, modernization, and the influx of foreign religious traditions, civilizations, science and technology, among others. As a corollary, the religion has some problems inherent in it. These include, pluralized forms (in its tenets, doctrines, traditions and ethics); secrecy (which has hampered its study), reliance on oral traditions (with it attendant problems of addition and subtraction of facts) and rigid rituals and worship pattern. Its study has witnessed numerous derogatory phrases that suggest that the religion not a living religion. These include, primitive, archaic, native is tribal, savage, pagan, and heathens, among others. However, in spite of these hindrances, African traditional religion has continued to survive among the people, even in the Diaspora. The question therefore is of what relevance will African religion be to a world, which has become highly secularized with the concept of globalization? Also, in what ways has urbanization affected its practice? In other words, will African traditional religion make any significant impact in a globalize and urbanize world?

This chapter attempt to answer these questions with the thesis that; African religion being a living religion (because, it is still being practice by living people) has serious impact for Africans and those who have been converted into it, in the world, that has been highly urbanized and globalize politically and economically. In this study, although reference shall be made to the whole of Africa, we would focus on the Yoruba who have been described as *"in all things religious."*[1] To articulate our thesis, this chapter will be divided into three parts: we shall examine African religion, its belief and practice vis-à-vis its spread. Globalization shall be briefly considered and we shall attempt to suggest and appraise the role African religion can play in the globalize world and conclusion will then be drawn.

African Religion: Belief and Practice

African religion is a form of religious tradition, which mirrors the socio-cultural as well as political orientations of Africans. These orientations, culminated in a belief system that is a product of the individual and collective experience of the divine and natural order. Therefore, it may be difficult for Africans to respond to these "*orders*" in the same way other cultures would have done. This will suggest that each religion must necessarily carry "*the* stamp of the characteristics, history and culture of people who practice it".[2] The scenario perhaps informed the submission of A. Abioye when he informs that:

> No human face is exactly the same with another. But it is like many others in having two eyes, a nose, two lips and two ears. In the same way, no two (groups) of people ever respond to God's presence in exactly the same way.[3]

Abioye's position suggests that African traditional religion like other religious traditions, are responses to the reality of the Numinous. The pattern and mode of response determines the system of belief as well as doctrines.

African religions are encapsulated in five major beliefs. These are, belief in the Supreme Being (the cause of all things including human beings), the Divinities (the lieutenants of the Supreme Being) the spirits (incorporeal being who are often conceived in diabolical terms, but whose benevolence is not in doubt) the ancestors (those who once lived as human, but has transited to spiritual existence after death) and to magic and medicine. Other beliefs in the religion are derived from these five major beliefs. These minor beliefs include, morality, judgment day, after life, social interactions, among others[4]. All these are better appreciated as a whole. This will explain the mystery inherent in the religion. However, perhaps due to ignorance, bias, or ego, some scholars[5] that engage in the study of the religion have concluded that it is not theism and even if it can pass for such description, it is polytheism. This may explain the submission of Emile Ludwig that:

> How, can untutored Africans conceive God? How can this be? Deity is a philosophical concept which savages are incapable of framing.[6]

A.B Ellis was reported to have claimed that the God known to the Africans was a "loaned and borrowed God from the missionaries".[7] P.A. Talbot, in trying to describe the beliefs of the people opined that it is all about anthropomorphism, polytheism, animism and ancestral worship.[8] Scholarship in African traditional religion has shown the contrary.[9] The general held opinion is that the continent has a rich culture that could have engendered a theistic belief system.

African traditional religion was the sole religion practiced in the continent before the advent of foreign religions. This religion, permeate all strata of their life and activities. In fact, nothing can be meaningful except given meaning and interpretation through the religion of the people. In Yorubaland, political authority and economic endeavors are always derived through the interaction with religious order. For example, the Oba (king) is the overall political authority in the land. He is assisted by chiefs (*Ijoye*) and heads of clans (*Baale*). All these political officers hold office in trust for Olodumare[10] and His divinities. Therefore, the *Oba* is praised as *Alase Ekeji Orisa* (the regents of the divinities). To disrespect any of these office holders is to ask for the anger and wrath of Olodumare and the Orisa. All economic activities are also subject to the approval or otherwise of Olodumare and the Orisa. This will explain why the Yoruba will always consult the Olodumare before making a choice of profession or even enter into a business deal. Some divinities (Orisa) are worshipped by the people because of their relevance to trade and commerce. For example, people in Aworiland,[11] will always worship Yemoja (the river, ocean, water divinity) to garner bountiful harvest in their fishing expedition. In Egbaland, the worship of Ogun (the iron and farming divinity) is prominent, because he is conceived as a hunter and farmer.

In socio-economic orientation, the Yoruba are noted for their reliance on Olodumare and the Orisa: Marriages are contracted with the blessing of spiritual agents, covenant relationships and social interactions are equally based on the sanction of these agents. This will show that the practice of traditional religion in Yorubaland is total. This is based on their belief in Olodumare and other functionaries as encapsulated in their belief system. In fact, Bolaji Idowu allude to this fact when he submits that "there is no atheist among the Yoruba".[12]

The belief and practice of African traditional religion has witnessed a decline in the continent. This is due in the main to the influx of foreign religions, especially Islam and Christianity. In Yorubaland, the introduction of Islam in the 18th century and Christianity in the 19th century affected the practice of traditional religion in Lagos.[13] These religions were introduced with the culture of their propagators, who not only convert people to the new traditions, but also instill in them new orientations, which are either Western or Arabian. The people were introduced to these cultures. Thus, leading to the abandonment of the religion of their ancestors. In Yorubaland, the turn of the 21st century has witnessed the resurgence of the belief and practice of traditional religion. This is often displayed in the syncretic tendencies observed among Yoruba Christians and Muslims, who now patronize traditional religious practitioners with the "cover of darkness". Where orthodox medicine has failed traditional medicine have come to the rescue. In Lagos for example, there are more than five hundred traditional herbal homes in the old Alimosho local government.[14] There are also renowned practitioners of traditional medicine. These include Akintunde Ayeni, Engineer Kunle Olowu, and Dr. Bamidele Ogaga among others. Their herbal formulas, which have now gained prominence, are exported to neighboring countries.[15] They claimed to have cure for Diabetes, Stroke, and Anemia weakness of sex organs, infertility, and typhoid fever, among others. In between 1997 and 2000, there was a claim by Dr. Abalaka that he can cure the dreaded Acquired Immune Deficiency Syndrome (AIDS)[16] through herbal formula. Apart from traditional medicine, there are people who are still committed to African religion. These people, though in small number, have re-organized the religion with some touch of modernity. This is obvious in the liturgy of *Ijo Orunmila Adulawo;* where, worship is pattern after that of Anglican

Church, with lesson drawn from Ifa corpus, (*odu ifa*) and sermon presented by the *Oluwo* (head of the church). They chant and sing lyrics in Yoruba language with all paraphernalia of Yoruba music.

African traditional religion has also been exported to Western countries as well as Asia. In fact, some Africans in Diaspora still hold steadfast to their belief in traditional religion. Ifayemi Elebuibon is reported to have established a School of Ifa Divination in Brazil and Cuba. In the United States of America, Santeria, which to this writer is a corruption of Yoruba belief system, is flourishing today, in Florida. The interest of foreigners in the traditions is growing steadily. In Osogbo, during the annual Osun Festival, many tourists of western background are seen in the Osun groove.[17] A school of divination of Ifa was established in Osogbo by Susan Wegner (Abeni Olorisa). When this writer visited the institution in 1999 and 2000, there are well over fifty students of different western countries (the prominent are Germans). On the whole, during the course of this study, we observed that many Yoruba people are not committed to the Yoruba traditional religion. However, their patronage cannot be denied nor ignored. Although, they may be accused of syncretism, but, the general belief among them is that *Olorun o ko ajo* (God is not against traditional care). Those who are nonchalant will submit that *Esin o pe ka wa ma soro* (religion, Christianity or Islam (in mind), is not against traditional religion). Based on the premises set above, it is obvious that Africans are still interested in the religion of their ancestor. In addition, non-Africans are equally interested in the religion. However, the shift in global attitude, from spiritualism to secularism has also taken its toll on the belief and practices of African traditional religion can we then suggest a future for the religion in the context of globalization?

Globalization and Religion

Globalization is a concept that suggests that growth and development of the universe vis-à-vis humanity should be global. This will point to the fact that human being must grow together with the removal or at least a reduction of political, economic and socio-cultural barriers to enhance worldwide interactions. The aim "is to develop humanity that will live to together in 'one world' and be more able physically, culturally and psychologically".[18] In the opinion of Julius Kiiza, globalization is "international economic and social intercourse".[19] The objectives of globalization as implied in its definitions, are to increase sense. That is, man no longer should think of himself alone, but in relation to others. It is also aim at improving the socio-economic conditions of man through global transportation, information technology and electronic mass media.

This new global culture has gained precedence over national claims in terms of development and socio-economic growth. Therefore, it is obvious, that it stands to benefit and favor dominant industrial and political powers compared to nation – states with growing economy. The example of the Asians manufacturing companies comes to mind. These multi-nationals now manufacture parts in Asia and assemble them in the Middle East (for example United Arab Emirate and Malaysia) to boost production and reduce labor cost and well as cut down on production tax. Neo-colonization has been alleged by anti-globalization movements,[20] which are spread globally. Their claim is that through improved information technology and communication system, it is now possible to monitor political activities and policies of governments in many developing countries by the "super powers".

Thus, we can argue that globalization has affected visually everything in human psyche since inception. To our mind, especially for Africa and its values, globalization has benefited the Bourgeois (elites) and the proletariats (masses) have suffered greatly. In fact, it has enhanced class discrimination. This could also be seen in gender classification. The implication is that those with access to global connections will benefits more from international financial back up and global territorial space. This will buttress our earlier position that globalization has given rise to inequality and encourage global apartheid, cultural imperialism and neo-colonialism. On the whole we can submit that globalization has affected the life of humanity at a level yet unseen. This is discernible in jet travel satellite communication, facsimiles the Internets and electronic media. It has also give rise to global concern to things that could endanger human existence. This is obvious in the reactions to global warming due to depletion of ozone layer.

With regard to religion, it could be said that religious traditions championed the cause of globalization. This is common in acclaimed world religions, such as Christianity, Islam, Judaism, Buddhism, Hinduism and Confucianism. The brotherhood engendered by these traditions, arguably give necessary background to globalization. It is possible to travel all over the world, and be welcomed by brethren of your religion. Thus, we can argue that some religions have been able to break political, economic, and socio-cultural barriers to enhance universal brotherhood. In Christianity, the church is conceived as a universal phenomenon where all who have accepted Jesus Christ, could express their new brotherhood. Interestingly, globalization has become secularized. Emphasis has changed from spiritualism to secularism. Therefore, religions that were once regarded as queen of all sciences have receded to play second fiddle to science and technology and economic advancement. The question to ask therefore will be that, can religion survive in a globalize world, based on science and technological advancement in area of information technology and enhance global communication. Our answer is in the affirmative.

African Religion in A Globalized World

A globalize world is technologically motivated. Such advancement is often rationalized on the desire of man to search for ways of making his existence comfortable. In a secularized world (that has been globalize) all technological achievements are ascribed to man. This is where the Africans exemplified by the Yoruba differ. To the people, all scientifically and technological achievement as well as discoveries which has enhanced globalization, are placed at the door step of Olodumare, who is conceived as omnipresent, omnipotent, and immortal. This belief is encapsulated in the aphorism common among the people thus:

a dun se bi ohun ti Olodumare fi owo si.
A soro se, bi ohun ti Olodumare ko fi owo si
(Easily done as if approved by God,
Difficult to achieve as what God disapproved)

Therefore, the Yoruba people like other African tribes will explain globalization as the will of Olodumare to better the lots of humanity.

The impact of African traditional religion in a globalize world could be measured in relation to how the Africans have been able to universalize their religion, adapting it to all functionality of globalization. To the Yoruba people, their culture is their bind factor. And wherever they go, they carry it with them. In addition, it is easy to observe and identify a Yoruba person in the West based on his affiliation to his culture. It follows that if religion is part of culture then wherever, Yoruba culture is on display their religion will automatically suffice. However, it may be difficult to x-ray the impact of Yoruba religion, universally beyond the fact that it has gained some level of prominence in countries earlier mentioned. Further, some non-Yoruba has been converted to the religion.[21] However, the basic features of globalization (information technology and communications) have enhanced the spread of the religion. There are websites on the Internet, where information on African religion can be studied. Access to informative literatures is also available on the web sites. In this regard, there are scholars of African religion (old and new) who are still committed to researches and studies in the field.

Globalization therefore can only assist the practice of African religion both in the continent and the world as a whole. It has the potentials to assist adherent of the tradition to open contacts with the outside world and educate people about the faith. The experience of this writer as a researcher of this tradition have shown that, perhaps, because of the low literacy level in Africa, rumors and hearsay are taken as truth about the religion. For example, it is funny that some people still believe that a king in Yoruba land must be buried with human heads.[22] There is also the obnoxious believe that when a new king is to be coronated human heads must be sacrificed to the divinities.[23] Therefore, it is my conviction that globalization will remove or reduce some of these misconceptions.

Globalization will also help to standardize the practice of the religions. The names of Yoruba divinities that have been corrupted could be connected and regulated. The same could be said about the stories and myths about the origin, death, and deification of these divinities. For example, the generally held opinion about the solar divinity in Yorubaland is that he was the 4th king in Oyo who was wicked and diabolical. Studies have shown that the contrary is the case. Sango was never a king in Oyo. However, some kings in Oyo are Sango incarnates who are often possessed by his spirit.[24] The same could be said about the unfortunate comparison between *Esu* of Yoruba theology and Devil or Satan of Christian tradition. Thus, the need to standardize the religion of our ancestors could be achieved through globalization. Although we are not running away from the reality that globalization can disrupt traditional relationships and cultural identity; but it has more to contribute to the upliftment of the practice of African religion.

Urbanization and African Religion

The *Cambridge International Dictionary of English*, define urbanization as a process through which people move from rural communities to live in cities.[25] *The Encyclopedia Encarta* describes it as a process of "removing the rural characteristics of a town or area."[26] Robert Lauer suggests that urbanization is a concept which points to increasing concentration of people living in cities.[27] Demographically, it is a process through which a redistribution of population from rural to urban settlements takes place. From the above definitions, urbanization involve the movement of people from rural areas (with all it attendant characteristics) to urban centers in order to seek comfort and better living conditions. The reasons for this may not be unconnected with the thinking that the urban cities hold promises of better socio-economic benefits to residence compared to rural areas and towns.

The world has become highly urbanized. In fact, Brown, et. al; projected that by 2010 more than half of the world population will live in urban areas.[28] This will affect the world population distribution. It also has the potential to stretch social services and infrastructures to the limit. In developing countries, it could make it difficult for effective management of human and material resources in these cities. Apart from the above, urbanization is associated with the problem of housing, crowding, congestion, poverty, urban decay and sprawl, as well as high crime rate. For example, in Nigeria due to urbanization, the cost of accommodation in cities have rise phenomenally in the last 20 years. As at 1974 a room apartment in Somolu/ Bariga of Lagos state Nigeria was eight Naira. The same apartment now goes for between one thousand and one thousand, five hundred naira. It is also observed that while in 1974 a room apartment is often occupied by a family of four, a two rooms apartment now accommodate over twelve people in these areas. Therefore, housing has become expensive and the efforts of government in building housing units in Nigeria have not solved this problem.

The effects of urbanization on religion may be minimal or negligible in environments where the practice of religion is not attached to natural phenomena. In Africa and Yorubaland in particular these natural phenomena are symbolic objects of worship. The symbols are often located in grooves, forests, hills, and valleys, among others. However, urbanization has necessitated the destruction of some of these structures to create space for more houses to be built in order to ameliorate the housing and traffic problems engendered by urbanization. Although in Yorubaland, some of these objects of worship are preserved, their influence and value reduces with time. For example, *Igbo Igunu* (Igunu groove) is often located on the outskirts of the town, but at Bariga, Lagos Island, Itire-Ijesha, Abule-Oja;

(all cities in Lagos state) the groove location has become urbanized.[29] This has reduced the myths that surround the *Igunuko* masquerade. The same could be said about *Igbale Egungun* (cult or shrine of *Egungun*). The *Oshun* groove in Osogbo, Osun state of Nigeria, is preserved with all its sacredness intact. Our study has shown that the Oshun groove survived because, Osogbo is still under-urbanized. According to a resident of the town "in the past nobody live near the groove (at least 20 kilometers) but now houses are been erected two kilometers form the groove."[30]

From the above discussion, we can summarize that urbanization has affected the practice and influence of traditional religion in Africa and the world at large. However it should be noted that this influence does not suggest a reduction in the value attached to the religion. We observed that "committed" practitioners of the religion live in the rural areas. This is not to say that those who are resident in urbanized cities are not involved in its practice.

Conclusion

In this chapter, we observe that the world has become a global village where political and economic barriers have been broken. This is due to the desire of humanity to interact globally and together brace-up against the challenges of human existence. In this regard, the world is becoming more secularized more than ever before. Also urbanization with it effects have taken serious dimension with implications for religious traditions like African religion which adopt some natural phenomena as objects of worship. It seems therefore that religion, and African traditional religion, for that matter, may not be relevant in the scheme of things. However, our study has shown that globalization and urbanization cannot remove cultural and religious identity. It will follow therefore that the traditional religion of the Africans, which emanated from their cultural realities, will continue to survive. Further, the Yoruba examples have shown that this developmental process with their attendant technological devices in communication and information technology is only to the glory and will of Olodumare. Consequently, the cultural identity of the Yoruba people will continue to play a significant role in a globalize world, because the people cannot but continue to be religious. Our position is further strengthened with fact that "men are incurably religious" thus globalization will enhance the practice of religion and African traditional religion cannot be an exception. This is expressed in the submission of Bolaji Idowu on the future of Yoruba traditional religion. He writes inter-alia:

> The traditional religion is at the moment striving to find a renewed life. It is rising to the challenges of competition with other religions in the country (world). In fact it would appear that it has stooped to conquer, in that it still has the unflinching loyalty of the majority of the Yoruba . . . Its magnetism is unfailingly effective for attracting . . . avowed Christians and Muslims. Indeed, it should not be denied a place among living religions of the world.[31]

The position advanced by Idowu suggests a strong future for African traditional religion. Therefore, man's developmental process and technological advancement epitomized in globalization and urbanization cannot be a hindrance to religion especially African traditional religion.

Notes and References

1. E.B Idowu, *Olodumare: God in Yoruba Belief* (Lagos: Longman 1996), p. 1.

2. Judaism bears the cultural traits of the Jews; while Christianity relied on the Jewish culture and Greek as well as Roman Culture to launch itself into universality.

3. S.A Abioye, "African Traditional Religion: An Introduction" in G. Aderibigbe and Aiyegboyin D., *Religion: Study and Practice* (Ijebu-Ode; Alamsek Press, 1997), p. 156.

4. I.S Aderibigbe, "African Cultural Beliefs" in A.O.K Noah, *Fundamentals of General Studies*, (Ibadan: Rex Charles Publication, 1990), pp. 245-360.

5. These include, Geoffrey Parrinder, R.S. Ratray, P.A Talbot, Emile Ludwig, A.B Ellis, among others.

6. Ludwig, was quoted by E.W Smith, *African Ideas of God* (London: Edinburgh House, 1950), p. 1.

7. A.B Ellis, *The Yoruba Speaking Peoples* (London: Chapman and Hall, 1894), p. 37.

8. J.O Kayode quoted P.A. Talbot; *Understanding African Traditional Religion* (Ile-Ife: University Press, 1984), p. 10.

9. There are many scholars in this regard, they include, Bolaji Idowu, John Mbiti, John Awolalu, P. Ade-Dopamu, J.O Kayode, John Bewaji, Ikenga Metuh among others.

10. This is one of many names through which the Supreme Being is known. Others include Olorun, Oluwa, Eleda, Elemi, and Eledua among others.

11. The Aworis, are the major stock of the aborigines of Lagos. However, they spread into the present Ogun State, but still maintain their hegemony through language, marriage and socio-economic activities.

12. Idowu, P. 3. There are some confessed cases of atheists in the land. Late Tai Solarin in his lifetime, claimed not to belief in God. He was however cited in a church during the funeral service of Late Pa Obafemi Awolowo.

13. I.S Aderibigbe, "Traditional Religion in Lagos" in A.O.K Noah (ed), *Fundamental of General Studies* (Ibadan: Rex Charles Publication, 1997), p. 227.

14. Oral interview with Mrs. Kudirat Ogunseye the vice chairman of the Association of Traditional Healers in Alimosho Local Government Area of Lagos State (15th February 2004) at her residence No. 15, Kamila Baruwa Close, Ipaja, Lagos.

15. Oral interview with Bamidele Ogaga (An Alternative Medical Practitioner) at the Premises of Nigerian Television authority, Tejuoso, Yaba, Lagos, Nigeria (10th July, 2001).

16. The claim of Dr. Abalaka was disputed by Nigerian Medical Association; they opined that Abalaka should published his findings in a reputable medical journal as ethically require in the practice. However, there are some people who have attested to the efficacy of the AIDS treatment in Abalaka's Hospital in Abuja.

17. This writer made this observation during his visit to Osogbo's (in the year 2000 and 2001) Osun Festival.

18. "Globalization" *Encyclopedia Encarta* (2002), http/Encarta.msn.com. Or Encarta. msn.co.uk.

19. Julius Kiiza, "Does the Culture of Economic Nationalism make sense in a Globalization World" in *Journal of Cultural Studies*, Vol. 2, No. 1, 2000, p. 14.

20. *Encyclopedia Encarta*, p. 10.

21. A lady of Australian origin who wanted to be converted into the faith contacted this writer. She contacted me via the Internet.

22. At the demise of late Oba Adeyinka Oyekan, of Lagos, it was rumored among non-indigenes that there was a search for 49 heads (of human beings) to be buried with the king. This writer discovered that the rumor was unfounded.

23. At the coronation of the new king of Ojo in Lagos State, the market was closed for seven days. It was also rumored that the people needed seven heads for rituals towards long reign for the king.

24. Danoye Oguntola-Laguda, "The Legend of Sango: A Critical Appraisal of His Personality in Existing Traditions" in JARS (Journal of Arabic and Religious Studies) Department of Religion, University of Ilorin) Vol. 16, December 2002, pp. 66-78.

25. P. Procter, et. al., *Cambridge International Dictionary of English* (South African: Cambridge University Press, 1996), p. 1601.

26. "Urbanisation" *Encyclopedia Encarta* (2002), http/Encarta.msn.com. or Encarta.msn. co.uk

27. R.H. Lauer and Lauer, J.C., *Social Problems and the Quality of Life* (New York: McGraw-Hill, 2002), p. 565.

28. L.R. Brown et al. *Beyond Malthus: Sixteen Dimensions of the Population Problem* (Washington: Worldwatch Institute (1998), p. 216.

29. Many of these locations are now by the side of major roads at Bariga, buildings now surround the Igunuko Groove. This allows those living in these apartments to see what goes on in the groove. The same could be said about other locations cited.

30. Oral interview with a court attendant of Ata-Oja of Osogbo (the king of Osogbo) Mr. Isiaka Adesoji (aged 63 years) at the palace of the king: 21st October 2001.

31. Idowu, p. 231.

14

Urbanism and Ethnic Crises Since 1980s

Olayemi Akinwunmi and Hakeem Tijani

Introduction

One of the problems associated with urban centers in Nigeria is ethnic conflict, which became a recurring decimal since the eighties. Before the eighties, there were instances of such crises but were not comparable to those from the eighties. This chapter attempts to explain the factors responsible for the upsurge of ethnic crises in some Nigerian urban centers as from the eighties and the inability of the government to contain such crises. This chapter will also explain the rise of ethnic movements and militias and their role in perpetuating the crises. In addition, the role of a non-governmental organization in conflict mediation and resolution is analyzed as an important departure from government inability to resolve perennial urban ethnic conflicts.

The Context

Urbanization is not a new field of study in Nigeria. Indeed, various studies have been done on migration and urbanization, which have given us a clue as to why people migrate to urban centers. Most of the researches done on these themes are of the opinion that economic consideration overrides other factors. Da Vanzo, in his "microeconomic approaches to studying migration decisions," notes "that an individual migrates in the expectation of being better off by doing so."[1] Nnoli holds the same opinion in his work, *Ethnic Politics in Nigeria*. According to him, conflict does not arise as a result of contact between groups. Conflict arises as a result of competing claims between the hosts and the migrants.[2] Samir Amin defines these competing claims "with reference to the economic and political problems of modern society, in which these groups are integrated"[3] It is in this light that we consider migration, urbanization, and conflicts in Nigerian cities which became prominent since the eighties.

Urbanization in Nigeria

In a separate study Olukoju and Tijani[4] maintained that urbanization in Nigeria predated the colonial period. However, colonial period marked the intensification of urbanization process in the country. This was so because of the establishment of Pax Britannica, which removed threats of insecurity in the country. As a result, movements in the country became unrestricted. Nigerians began to move or migrate across borders, which was not popular in the pre-colonial period. Colonial policies encouraged such movements. For example, the decision to link the interior (cash crops producing areas) to the coast by constructing railway lines encouraged movements to areas where the lines went through. It also led to establishment of new settlements or cities in the country. Jos, Maiduguri, Enugu and Port Harcourt are urban centers that emerged in response to colonial government's decision to open up the country for exploitation.[5] Lagos, Ibadan, Abeokuta and Kano benefited from the constructions of rail lines, roads, and ports constructed by the colonial government.[6] In the case of Osogbo, Olukoju mentioned, "it was 'transformed' almost overnight" as a result of railway that went through it.[7]

Under the colonial rule too, administrative centers became attractive too for migrants. Cities like Kaduna and Lagos began to receive migrants because of their administrative status. Kaduna was the administrative city of the northern regional government, while Lagos became the center of the colonial government in the country. It is interesting to note that the fortune of Zungeru in northern Nigeria declined as soon as the colonial administrative machinery was moved to Kaduna. This is a confirmation of the attractive nature of administrative centers in the colonial period. (See below population table of some cities during the colonial period).

Rail transportation facilitated movements in the colonial period. Because of the linkages provided by the construction, many Nigerians began to cross their ethnic boundaries to other areas. As pointed out by Olasiji Oshin, the opening of the eastern railway from Port Harcourt to Kaduna in 1927 facilitated movement from Southern Nigeria to Northern Nigeria. Igbo of the Eastern Nigeria took advantage of this to establish in various parts of Northern Nigeria, especially Kaduna, Kano and Zaria.[8] Yoruba's and other ethnic groups were not left out in the migration. There were movements from Yoruba land, Southwest Nigeria to Northern Nigeria as early as 1903. The first group of Yoruba migrants in Hausa land, especially in Kano came with the colonialists as aides. It was however the railway system that facilitated their movements to the North.

The Hausa in the North too were involved in migrating to other regions in the country. As pointed out by Albert, by the second decade of the twentieth century, Hausa settlements had been established in the following urban centers in Igbo land: Ibagwa, Awka, Aguleri, Abakaliki, Aba, Umuahia-Ibeku, Omoba, Mbawsi and Afikpo.[9] In Yoruba land, more and more Hausa began to establish settlements in cities like Ibadan, Ogbomoso, Lagos and etc.

The migrants in the period under discussion were involved in many professions. Some became employees of the colonial government in their new environments. Railway system absorbed many of them. This was true of many of the Igbo and Yoruba migrants in the North, especially in Kafanchan, Kaduna, Jos and Kano. Those who were not in the employment of railway department were employed as clerks in many of the colonial departments, industries or mining companies as was in Jos. Others were self-employed. In this category were traders. These traders utilized the opportunity provided by railway to sell the products from their areas in their new settlements and vice versa. Traders from the south specialize in foodstuff while Hausa traders from the north are predominantly cattle traders.

On the eve of independence, there was no urban center in the country without migrants. With reference to Kano, R.L. Maiden, a colonial officer, wrote in his report that Kano was to the "ubiquitous Ibo and the other tribes from the distant south."[10] This was also true of Lagos, which became a Mecca and a place to settle for many migrants because of the economic potentials in the city. On the eve of independence, Lagos population was about 600,000.[11]

Table 14.1. Population of the Largest Towns in Nigeria, 1921 – 1963

Town	1921	1931	% Increase	1952/53	% Increase	1963	% Increase
Lagos	99,690	126,108	26	267,407	112	665,246	148
Ibadan	238,094	387,133	62	459,196	18	627,379	36
Ogbomoso	84,860	86,744	2	139,535	60	319,881	129
Kano	49,938	89,162	78	127205	142	295,432	132
Oshogbo	51,418	49,599	-3*	122790	107	208,966	70
Ilorin	38,668	47590	23	40994	-13*	208,546	408
Abeokuta	28,941	45,763	58	84,451	84	187,292	122
Port Harcourt	Na	15,201	-	71,634	371	179,563	122
Zaria	22,680	21,953	-3*	53,974	145	166,170	207
Ilesha	N/A	21,892	-	72,029	229	165,822	130
Onitsha	N/A	18,084	-	76,921	325	163,032	112
Iwo	53,588	57,191	13	100,006	74	158,583	58
Kaduna	N/A	10,628	-	44,540	319	149,910	236
Mushin	N/A	N/A	-	32,079	-	145,976	355
Maiduguri (Yerwa)	N/A	24,359	-	56,740	132	139,965	146
Enugu	30,000	12,000	300	62,764	423	138,457	120
Ede	48,360	52,392	8	44,808	-14*	134,550	200
Aba	N/A	12,958	-	57,787	345	131,003	56
Ile-Ife	22,184	24,170	9	110,790	358	130,050	17

Source: Ajaegbu, "Urban and Rural Development" in Toyin Falola and Steven J. Salm ed. *Nigerian Cities*, 130

* Negative growth or decline   Na: not available

In postcolonial period, many of the cities continued to receive more migrants, especially from rural areas because of negligence of agriculture in the seventies as a result of the oil boom. Since agriculture was no longer the mainstay of the country's economy, more and more Nigerians migrated into cities to look for jobs.

Cities that became attractive to migrants in this category were Lagos, Ibadan, Kano, Port Harcourt, Enugu and etc. Margaret Peil's description of Lagos attested to the above. According to her, "Lagos has been a magnet for migrants since its foundation, and the increasing complexity of the modern-day city reflects the various factors in this attraction . . . The quickening political, industrial and commercial life of Lagos, especially at independence and during the oil boom of the 1970s has proved irresistible, not only to Nigerians, but to emigrants from neighboring countries . . . Growth rates have been largely due to migration.[12]

Other areas that received influx of migrants in the period under discussion included new centers of administrations, which came into existence as a result of creations of more states and local governments in the country. These centers of administrations continued to receive population from surrounding areas, especially the youth who wanted gainful employment.

One characteristic feature in all the urban centers, especially with the influx of migrants from other areas, is the establishment of hometown associations and ethnic associations in the cities of Nigeria.[13] While the hometown associations are more restricted and composed of people of the same town, the ethnic associations embrace people of the same ethnic group. The latter are more vocal in presenting the grievances of their members and ready to defend the interest of their members in their new abode. In deed, it should be mentioned that these ethnic associations, whether it was Egbe Omo Oduduwa and Ibo State Union, welded so much influence and power over their members in the fifties and sixties that the first military administration in the country had to ban all ethnic unions. These unions have emerged today under different names and with branches in every cities of the country.

Conflicts in Nigerian Cities

As mentioned above, conflict arises as a result of competing claims between the hosts and the migrants.[14] The indigenes are afraid that their economic and political advantages are likely to be lost as a result of the encroachment of the migrants. Toyin Falola and others rightly capture the suspicion between the indigenes and the immigrant thus:

> As in other aspects of social development during colonial rule, urbanization had serious adverse effect on the Nigerian society. It is true it encouraged integration but at other times it left permanent division among Nigerians. This was because the rise of urban centers often involved the dislocation of the original owners of the land on which the urban city developed. The arrival and permanent settlement of non-indigenes in the urban centers meant that the owners of the land were required to make adjustment to their usual ideas about land use, and other property rights that would enable the 'immigrants' have a sense of belonging in the city . . . The tension, which arose between indigenes and non-indigenes, was to have lasting adverse effects on Nigeria's political culture both during and after colonial rule.[15]

The 1953 Kano riot, in spite of the attempt to read politics into it, was primarily economy and fear of Igbo domination. John Paden wrote that the riot was an "outpouring of resentment by the indigenous Hausa population" against what was perceived as the Igbo domination of the commerce and civil service in Kano.[16] It should be recalled that the Igbo had migrated to the northern Nigeria as a result of population explosion and scarcity of land to establish successful businesses and to be employed in the civil service. The killing of the Igbo and the destruction and looting of their various commercial centers supported the economic motive of the riot and the fear of the Igbo domination. The political crisis in the country in 1953 only ignited the riot.[17]

The period before the eighties did not witnessed much violence in the urban centers compared to the period from the eighties. By the eighties the country's economy has nose-dived for the worst. Attempts by the various governments to correct the situation did not succeed. Babangida Structural Adjustment Program (SAP), which "has been the most far-reaching attempt to reform the economy",[18] did not solve the economic problem as it was intended. As a result of the devaluation of the naira, the cost of all imported items increased and many industries that relied on goods from abroad could no longer afford them. These industries folded up and the workers ended up on the already saturated labor market. The effect of the implementation of the SAP is "the pauperization of the great majority of Nigerians."[19] The May/June 1989 riots in most of the cities, especially Lagos and Benin, were a reaction to the hardship from the implementation of the SAP.

As a result of the economic crisis, there was competition for the limited scarce resources in all the urban centers, which have resulted in conflicts. Olukoju wrote that conflicts are inevitable where there is "communal competition for scarce social and economic resources and in conditions of poverty, insecurity and lack of opportunity for satisfying employments."[20] The conflicts came in the camouflage of religion in a section of the country, while in other areas they were purely ethnic clashes - The objective was the same; to attack non-indigenes perceived to have denied the indigenes the right to employment and economic advancement. This is basically the explanation for the crises in the following urban centers: Lagos, Kano, Kaduna, Jos, Ibadan, Aba, and Umuahia in the period under focus.

The militia groups that emerged in the various cities in the country promoted ethnic violence in the period under discussion. The Oodua Peoples Congress (OPC) emerged among the Yoruba to defend the interests of the Yoruba, which were perceived to be under threat by other groups. Their operations in Lagos, Ibadan and other Yoruba cities have been against other groups. The Hausa, Ijaw and the Igbo were attacked at various times. In November 1999 at Ketu, Mile 12 market, the Hausa were attacked and in July 2000, at Alaba International Market, the Igbo were attacked. The Igbo were believed to have taken over the market to the detriment of the Yoruba.[21]

In the South-South, ethnic militias such as the MOSOP, the Egbesu Boys and etc also emerged to defend the interest of their ethnic groups in their cities too. The Egbesu Boys had to engage the OPC in Ajegunle, Lagos to defend their Ijaw people against the OPC. The Egbesu also engaged the State Security because what the group perceived to be injustice perpetuated by the Nigerian State against the Ijaw. In the South East, the Bakassi Boys came into existence to do the same for their Igbo group. In the north, though the Arewa Peoples Congress (APC) was not as active as the others, there were other groups operating in some northern cities were deadly in major conflicts in the northern cities. Olawale Albert has identified some of these groups in Kano. They were Yan Daba (or Yan Tauri), Yan Danga and Yan Daukar Amarya. These groups have been responsible for the religious, political and ethnic violence in Kano.[22]

The various ethno-religious crises in the country since the period under discussion had resulted in the death of many Nigerians in the various urban centers in the country. Apart from that, the conflicts had affected the economy of many of the cities, if we have to take into consideration the levels of destruction that took place in these cities. It is however necessary to point out that not all the cities are involved in conflicts. There are some cities where non-indigenes have been integrated into the traditional political system of their hosts. In such cities, mechanism for resolving inter-group crisis has been established.

Heinrich Boll Foundation and Communal Conflict Resolution in Lagos

The *Heinrich Böll Foundation (HBF)*, named after the German Nobel Prize winner in Literature who stood for the values of peace and social justice, is associated to the German Green Party. In Germany and abroad, the main objectives of the Foundation are the promotion of democratic and civil-societal structures, social justice, gender democracy, universal human rights and sustainable development. The Foundation is active world-wide with more than 20 regional and country offices. It has been active in Nigeria since 1994 and established a full-scale Nigeria country office in Lagos in May 2002.

Programs on women and gender, ecology and sustainability, democracy and human rights form the core of the Foundation's work in Africa. The democratic transformation of Africa since the 1990s has been a major focus of the Foundation, as have the rapid cultural changes occasioned by the transition from traditional forms of society to modernity. Here the Foundation's work concentrates on the particular opportunities and vulnerabilities of women.

HBF Nigeria co-operates on a long-term basis with Nigerian partner organizations, both at the grassroots and policy-making levels. Internationally, the Foundation provides an interface that links national and international debates, and supports training and exchange programs for its partner organizations. In its Lagos office, HBF Nigeria organizes workshops and media-oriented events on current issues, as well as capacity building workshops for non-governmental organizations exploring new fields of activities, helping to establish networks among themselves and with other actors, and supporting them with practical advice and training on project and financial management.

Currently, HBF Nigeria runs three programs, supporting projects in the fields of

- women's rights and women's empowerment,
- democracy and good governance, with special focus on economic and structural reform ("economic literacy"), and
- conflict management.

In February 2002, severe ethnic clashes broke out in the Idi-Araba area of Mushin Local Government, Lagos. In November 2002, an Ethnic Forum Council was formed that brings together leaders from resident and professional groups and establishes a conflict management mechanism in the locality. Work towards the establishment of the Ethnic Forum Council began with a series of meetings of community leaders, involving the traditional rulers of the Yoruba and Hausa communities, the leader of the market women, local representatives of the Oodua People's Congress, and many others. Training about methods of conflict resolution and mediation followed. A formal Ethnic Forum Council consisting of seven members was then created, chaired by Major (rtd.) Ajao. The Seriki Hausawa of Idi-Araba acts as the Council's patron. The Council made contact with the area police commander and secretary of the local government, both of which expressed their satisfaction that such a local initiative had emerged, and promised their support for it. The Forum Council's members meet regularly and were supplied with GSM phones, in order to enable them to inform each other and react quickly in case of any communal tension. The reconciliation between the Yoruba and Hausa communities of Idi-Araba was manifested on January 25, 2003, with a public "peace walk" by the Baale Yoruba and the Seriki Hausawa, in the presence of TV and newspaper journalists. The walk led through the central area of Idi-Araba, where numerous ruins from the riots one year ago are still to be seen. The establishment of the Ethnic Forum Council was facilitated by Gregory Okwodu. He is the co-coordinator of Inter-Ethnic Forum, a small NGO formed by a number of concerned citizens of Lagos, worried about the rise of instances of communal violence in the city since Nigeria's return to democracy. With continued support by HBF, Inter-Ethnic Forum in 2003 extended its work towards conflict management on the community level to other volatile Local Government Areas in metropolitan Lagos. In the course of the year, Ethnic Forum Councils began to work in the Agege and Kosofe Local Government Areas as well. On 11 November 2003, the Ethnic Forum Council Agege commissioned a Youth Center, offering training of computer skills for youths of the community. The Center started its work in January 2004 with two groups.

Other Non-Governmental Efforts

It is pertinent to discuss the role played (and continued to play) by other non-governmental organizations such as the United States Agency for International Development (USAID), West Africa Regional Program (WARP), and various interfaith centers in Nigeria. These organizations were concerned that within two years of return to civilian governance there had been "sudden bursts of communal violence" that resulted in about 7000 deaths.[23] It was in the light of this that both USAID and WARP intensified assistance toward the various civil society organizations (CSO). Through the CSO they engaged in conflict management, prevention, peace education, women empowerment, dialogue and town meetings, advocacy for intercommunal conflict resolution, public complaints, research, education, alternative dispute resolution (ADR), visions of peace (VOP), media campaign, and rapid response etc.[24]

The Interfaith Mission Center and the United Methodist Church deserve a mentioning in this analysis. Through supports from Iowa based United Methodist Church, inter-denomination roundtable meetings were organized for leaders of the two religious faiths – Christianity and Islam, at different locations in the State of Iowa between October 2 and November 27, 2001.[25] The participants interned at churches and mosques in various part of Iowa learning experiential aspect of conflict management, resolution, mediation, and peaceful cohabitation. The participants in turn trained youths and other interested parties upon returning to Nigeria. This and exchange of personnel in the future was among the goals of Iowa Resource for International Service (IRIS) chaired by Iowa's Lieutenant Governor, Robert Anderson. Suffice it to say that such internationalism and interest from remote Iowa is predicated upon efforts earlier made by different groups, including the local United Methodist Church, at conflict management and ethnic crises in post-1999 Nigeria. Mention should be made of Sisters' Fellowship (the women wing of the Association of Muslim Brotherhoods of Nigeria) and the Kaduna based Interfaith Mediation Group. Perhaps of more significance is Reverend John Auta Pena's "Let Love Rain" project that aimed at bringing together followers of Christianity and Islam and the community at large to a roundtable to amicably resolved differences. The project emphasis mediation techniques and focus was placed on youth education.[26]

Conclusion

The causes of Nigeria's incessant ethnic and religious conflicts can be outlined thus: Colonial legacy of unresolved ethnic and traditional power structure; Intolerance for diversity and values of the two hundred ethnic groups; Inequitable distribution of the wealth of the nation; Military and police lack of ethics and gross abuse of power; Tensions between "ruralites" and "urbanites"; Students and student unions militancy and cultism (This we did not cover in this study). We conclude that while the role of civil society organizations cannot be over emphasized the government must reorientate it and provide both structural and non-structural supports for a peaceful society in other to stall perennial ethnic and religious conflicts. Suffice it to say that civil society organizations seem to have a strong foundational capacity to undertake conflict management, prevention, and resolution. Their continuous success would depend upon both government and non-governmental agency supports.

Notes and References

1. J. Da Vanzo "Microeconomic approaches to studying migration decisions In: Gordon F. de Jong and Robert W. Garden (eds.) *Migration Decision Making* (New York: Pergamon Press, 1981, pp90 – 129.

2. O. Nnoli, *Ethnic Politics in Nigeria* (Enugu: Fourth Dimension Publishers, 1978).

3. Samir Amin, Introduction in Samir Amin (ed.) *Modern Migrations in Western Africa*, London, Oxford University, 1974.

4. See Ayo Olukoju, "Nigerian Cities in Historical Perspectives," *Nigerian Cities* Ed Toyin Falola and Steven J. Salm (Trenton: Africa World Press, 2004); HI Tijani, "Urban Politics in a Yoruba Frontier – Mushin," Falola and Genova (eds.) *The Yoruba in Transition: History, Values and Modernity* (Durham: Carolina Academic Press, 2005)

5. Jos, Maiduguri, Enugu and Port Harcourt were established in 1903, 1907, 1909 and 1912 respectively.

6. Olukoju, *Nigerian Cities*, 26.

7. Olukoju, 26

8. See Olasiji Oshin, "Railways and Urbanization", in Falola and Salm (ed.) *Nigerian Cities*, 112. See Olubomehin's analysis in chapter four for a different conclusion.

9. See Isaac Olawale Albert, Inter-Ethnic Relations in a Nigerian City: A Historical Perspective of the Hausa-Igbo Conflicts in Kano 1953-1991. *Occasional Publication* no.2, 1993 by the French Institute for Research in Africa in Ibadan, 4-5.

10. See National Archives Kaduna file (NAK. Kano Prof.5/1 4292 in Albert, Inter-Ethnic Relations, 6.

11. David Aworawo, "The Stranger Problem and Social Ferment in Lagos" in Falola and Salm ed. *Nigerian Cities*, 277.

12. See Margaret Peil, *Lagos: The City is the People* (London: Belhaven Press, 1991) 30-31 and Aworawo, "The Stranger Problem" 280

13. See Charles Abbott, "Hometown Associations and Ethnic Unions," in Toyin Falola ed. *Nigeria in the twentieth century* (Durham: Carolina Academic Press, 2002) for details

14. Nnoli, *Ethnic Politics*

15. Toyin Falola et al; *History of Nigeria 3: Nigeria in the 20th Century* (Lagos: Longman, 1991), 46.

16. See John Paden, "Commununal Competition, Conflict and Violence in Kano" in Melson and Wolpe (eds.) *Nigeria: Modernization and the Politics of Communalism* (Michigan State University Press, 1971).

17. See also Olayemi Akinwumi, *Crises and Conflicts in Nigeria: A Political History Since 1960* (Muster, Germany: LIT Verlag, 2004), 43-44.

18. Toyin Falola, *The History of Nigeria*, 184.

19. See I.O. Albert ed., *Urban Management and Urban Violence in Africa* (Ibadan: IFRA, 1994), 227.

20. Ayodeji Olukoju, "The Dynamics of Cultural Nationalism in Colonial in Nigeria" in *Nigerian Peoples and Cultures*, Eds. A Osuntokun and A. Olukoju (Ibadan: Davidson Press, 2005), 300.

21. Olayemi Akinwumi, "Ethnic Militias and Violence" In Falola, *Nigerian Cities* (Trenton, NJ: Africa World Press, 2003), 347-362.

22. See Olawale Albert, "Kano: Religious fundamentalism and violence" and Akinwumi, "Ethnic militias"

23. See E McCandless et. al; *West Africa: Civil Society strengthening for conflict prevention study* (USAID and WARP Publication, 2001), 5

24. Ibid. 29-35

25. See Program of African Studies (PAS), Winter 2002, vol. 12, No 2, Northwestern University, Evanston, Illinois. 1& 6

26. Ibid. 1

15

Managing Rural and Urban Poverty

Adoyi F. Onoja

Introduction

One of the many epitaphs the continent of Africa has endured in its relationship with the outside world, particularly the developed economies, is the one that described it as one universal den of misery, death, and desolation.[1] The validity of this statement made centuries ago today cannot be questioned. Just after the 9-11 attack, a release by Voluntary Service Overseas (VSO) described the region as permanently marred in poverty and doom. The British prime minister,[2] acting as the coalition spokesperson, implied that poverty, misery, and injustice informed the attack against western interests.

There is a coalition of interests in the anti-poverty campaign in the west.[3] The World Economic Forum meets regularly in Davos, Switzerland and the 2005 theme was tackling poverty in Africa and climate change. Bill Gates called on the world's rich to share their wealth with Africa and he donated a quarter of a billion dollar to save African[4] children whose plight he described as scandalous. Blair also chipped in a word on the condition in Africa and along with his chancellor of the exchequer committed their government to the cause of alleviating poverty. Coming at the heels of the Davos meeting was the G-7 meeting in London where Mr. Nelson Mandela, with the support of Britain, Germany, and France, addressed a crowd at Trafalgar square to call for massive aid to fight poverty and disease in Africa.[5] The common place statistics of Africans living on a less than a dollar a day, the devastating onslaught of disease such as malaria, tuberculosis and HIV/AIDS, war and civil conflict, the effect of climate on agricultural productivity, the policies of the Word Trade Organization, and the promise to review the debt question especially the service obligations which has crippled most sub-Saharan Africa States, were some of the dish on offer.

In Porto Allegre, Brazil, President Ignacio Lulla Da-Silva hosted the World Social Forum as a counter weight to the Davos meeting where it called for the cancellation of debt; increase aid, and the reform of the global trading system. The United Nations System, in preparing for the new millennium, had declared the attainment of many objectives by the year 2000.[6] It would appear that these objectives were slogans for the world body as none of them has been attained. What we have now is the 2015 Millennium Development Goal, another postponement of the evil days, as an indication that many in Africa may not catch the train to this destination.

Through the agencies of the international monetary fund and the World Bank, numerous anti-poverty schemes were initiated with each failure succeeding the other. The context of this new poverty campaign was the deregulation of economies worldwide and its enhancement of the marginal position long occupied by the African continent. As part of the forward approach of the new genre of African leadership post cold war, the New Partnership for African Development (NEPAD) scheme was launched in 2001 as an indigenous continental solution to poverty and bad governance. The scheme has since started gathering dust,[7] and like others, it is long on promise and short on achievement. There was the AGOA scheme, which a conditional bilateral trading access granted to specific African States. These measures have not addressed the crisis of poverty on the continent.

Since the late 1980s, the Nigerian government has been concerned with the question at least in theory. But the measures adapted to addressing poverty have been inadequate. The adoption of Structural Adjustment Program resulted in government divesting from the public sector with the loss of jobs and spiraling insecurity. This was aided by the mismanagement occasioned by the politics of the Second Republic. General Ibrahim Babangida initiated the economic restructuring program and the measures to cushion the effects. He launched the National Directorate of Employment (NDE) and the Directorate of Food, Roads, and Rural Infrastructures (DFRRI).

The former was aimed at unemployed youths through apprenticeship scheme and loans to graduate after training. It also includes employment for public works, but it was inadequate and above all, those in charge who used it to alleviate their own poverty hijacked it. The latter was charged with the provision of infrastructure such as rural roads, electricity, a borehole, etc. as part of making the area habitable and as an incentive to curtail rural-urban drift. It started with initial fanfare but lost its steam long before the contradiction that tore through the regime manifested. It was within the context of the SAP that commercial motorcycling[8] emerged in Nigeria employing considerable amount of unemployed Nigerians.

The present leadership of Nigeria resumed the fight against poverty. It created the NAPEP agency with an initial capital of ₦10 billion and the agency was charged with managing the poverty problem. It also incorporated the campaign against poverty in the National Economic Empowerment and Development Strategy (NEEDS) plan of action. NEEDS was described as Nigeria's homegrown poverty[9] reduction strategy. Implicit here was the admission of the failure of the previous program driven by the development school.[10] Like its predecessors, government enthusiasm was sustained in the launch and since then cynicism and despair[11] had set in as it has not done much to addressing the problem.

The scorecard of the government's poverty reduction measure was voiced when the president said that there was no abject poverty[12] except poverty in Nigeria. The same president made a Volta face when he urged the U.N System to use its initiative to help the government alleviate abject poverty in country.[13] There seem to be no consensus on the question and this contradictory statement from the head of the regime mirrored the way the scheme is being addressed.

It is against the backdrop of the inadequacies of the measures introduced since the late 1980s that we must understand the rise of the faith-based group in the anti-poverty campaign. To a large extent the relative peace subsisting in Nigeria amidst grinding want is the creation of this group. This chapter examines the DRFFI and NAPEP scheme in the context of rural and urban poverty management, with the urban one complimented by the growth of faith-based organization.

The Anti-Poverty Politics

Fighting poverty in Nigeria is a popular venture whose political value has been appreciated. The awareness over this could not have been more noted in the present dispensation. Even in the colonial period the nationalists[14] jump-started their campaign to replace the colonial authorities promising better life for Nigerians under indigenous rule. No government since independence has lost sight of the need to provide for the poor.[15] As much as there was the awareness and programs put in place, the net result is that Nigeria's place in the poverty index kept deteriorating.[16]

At independence, according to the federal office of statistics, about 15 percent of the population was poor, but by 1980 this had grown to 28 percent.[17] By 1985, the extent of poverty was about 46 percent although it dropped to 42 percent in 1992. In 1996, ten years after the adoption of the SAP,[18] poverty incidences in the country was 66 percent or 76.6 million Nigerians out of a population of 110 million. The U.N human poverty index in 1997, which gave Nigeria 41.6 percent, ranked her as the 25 poorest countries in the world. Today it is estimated that two-thirds of the population, or 80 million, are poor in spite of the fact that Nigeria has earned over 300 billion dollars in oil and gas revenues and development aid.[19]

As the figure of those falling into poverty appreciates, so does the other elements such as absolute poverty, relative poverty, subjective poverty, and structural poverty.[20] In the Nigerian case, the poor in fall within these criterion and they refer to the ignorant, the hungery,[21] the disease ridden, and those settled in miserable tin-shark habitation's without regular occupation (with irregular or low income) who are routinely deprived of the very essentials of good life.[22] While in some instances like rural communities, they may run ancestral lands, yet in life are at subsistence level. In the urban areas they are those who combine low average income with considerable instability and insecurity of income, employment, shelter, nutrition, and health care.[23]

While attempts to alleviate poverty has been on since independence,[24] those expressed since the 1980s is the by-product of the World Bank's activities since we became a regular patient in her economic clinic. The Bank's portfolio in the area of anti-poverty campaign – in a way picking the pieces of its more sinister twin partner, the IMF – has expanded. In 1994 it observed that progress was made in implementing the poverty-reduction strategy such as lending operations, country-assistance strategies and the policy dialogue, and in strengthening poverty analyses.[25] Also, it contended that future challenges had to be addressed in future poverty-reduction work. These included an integrated poverty-reduction effort in country-assistance strategies, the completion of and improvements to poverty assessments for all borrowers, and the development of poverty-monitoring systems and expansion of countries' capacity to implement them.[26]

Since the 1980s, Nigeria has been an active member of the World Bank family as well as a beneficiary of its poverty reduction program, which is a program being implemented by virtually all its patient countries whose most important feature is its top to bottom origin. It is lacking in originality and environmentally insensitive to country-specific needs. In fact, since the commencement of the structural adjustment program, a concoction of its sister agency, the IMF, the relationship between the two has deepened spanning different sectors. However, the incidence of political instability, policy discontinuity, and the politics of winning support characteristics of the turbulent 1980s, meant that embarking on anti-poverty campaign did not equate to alleviating poverty as the Bank's resolve of "poverty-monitoring and expansion of countries' capacity to implement them", was scarified at the alter of expediency. As the portfolio of the Bank increased,[27] so did the claim of poverty reduction and the experience on the ground in individual countries. In fact, since the 1980s, there was more change in nomenclature of its varied poverty reduction schemes than actual impact on the people. Areas needing reconciliation in the Bank's claim and what is happening in Nigeria include: what constitute growth? What constitute result? What are the yardsticks for success? Is there difference in standards of measurement? Does the Bank's criterion include jobs, accessible and affordable health, education, infrastructure, rising living standards in both relative and absolute terms? Can the years of reforms in Nigeria be said to have produced the most of these? Do these case studies present an overwhelming picture of these? A survey of the anti-poverty structure of the 1980s to present especially the DFRRI and NAPEP would help answer these questions.

General Babangida DFRRI

It has been remarked that the good intention of anti-poverty structures have been sacrificed for political expediency. Nowhere is this claim the case than in the General Ibrahim Babangida schemes for rejuvenating the Nigerian economy. Of all the leadership since the 1980s, his case has stood out as the most comprehensive in terms of programs. But how much of these stood the test of time? Most of them petered out even before he was hurried out of office in 1993.

Among the schemes introduced were the Directorate of Food, Roads and Rural Infrastructures, the Peoples' Bank, Community Bank, National Agricultural

Land Development Authority, and the Better Life for Rural Women, which under his wife, was directed at women.[28] The noble objectives of DFRRI in its rural focus was well conceived as the areas constitute over 90 percent of the Nigerian population regarded as the largest single population and social category.[29] It offered the most comprehensive program on the nation's war against poverty, this considering the truism that rural populations in Nigeria are significantly poorer than their urban counterparts, this program targeted this core group. The rural area being the generating seam of urban squalor became the focus aimed at promoting rural employment based on the assumption that if rural infrastructures (water, electricity, roads, etc.) was available, many people would operate there instead of scrambling for spaces in congested urban centers.[30]

The DFRRI was established in June 1986 with the attainment of three major objectives envisaged. First was to improve the quality of life and standard of living of the people in the rural areas by raising the quality of rural housing, and the general living environment as well as creating greater opportunities for human development and employment, particularly self-employment. Secondly, it aimed to use the enormous resources of the rural areas in order to lay a solid foundation for the security, socio-economic growth and development activities of the rural areas to complement those of the local government areas, states and those of the local government areas, and states and the federal government. And thirdly, through DFRRI, the government aimed to secure a deeply rooted and self sustain development process based on a well-mobilized mass participation.[31]

Most of these objectives outlined for DFRRI and other agencies under General Babangida were never realized. The agency was launched with all the glitters at the national and state levels. The extension to the rural areas was limited where it was needed. Scattered on the landscape of the country are the sparse evidence of its existence. People's recollection of its impact differed. As the capitals and local government headquarters mentioned were made of the agency while at the rural setting, one is more likely to hear of P.T.F. intervention in rural water supplies them the distance DFRRI. Boreholes that yielded no water were evidence in some communities.[32]

No doubt the organization became a corruption conduit of regime officials like most others in the period. It was the views of many Nigerians that like other programs by the regime, they were good but their impacts on the populace and poverty were minimal because of the shortcomings in their implmentation.[33] Since the scheme became a pawn in the power play of the period, it never achieved its objectives of creating the enabling environment for development, material and human, to take place and did not check rural urban drift. By 1993 DFRRI has been consigned as one of the failure of government program.

Poverty and Urbanization post-SAP Era

One of the enduring legacies of the Babangida administration is the exacerbation of poverty and the consequent rise in urbanization. Both phenomenon complimented each other. Poverty resulted in urbanization and urbanization produced the poverty situation. Modernization, reforms and the process of advancement has made it possible for people, who had been mainly rural for most of their history, to begin to experience a rapid and profound reorientation of their social and economic lives toward cities[34] and urbanism. Nigeria post-SAP intensified this process and the result of the movement of people to cities is that the entire fabric of life in both urban and rural areas witnessed massive changes.[35]

The phenomenon of urbanization dates back to the colonial period and the attempts to ameliorating the conditions of poverty it produced captured the attention of the new rulers to the disparaging neglect of the rural areas.[36] In 1944, it was posited that the colonial social welfare policy should concentrate in towns instead of worrying about rural communities because:

> there is no problem of delinquency in a village where the authority of chiefs
> or elders is respected and therefore effective, no unemployment or destitution
> where everyone draws his living from the land.[37]

However, such a pristine situation described above was no longer obtained since the levels of deprivation has impacted on the rural communities through reforms, government neglect, the spread of white collar job culture, the need to benefit from town-centered infrastructures such as roads, schools, electricity, water, health service, and the all pervasive influence of globalization[38] producing rural-urban migration that is responsible for the depopulation of some rural areas and the influx of people into towns and cities.[39]

As a Low Developed Country (LDC), Nigeria has been described as producing a paradox in her urbanization trend.[40] The 1991 census reported Nigeria to be about 36 percent urban leaving some 60 percent as predominantly rural, living in small, remote communities.[41] Globally, Nigeria is one of the least urbanized countries in the world simultaneously experiencing the discomfort of over-urbanzation.[42]

The structural adjustment program compounded the prevailing scenario and the inability/inadequacies of the measures put in place to check its social consequences. Thus, the paradox was explained in terms of urbanization running far ahead of industrialization; hence, there is high level of unemployment/under employment, low productivity, the existence of a rather bloated administrative and service sector, the existence of a great disproportion between the costs of urban growth and the maintenance of proper facilities of urban dwellers, and the marginalization of the labor force in the urban centers.[43]

Examined point by point in the context of the requirement of the SAP, the above situations were worsened. Industrialization slumped as available companies closed shops due to hostile operating environment, those that operated at all reduced their workforce and hours of production and new ones refuse to come in, unemployment shot over the roof, low productivity was heightened as a result of decaying and dying infrastructures, the pruning of the over-bloated administrative and service sectors increased, the heightening of the costs of urban growth and maintenance of facilities and, in some cases, the total lack of such provision through the corrupt siphoning of available resources as well as the over marginalization of the labor force. The situation produced urban overcrowding and congestion, unemployment, poor environmental practice, poor and inadequate housing, crimes, violence, prostitution, destitution which are identified with the urban centers in Nigeria.

The preceding trends were well registered in Nigeria prior to the SAP. The introduction of the SAP exacerbated these conditions beyond what used to exist. In the propaganda campaign that ensued among civil right and pro democracy groups, and their attempt to sell the democracy option, the prevailing conditions then were linked to the military and that democracy would provide limitless opportunities for all. There was heightened expectation that poverty would become a thing of the past with a democratic government in place.

The Obasanjo Regime's Anti-Poverty Program

Little was expected of General Babangida in his anti-poverty scheme because he never had the mandate of the people to rule. This is not so with President Obasanjo who was voted into office in 1999 amidst heightened expectations that considering his experience and travails, the salvation of Nigeria is in the proper hands. However, this expectation appears set to being dashed as cynicism and foreboding has taken over.[44] Among the reasons given for this position is the politics of personal rule and the top-down-approach.

The latter criteria would be well appreciated given the antecedence of the regime in its commitment to economic reforms, most of which it claimed was indigenous, but whose origin, considering the caliber of the regime economic think-tank, cannot be disputed.[45] President Obasanjo had set out to deal with the twin evils of corruption and poverty, two ailment that complimented each other. The government approved the blue print for the creation of the National Poverty Eradication Program (NAPEP), a central coordination point for all anti-poverty efforts from the local government level to the national level by which schemes would be executed with the sole purpose of eradicating absolute poverty.[46]

It recognized the threat poverty constituted to the attainment of its project for a new Nigeria in its NEEDS reform package, claiming that available statistics from 1996 survey indicates that poverty is deep and pervasive with an estimated 70 percent of the population living in poverty.[47] It appreciated, in fine words, the implication of poverty whose social conditions present a startling paradox in spite of a robust endowment in natural and human resources. It admitted that the deepening incidence and dynamics of poverty has polarized the country in divergent dimension.[48] The way forward is in the embrace of NEEDS that is a long-term plan. The short-term palliatives have been on since 1999 and have more than proved their insufficiency.[49]

The difference between NAPEP and past schemes is that it is not a sector project implementation agency but rather a coordination facility that ensures that the core poverty eradication ministries were effective. Under its secondary mandate, which gives it the right to provide complementary assistance to the implementing ministries and parastatal nationwide, it would only intervene when necessary. The schemes it promoted include Youth Empowerment Scheme (YES), Rural Infrastructures Development Scheme (RIDS), Social Welfare Services Scheme (SOWESS) and Natural Resource Development and Conservation Scheme (NRDCS); all of these were directed at eradicating absolute poverty. NAPEP got a take off grant of N10 million in 2001. It claimed it has trained 100,000 youths under its Capacity Acquisition Program (CAP), with 5,000 others trained as tailors and fashion designers resettled. 50,000 graduates also benefited from its Mandatory Attachment Programme.[50]

These claims and institutions in existence are merely on paper. In a population of over 120 million with 70 percent actively poor with no jobs, access to facilities that enhanced good living, providing for just one hundred and fifty five persons when it claimed that 6.4 million[51] people were actively looking for jobs without getting any in 2003, is like a drop in the ocean, assuming its statistics are correct. Indeed, the largesse dispersed under its numerous schemes goes to the beneficiaries who are mostly connected to the implementers. Most of the benefits are confined to the state capitals and local government headquarters, and even then it is grossly insufficient. The amount of N10 billion and subsequent disbursement is inadequate and subject to abuse. In spite of the claim to fighting corruption[52] Nigeria's position in the Transparency corruption index has remained constant clocking the scale as one of the five most corrupt countries in the world. No doubt the anti-poverty scheme formed part of these corruption conduits.

While oblivious of its failing, the government is busy worrying about missing the train of the U.N inspired Millennium Development Goal of halving global poverty by 2015[53] when its definition and perception of what constitute poverty is convoluted. In outlining its own Poverty Reduction Strategy Process (PRSP) it worried most about meeting the global thinking than on its impact on the people.

Poverty in Nigeria has many manifestations including joblessness, over-indebtedness, and economic dependence at adult age, lack of freedom, and inability to provide the basic needs of life for self and family. Other characteristics falls within the categories of poverty of money, access, and power.[54] The NEEDS document, the current obsession of the regime, gave on extensive assessment of causes of poverty and past measures to forestall them, providing the groundwork for why this particular approach (using NEEDS) is the panacea.[55] But an agreeable conclusion is the difference of opinion on definition and what constitute success between the government and the governed.

The net result is the rising crime wave, resistance, and clamor for resource control, sharia, state police, and the call for sovereign national conference. There is unanimity that democracy is failing Nigerians; that the pre-democracy claims and post democracy attainment differed that rationality is beyond the grip of government, and that people must learn to live outside the state. Since the state has failed them, none bothered about the survival of the state and an atmosphere of uneasy calm prevails all over. This is heightened by the display of insensitivity as the elite are already fighting for who controls power come 2007. It is within this climate that the faith based organizations were nurtured into being.

The Faith-based Organization and Poverty Alleviation: "Titty-tainment" and Hope

The position of Nigeria vis-à-vis rising faith in God and the church was underscored by two surveys carried out by the BBC in 2004. The first claimed that Nigerians were the happiest people on earth. The second posited that Nigerians were the most religious minded people in the world with the fastest growing number of churches. The late Afro-beat king, Fela Anikulapo-Kuti, would sum up this view as the case of "suffering and smiling". Either the BBC was dead right or grossly off the mark. But the connection between happiness and religion cannot be missed. It is the paraphrase of the Marxian thesis of religion being the opiate of the people.

Indeed, Nigeria has the fastest growing churches in the world, and these churches are located in the urban centers. The timing of their proliferation fits into the dawn of economic decline, government's failing, and the redefinition of the state. In fact, it is the result of the world after the cold war. But to say that Nigerians are happy as a result is to miss the point and send the wrong signal to the government.

The setting for the growth of faith-based institution in the lives of Nigerians, specifically the deregulation of the institution, was the onset of economic crises in the 1980s following the rise to power of rightist free market leaning governments in the hearing centers of capitalism. The event radically altered the theory and practice of development across the world.[56] The shift in economic and political orientation produced a dramatic result most evident in the systematic attack on the state and its interventionist role in the development process. The new clarion call was rolling back the frontier of the state and the enthronement of the unfettered dictatorship of the market as the central goal of policy and the direction in which all countries must move. Inflation rather than unemployment was defined as the new public enemy.[57]

The social consequences of the new orientation were enormous – unemployment, destitution, lawlessness, drug trafficking, general apathy, and the peoples' remaining faith or what was left of it slide with each new incapacitation of the government.[58] It is within this mass of crises that the churches stepped in not only to restructure themselves along the prevailing line and in line with the perceived failing of the orthodox churches (the equivalent of the old state) in the face of so colossal a deprivations, but also to take advantage of the situation and engineer into being a set of structure that feeds on the discontent pervading the society.

The preceding fits the framework canvassed by Marxists that excessive religiosity and/or the mass embrace of religion was because of the failure of rationality.

Religion as the opinion of the people becomes much more poignant in the social setting of Nigeria since 1980s.

The former Archbishop of Canterbury, George Carey, captured the situation in Africa. According to him, "Life is not as dramatic in Britain as it is in Latin America or Central Africa and unlike the later, it does not require a Christian revelation to interpret it".[59] It also burrowed into what Karen Armstrong described as Christianity's ability to transformed itself under changing tide. Any major faith has had to undergo constant transformation in order to "speak to the peculiarities of each new modernity and Christianity has gone this far because it had this flexibility."[60]

While religion in Europe mirrored social and economic life, a life of seeming conquest of the world, the one in Africa and Nigeria exposed the gap between material attainment in Europe and deprivation in Africa and it is this that explained the disparity in church growth between the two. Consequently, the new churches stepped in to provide for the deprived in the society.

The real impact of a deregulated economy, which translated into deep social crises of a proportion that defied all the state anti-poverty palliatives, left a permanent scar on the populace that the consolation industry[61] i.e. the church became the suction that held the people from falling deeper into aimless abyss. A Ghanaian expert located the link in the rise of the Pentecostal movement and deepening poverty, a view endorsed by Dr. David Maxwell who described modern pastors as doorkeepers of hell controlling the hopes of desperate sinners.[62] Unfortunately, the proliferation of these brands of sinners seemed to point to a conspiracy between the emerging new state and its equally new spiritual counterpart. These sinners did not sin of their own volition but were compelled by forces beyond their understanding.

While alarm is being voiced about the Anglican Church in England being one generation away from extinction,[63] churches in Europe are becoming tourist sites with attendance plummeting compelling their conversion into garages, galleries, and supermarkets as young people are being paid money[64] to woo them into attending churches to continue the tradition in Denmark; the reverse is the case in Nigeria. Church is a major growth industry[65] as properties in choice locations and commercial districts are being bought and turned into worship centers.

Among the features of the new churches that appeal to the people are its strong economic presence and their desire to tackle the question of man's material existence. Gone was the conception that business affairs should be left to the businessmen unhampered by the intrusion of an antiquated morality or by misconceived arguments of public policy. Money making, it insisted, if free from spiritual dangers and prejudice, was not a danger, but rather it could be and ought to be carried on to the greater glory of God. It was its view that the "church has known salvation, divine healing, deliverance, signs and wonders for long. It is now time for it to embrace[66] wealth." It does not just encourage, it also led the way.[67] Other features include its claims to solving all problem, a situation that attracts followers to its camp. The manner it advertised its program reflect this view. These two features summed up the concerns of Nigerians in the present.

The overwhelming focus on wealth creation, material prosperity, and the magic of giving is another of its stock in trade. Majority of the churches are city-bound and urban center oriented and cannot survive in the rural areas. Most of those who attend them are the urban proletariats, the wealthy class especially the genre called the nouveau riche, what is left of the vanquished middle class, and the intellectually minded. Also, peculiar to the church is the caliber of pastors who operated them. Most of them are professionals who abandoned their different callings for the pulpits. Their education ruled out their resident in the rural areas. Finally, is their tendency to proliferation largely due to personality clash and quarrel over church finance?

It is the activities of these faith-based organizations that have provided for the numerous distressed members of the society especially the urban dwellers. Their energies are being redirected to creative venture and above all their sermon of hope provided a sort of "tittytainment"[68] that kept them out of trouble. The following questions remained unanswered: When will the government's reform start yielding the desired result in jobs, housing, health care delivery, adequate and stable infrastructure that will encourage productivity and raise standard of living? And for how long will the people continue to hope that one-day it will be better? Would Nigeria experience the situation in Europe where as a result of material prosperity church attendance plummeted? Is there a conspiracy between the state and the faith-based organization as both profits from each other? Is it in their interest that material prosperity should return?

Conclusion

Nigeria is definitely high in religion and low in morals.[69] This is because the development was induced by the failure of the government government's anti-poverty provision making their embrace of religion very tenuous and tran-sient. The General Babangida scheme of DFRRI was a noble cause, which was sacrificed in the contradiction that rocked his regime. If it had succeeded in its objective in the rural area, Nigeria would have reaped enormously from it. The present democracy seems set on leaving a legacy of unfulfilled expectation as its poverty reduction strategy is set on a similar course. Currently, the goal post has been extended to the maturation of the NEEDS reform. The inadequacy of NAPEP and the top-down approach that conceived it indicated that it was, right from inception, cut off from the realities of Nigerians. But the government is not relenting in its claim of creating jobs and attracting investment. The latter of the environmentally unfriendly type such as cigarette and beer production factories.[70] Nor are the managers short on complacence.[71] For now managing poverty from the rural to the urban areas is the joint endeavor of the government and the faith-based groups. Both are complementing one another and are generating motions rather than movements.

Notes and References

1.   Adoyi Onoja "To the Rescue" Nigeria Standard. PPC: Jos: 2nd August, 2000; Robert
     S. McNamara described poverty as a fundamental problem in Sub-Saharan Africa.
     See "Africa's Development Crisis: Agricultural stagnation, Population Explosion and
     Environmental Degradation. Address to the Africa Leadership Forum, Lagos: Nigeria,
     June 21 1990. P. 3.

2.   Mr. Blair in a speech at his Party's annual convention at Brighton in 2002 described
     the poverty in Sub-Saharan Africa as a dent on the conscience of the world. In terms
     of rhetoric, Mr. Blair and lately Gordon Brown have been foremost in the fight against
     poverty in Africa; *Africa Today* Vol II, No.1. January 2005. United Kingdom. "2005:
     Blair's Year of Africa". See P.12.

3.   Apart from individual governments, are non-governmental organizations like Oxfam,
     the Bretton-Wood Group, a genre of elite protesting against discriminatory trade prac-
     tices and others focusing on specific areas. The timing of these campaign coincided
     with the emerging world order following the recession in power play.

4.   Read BBC News 27/28-01-05

5.   The support of this power was noted and the cold feet in the G-7 plans are the United
     States. BBC News 31/01/05

6.   The Year 2000 was declared as the magic year when most indices of poverty would be
     eradicated – education, food, employment, housing etc for all by the magic year. See
     Adoyi Onoja "Checkpoint 2000' Nigeria Standard, PPC: Jos 16th and 17/12/1999;
     "Echoes from U.N Summit" Nigeria Standard 16th/10/2000; - "The African Month?"
     Nigeria Standard, 21st/01/2000; The World Economic Forum in Davos with "Tackling
     Poverty in Africa" as its theme and the World Social Forum in Porto Allegro, Brazil,
     an alternative anti-poverty forum reported by Steve Kingston BBC world service
     news, 04:20, 28/01/05.

7.   The New Partnership for African Development (NEPAD) was the brainchild of
     Nigeria, Senegal, South Africa and Ghana. Since its inception, it has not brought any
     tangible change on the lives of Africans. This was aptly demonstrated in Abdullahi
     Wade's criticism that NEPAD was enmeshed in conferences alone. Recently, the
     leaders met in Nigeria to review economic development and anti-poverty measures
     under the NEPAD. Read BBC world service news 04:25 28/01/05 and Network Africa
     BBC News bulletin, 04:33, 28/1/05

8.   Adoyi Onoja 'Anatomy of the Achaba Man' Nigeria Standard, 20th December, 2000,
     p 2.

9.   See "Executive Summary" in Nigeria: National Economic Empowerment and
     Development Strategy (NEEDS). National Planning Commission: Abuja. March
     2004.

10. For views on the Development School-the externally developed and imposed salva-
     tion scheme for third world ills, See Majid Rahnema with Victoria Bawtree. The Post
     Development Reader. Zed book: London. 1997.

11. The mayhem witnessed in Jos on 7th September 2001 in which thousands died and
     properties worth millions were destroyed was predicated on the inadequacy of the
     anti-poverty program. Specifically, it was the disputed headship of the local office of
     the poverty agency that unleashed the carnage.

12. The President made the declaration when he accepted the NDDC Master Plan for the oil producing areas. It was his view that no Nigerian exists who goes to bed without knowing what to eat the nest day.

13. While commissioning the $16million house donated to the U.N in Abuja, Mr. President urged Kofi Anan to use his office to reduce abject poverty in Nigeria. AIT News, 31st/01/05.

14. G. O. Olusanya "The nationalist movement in Nigeria", Obaro Ikime (ed) Groundwork of Nigeria History. Heinemann: Ibadan, 1980; Michael Crowther, The Story of Nigeria, "The Rise of Nigerian Nationalism". Faber and Faber. 1960.

15. For explanation of the poor, See Waxman, Chaim I., The Stigma of poverty: A critique of poverty theories and policies, 2nd ed., Pergamon Press. 1983, P. 1.

16. Poverty Alleviation in Nigeria – A perspective in www.dawodu.com/poverty1.pdf.

17. Ibid.

18. Nigeria and the World Bank: Learning from the past, looking to the future. World Bank: U.S.A. 1995. Pp. 13-24.

19. See www.dawodu.com

20. See M. Haralambos, with R.M Herald Sociology: Themes and Perspectives, Cambridge: Oxford University Press, 1988. Pp. 140-171 for a discussion of these nations.

21. The president recently offered a seminal explanation of abject poverty and poverty with the former being a state where you are not sure of your next meal. He conceded that the former was absent in Nigeria. Later he contradicted himself when he told Kofi Anan that he should use his office to alleviate abject poverty in Nigeria. Such insensitivity and lack of understanding have been the stock-in-trade of Nigeria's ignorant elites. Umaru Dikko once claimed that Nigerians don't eat from the dustbin yet. That might be true for the sole reason that not enough can be found there. While David Mark claimed that telephone was not for the poor.

22. Browne Onuoha "The poor and the social implications of the political transition Programmes in Nigeria" Browne Ohuoha and M.M. Fadakinte (eds.) Transition politics in Nigeria – 1970-1999. Malthouse: Lagos. 2002. Pp. 244-245.

23. Bromley R., and Gerry, C. (eds) Casual work and poverty in the Third World cities, Pp. 12-14.

24. See www.dawodu.com

25. The World Bank Annual Report. World Bank: Washington D.C. 1994. p. 11.

26. Ibid.

27. Ibid. p. 33.

28. See "Community Banks as economic prop for democracy" in S. Oyovbaire & T. Olugunju Crisis of Democratization in Nigeria, Selected speeches of IBB Volume, III. Malthouse Press: Lagos 1996. Pp. 229-231. In the speech he claimed that the "establishment of community banks in Nigeria at this time is a clear demonstration of the unflinching commitment of this administration to a grassroots development. Indeed, various activities of DRFFI, MAMSER, BLP, NALDA, the Peoples Bank and now your Community Bank etc. stand out as eloquent and practical testimonies of our commitment to rural development . . . (since) more than 80 percent of the country's resources for development are rural based."

29. Browne Onuoha "The Poor and the social implications" p. 242; for assessment of rural areas, see Francis Enemuo: "Transition and the challenge of rural development in Nigeria", Onuoha & Fadakinte (eds.) Transition politics in Nigeria; O. Obasanjo & Akin Mabogunje (eds) Elements of Development. ALF: Nigeria, 1991. p. 139-151.

30. www.dawodu.com

31. T. Falola, M. Mahadi, M. Uhomoibhi, U. Anyanwu History of Nigeria 3: Nigeria in the Twentieth century. Longman: Nigeria. 1991. p. 194-196.

32. Mr. Okechukwu Akanonu recalled a case at FSAS Suleja where the student rioted because a purported borehole dug by DFRRI and filled with water on commissioning day, dried out as soon the water ran out.

33. www.dawodu.com

34. Michael M. Ogbeidi "Urbanization and Social Reforms," In Nigerian Cities edited by Toyin Falola and Steven J. Salm. Africa World Press. New Jersey. 2004. p. 333.

35. Ibid. p. 333-334.

36. Ogbu U. Kalu "Poverty and Its Alleviation in Colonial Nigeria: In The Foundations of Nigeria: Essays in Honour of Toyin Falola edited by Adebayo Oyebade. Africa World Press: New Jersey. 2003. P. 425.

37. Lucy P. Mair. Welfare in the British Colonies. London. 1944. Pp. 109-110.

38. For definition and consequences of globalization including destruction of local cultures, regional tastes and national tradition, see Kofi Annan "The Politics of Globalization" in Globalization and the Challenges of a New Century A Reader edited by Patrick O'Meara, Howard D. Mehlinger and Mathew Krain. Indiana University Press: U.S.A. 2000. Pp. 125-120.

39. Akin Mabogunje "Urbanization in Nigeria – A Constraint on Economic Development", Economic Development and Cultural Change, Vol. 13, No. 4 (1965): 436-8.

40. Michael Ogbeidi "Urbanization and Social Reforms" in Nigerian Cities, P. 334.

41. World Bank Report "Trends in Developing Economies" (1993): 365 quoted in Ibid. P. 335.

42. Ibid. P. 335.

43. Ibid.

44. Anthony Madugwu "Alleviating poverty in Nigeria" in www.afbis.com/analysis/alleviating-poverty

45. There is Dr. Ngozi Iweala a former Vice President of World Bank, Dr. Magnus Kpakor – an official of the World Bank, Professor Charles Soludo the C.B.N. Governor and architect of bank merger for global positioning, Malam Nasir El-Rufai, a Harvard trained economist and former head of the privatization bureau.

46. www.dawodu.com

47. Nigeria; National Economic Empowerment and Development Strategy (NEEDS). National Planning Commission. Abuja – 2004. Pp. 21-24.

48. Ibid. Pp. 95-96

49. Such inadequacy was behind the conflicts all over the country.

50. For detail, See www.dawodu.com.

51. See Nigeria: National Economic Empowerment and Development Strategy. P.6.

52. Numerous agencies are in place to fight corruption since 1999. There is the ICPC, Due Process, E.F.C.C.

53. Nigeria: National Economic, p. 19.

54. "Urban Poverty Alleviation" Paper presented at the Regional High-level Meeting in Preparation for Istanbul +5 for Asia and the Pacific, 19 to 23 October 2000 Hangzhou, People's Republic of China. www.unescap.org/huset/haugzhou/urban-poverty.

55. Nigeria: National Economic, pp. 97-100

56. Olukeshi, A and Oyekanni, F. "Editorial" CODESRIA's Bulletin, Nos. 1 & 2, 2002. P.2.

57. Ibid.

58. Adoyi Onoja "The Deregulation of Salvation: The Nigerian Pentecostal Movement in perspective". A paper presented at the Faculty of Arts Seminar, No. 1 26th August 2004, Nassarawa State University, Keffi. P.6.

59. Newsweek "Is God dead?" 12th July, 1999. New York. P. 52.

60. Ibid. P. 57.

61. Interview Mrs. Iberi Odoh 75 years. The term consolation is a direct translation from the Idoma language. 26/10/2002.

62. BBC Postmark Africa 9th/02/2003

63. Newsweek Ibid P.52.

64. BBC News hour 23/02/2003

65. Adoyi Onoja "Deregulating Salvation" Nigeria Standard. PPC: Jos. 6th, 9th, 10 June 1997.

66. Newswatch "Highest paid pastor, their money, their life styles and their wives" 23rd December 2002. P.24; Newswatch "Raising Godly Billionaires" 25th August 2003. Pp. 9-10.

67. Africa Today "A circle of Winners" by Pelu Awofeso. Vol. 10 January 2004. P.5. United Kingdom.

68. A phrase coined by Zbigniew Brzezinski. He thinks of 'Titty-tainment' ('tits' plus 'entertainment') in terms not so much of sex as of the milk flowing from a nursing mother's breast. It describes a mixture of deadening entertainment and adequate nourishment, which will keep the world's frustrated population in relatively good spirits. This is what is on offer Sunday after Sunday and in most revivals, which are frequent. See Hans-Peter Martin and Harald Schumann The Global Trap: Globalization and the assault on prosperity and Democracy trans. By Patrick Camiller. Zed books: London. P.4.

69. Abraham Ogbodo "High In Religion, Low in Morals" The Guardian, Sunday, December 26, 2004. P. 24.

70. In 2004 President Obasanjo commissioned the $150 million BAT factory in Ibadan and later the ₦60 billion Ama Brewery in Enugu. These and the G.S.M revolutions are triumphant cards in his quest for investment and jobs creation. Driven from Europe and America by incidence of cancer-induced litigation running into billions of dollar, tobacco factories are relocating into Africa where weak law and quest for investment is attracting them. Unwittingly we are creating the next generation of public health crisis we have no resources to checkmate.

71. Ojo Maduekwe described Nigeria as "work in progress".

16

The Development of a
Federal Capital Territory – Abuja

Ibrahim Umaru

Introduction

> *"The panel on the location of the Federal Capital has recommended that the nation's capital should move out of Lagos to a Federal Territory of about 8,000 square kilometers to the Central part of the country . . . The site recommended satisfied the panel's criteria of centrality, good and tolerable climate, land availability and use, adequate water supply, low population density, physical planning convenience, security and multi-access possibility. The area is not within the control of any major ethnic groups in the country. We believe that the new capital created on such virgin land as suggested will be for all Nigerians as a symbol of their oneness and unity. The Federal Territory will belong to all Nigerians."* (Emphasis mine).

GEN. MURTALA MUHAMMED - February 3, 1976

Nigeria's capital city was born out of the necessity to create on a 'virgin and neutral land', a more accessible and befitting nation's capital and to relocate the seat of government from the congested and strategically unsecured commercial city of Lagos to the environmentally friendly Abuja. This has created two historical fallacies namely, that the new federal capital territory (FCT) was initially literally vacant with insignificant population as well as economic activities; and that the scanty population was at subsistence level scattered in "sleepy and sick" villages. This discourse attempts an in-depth review of the origin and development of the area in a bid to put the history of the FCT Abuja in proper perspective. In pursuance of this objective, the discourse walks through the origin and existing traditions of the people who occupied the area before 1900 A.D; the development of new settlements under British colonial administration; and the dramatic transformation of the territory from 1976 to 1995. Finally, the discourse examines the settlement schemes undertaken by the FCT development authorities aimed at relocating the inhabitants and aborigines and came to the conclusion that the modus operandi of the development of Abuja had been unjust to the indigenous communities as they were poorly compensated and resettled.

After going through the above-quoted passage of the speech proclaiming Nigeria's new federal capital territory (FCT),[1] one gets the impression that the land on which Abuja is founded was not only recently literally vacant but its history quite recent. On the contrary, by 1975 the area that now constitutes the FCT was actually made up of ethnic groups such as the Gbagyi (Gwari), Koro, Gade, Gwandara, Ganagana (*Nupe*) and Ebira. Archeological and linguistic sources suggest that the history of human activity in the area, especially of the Gbagyi dates back to five centuries ago.[2] Indeed, with the exception of the Gwandara group, there is evidence that draws a linkage between the past and the present groups found today in the area.[3]

An in-depth review of the origin and development of the area will therefore help in no meager measure to put the history of the FCT in proper perspective. The rest of this discourse is divided into four main sections. Section I traces the origin and reviews existing traditions of the people who occupied the area before the year 1900; Section II discusses the evolution of settlements in the area in the first three quarters of the 20th century A.D.; and a review of the rapid transformation of the area from rural settlements to capital territory from 1976 to 1995 forms the subject of the last section of the discourse.

Origin and Traditions of the People of the Area Before 1900 A.D.

The history of the area before 20th century is largely a history of the dynamics of the inter-group relations which existed between the various groups found in the area, especially those of Koro, Gwandara, Gbagyi, Gade, Bassa, Ganagana, Ibirra, Hausa and Fulani. However, historical evidence points to the fact that the three earliest groups that were to inhabit the territory were Koro, Gwandara and Gbagyi.

The Koro people are predominantly found in places like Zuba, Kawu, Shere, Dutse-alhaji, Tungan-maje and Dogun-kurmi. Outside the FCT, they are to be found at Ija-Koro, Kafin-Koro in Niger State.[4] The Koro people of Abuja are of three basic groups, namely Koro-Ganagana, Koro-Nuku and Koro-Hunta.[5] Though all the groups are of the same ethnic configuration, they however have slight cultural and linguistic difference. For example, Koro-Ganagana had over decades intermarried with the Ganagana people and developed a distinct dialect that could be aptly described as an admixture of Koro and Kanuri languages.[6] The differences notwithstanding, all the sub-groups trace their ancestry to Kwararafa who, according to traditions conquered the whole of the Hausaland in the 17th century. One tradition has it that some Koro people settled at Zazzau (Zaria) while others at Kano during the reign of the last Hausa ruler (Alwali) Ali Wali who was later driven out and eventually killed by the Fulani. The tradition has it that after his death, some of his followers moved down to Zazzau and fought against the Bassa and the Ganagana and eventually took over their lands.[7] Whether one accepts this tradition or not, the fact that Zuba Koro were also called Koro Kutumbawa and the famous Zuma Rock seems to have derived its name from the Koro word 'Zu-ma' meaning 'big-rock' is enough evidence to point to long habitation by Koro people in the area and also that they might have had close ties with Aliwali of Kano (c.1623) as the migration might have taken place about the same time as the Gwandara's from Kano.[8]

The Gwandara group has been living with the Gbagyi and Koro in the area for a long time. They are mostly to be found in Fadan Karshi, Ankara, Madidi Nyanya (Tudun Gurku), Kakyama, Shangado and around the Bwari-Asokoro-Nyanya chains of hills. The Gwandara people are known for their attachment to their traditional religious system. According to one tradition, Nyanyaya was one of the leaders of the people that migrated from Kano in the year 1366 due to unfavorable conditions they were exposed to, due to their beliefs and practice of traditional religion.[9] Nyanyaya with his brothers founded what is today known as Nyanya in the FCT as well as some intermittent settlements such as Fadan Karshi, Madidi Nyannya (Tudun Gurku) Shangado and Ankara in the present-day Nasarawa State.[10]

The Gbagyi has been the dominant group in the area which later became the FCT. They are made up of two demographically distinct but linguistically similar sub-groupings namely, Gbagyi-Ngenge and Gbagyi-Matayi.[11] There are many traditions of the origin of the Gbagyi people. One of them claims that the origin of Gbagyi people emanated from Bornu through Zazzau (Zaria). According to the tradition, it was from Zazzau that their ancestors brought dogs for hunting and security and settled at Shepei and Zhigakuchi; and from the latter some of them left only to settle at Gbaduma (Aso-Pada) in the present Nasarawa State. Other settled in Nyanyayi (present Nyanya); Peyi (Garki) and Lugbe.[12] Another tradition tries to trace the origin of the Gbagyi people of the area through the Bayyajida legend. In fact, the tradition claims that the evolution of settlements like Karu, Nyanya, Garki and Kurudu is linked to chains of migrations from Zazzau through Birnin Gwari, Keffi and Kurape between the c.1400 and 19th centuries A.D.[13] While a critical assessment of these traditions reveals fantastic dating that is questionable as the traditions might merely be attempts to justify the long standing relationship between the Gbagyi settlements and their ties with Zazzau following the waves of immigration from Hausaland and Zazzau into the area in the 18th and 19th centuries, however other traditions collected from Hausaland seem to suppose the existence of the Gbagyi group in the pre-FCT surroundings as well as major settlements in Zaria area between the speculated period, and seem to agree with the claims of the Gbagyi traditions.[14] What is more, the Gbagyi are said to belong to the Kwa-speaking people of the Niger-Benue confluence area[15] and linguistic evidence shows that together with Yoruba, Igala, and Nupe and so on have been where they are and separated as distinct languages from a period varying from 1,500 to 6,000 years ago.[16]

Whatever the situation might have been, it is evidently clear that following internal dynamics and the impetus from the influx of people from outside as a result of the trade routes that cut across the entire region from Panda kingdom on the confluence of River Niger and Benue in the South and Zazzau kingdom in the North, small independent states and polities emerged at about the 17th and 18th centuries.[17]

Aside from Hausa and Fulani powerful kingdom of Abuja, Nassarawa Kwato and Keffi, Karu emerged as a centralized authority in the beginning of the 19th century after been under suzerainty of Kurape kingdom for about 100 years.[18] A tentative reconstruction of the king-list of the latter settlement points to c.1600 A.D. when it started to exercise cultural and political influence over the neighboring settlements and became powerful when it received waves of immigrants about that period.[19] Kurape maintained her dominance for quite sometimes until the emergence of powerful sister polities like Waru, Kurudu, Karu, Jere and Gyinu (Kupan Gwari), Abuja, Nassarawa Kwato and Keffi.

With the exception of the Pai Fulani, all these polities paid tributes to Zazzau not as a result of conquest but because the latter could provide protection in times of need. This allegiance continued until the Habe rulers of Zazzau relocated to Abuja (now Suleija) at the beginning of the 19th century following the advent of the Fulani Jihad.[20] For almost eight decades that followed, these states came under constant military incursions by the Fulanis led by Makama Dogo and his lieutenants from Nassarawa Kwato, Keffi Fulani and sometimes Habes of Abuja. These military sorties notwithstanding, the resilience of the people, tenacity and resolve to survive as independent people helped to resist such attacks until the advent of the British colonial administration in the first half of the 20th century.[21]

Evolution of Settlements in the Abuja Area (1902 – 1974)

By the turn of the 19th century all the area in which the present FCT lies had witnessed the development of well-established settlements as well as the mixture of peoples. The area comprised of what was later to become Abuja Emirate together with adjacent parts of Nasarawa and Minna Divisions, and parts of southern Zaria. The Gbagyi still remained the most dominant group. Others included Gwandara, Gade, Igbirra and Bassa. Also included were a scattering of nomadic Fulani, and some Hausa and maybe settled Fulani in the larger settlements.[22] The political situation as at that time was disturbed as the Hausa Emirate of Abuja was still under pressure from the settled Hausa, who dominated the surrounding area from settlements such as Keffi, Nassarawa Kwato, Lapai and Lafia.[23] While the Hausa and Fulani protected themselves from sporadic raids within their walled headquarters, others found safety in nucleated settlements on hill tops or within the protection of hills and settlements within the forests.[24]

The establishment of colonial rule in this area brought relative stability to rural settlements. Beginning from the first quarter of the century, significant changes especially with respect to the settlement pattern began to emerge. Evidently, the movement away from the earlier sites, though of short distance, by peoples in the area was marked. Historical sources show that 25 per cent of the people moved less than 1 km and 29 per cent less than 5 km away from the old sites in the area.[25]

These movements were to familiar areas and only in rare occasion were movement of 80 km and 240 km involved to warrant significant changes in the way of life.[26]

It goes without saying that effective stabilization of rural settlement within this period came on the heels of the establishment of colonial administration. This was as a result of three closely related factors namely, administrative measures which encouraged or forced fixed settlements; restriction the land available by defining boundaries creating forest and game reserves and the division of lands between settlers and natives; and road construction.[27]

Colonial administrative policy largely determined the movement and fixation of settlement in the Abuja area. For example towards end of the 19th century, Gwazunu, a Koro settlement, was relocated from its earlier site to just outside the boundaries of the Abuja (Suleija town) following Gbagyi raiding from Ija.[28] But because the colonial administration wanted Gwazunu for a small governmental residential area (GRA), it was again relocated to across the Iku River near its earlier site. In a similar move, Gussorro, initially a forest settlement was forced to relocate southward following the death of a British colonial officer, was reorganized into a village area in 1933 and in 1936 official intervention prevented fission with a group of Afo in the Onda area.[29]

This was in tune with the fact the colonial administration disliked too dispersed and too concentrated settlements. In deed in some instances, growing settlements integrating several groups were forced to disperse and settle in different wards; the case of Kuta in which a compulsory downhill movement was imposed on it, was followed by the scattering of the large settlement into 23 widely dispersed wards[30] is instructive. In other instances, forest- and hill-dwellers were encouraged to move to healthier and more accessible sites.

Creation of forest reserves was an effective way of regulating land available to farmers or restricting the movement or relocation of settlements in the Abuja area by the colonial administration, especially up to the 1950s. Identifying and declaring an area as a forest reserve meant that any settlement within that area would have to be relocated. For instance, between 1926 and 1936, the noticeable decrease of population in Koton Karfi Division was attributed partly to the emigration of farmers who saw the forest reserves which occupied two-fifths of the Division as restrictions on their farmland.[31] This settlement policy even endured into the post-independence period. In 1961, when Madalla Reserve was established, the settlement within Zuma *kurmi* (forest) was moved.[32] On the other hand, in a sizeable reserve the policy could change to create an enclave as was the case when the first Abuja Native Authority reserve of the size 100 square km was created in 1942.[33]

Road construction was another measure that influenced the fixation of settlement in the Abuja area within the period. The construction of motorable road actually began in c.1930. A key feature of this development was the development of settlement close to the market; and markets close to roads thrived while those far off the roadside eventually withered away. For instance, Madalla initially provided trading opportunities and later attracted Hausa settlers. By 1932, these traders had formed their settlement around the market, almost exclusive of the existing Gbagyi settlements. The Hausa settlement rapidly expanded, thanks to the construction of Abuja-Keffi Road. By 1965, a new Hausa quarter right beside the road junction sprang up in a bid to cash in on the trading opportunities provided by stopping lorries and passengers.[34] Down the eastern part of the Abuja-Keffi Road, Maitama and Mabushipe (Mabushi) moved in the 1960s to closer sections of road. Also, farmers from far-off and isolated settlements like Jawu relocated to establish Masaka from as early as 1945. By 1972, Masaka was already occupied by 340 farmers; only 30 remained in Jawu.[35] The period 1930-1945 saw a new settlement springing up at Awtabalaifa (the present day Auta Balefi) near the Karshi junction. The Gbagyi and Gwandara were attracted to the new site from off-road settlements by abundant farmland close to a site which had become an important stopping place for lorries. Similarly in the Toto-Umaisha area, several new settlements sprang up following the construction of Toto-Umaisha road at the end of the 1930s in order to link the flourishing riverside trading centre with the interior of Nasarawa.[36] By 1950, the area between Gadabuke and Buga, the Gade dominated politically. In 1953 the Gbagyi who earlier settled at Buga relocated to Gudun Kariya and Nakuse. As the chieftaincy dispute heated up at Buga, in 1959 some Gade dissenters left Buga and resettled at Toto while others headed for Nasarawa. After the river traffic dwindled, the Toto-Umaisha Road lost its importance to the Koton Karfe-Abaji-Toto Road which under the former Benue-Plateau State was tarred towards the end of the 1960s. This led to establishment the growth of settlements like Koton Karfe, Abaji, Yauye, Rubuchi, Ukya Kulo, Achido and Ahinza.[37]

Considering the turbulence in terms of military raids and counter-offensive among the states and polities that characterized area in the period before colonial intervention, matters of defense and security were major considerations in the establishment of settlement sites in the Abuja area.[38] Constructed walls were popular with Hausa and Fulani settlements; but for others, hills and other natural barriers were more effective. Majority of settlements that became established after the British stabilization were as a result of voluntary and piecemeal movements over an extended period as well as forced and direct intervention by the colonial government officers in order to facilitate administrative convenience. Evidence shows that around the ancient Abuja city (Suleija), most of the hill settlements were associated with isolated or grouped inselbergs on which farmlands were scanty or rarely in use; in the Kuta area, small and rocky ridges were used; in parts of Nasarawa, larger hill masses such as the Afo hills provided convenient sites.[39]

The Gbagyi of Madalla was one of the first groups to abandon their hill site. Historical sources show that the earlier site was on a platform 250 meter above the base of a very large inselberg. During rainy season, water was obtained from natural pits on the platform and from seepage further down. In the dry season, water was got from stream downhill. Following persuasion by colonial administration 1909, the site was abandoned and a new village was established on the nearby plain. Similarly several other hill sites were abandoned voluntarily; such include Garki, Dikko, and Idu in Abuja (Suleija); and Karu and Jawu in Keffi.[40] However, in other hill sites, the colonial administration had to use force. For instance, disturbance among the Afo in 1919 invited the dispatch of a British military expedition that had to force the Afo to move down to the plains.[41] The process of hill site abandonment became accelerated in the 1920s in both the Keffi and Abuja Divisions; Ija Koro was relocated down in the early 1930s; the Gbagyi of Bwari moved towards the end of 1936.[42]

With the issue of security settled, many nucleated settlements created by unsettled conditions began to break away. Discontented groups broke away from the rule of unpopular chiefs and fission became the order of the day. For instance, among the larger Gbagyi concentration in the north, dispersion occurred in the first quarter of the 20th century. Fission among people and groups was marked in the ancient Abuja town (Suleija) and walled Fulani centers which were occupied largely by farmers even though those settlements were not villages. As at c.1900 A.D. Abuja (Suleija) was a home to the descendants of the original Hausa settlers, Hausa from elsewhere, the Gbagyi and Koro seeking shelter from Fulani attacks. Within a few years there was a noticeable spread of some of the town population which started about 1914 and accelerated until the 1930s.[43] Several scores of the Gbagyi, Koro and Hausa relocated to set up new farming hamlets within a few kilometers from Abuja town (Suleija). While some of these settlements were located to the north and east of the town, others were sited close to the perennial River Iku. Also evident were the settlements located near the base of the inselbergs to cash in the advantages offered by favorable water conditions that could be found than on the open plains.[44] Because of their unsuitability for farming and habitation, areas to the west did not attract migration. In order to take advantage of trade, some Hausa moved to the larger rural settlements, such as Bwari and Garki. In these areas, they built near yet carefully detached from the existing Gbagyi settlements.[45] In Karu District, the Gbagyi and Koro likewise carefully maintained separate villages established in pairs. The characteristic settlement pattern was common in the Abuja Emirate and might have involved other groups, for instance Gwandara and Gbagyi, Ganagana and Gbagyi, Gade and Gbagyi. However, the Gbagyi always appeared to be the politically dominant group.[46]

By the mid of the first quarter of the 20th century, outward movement had gathered momentum. The population of Abuja (Suleija) was estimated at 4, 157, far larger than any other emirate (Keffi, 3, 030; Jemaa, 1,466; Lafia, 2,194; and Nasarawa, 1, 033).[47] While integration (the assembly of dispersed or small settlements into a new nucleation) was not common, amalgamation (voluntary or forceful joining of existing large settlements by smaller ones)[48] occurred frequently and often resulted in relatively large ethnically homogenous settlements in the areas that later became the FCT. In the south of Abuja (Suleija), the Gbagyi and other groups as well as the Hausa from nearby settlements formed compounds at Gadabuke, in addition to the migrants from Buga. However, each ethnic group formed its own ward or hamlet. Also, a village complex emerged at Izom, which had five distinct sections. Though the core was a Gbagyi settlement, divided into two parts by wet land, other parts were added in 1926; first, Ko was[49] established by Hausa traders from Zaria but moved from there when motor traffic started using the Bida-Abuja Road and at a time when the Gurara River was crossed by a ferry. Later on, more Hausa and Muslim Yoruba traders moved into the same section; with others, mostly the Gbagyi from various settlements nearby and Izom proper came to form a new section near the market, the fourth largest in the Emirate. Then, came a large group from Chini, who abandoned their old settlement some kilometers down the Gurara River to form a separate section besides the market. Finally, in 1958, migrants from a settlement in Koton Karfe Division built the new section at Gudugudu. Izom became an attraction because of its advantages which included concrete-lined wells, a perennial river, shops and a primary school.[50]

The development of Madalla village complex within the same period share similar characteristics.

At Karu, a predominantly Gbagyi settlement which had emerged from its ancient settlements and grown considerably since mid 1950s was a population which included Jaba, Tiv, Hausa, Yoruba, Ibo and Gwandara people.[51] The Hausa and Gwandara and most of the Yoruba live in a section separate from the rest; because the Hausa, Gwandara and some Yoruba were Muslims, they lived in a separate section, while the rest who were either Christians or animists (pagans) had different quarters.

In some other settlements in the Abuja territory however, there were no such clear-cut distinction between the existing groupings. For instance, in Abuja town (Suleija) there were strangers, yet there was no *sabon gari*. At Nasarawa, the situation was similar. Also at Dikko and Kuta, the Hausa were not cut off distinctively from the intermixed Gbagyi traditional and Christian communities even though the former tended to reside around the market.[52]

Another key feature of the period was the functional transformation of settlements, a process where villages change into urban centers. It has been suggested that the most important factor responsible for such transformation in the Abuja area was the selection of a particular village as the seat of a district or provincial administration or the building of a segregated residential area for government officers (the GRA) and for strangers (*sabon gari*).[53] For the Abuja area, most of the changes had been restricted to the capitals of the 19th century emirates though the extent of change among such settlements varied. For instance in 1919, the population of Abuja (Suleija) was larger than that of Keffi (4,157:3,030); but by 1963 Abuja was far more than Keffi (7,700:31,700). In spite of this, Abuja remained the centre of an Emirate, became the headquarters of a Native Authority and was host to a police barracks, road maintenance yard, dispensary, post office, two primary schools, a secondary school, a pottery; and from 1967, a general hospital and yet another secondary school. This was in addition to increased tempo of trading and marketing and the establishment of a GRA, however without a *sabon gari*.[54]

The development of Keffi was similar but slightly varied. Keffi became the headquarters of the old Nasarawa Province for a while because of the killing of a colonial officer, Captain Maloney. It became the host of a Second Class Chief after it had grown just the same way as Abuja. In 1952, when the Keffi project which included building of a large secondary school, a hospital, a training college, a GRA and a water scheme was conceived and executed, the settlement witnessed rapid growth and development[55] so much so that by 1954, a vibrant cotton market had emerged which was followed by the establishment of a ginnery. Its development was further boosted by the spread and influence of mission activities as well as the construction of the Kaduna-Keffi Road in 1958.[56]

Other settlements within the area, such as Kuta, Karu and Dikko developed in like manner, though on a lesser scale. By 1970, Kuta had a rural health centre, secondary school, Area Development Board Office and a residence for the Divisional Officer who moved from Minna. Likewise, at Karu and Dikko, mission influence aided the functional transformation of the settlements.[57]

In sum, under colonial rule, the area that was soon to become Nigeria's FCT witnessed many administrative restructuring which put them under various administrative units and arrangement. Thus, the once independent polities and settlements were treated as villages and District areas and brought under Abuja Division in Benue-Plateau province and Koton-Karfe Division in Kabba province.[58] Abuja Division came under Niger Province and had Abuja (Suleija), Ashere, Kuje, Bwari, Dikko, Gwagwalada and Kwali as District areas. Nasarawa Division was under Benue Province and had Keffi, Karshi, Lafia, Karu and Toto as District areas. Koton Karfe Division under Kaba Province consisted of Koton Karfe, Tawari, Umaisha and Abaji as District areas.[59]

After these administrative restructuring, there was essentially no major changes that took place in the area even to the period immediately after Nigeria's political independence in 1960. However, as a result of the creation of states in 1967, the three provinces became part of newly created North-Western, Benue-Plateau and Kwara States, until 1975 when the area was carved out to form the present FCT.[60]

Development of the Federal Capital Territory (1976 – 1995)

It is on record that the desire to relocate the nation's capital from Lagos started with Lord Frederick Lugard when he initiated the 1914 Amalgamation Policy.[61] However, it was not until the early 1950s that politicians revisited the issue during the review of the Richard's Constitution. The agitation for it became more vociferous after Nigeria's political independence, especially in the early years of 1970s following reports and studies that revealed the land availability, environmental and security problems of Lagos as a nation's capital.[62] The then military administration under General Yakubu Gowon ignited public debate on the issue and initiated policies for realizing the new FCT. It was General Murtala

Ramat Mohammed that laid the concrete foundation for the creation of a new FCT by establishing *Ad-hoc* committees (one of which was the Aguda Panel[63]) and subsequently the promulgation of Decree No. 6 of 1976. Two years later, work commenced at the new FCT.

The location and size of the FCT was defined and limited by the *Abuja Master Plan* which was approved in 1979.[64] The piece of land that was carved out was 8,000 km², located and bounded in the north by Kaduna State, bordered by Niger State in the west, to the southwest by Kogi State and Nasarawa State in the east. The settlements that came within the FCT were neither under one traditional authority nor one local government area (LGA). The naming of the new nation's capital as Abuja seems to have been influenced by the suggestion of the site during the debate for a new FCT and by the proposal and feasibility study undertaken which included the settlement, Abuja (now Suleija). It was then obvious that Abuja was the biggest town in the proposed site and its map a clean square.[65] However, the settlement itself was carved out of the new FCT and renamed Suleija after the name of the incumbent ruler, while the land of the surrounding villages were added to others in Plateau and Kwara States to form the FCT.[66]

The *Abuja Master Plan* was a combination of several variables namely, aesthetics, quality of space, color, order and health. Abuja was designed to be an administrative city, not oriented to developing broad economic base characteristics of other larger cities of Nigeria but the nation's expression of unity as well as responsive to Nigerian urban tradition and lifestyles. Sandwiched within the natural solitude of Zuma-Bwari-Aso hill, the new capital city was envisaged to occupy an area of some 250 square kilometers. This would mean the city would occupy only 3 per cent of the FCT land area of 8,000 square kilometers. Provision was made for phased incremental growth and use of loose disposition in the city. It was estimated that the city will house a projected population of three million. The design also incorporated all the city functions, from cemeteries through residence to the business districts, parks, green areas and open spaces.[67]

Table 16.1. Phased Development of the Capital City Plan

PHASE	PROJECTED TARGET POPULATION
Phase 1	230,000
Phase 2	585,000
Phase 3	640,000
Phase 4	1,700,000
The phase 1 which comprised the most important and glamorous functions of the city was made up of six districts which included:	
Maitama District	Residential
Wuse District 1 & 2	Residential
Garki District 1 & 2	Residential
Asokoro District	Residential
Central Business District	Business

Source: Ministry of Federal Capital Territory (1992) *Abuja: So Far, So Good,* Efua Media Associates Limited, Lagos, pp 17.

In order to achieve the target of orderly growth of the new capital, the city was divided into four developmental phases. Aside from the Central Business District, all the other areas were developed for residential purpose (Table 16.1). However, due to office accommodation constraints, many residential quarters were temporarily converted to offices.[68]

Each residential district was further divided into smaller units called neighborhoods. Garki Districts 1 and 2 had 8 neighborhoods; Wuse District 1 and 2 had 15; Maitama District had 6; Asokoro District has 4 neighborhoods in the residential district of phase I of the plan. Each district and neighborhood was served with a centre, respectively, to serve as market/distribution points of goods and services for the residents. Area 1, 2 and 10 of Garki District had neighborhood stalls containing 148 stores, while one district shopping complex with 25 stores was sited at Wuse. Additional expansion was carried out at Wuse Shopping Centre with the construction of 38 lock-up shops and a neighborhood centre in Area 1 of Garki District. The Garki Neighborhood Centre "B" had 100 lock-up stalls, a post office, a clinic and a supermarket. Also in addition to 180 lock-up shops, the Garki District shopping complex had two banking halls and two supermarkets.[69]

The Central Business District was arguably the most important and imposing of all districts in the entire capital city, both in symbolic sense and in physical actuality. It was home to the Three Arms Zone, which comprised the Presidential complex, the National Assembly complex, the Supreme Court Building, the Federal Ministries complex, States Liaison offices and other extra-ministerial bodies' offices. It has also been designed to accommodate the National Mosque, National Ecumenical Centre, National Theatre, National Archive, National Conference Centre, National Stadium, and so on. The District's phases I & II form the nerve centre for all modes of transportation in and out of the city. It was home to urban shopping markets. Also two Diplomatic zones were located to east and west of Phase II of the District.[70] Perhaps the most outstanding features of the Business District were the three-line wide streets with expansive sidewalks and planted median strips called Boulevards; it is clear from the design that this District was envisaged to be the most attractive of the whole of the FCT.

It will also be instructive to mention that provision of social amenities such as educational facilities; police service posts; fire prevention facilities; post and telecommunications; and sporting and health facilities were not only adequately incorporated in the design but sited around the capital city to maximize efficiency and use.[71]

Administratively, the creation of FCT by the instrumentation of Decree No. 6 of 1976 bore out the need to administer the nation's new capital and its people directly as a state by the Federal Government (FGN) through the appointment of Minister of Federal Capital Territory (MFCT). For effective administration of the territory, therefore, the creation of an efficient local government system became imperative. In response to this, the military administration of General Muhammadu Buhari created Abuja Municipal, Gwagwalada, and Abaji Area Councils on 1st

October, 1984. Later on, on 27th August, 1989, General Ibrahim B. Babangida created Kuje and Kwali Area Councils. In a similar vein, the General Sani Abacha Military Administration added the list with the creation of the Bwari Area Council in 1996 to bring to the total of area councils in the FCT to six.[72]

Interestingly, the low population of the territory by 1976 largely informed its choice as an FCT. The total population of the FCT was put at 109,000 and 125,000 in 1963 and 1977, respectively.[73] However, the regional development authority of the FCT envisaged the population of the area to grow from about 171,000 in 1985 to a modest figure of about 825,000 in 1991, representing a 48.2 per cent increase in ten years. However, the territory witnessed unprecedented massive peopling due to the forceful movement of ministries, parastatals, extra-ministerial departments and some government agencies from Lagos starting 1985 and accelerated into the first half of the 1990s, as well as the influx of people from neighboring states in search of better working and living conditions. By 1988, the total population of the FCT estimated to had stood at 555,668 (Table 16.2).

The growth of population in the territory made a dramatic turn especially from 1990 upward after the seat of government had been officially brought to Abuja (Table 16.3).

Table 16.2. Estimated Population of the FCT by Area Council (1986-1988)

Area Council	Estimated Population		
	1986	1987	1988
Abaji	62,300	65,400	70,305
Municipal	198,500	208,400	224,030
Gwagwalada	121,300	127,400	136,955
Kuje	110,200	115,700	124,378
TOTAL	492,300	516,900	555,668

Source: Federal Capital Territory, *Digest of Statistics*, 1989.

Table 16.3. Estimated Population of the FCT by Area Council (1990-1995)

Area Council	Estimated Population					
	1990	1991	1992	1993	1994	1995
Abaji	15,239	23,642	24,891	25,762	26,626	27,403
Municipal	157,603	212,854	214,931	215,912	217,604	218,696
Gwagwalada	69,441	80,841	81,110	81,576	82,206	82,475
Kuje	53,456	61,329	61,782	63,333	64,404	65,022

Source: Federal Capital Territory, *Digest of Statistics*, 1990.

A review of the origin and development of the FCT would certainly not be complete without briefly discussing the resettlement scheme in line with Decree No. 6 of 1976. In 1980, the new civilian administration of Alhaji Shehu Shagari constituted two Presidential committees charged with the duty of settling the aborigines and ensuring the acceleration of development of the FCT. First, the *Ad-hoc* Committee on settlement was inaugurated on 6th June 1980 and had as its members Senator A.D. Rufai (Chairman), Alhaji Abubakar Koko, Alhaji Ibrahim

Aliyu and Mr. S.S. Gofwen. The Committee's terms of reference were: (1) to determine the number of inhabitants who wish to move out voluntarily from the FCT; (2) to bring up a plan for the phasing of movement and settlement in accordance with available funds and to determine the extent of Federal Government assistance; and (3) to determine priorities of resettlement of inhabitants in peripheral towns and villages.[74]

Consistent with the provisions of the Decree No.6 of 1976, the Committee recommended that all inhabitants in the FCT should be evacuated and resettled outside of it at the expense of the FGN. However, it was quick to recognize the likely difficulties to be encountered in implementing such an exercise alone. Following due consultation with the Federal Capital Development Authority (FCDA) and officials of the affected states (Niger, Plateau, Kaduna and Kwara), the latter were requested to set up their own resettlement committees with representatives from FCDA.[75]

One of the decisions reached by the FCDA officials and state resettlement committees was that the latter would provide resettlement areas for each village or a combination of villages displaced from the FCT. Individual persons affected by the exercise were to be provided with new dwellings comparable in size to the ones abandoned in the FCT. In addition, the cost of community facilities within each of the new settlements such as schools, rural health centers, local water supply, community centers and market stalls were to be borne by the FGN.[76] However, following complaints and disaffection from the indigenes as well as Prof. Akin Mabogunje's recommendation, the FGN was compelled to reverse the initial decision to wholesomely uproot the inhabitants occupying the expanse of land of the FCT and into much smaller areas without their consent. Thence, the people were allowed to continue staying where they were unless their lands were required for development, after which they were to be compensated before they were reallocated[77]; a move consistent with the spirit and provisions of the 1972 Land Use Decree (and 1978 Amendment).

Subsequently, the activities of FCDA as regards resettlement were limited to monetary compensation to the displaced persons. Little or nothing seems to have been done by the Federal Capital Territory Administration (FCTA) in terms of physical development as at 1983 when it was dissolved.[78] After the dissolution of FCTA, a task force on resettlement was inaugurated in November, 1983 charged with the responsibility of: (1) assessing the worth of crops and economic trees to be affected by development of the territory; (2) paying compensation due to affected villages; (3) selecting of sites, preparing and implementing development plans for affected villages; (4) overseeing the implementation of plans prepared; and (5) arranging and supervising the movement of the villagers into their new locations.[79]

The first effort at resettling the affected persons was consummated under the Usman Town Resettlement Scheme, which was commissioned in 1986. About

1,200 displaced persons from 3 villages namely Peyi (Garki), Jigo and Kwabara were accommodated at the lower Usman Dam site.[80]

By 1995, the resettlement task force unit through the progress made in the preparation of the master/detail development plan was able to start on other resettlement schemes at Kuje, Giri, Karu and Ushafa. The Kuje Resettlement Scheme was able to accommodate displaced persons and aborigines by the accelerated development of the various projects in Phase II of the FCT; the Giri Resettlement Scheme accommodated about 26 villages within the Abuja University site area of Giri; the Karu Resettlement Scheme was able to accommodate 2 hamlets located within the Federal Housing Authority Estate at Karu; the Ushafa resettlement Scheme was planned to accommodate the inhabitants of the old Ushafa village because of its proximity to the lower course of the river that feeds Usman Dam. Also villages affected by the expansion of the existing Airport expressway were relocated to Dutse/Kubwa, Gawu-Babangida and Sabon Wuse Resettlement areas in Niger State.[81] These resettlement towns consisted of 186 housing units ranging from one to three bedrooms with full range of facilities/infrastructure like school, road, sewage, health clinic and water supply.

The second major scheme was the Kubwa Resettlement Scheme which consisted of 500 housing units expected to provide accommodation for about 10,000 persons displaced from villages located in the Phase I and II of *Abuja Master Plan*.[82]

In all these cases, the MFCT claimed to have adequately taken care of the interests of the displaced inhabitants and aborigines by way of providing adequate compensation in respect of crops destroyed and economic trees as well as in the provision of infrastructure/facilities.[83] However a five-year study of the economic and social consequences of these resettlement schemes by Mailafiya Filaba[84] reveals that the people had suffered from denial of right to property; under-valuation of assets and under-compensation; social and economic alienation and insecurity. This is how the author sums the mood of the people:

> the modus operandi of the development of Abuja FCT was violent to the agrarian communities by denying them their fundamental human rights. The initiators of the FCT did not deem it fit to first negotiate with owners of the land before promulgating Decree No.6 of 1976. Only 15% of the indigenous communities were poorly compensated and resettled. The remaining indigenes were left in quagmire and torture. Government has failed to tell them their fate while their land was being forcibly taken away for the rich and allocation of plots to commercialists and Multi-National Corporations (MNCs).[85]

Notes and References

1. The Justice T. Akinola Aguda Panel on the Location of the Federal Capital Report recommended that the demarcation for the new FCT should start from Izom on 7°E Longitude and 9° 15' Latitude, projected on a straight line westwards to a point just North of Lefu on the Kemi River; then projected on a line along 6047½ 'E southwards

passing close to the villages called Semasu, Zui and Bassa down to a place a little west of Ebagi thence project a line along parallel 8^0 30'N Latitude and 7020'E Longitude; thence projected on a line northwards joining the village of Odu, Karshi and Karu. The line should proceed along the boundary between North-West and Benue-Plateau (Nasarawa) State as far as Karu; thence the line should proceed along the boundary between North-Central (Kaduna) and North-Western (Niger) States up to the point just North of Bwari village; then it should go straight to Zuba village; thence the line should go straight to back to Izom (For the location of the federal capital territory see diagram 3).

2. Baba, I. (2003) "Federal Capital Territory, Abuja: A Reflection into its Past", *Gbagyi Journal Vol.2 No.1*. (Special Edition), Mazlink Nigeria, Jos, Nigeria; Mahdi, A. (1974) "The Hausa Factor in West Africa", an unpublished PhD Dissertation, Centre of African Studies, University of Birmingham, London, pp 43.

3. Scoper, R.C. 91980) "The Stone Age in Northern Nigeria", *Journal Historical Society of Nigeria (JHSN)*, Vol. III No.2, Ibadan University Press, Ibadan, Nigeria.

4. Ichaba, A.E. (1993) *A Social Cultural Study of the People of Abuja Vol.1*, Research and Documentation Unit, Council for Arts and Culture, Abuja, Nigeria, pp 2.

5. Hassan, M. and M. Shuaibu Naibi (1962) *A Chronicle of Abuja*, African University Press Lagos, Nigeria, pp 83.

6. Yinusa, A. (1998) "A History of Zuba Settlement Pattern in the Federal Capital Territory", an unpublished B.A. Project, Department of History, University of Abuja, Nigeria, pp 2.

7. This account is from oral traditions collected by Amina Yinusa in March, 1998 and cited in Yinusa, A. (1998), *op. cit.*, pp 11.

8. Mahdi, A. (1974), *op. cit.*, pp 29.

9. Anyanwu, E.M.U. (1998) "A History and Development of Nyanya Up to 1975", an unpublished B.A. Project, Department of History, University of Abuja, Nigeria, pp 12.

10. Anyanwu, E.M.U. (1998) *op. cit.*, pp 9.

11. Okpave, S. (1998) "The Evolution of Karshi in the Federal Capital Territory", an unpublished B.A. Project, Department of History, University of Abuja, Nigeria; Anyanwu (1998) *op. cit.*, pp 13.

12. This account emanated from oral interviews with Elder Danladi Iyah at Garki (6/8/98) and Chief Adamu Iyah (JP) and members of his cabinet on 20/12/97 at his Palace in Nyanya, conducted by Anyanwu (1998), *op. cit.*

13. This account follows traditions collected by Bitrus Narai reported in Filaba, M.A. (1994) "Karu, Kurape and Kurudu Kingdoms: A study of Cultural, Economic, Social and Political Changes among the Gbagyi of Central Nigeria in the 18th and 19th Centuries", an unpublished M.A. Thesis, Ahmadu Bello University, Zaria-Nigeria; and by Mailafiya Aruwa Filaba as well as others cited in Filaba, M.A. (1994).

14. Arnet, F. (1920) *Gazetteers of Zaria Province*, pp 8-9; Usman, Y.B. (1988) "Facts, Values and Nigerian Historiography" Department of History, Ahmadu Bello University, Zaria, Nigeria, pp 170ff; Gunn, H.D. and F.P. Conant (1960) "People of the Middle Niger Region of Northern Nigeria", *Ethnographic Survey of Africa*, Part XV, International African Institute, London; Temple, O and C. Temple (eds) (1965) *Notes on the Tribes of Provinces, Emirates and States of Northern Provinces of Nigeria*, Frank Cass and Co. Ltd, London.; *NAK SPN 172245 KARGI MANUSCRIPT*: "The

History of Kargi"; Oyedele, E. (1987) "Colonial Urbanization in Northern Nigeria: Kaduna 1913-1960", an unpublished PhD Dissertation, department of History, Ahmadu Bello University, Zaria, Nigeria, pp 24; Sciortino, J.C. (1972) "Nasarawa Province", *Gazetteer of Northern Nigeria*, Vol. III, Central Kingdom, Pref. Notes by A.H.M. Kirk Greene Frank Cass, London; Hassan, M. and Mallam Shuaibu Naibi (1962) *op. cit.*

15. Ichaba, A.E. (1993) *op. cit.*

16. Martins, F.F. (1975) "A History of the Origins and Development of Karu in the FCT up to 1990", an unpublished B.A. Project, Department of History, University of Abuja, Nigeria, pp 26.

17. Scoper, R.C (1965) *op. cit.*, pp 185; Obayemi, A. (1980) "States and People of the Niger-Benue Confluence Area", Obaro Ikime (ed.) *Ground Work of Nigeria History*, Heinemann Educational Books Nigeria Limited, pp 145.

18. Filaba (1994), *op. cit.*, pp 28.

19. *Ibid*, pp 20.

20. Sciortino (1972), *op. cit.*, pp 18; Hassan and Naibi (1962), *op. cit.*

21. Baba (2003) *op. cit.*, pp 10; Sciortino (1972), *op. cit.*; Hassan and Naibi (1962), *op. cit.*

22. Hocking, J.A. (1977) "Twentieth-century Evolution of Rural Settlement in the Abuja Area", *Savanna* Vol. 6 No.1 (June); Gunn and Conant (1962), *op. cit.*, pp 80.

23. Hassan and Na'ibi, (1962) *op. cit.*, pp 4; Smith, M.G. (1920) *The Economy of Hausa Communities of Zaria*, London, pp 3.

24. Hocking, J.A. (1977), *Op. cit.*

25. Hocking, J.A. (1977), *Op. cit.*, pp 57; Hassan and N'ibi, *op. cit.*, 1-45.

26. Hocking, J.A. (1977), *op. cit.*, pp 57; Prothero, R.M. (1970) "Population and Pioneer Areas in Tropical Africa: A Review", *Symposium on Population Problems in Pioneer Areas*, Institute of British Geographers (mimeo).

27. Hocking, J.A. (1977), *op. cit.*, pp 57.

28. Hocking, J.A. (1977), *op. cit.*, pp 58; Hassan and N'ibi, *op. cit.*, 43.

29. Wilson, G. (1939) *Touring Diaries of an A.D.O., 22 July, 1938 – 19 January, 1939*, Rhodes House Library, Oxford (mss Afr. S.549).

30. Hocking, J.A. (1977), *op. cit.*, pp 58; Wilson, G. (1939) *op. cit.*; Gunn and Conant (1962), *op. cit.*, pp 93.

31. Sessional Paper 22 of 1937, *Annual Report for the Northern Province, 1936*, Lagos, pp 27.

32. Hocking, J.A. (1977), *op. cit.*, pp 59.

33. *Ibid.* pp 59.

34. *Ibid.* pp 60.

35. *Ibid.* pp 60.

36. Nigeria, Government of (1930) *Communication Guide*, Lagos; Sessional Paper 22 of 1937, *op. cit.*

37. Hocking, J.A. (1977), *op. cit.*, pp 60.

38. Udo, R.K. (1966) "Transformation of Rural Settlements in British Tropical Africa", *Nigerian Geographical Journal*, 9, 1966, pp 129-44.

39. *Ibid.* pp 61.

40. *Ibid.*
41. Sciortino, J.C. (1972), *op. cit.*, pp 93.
42. Sciortino, J.C. (1972), *op. cit.*; Hocking, J.A. (1977), *op. cit.*, pp 61.
43. Sciortino, J.C. (1972), *op. cit.*
44. Mortimore, M.J. (1970) *Zaria and its Region*, (ed.), pp 112.
45. Gunn, H.D. and F.D. Conant, op. cit., pp 98.
46. Hocking, J.A. (1977), *op. cit.*, pp 62.
47. Sciortino, J.C. (1972), *op. cit.*, pp 24.
48. Udo, R.K. (1966), *op. cit.*
49. Hocking, J.A. (1977), *op. cit.*, pp 63.
50. *Ibid.* pp 64.
51. Martins, F.F. (1995) "A History of the Origins and Development of Karu in the Federal Capital Territory Up to 1990", an unpublished B.A. Project, Department of History, University of Abuja, Nigeria.
52. Hocking, J.A. (1977), *op. cit.*, pp 64.
53. *Ibid.*
54. *Ibid.* 64.
55. Northern Region of Nigeria, *Provincial Annual Reports, 1952*, Kaduna, 28.
56. Hocking, J.A. (1977), *op. cit.*, pp 64.
57. *Ibid.* 64.
58. Gunn, H.D. and F.P. Conant (1960), *op. cit.*, pp 86.
59. Baba, I. (2003), *op. cit.*, pp 10.
60. Ministry of Federal Capital Territory (1992) *Abuja: So Far, So Good*, Efua Media Associates Limited, Lagos, pp 7.
61. Awa, E.O. (1964) *Federal Government in Nigeria*, California, pp 51-52.
62. Such studies and reports include Sovani, N.V. (1964) "Analysis of Over-urbanization", *Economic Development and Cultural Change* 12 (January), pp 113-122; Hauser, P.M. (1963) "The Social, Economic and Technological Problems of Rapid Urbanization", in Hoseltiz, B.F. and W.E. Moore (eds) *Industrialization and Society*, UNESCO; Marris, P. (1967) "Motives and Methods: Reflections on a Study in Lagos", in H. Miner (ed) *The City in Modern Africa*, Pall Mall, London, pp 39-54; Mabogunje, A.L. (1967) *Urbanization in Nigeria*, Uni. London, pp 238-297; The *Nigerian Chronicle*, 13th February, 1914, pp 8; Ademilehin, B. (1971) "Should Lagos Remain Federal Capital? The Debate in 1914", *Sunday Times* (20th June), pp 8; Lawal, W.G. (1970) "For Security Reasons, Let Move Capital Up Country", *Sunday Times* (3 May), pp 7.
63. Which had as members Hon. (Dr) Justice T. Akinola Aguda (as Chairman) Dr. Tai Solarin, Col. Monsignor, Pedro Martins, Alhaji Muhammed Musa Isma, Chief Owen Fiebai , Dr. Ajato Gandonu and Prof. K. Ogan.
64. Abumere, S.A. (1995) "The New Federal Capital Territory: Regional Development and Planning", in Tamuno, T.A. *et. al.*, *Nigeria since Independence: The First 25 Years*, Vol. 4. Government and Public Policy, Federal Government of Nigeria, Lagos, 189; T.A. Aguda, T.A. *et. al.* (1976) *Report of the Committee on the Location of the Federal Capital Territory*; Federal Government of Nigeria (1976) *White Paper on the Report of the Committee on the Location of Federal Capital*, Lagos, Nigeria.

65. Azikiwe, N. (1994) *Dialogue of a New Capital for Nigeria: A Political Analyst*, Ahmadu Bello University Press, Zaria, Nigeria.

66. Filaba, M.A. (2003) "Violations of the Fundamental Human Rights of the Rural Communities in the F.C.T. Abuja: Perception of the Indigenes", *Gbagyi Journal* Vol. 2. No.1 (Special Edition), Mazlink Nigeria, Jos, Nigeria. Abuja in 1981 had substantial settlements with about 200,000 people under 15 Districts: Karu, Bwari, Gadabuke, Gawun, Karshi, Koton Karfe, Kuje, Kwali, Lapai, Suleja and Toto.

67. Ministry of Federal Capital Territory (1992), *op. cit.*, pp 16-17; Ministry of Federal Capital Territory (1999) *Report of Ministerial Committee for the Appraisal of Physical Planning and Development Issues in the Federal Capital Territory Abuja*, Vol. 1 (November).

68. Ministry of Federal Capital Territory (1992), *op. cit.*, pp 17.

69. *Ibid.*

70. *Ibid.* pp 18.

71. Owan, M.A. (1997) "Healthcare Delivery in the Federal Capital Territory from 1976-1996", an unpublished B.A. Project, Department of History, University of Abuja, Nigeria; Ede, B.N. (2002) "Igbos and Transportation Business in Northern Nigeria: A Case of FCT Abuja from 1976-2002", an unpublished B.A. Project, Department of History, University of Abuja, Nigeria; Abdullahi, R. (1995) "A History of Industrialization in the Federal Capital Territory since 1975", an unpublished B.A. Project, Department of History, University of Abuja, Nigeria; Salau, A.H. (2004) The Evolution of Local Governments in the Federal Capital Territory (FCT): A Case Study of Abuja Municipal Area Council (A.M.A.C.) (1976-2003), an unpublished B.A. Project, Department of History, University of Abuja, Nigeria; Tador, V.T. (1998) "Development of Western Education in Gwagwalada Area 1940-1997", an unpublished B.A. Project, Department of History, University of Abuja, Nigeria; Ministry of Federal Capital Territory (1992), *op. cit.*, pp 18.

72. Salau, A.H. (2004), *op. cit.*, pp 20-28.

73. *Ibid.* pp 29.

74. Federal Government of Nigeria (1980) *Interim Report of the Presidential Ad-hoc Committee on Resettlement of the Inhabitants of the Federal Capital Territory (FCT)* (September), pp i-iii.

75. *Ibid.* pp 3.

76. *Ibid.* pp 4.

77. *Ibid.* pp 7.

78. Ambrose, U. (1998) "Changing Population Trends in the Federal Capital Territory 1985-1995", an unpublished B.A. Project, Department of History, University of Abuja, Nigeria, pp 27. It should be noted that resettlement activities from the beginning was the sloe responsibility of the Federal Capital Territory Administration (FCTA) which was then a sectional unit of the FCDA.

79. Olusola, A. (1993) *Abuja, Nigeria, New Capital*, Concept Inc. (Nig.) Limited, pp 71-72.

80. Ministry of Federal Capital Territory (1992) *Abuja: Achievements of the Ministry of Federal Capital Territory*, Efua Media Associates Ltd, Lagos, pp 73.

81. *Ibid.* pp 75.

82. Ambrose, U. (1998), *op. cit.*, pp 28.

83. Ministry of Federal Capital Territory (1992) *op. cit.*

84. Filaba, M.A. (2003), *op. cit.*, pp 28-52.

85. *Ibid.* pp 43.

About the Editor

Dr. Hakeem Ibikunle Tijani, editor of this volume is currently an assistant professor of history and social sciences at the University of St. Francis, Joliet, Illinois. He previously taught at the Lagos State University and Henderson State University in Nigeria and Arkansas, United States respectively. He was a Commonwealth scholar at SOAS, University of London; a recipient of the prestigious U.S. Military National Merit Award; he has received research grants from Harry Truman Library and Institute, the MacMath Endowment Foundation, and Henderson State University Faculty Development. His most recent grants are from University of St. Francis Academic Professional Growth and the American Historical Association Schmitt 2005 award. His research interests are: intellectual and nationalist history, anticommunism and decolonization in West Africa, urban history, and Anglo-American relation in post-1945 West Africa. A 2005 Reader for The College Board Advanced Placement World History examination, he is the author of *"Britain, Leftist Nationalists, and the Transfer of Power in Nigeria, 1945-1965"* (New York/London: Routledge Publisher, 2005) [ISBN 0415978122].

About the Contributors

Abolade Adeniji, PhD, is a senior lecturer at the department of History and International Relations, Lagos State University, Nigeria. He has published articles in learned journals and books. He is also the coordinator of International Studies diploma program at the Lagos State University.

Adewole Atere, PhD, is a senior lecturer and chair of sociology at the Lagos State University, Nigeria.

Adoyi Onoja, MA, is currently a lecturer at the department of History, Nasarawa State University, Nigeria. He has published widely and contributes to newspapers on current affairs.

Akeem Ayofe Akinwale, MA, is currently completing a doctoral degree in sociology at the University of Ibadan, Nigeria. He has attended many local and international conferences where he presented studies on sociological implication of urban development.

Dan-Oye Laguda, PhD, is a lecturer at the department of Religions and Philosophy, Lagos State University, Nigeria. A journalist and teacher, Laguda currently teaches African philosophy at Lagos State University.

Hakeem Ibikunle Tijani, PhD, editor of this volume is currently an assistant professor of history and social science at the University of St. Francis, Joliet, Illinois. He previously taught in Nigeria between 1988 and 1998. His research interests are: intellectual and nationalist history, anticommunism and decolonization in West Africa, urban history, and Anglo-American relation in post-1945 West Africa. His work published by Routledge, New York/London is titled *Britain, Leftist Nationalists and the Transfer of Power in Nigeria, 1945-1965*. Greenwood Press, Westport, Connecticut in 2006, will publish his volume on Culture and Customs of Ethiopia.

Ibrahim Umaru, PhD, teaches Economics at Nasarawa State University. He was formerly a journalist and a web developer.

Jare Ajayi, MA, is an associate member of Institute of African Studies, University of Ibadan, Nigeria, and the Executive Director, African Agency for an Enhanced Socio-Ethics and Traditional Order (ASETO), Ibadan, Oyo State, Nigeria.

Mosope Fagbongbe, MA, has degrees in history and international relations and law from Lagos State University and the University of Lagos respectively. She completed a Master's degree in Law at the University of Manitoba, Canada. She is on the faculty of law at the University of Lagos, Nigeria. Mosope is currently a doctoral candidate at the University of British Columbia, Vancouver, Canada.

Saheed Aderinto, BA, was formerly a research assistant at French Institute in Africa, Institute of African Studies, University of Ibadan. He is at present a graduate student at the University of Texas, Austin.

Rasheed Olaniyi, PhD, is SEPHIS-CODESRIA's Young Historian and AAPS-HF Guggenheim Foundation's African Young Scholar. He completed a doctoral degree at the Department of History, Bayero University, Nigeria. Formerly a program officer at the Centre for Research and Documentation, Kano, Nigeria; He is a lecturer at the department of history, University of Ibadan, Nigeria. His research interests include ethnic relations, Diaspora studies, and urban development.

Patrick Ebewo, PhD, is a senior lecturer in drama and theater arts at the National University of Botswana. He was formerly an assistant director of Arts and Culture at the Nigeria Arts and Culture Center. He is widely published in learned journals and referred books.

Dipo O. Olubomehin, PhD, is a senior lecturer and chair of History and Diplomatic Studies at Olabisi Onabanjo University, Ago-Iwoye, Ogun State, Nigeria. A specialist in economic history, Olubomehin's works has appeared locally and internationally.

Olayemi Akinwunmi, PhD, is the founding chair of history department at Nassarawa State University and a professor of history. A recipient of many distinguished fellowships, Professor Akinwunmi is well known for his works particularly concerning German colonial rule in West Africa, and the development of African metallurgy.

Seyi Fabiyi, PhD, lectures at the University of Ibadan in the department of Geography. He holds a BSc in Urban and Regional Planning, and M.Tech and PhD in Geography. He specializes in urban environmental analysis with geo-statistical techniques and sensitivity index mapping. He has published in both local and international journals and attended many conferences. He is a member of many professional bodies such as Nigerian Institute of Town Planners, Nigerian Geographical Association, and the Nigerian Environmental Society GIS Users Association.

Index

Abakaliki 8, 9, 202

Abeokuta 5, 31, 49, 51, 52, 54, 122, 154, 158, 202, 203

Abioye 192

Abubakar Umar 23, 238

Adeniyi, Tola 59, 157

Administrative Areas 153

African Anti-Colour Bar Movement 139

African religion 191-193, 195-198

Agaja Trudo 120

Agbabu 48-50, 52

Agbese, Dan 61

Agriculture 4, 20, 38-40, 45, 53, 128, 203

Akin Mabogunje 2, 123, 145, 146, 148, 154

Akure 31, 46, 48

Alaukwu, Georgina 67

Amalgamated 7

Ancestors and Religion 69, 145, 192, 193, 197, 229

Annexation 123

Ansar-ud-deen 138, 141

Anti-prostitution laws 78, 92, 101, 102, 109-111, 113

Apartment for Religious Functions 145

ARCHCON 22, 24

Archetypes in Residential Precincts 145, 162

Architecture of Central areas 153

Arikola 49

Aristophanes 59

Arochukwu District 8

Athol Fugard 58

Aworis 126

Babangida Structural Adjustment Program (SAP) 205

Babangida, Major-General Ibrahim 62, 238

Badagry 5, 119-130

Badagry Local Governments 127, 128

Baptist Primary School 141

Belief and practice in Religion 192

Bere 147

Betrothal 82, 89, 103, 107, 108

Biological Theory 121

Bode Sowande 60

Boma boys 104, 110, 111

Border markets 125, 130

Border town 119, 125, 130

Boundary treaty 121

Brazilian style 150-152, 158

Bridges 11, 122

British 4, 6-9, 32, 45-47, 52, 61, 80, 82, 83, 86, 90, 101, 102, 108, 121-124, 133-139, 148, 149, 152, 153, 168-170, 211, 227, 230-233

Buhari, Major-General Muhammadu 62, 66, 237

Building process in Pre-Colonial times 146, 152

Business or Commercial Districts 153

Businessmen 152

Calabar 5, 8-10, 154

Cantonment proclamation 135

Central business district 163, 236, 237

Central market 4, 149

Central place theory 4, 119, 183

Chief's houses 146

Child prostitutes 90, 109

Church Mission Society Primary
    School 138, 141

Civil war 62, 154

Cognizance 20, 24, 27, 177

Colonial 1-7, 11, 12, 18, 21, 27, 32, 33,
    38, 45-49, 51-55, 60, 61, 71, 75-87,
    89-92, 99-103, 106-109, 112-114,
    119, 124-126, 130, 133-137, 139,
    142, 145-153, 155, 157-159, 161,
    163, 169, 170, 184, 202-204, 208,
    213, 216, 227, 230-233, 235

Colonial policy 11, 124, 126, 139

Colonial road transport 45

Colonial Urban Centers and Urbanism
    148

Commoners' houses 146

Convertible currencies 129

Cultural Determinant Theory 32

Cultural factor 21

Customary law 169

Dahomeans 126

Declaration of protectorate 121

Decree No. 22 184

Demobilizations 91, 113

Dependency school 45

Dependency theory 35

Derelict old buildings especially at the
    core of old traditional cities 163

Development 1, 5, 6, 11, 12, 15-17, 21,
    22, 28, 31, 34-39, 43, 45, 57-61, 63,
    67, 69, 72, 112, 123, 126-128, 138,
    141, 154, 159, 161-163, 167, 168,
    170-173, 175, 176, 183-189, 206,
    207, 212, 215, 227, 231, 235, 239

DFRRI 127, 212, 214, 215, 221

Dilapidation 22

District officer 89, 103, 109, 149, 152

Dual system of law 167

Economy 16-18, 34, 45-47, 52, 54, 55,
    62, 84, 88, 89, 103, 106, 122, 124,
    130, 149, 154, 175, 194, 203, 205,
    206, 214, 220

Ede 46, 203

Ejinrin 48-50, 52

Eket 8

Elective mechanism 168

Elite 67

Ellis, A.B. 192

English 197

English laws 169

Environment 1, 3, 17, 29, 30, 47, 59,
    72, 102, 110, 128, 155, 160, 162,
    169, 173-175, 215, 216

Epe 48, 52, 66, 127

Equal Pay Act 33

Estates 6, 11, 155, 184, 186

European norms 168

European Reservation Areas 149, 152,
    170

European residential 135

Exploitation 11, 18, 40, 45-47, 55, 57,
    67, 119, 168

External trade 45

Faith based organizations 213, 219,
    221

Federal government of Nigeria's
    Directorate of Food 212, 214

Federal Housing Authority 30

Fee tail 169

Feminism theory 33

Fishing Cooperatives 129

Forced labor 46

"French Village" 127
From Zia with Love 66

Gargantuan designs 21
Gbilekaa 58, 67
Gender 27, 29, 31, 33, 35, 37-39,
   41-43, 206
Gender and Sex roles 28, 29
Gender Issues in Development
   Planning 31
George Carey 220
Globalization and Religion 194
Government housing schemes 152
Government Reserved Areas 133
GRA 5, 6, 22, 133, 158, 231, 234, 235
Great depression 137

Harem apartment 146
Hausa 4, 5, 32, 78, 79, 81, 87, 90, 112,
   121, 124, 133-138, 140, 202, 203,
   205, 207, 228, 230, 232-234
Heinrich Boll Foundation (HBF) 206,
   207
High income earners housing 164
Hodder, B.W. 49, 123
Holy Trinity Primary School 138, 141
Housing 4, 6, 11, 17, 20-23, 29-31, 35,
   140, 146, 149-152, 154-164, 168,
   175, 176, 178, 186-188, 197, 215,
   217, 221, 240
Housing shortage 168

Ibadan 5, 7, 31, 46, 49, 51, 52, 54, 59,
   68, 83-87, 89, 90, 100, 107, 111,
   113, 114, 145, 149, 154, 157, 158,
   202-205
Idowu, Bolagi 193, 198, 199

Igbokoda 48, 52
Ijebu 48-52, 54, 126
Ikare 46
Ikirun 46
Ikorodu 48-50, 52, 122, 185-187
Ilaro division 122, 125, 129
Ilase 46
Immigrants 17, 53, 126, 134-140, 151,
   156, 230
Indigenous economy 46, 54
Indigenous trade 48
Industrialization 34, 35, 86, 175, 216
Industry 16, 39, 57, 155, 158, 161, 185
Informal dwellings and shanty struc-
   tures 163
Informal settlements 168
Infrastructure 16, 212, 214
Institutional buildings 164
Internal trade 48
International boundaries 119
Intraregional trade 48
Islam 107, 193-195, 208

Jankara 46
Johnson, Colonel Mobolaji 62, 81,
   183, 185

Kaduna 6, 21-23, 31, 79, 83, 84, 105,
   136-138, 140, 143, 154, 202, 203,
   205, 208
Kajola 46
Kano 4-6, 29, 31, 38, 79, 80, 83-85,
   87, 89, 100, 105, 112, 114, 122,
   134-143, 145, 149, 154, 158, 202-
   206, 228, 229
Kano Riot 205
King Palace 145, 146
Kole Omotosho 60

KSHA 23
Kuti, Chief T.O. 51, 52, 219
Lagos 4, 5, 7, 29-32, 49-51, 53, 54, 71, 72, 83-85, 88-90, 100, 103, 104, 107-109, 111, 113, 114, 120-124, 126-130, 139, 145, 148-152, 154, 157, 158, 161-163, 167, 169-176, 178, 183-186, 188, 193, 197, 198, 202-207, 227, 235, 236, 238

Lagos Badagry Expressway 127
Lagos Executive Development Board 148, 170
Lagos State 127, 128, 162, 167, 171, 173-176, 183, 185, 188, 197, 198
Lagos State Development and Planning Corporation 188
Lagos State Industrial policy 183
Land holding 158, 169
Land Tenure System 172
Land Use Act 169, 171-174, 177
Lander, Richard and John 121, 122
Legally planned development 168
Life span 169
Little, Kenneth 2
Local craft industry 45
Local statutes 169
Lord Haldane 169
Low income planned housing 163
LSDPC 188
Ludwig, Emile 192

Magic 192, 221
Mandela, Nelson 211
Manufactured goods 46, 47, 49
Marx, Karl 33
Marxian Approach 33
Medicine 193

Medicine for Love 63
Middle income earners 152
Migration 17, 27, 83, 120, 123, 168, 201
Ministry of Housing and Urban Development 30
Modernization theory 35
Mofereyi 46
Moslem 169
Murdock, George Peter 32
Mushin 184, 186-189, 207
Mushin local government council 186-188

NAPEP 212-214, 217, 218, 221
National objective 20
Native authority 137-139, 231, 234
Native land 169
Nature and Types of Urban Architecture (Colonial Period) 150
NDE 212
NEEDS 1, 6, 16, 24, 28, 30, 37, 88, 141, 164, 168, 178, 185, 186, 188, 212, 214, 217, 218, 221
New low quality residential 151
Ngugi wa Thiong'o 58
Nigeria 2-7, 9, 11, 15, 27-33, 38, 43, 47, 49, 50, 52, 58-61, 63-65, 67, 70, 76, 77, 80, 81, 84, 86, 89, 90, 100, 102, 104, 108, 111-114, 123, 124, 127, 133-135, 138-140, 148, 154, 158, 159, 168, 170-172, 176, 198, 202, 203, 208, 216, 217
Nigerian legal system 167
Nigerian Motor Transport Union (N.M.T.U.) 51
Nigerian Urban and Regional Planning Act 173, 176
Nixon, Richard 59

Nok culture 3
Northern Elements Progressive Union 139
Nupe 133, 136, 137, 228, 229

Obasanjo, Olusegun 31, 62, 217
Obligations 52, 121, 168, 211
Obubra District 8, 9, 103
Oja Oba/Oja'ba 46, 187
Okitipupa 48, 49, 52
Olodan 46
Olusanya 51, 135
Ondo 48, 52
Onitsha 9, 10, 31, 154, 203
Oodua Peoples Congress 205
Opeji 49
Oshele 46
Oshogbo 46, 52, 203
Osita Agwuna 139
Owena 46
Owene 46
Oyo 31, 46, 51, 54, 122, 123

Pimping 111
Pioneers 60, 67
Pioneers and Political Development 60
Plato 57
Pluralistic 169
Political Power Plays 61
Population 5, 17, 53, 119, 120, 123, 138, 154, 164, 168, 183, 188, 213, 218, 233, 234, 236, 238
Postcolonial urban forms and urbanism 154
Poverty 27, 35, 36, 38, 71, 119, 168, 197, 205, 211-215, 217, 218, 220
Poverty and Urbanization 215

Preboundary routes 122
Prostitution 2, 34, 75-92, 99-114, 134, 217
Public works 212

Queen Amina 32

Radicals 60, 63, 67
Radicals and Political Development 67
Raji Abdallah 139
Rate of urbanization in Nigeria 29
Renaissance 61, 126
Repatriation 91, 92, 99, 114
Rights 43, 80, 82, 135, 168-173, 204, 206, 207, 240
Rise of Modern Architecture in urban Nigeria 159
Rivers Province 10
Road network 178
Road transportation 45-55
Royal Niger Company 9
Rural 2-6, 11, 17, 18, 27, 29, 31-33, 36, 52, 53, 76, 83, 84, 87, 88, 108, 127-129, 140, 149, 154, 155, 157, 168, 172, 173, 176, 183, 184, 187, 197, 198, 203, 211-219, 221, 228, 230, 231, 233, 235, 239

Sabon Gari 4, 87, 105, 112, 133, 135, 137, 139, 141, 143, 234
Saharan 3, 4, 121, 211
Sani Abacha 238
Sasa 46
Sekona 46
Shehu Shagari 62, 238
Socialization 15, 133
Society of Nigerian Theatre Artists 59

Socioeconomic 27, 28, 43, 136, 140

Southwestern Nigeria 45, 46, 81

Spoliation 18

Squalor 168, 215

Stagnation 130

Structural Adjustment Program 205, 212, 213, 215-217

"Symbolic Peace, Symbolic Gifts" 64

Talbot, P.A. 82, 90, 192

The Raft 63, 69

Throne Room 146

Trade 4, 5, 7, 18, 20, 39, 45, 48, 49, 85, 89, 104, 105, 113, 119-126, 128, 130, 134, 148, 193, 211, 221, 229, 233

Unhealthy 105, 168

Urban biography 2

Urban growth 12, 175, 216

Urban migration 27, 29, 83, 154, 168, 176

Urban programs 21

Urban slum 18, 138, 139, 168

Urbanism 145, 148, 149, 154

Urbanization 1-4, 7, 11, 12, 15-17, 19-21, 23, 24, 27-29, 31, 33, 35, 37, 39, 41, 43, 54, 73, 82, 83, 91, 102, 123, 130, 135, 140, 142, 145, 167, 168, 171, 172, 175, 176, 178, 183, 191, 197-199, 201, 202, 204, 215, 216

Urbanization and African religion 197

Urbanization process 2, 202

Uyo Province 8, 31

Venereal disease 109

Vertical nuances 19

Victorian model 168

War Against Indiscipline (WAI) 66

Water transportation 49, 50

Wole Soyinka 60, 64

Women 27, 30-34, 36-43, 72, 77, 80, 81, 84, 87, 88, 90, 105, 113, 206-208, 215

Women police 110, 111

World Bank/ IMF 17, 188, 212, 214

World economic forum 211

World Social forum 211

World War II 76, 84, 99, 100, 102, 108, 114, 138, 139

Yaba College 158, 186

Yoruba 4-6, 32, 63, 66, 81, 82, 88, 107, 120-124, 133-138, 145-148, 151, 191, 193-196, 198, 202, 203, 205, 207, 229, 234

Yoruba belief 194

Yoruba central mosque 138

Yoruba religion 196

Yorubaland 124, 192, 193, 197

Zakes Mda 57